A Life Against the Grain

A Life Against the Grain

The Autobiography of an Unconventional Economist

Julian L. Simon

Transaction Publishers
New Brunswick (U.S.A.) and London (U.K.)

This book is printed on acid-free paper that meets the American National Standard for Permanence of Paper for Printed Library Materials.

Library of Congress Catalog Number: 2001054002
ISBN: 0-7658-0073-X
Printed in Canada

Library of Congress Cataloging-in-Publication Data

Simon, Julian Lincoln, 1932–
A life against the grain : the autobiography of an unconventional economist / Julian L. Simon.
p. cm.
From his manuscript posthumously edited and prepared by Rita J. Simon for publication.
ISBN 0-7658-0073-X (alk. paper)
1. Simon, Julian Lincoln, 1932– 2. Economists—United States—Biography. I. Simon, Rita James. II. Title.

HB119.S475 A3 2001
300'.092—dc21
[B]

2001054002

Contents

Comment

Julian Simon died suddenly and, according to the doctor's report, instantly of his first and only heart attack on February 8, 1998. He had just returned from a trip to Spain where he had been awarded an honorary degree from the University of Navarre. He was in very good spirits and showed no signs of fatigue or illness.

Julian had been working on his autobiography from 1994 until the end of 1996. I found no disks or manuscript pages after the end of 1996. But in the year or so before his death and his last written account, he talked about his autobiographical manuscript and how much it meant to him. He very much wanted to finish it and see it published. With the help of my children, his wonderful secretary, Helen Demarest, and the support of Irving Louis Horowitz, I edited and prepared Julian's manuscript for publication. As I went through the manuscript (Julian left over 900 pages), I tried very hard to be sure that it was Julian's opinions beliefs, likes, and dislikes that were being expressed and not mine. When I was doubtful I almost always decided to leave things as Julian had written them. I believe if he had had an opportunity to read this edited/published version he would agree, it is his autobiography.

RITA J. SIMON

Preface

"From the moment I picked this book up until the moment I put it down, I could not stop laughing. Some day I hope to read it."— Groucho Marx

By some quirk of fate this volume has fallen into your hands. So you now wonder: Should you spend some of your most valuable capital—the minutes and hours of your life—in reading this book? I'll now try to persuade you to do so.

The book aims to give you some pleasure—a few laughs, some curious stories of the life of a fellow human being, and perhaps a few interesting ideas. That's why I copy from Pablo Casals's autobiography in starting off with a joke or two. You don't find much humor in most autobiographies, just as you don't see many smiles on their faces when people walk alone on the street. Maybe it's because we take ourselves very seriously and we don't see much absurdity in our lives. And maybe it's wise to take ourselves seriously. Adam Smith advised us to think a bit more highly of ourselves than the facts warrant, so that others will take us seriously, too.

Here is another joke that portrays one of my basic attitudes:

The two women were fighting over a chicken. One pointed out to the rabbi that she had three witnesses who would say they saw her buy the chicken, and demanded that he award it to her. "You're right," said the Rabbi.

The other woman then produced a statement from the butcher that she had purchased that very same chicken, and demanded that the Rabbi award the chicken to her. "You're right," said the Rabbi.

The Rabbi's faithful disciple pulled him aside and pointed out,

"Rabbi, there is only one chicken and you said that both of the women are right." "You're right," said the Rabbi.

The eminent biologist E. O. Wilson referred to me in a newspaper as "a buffoon." When a reporter asked me for a response, I leaned with the blow and said, "Wilson is right." Indeed, I play the clown and occasionally take pratfalls in class to keep my students amused. I have put on rubber horns when giving public lectures to make the point that a lot of persons think I'm the devil himself. I wear two wigs, a raincoat up to my ears, and a Viennese psychiatrist's accent when I teach about the need to gain people's attention when advertising. And in this book I'll tell you my best ludicrous episodes, and try to make the volume enjoyable and amusing.

Another reason to spend some time on this book: You might benefit by learning from my mistakes. From the standpoint of having a successful "career," I've done just about everything wrong, and the outcomes prove it. Maybe my back-and-forth, in-and-out, around-and-about mentality inevitably kept me from being more sensible and prudent, but you need not blunder as I have. (However, you may well know already how not to make the mistakes I've made; most people do, as some of them are glad to tell me.)

You might also learn something from this book about how your own mind works. Our minds are fascinating in their absurdities as well as in their powers. I'll give you examples of the peculiar workings of this particular human's brain, whose operations—which I assume are like those of most other people's brains—are frequently absurd.

You may also pick up some devices for improving the practical quality of your thinking. I'll say a bit about some methods of gathering useful information and making sound decisions.

I hope you will share with me the joy of the extraordinary good luck I have had in life in the most important of matters: my own health and that of my family; my friendships; the lack of any tragedy or privation that twisted me physically or mentally; great command over my own time since I got out of the Navy and quickly stopped working for others in business; enough money that I haven't had to scrounge for it since I was in my thirties; in general, the absence of hellish hardship; and most important, the fun of doing the work I wanted to do.

I emphasize the role of luck because much of my work life may seem to you to have been simply a painful waste—a mess of useless effort and fruitless fights. I don't want that sense of waste to miscolor the larger picture and give you the impression that I am at all bitter about what life has treated me to. (X: "How is life treating you?" Y: "It's not treating me; I'm paying my own way." Yes and no. Always yes and no.)

Aristotle taught that great art portrays people who are very different from you and me; the tragic heroes are his subject. But I lack gravitas—weighty dignity. I was not cut out to be a Mafia boss; I'm more like a competent and hard working plumber or building contractor or burlesque-show baggy pants comedian, though I have more kooky ideas than most of them. Yes, the results of my studies and my writings have turned out to be correct. As I told a reporter in a loose moment, I'm still just another shithead, and I don't believe that the idea of being "smart" is useful or even harmless. (His editors changed the s-word to "jerk" in his *Wall Street Journal* story.) So soaring drama about tragic heroes that will move your great emotions I can't promise or deliver.

Because my work has been a large part of my life, and the professional" autobiography part that is significant to anyone other than my family, this book describes my adventures in doing my work and discusses the consequences of the work. I shall also talk about those aspects of my life history and psychology that involve my intellectual development and hence affect what I have done professionally, and how the work has been received. All this is much less interesting to me than some other aspects of my life—sex, family relations, and emotions—which I much more enjoy talking about. But sex and family are too private for me to write much about—at least, at this stage of my life—and one person's emotions are usually dull to another person.

Isaac Bashevis Singer said in his autobiography that his watchword was "Maintain suspense." I'll try to do that for your reading enjoyment. Indeed, there is real suspense in the course of my professional life, up to this very moment. How will it end? Will the best of the scholarly works that I've planted in the scholarly ground—my very best ideas either never having been published yet, or having been published but never even been noticed—will they ever be presented to the scholarly world so that the seeds will have a chance to grow to be fruitful?

Consider in particular the revolution in statistical inference that I tried to initiate in 1969—having people do most or all of their statistical inference with formula-free, perfectly understandable Monte Carlo experimental simulation methods—when will that revolution come about? Will it be long after my lifetime? When I first published those methods, I knew that the professional literature and daily practice must *eventually* go that way, but I could not know when. That forecast has so far proven right with respect to scholarly research in advanced statistics. These methods—now called "resampling"—have indeed been hailed as the greatest breakthrough in statistics since the 1970s (though not attached to my name). But when will the most important step—the routine use of these devices in everyday practice by nonstatisticians—come about? Along with my colleague and partner Peter Bruce, I continue every day with this struggle through mostly unorthodox channels, such as commercial distribution of the computer program, to make these methods convenient. We're making some progress, but the adoption of new ideas is always slow, especially when the idea must penetrate introductory courses of instruction. When will it happen? Will the onset of the Internet—which will be the greatest innovation in scholarly communication since the invention of printing at the end of the fifteenth century—speed the widespread adoption of resampling methods? (It *must* happen *eventually*.) Maybe by the time this book has fallen into your hands, some better answer will be available.

A novelty of this book among scientific autobiographies is that it is not written by a person who is a success. Every other scientific autobiography I know of is by an acknowledged major figure—a Nobel prizewinner or what have you. For example, all the authors of the excellent collection of autobiographies sponsored by the Sloan Foundation in the 1970s to the 1990s are people who have been thoroughly successful. None is by a professional outcast, a failure, or the inventor of questionable ideas. In contrast, most of my best scientific work has gone for naught. I consider myself lucky even to survive at all. There may be something to learn from my ups and downs that resounding success cannot teach.

Yes, I've had clear-cut successes, as with the airline oversales volunteer scheme that everyone laughed at, resisted ,and denounced for twelve years but that now delights and profits tens of thousands of U.S. air travelers every day without loss to anyone. But even this achievement has not been a scholarly success that has led to further scholarly work. Rather, it has been a success in the working world, but a success whose inventor goes unacknowledged except by a few cognoscenti.

My statement that most of my professional life may have been a waste of time will surely seem false to most friends and acquaintances. They point to articles by and about me in national newspapers—though many are denunciations—as evidence that I have made a mark (an apt term). Indeed, the wonderfully ugly things that have been printed about me are my main marks of success. But the marks that others see are ephemeral, and they are only the by-products of the fundamental professional research that occupied all of my work time (except for teaching) until about 1980, and perhaps 90 percent of my time since then.

What others don't notice when they kindly praise me is that in my entire professional life, spanning more than three decades, I have never (I mean literally *never*, truly an amazing statistic) had a single standard mark of professional respect (let alone honor) in my academic professions. I've never held an office in a professional association (not even membership on the committee that nominates *other* people for offices and honors or on the committee that counts the ballots for the candidates); never been offered a prestigious teaching job; never been asked to give a to-be-published paper at an annual economics association meeting. Any scholar must be amazed that anyone could publish as huge a pile of books and papers as I have over many years and never be asked to referee a paper for the major "official" journal in my three fields of economics, demography, and statistics, or with two or three exceptions in 30 years, by almost any other top journal. Shake your heads at that, brothers and sisters. You can hardly get any less formally distinguished than that. It's true that I can't claim to have done much (if any) solicitation for such positions and honors, but even so, that's a hell of a performance.

The acid test for someone with my goals is whether others build upon one's technical/empirical and theoretical work. There has been precious little of that for me until now, a matter I'll talk about at greater length later. Yes, some population economists credit me with changing the direction of that field in the 1980s; how true that is, and how much lasting effect it will have, is very unclear. I have changed some people's thinking, but not necessarily the thinking or the work lines of scholars in the field. So there is still suspense about what the outcome will be.

What is *not* in suspense is whether my basic prediction since 1970 would be correct: That the world will continue to become better-off in all material ways for the foreseeable future has so far been confirmed completely. It is also not in suspense whether my having been correct would gain me credibility with a wider public and the press; the answer to that is an unequivocal "no." Being right brings out almost nothing except vilification, as many have learned before me.

Conflict heightens reader interest. You may find conflict in the sagas of my many professional hassles and also in my service as a soldier in the unnoticed War of the Two Cultures, the struggle between the clever people and the competent people. In part because I know (or at least can guess at) how unsmart I myself am, the clever people have been my main obstacle at every turn—in the case of the airline oversales auction scheme, for example, and in the case of my radical experimental approach to inferential statistics. This two-culture war makes C. P. Snow's saga of the struggle between the cultures of science and humanity seem like a tea party.

The book will give you the opportunity of joining the moral parade of the good guys with three degrees after their names and chairs at the fanciest institutions in the U.S. and abroad, as they blast the bad guy (me) during their commencement speeches and presidential addresses to their associations for being (just a few examples) "a terrorist," a scholar who "lays a smoke-screen of statistics," whose work is "Intellectually dishonest . . . immoral," "an insult . . . filled with incomplete analysis, selective documentation, and false analogies," and "Schizophrenic nonsense and baloney . . . sabotaging the human race," "like the fast-change artist at a county fair, befuddles the reader with rapid rhetorical interchanges . . . [and] sleight of hand." But maybe you'll wonder, with me, what it is about my work and person that brings this on? After all, my research shows the economic value and material benefits of freedom, sound statistics, and the presence of additional human beings as babies and as immigrants. What is so vile or threatening about all that?

Of course you'll wonder about what I'm not telling you, as one always should when reading an autobiographical account. Therefore, I'll copy an ingenious device in Muhammad Ali's autobiography: He turned over one chapter to his divorced wife and wrote another as a dialog with Joe Frazier, his greatest ring opponent, letting them tell it as they saw it. My first wife is still with me after more than three decades, so she has had an unusual amount of time to see and recount my rough side and tell you all that I prudently leave out. I lack Ali's guts, however, so I won't invite any of those who call me a terrorist and liar to testify against me on my time.

As I waited in the spring of 1983 to hear whether the University of Maryland would come through with its tentative offer of a job, after Rita's job in Washington was all set, I was on tenterhooks. Throughout every ordinary day, my mood rises and falls many times as I first remember something to lament or worry about and then lay the worrisome thought to rest. That spring I promised myself—as we all make vows in order to bargain with fortune—that if the job came through I would not let myself be unhappy for a single moment until we left Illinois. The job came through; I kept my vow. Now as I write this book and a troubling thought comes to me I remind myself: of all the situations I might be in today, writing this is the most desirable situation. If I can't enjoy this moment, what better could I hope for? That should tell you the most powerful reason for my writing this.

A problem with which every autobiographer struggles—aside from those whose entire story is kiss-and-tell—is how much to say about the people close to you. Especially if you aim to write about the most important parts of your life and about your deepest feelings—your parents, spouse, and children—plus friends and other relatives—enter importantly into the story. No person of decency or delicacy can tell much about these intimate relationships without taking a chance of making others uncomfortable or angry. Certainly one cannot come close to telling the unvarnished truth about others in the way that one dares to about oneself. It seems as if the only choice is to leave out most of this material. But this also has its drawbacks. It biases the account, and it also can distress those who are close to you because it seems as if they do not matter enough to deserve mention. This was the case when I wrote my own story for my book on depression. I know that Rita felt bad that I mentioned her so little, and I worried so much about my mother's reaction that in all the early drafts, until she died, I affixed a pen name to the book.

This difficulty is a special disability for a person to whom sex is particularly important—even holy. The telling of my life story will be very imbalanced because the amount of space devoted to sex is so little. I'm sure that our views of the role of sex for human beings are biased because of biased autobiographical accounts such as this one. The solution to the problem? There is none. Just do the best you can, I guess, even though it will be extremely inadequate.

I worry that people will think me egoistic and stuck-up (do people still use that word?) for writing an autobiography. I'm embarrassed to imagine them saying: "Why would he think that anyone would be interested enough in him to read his story? What a self-indulgent, self-regarding fool." But in his excellent book about autobiographies, Roy Pascal says that writing an autobiography does not signify that you love yourself a lot. "It is misleading to talk of the 'self-love' of autobiographers; most of us love ourselves too dearly to be autobiographers" (Roy Pascal, *Design and Truth in Autobiography*). I take some comfort in that.

Will anybody actually want to read natterings like the above paragraph? Certainly when young, I never had the slightest interest in reading Marcel Proust's unceasing musings in *Remembrance of Things Past*. But maybe a few relatively brief examples of this sort of mental wheel-spinning are useful to put my life—or anyone's—into perspective. Maybe these wandering records of the byways of thought will help make clearer how the usual picture we get of people's thought processes—neatly connected, proceeding in a straight line, relatively economical, with everything included being relevant—is only the cleaned-up product seen from the outside of the machinery. And maybe an occasional helter-skelter style of disconnected and unexpected observations and recollections, rather than the tight discipline of scientific writings, will keep the reader from dozing off, as the occasional joke or aside in the classroom can.

Of course, a writer of an autobiography has a wonderful excuse for discursions, saying to himself or herself: But the purpose of an autobiography is to show me as I am, and these digressions are part of how I am. In truth, some art is required in autobiographies just as in all other writing, and trimming out unnecessary verbiage is a crucial part of this art.

Should this book be lucky enough to get reviewed, a reviewer is likely to apply a favorite word of the reviewer's trade: "uneven." But it is my actual life that is uneven, even more than my *description* of the life. So there must be different styles of writing, differing degrees of detail, different moods, different attitudes toward life and work, in different parts of the book if the book is to describe my life with any fidelity.

Here's the deal I offer you: I'll try to avoid writing anything that is humdrum or routine or trivial that would make the reading a bore, unless for me it is so delicious that leaving it out would take the fun out of the writing.

Please do not be fooled by the casual writing style into thinking that I am revealing all. For the 13 years that I was depressed I never said one word about it to anyone at work or to most close friends or even to my children; I deemed it too dangerous to do so. A person who, out of prudence, is that close-mouthed about such a matter obviously is capable of guarding his words about other crucial matters.

One of my mistakes is affronting and thereby alienating those very people (the few of them) who might otherwise share some of my ideas. Now I'll do it again. J. M. Keynes made a famous remark about the influence of long-dead economists, and Friedrich Hayek quoted that remark with some approval, saying, "I agree with Lord Keynes that `the ideas of economists and political philosophers, both when they are right and when they are wrong, are more powerful than is commonly understood. Indeed, the world is ruled by little else.'"

This is one of the few matters on which I disagree with Hayek. All of us like to think we are important—intellectuals certainly at least as much as anyone. And yes, ideas can be powerful in the intermediate run, as witness the disaster caused by Marxist thinking for much of a century in eastern Europe and China. But in the longer run, the elemental forces of peoples' desires to carve out a good living for themselves and for their families, to have children and raise them happily and well-educated, to employ their talents and energies and to possess their fruits—these forces will eventuate in government policies that allow people these fundamental freedoms. There probably always will be temporary reversals and reversions to totalitarianism for a while. But we can hope that in an ever-ramified world where people can move ever more freely with each passing decade, these reversions will be of shorter duration and of lesser magnitude.

All we need from philosophers and economists is that they manage to pry from rulers a small chink of living and operating space for individuals, and some modicum of the rule of law. All the rest will be done by the individuals, without recourse to any grand ideas. Indeed, this is the very heart of the doctrine of Hayek—and of Friedman, Smith, and Hume. In this rare respect, Hayek and his teacher von Mises contradict themselves. Indeed, they know well the power of black markets even in the teeth of the most fearsome sanctions. Such markets are not driven by grand ideas, but by human desires and economic incentives.

The more that humanity progresses, the less that the ideas will matter, because the variety of regimes offered competitively by the various countries and the easy movement from one country to another will provide the necessary opportunities for entrepreneurs and other talented persons. The need then grows less for the philosophers of liberty to eke out for society a bit of freedom from the clutches of politicians intoxicated with the chance to put into operation their delusions of social improvement by central control (theirs). People will achieve it anyway.

Saying this to my colleagues in the idea business, who fancy themselves as being crucial to progress, will not endear me to them. But some dybbuk keeps me saying these things even though I understand the cost of doing so.

(On the other hand, with greater progress comes greater freedom from pressing survival needs, which enables people to indulge themselves in foolish, irrational, and counterproductive thinking, and can lead to mass movements that impede progress. I am hopeful that this perverse process will be kept from going too far by the pressure of basic needs. Farmers and small retailers, who are inevitably in close touch with economic reality, are—or at least I so think—somewhat protected from being enamored of foolish economic ideas.

The chapters are mostly titled by place. This does not mean that places have been of huge importance to me. Rather, this was a helpful device for defining periods of time when I was sorting out the various events and reminiscences.

A considerable range of writing styles appear in the book, depending on what I'm writing about. You will find differing (though I think not conflicting) aspects of personality and character. That variety is an essential part of me, and I therefore have not tried to suppress the variety by imposing consistency on the writing or the facets of person that appear.

The brevity and the modesty of David Hume's wonderful 13-page autobiography (not much longer than this introduction) are a challenge to every autobiographer. Maybe there is an inverse law for idea people: The greater and clearer are your other books, the less autobiography you need to write. That will provide me a justification for writing long. But if this book is boring, there can be no excuse.

1

Newark, New Jersey: 1932–1937

My mother have birth to me just before midnight on February 12, 1932. She was anxious that the event take place before 11:59 P.M. because February 12 is Abraham Lincoln's birthday and she wanted my middle name to be "Lincoln."

As an adolescent, I once complained to my father that I did not like the name "Julian." He banteringly suggested I call myself "Linc." It was a good idea, and I should have thanked him for it, even though it seemed ridiculous to me at the time; outwardly well-socialized as I was, it seemed illegitimate to alter my identity. But 40 years later, I am sorry that I did not take that suggestion seriously and actually do it. The name of Lincoln stirs in me thoughts of a man of courage, wisdom, love of humanity, and good judgment, whereas Julian was just an effete Roman emperor with peculiar tastes, with whom I feel no kinship of any kind. When I have occasionally written something under a pen name, I have used "Lincoln Pashute," the "Pashute" meaning "simple" in Hebrew. I have also written "J. Lincoln Simon," for example, to avoid the possibility that a journal will reject an article just because it is by Julian L. Simon. (That's the sense of the world that comes with the reputation I have spent a lifetime earning.)

As I look back now and assess the years since then, it seems to me that the consequences of my birth, and of the average boy or girl born that year (or any year) in the U.S., square with my studies of the economics of population: We have created a bit more than we have used up, and hence the world will be left a bit richer because of our having lived. I judge that the same is true of the average person born that year even in poor places such as India, China, the poor parts of Africa, and the poor countries of Latin America. (The case is hardest to make for modern China, because an authoritarian regime has shackled people's free creative powers and engendered violence.)

Some people's childhoods are worth reading about because they were extraordinarily eventful. Irving Louis Horowitz grew up a Jewish boy in the middle of black Harlem with a sadistic father and a terrible harelip that required a series of painful operations; that's inherently interesting. G.C. Jones grew up in Harlan County, Kentucky, and was forced to leave home at the age of twelve because the truth came out that his mother's husband was not his father; then, before he was out of adolescence, he did everything from driving mules to being an undercover "man" for the United Mine Workers; that's inherently interesting, too. William Owens grew up just after the turn of the century in Pin Hook, Texas, so poor that he could not manage to get more than a few months of schooling in each of the few years when he got any education at all, and he could obtain literally nothing to read; some old newspapers pasted onto the walls of a shack in which he lived, to keep out drafts, were the most he could find for a while. (Owens miraculously became a professor of literature and folklore at Columbia University.) Willie Ruff grew up rock-bottom poor in a black area of a small South Carolina town, lost his mother, went alone to join his father in Detroit, dropped out of school and faked his age well enough that he got into the Army at fourteen years old, even though he was not a big kid—just big enough to make the minimum height. By the time he had left the army at age seventeen, he was a star member of the greatest black army band, had passed his high school equivalency test, and had been admitted to the Yale School of Music. That's interesting stuff.

In contrast, my early life was unexceptional—worth talking about only for the light it throws on what I later became (or did not become) and because of some funny happenings.

I remember with pleasant warmth the first nine years of my life. My first memories are in a building on West Market Street in central Newark. Grandmother Goodstein and my then-unmarried aunts Ruth and Anna lived upstairs in a sprawling second-floor apartment, and downstairs was Grandma's hardware store. I'm told that during the first visits there as a small baby, I was put into a dresser drawer for safekeeping. A nice story.

Mother, Dad, and I—no brothers or sisters were to come—lived in a second-floor apartment somewhere in the Weequahic area of Newark. I'm told that when I could stand up I was put outside a second-floor window in a screened-in box that my father built; it was suspended by wires, and Harris Solman, whom I called "Uncle" and was a civil engineer who built bridges, certified it as safe. The contraption saved my mother from having to haul me down the stairs in order for me to get fresh air. (This was a time when fresh air was regarded—especially by the mother—as the best all-purpose preventive medicine. Lots of open windows and all that, à la the British. But unlike with the Brits, among Jews—even Jews with higher cultural pretensions such as Mother—it was a time when apartments also were overheated.)

Naturally I don't remember, but it is said that at first I cried when I wanted my mother and/or I wanted to come in. But my mother taught me early lessons in independence and steadfastness by painfully shutting her ears to my cries until I learned to stop. Maybe here was the template for my life: Yearning to be held close, but not expecting that my yearning would be fulfilled.

When years later I asked her about it, Mother said that they did not have any more children because she and Dad did not think that they could afford any more. This assertion certainly was in tune with the very low urban birthrate in the early 1930s. Yet Mother's statement somehow never seemed convincing to me. Expenses for food and clothing were not great at the time; there would have been little or no additional expenditure on housing; Mother already was staying at home taking care of me, so another child would not have affected her earning power or the cost of child care; and there were no other major child-raising expenses. But perhaps I am projecting onto my parents my own feelings about the importance of having children and my own risk-averse attitude toward life; it has always seemed to me that having just one child placed parents in intolerable danger of losing everything if the child were to die. And in the 1930s, the death rate for young children was nowhere near as low as it is the 1990s in the United States.

Harris Solman, who certified that the window-porch was safe for me, was an interesting and attractive human being. He was the husband of Frances Solman, one of my mother's many close friends from high school and early adulthood. Mother's friendships spoke very well for her. The friendships endured for her entire life, genial and reliable.

In contrast, Dad never had a single friend other than Mitchell Sabol, with whom he had gone to high school and with whom there were a few phone calls during my lifetime. I never met Sabol, nor do I believe Dad ever saw him during those years. Dad never invited anyone to the house, nor did anyone ever invite him (aside from Mother's friends and relatives). I was very aware of this asocial aspect of Dad's life from about the age of nine, and it made a big impression on me. More about this in the chapter on the family.

Harris was born in Europe and had "smicha"—that is, ordination as a rabbi—before he came to the U.S. When he came to the U.S., he trained as a civil engineer at Rutgers, the New Jersey state university. He was hit particularly hard by the Depression and could not find work in his field for several years. He finally found work with New York State as a bridge designer, and the childless couple went to Albany to live.

During World War II, Harris was first assigned to the federal government to work in Washington, and I visited them there in 1941. Harris toured me over a half-completed bridge he was working on, and I was fascinated; the fascination with building has continued to this day, but I am glad I never considered engineering as a career; the frustrations of not being able to build as I would have liked, because superiors or clients would have given me my head, would have been very hard for me to take.

Harris was perhaps five feet three inches, about the same height as my father, with a round face, eyeglasses, and a bend in his back (perhaps due to a terrible auto crash) that may have been enough for him to qualify as a hunchback. He was the most benign person I ever met. (Frances was something of a shrew, which Harris handled with remarkable grace and serenity.) Harris also was one of the people whom I recognized early on as knowing what he was talking about; he knew about engineering, Judaism and the Talmud, and many other subjects. This was in contrast to my father and (to a lesser degree) many other adults I knew, who happily talked of many topics in a way that convinced me that what they said should not be completely believed, or not believed at all.

When I stayed with them in Washington, Uncle Harris took me one day to the Smithsonian Museum, and we wandered through the exhibits of weaponry. We halted before a case of machine guns and he pointed to one and said, "That's the kind that I manned in France in World War I." He, who had the least martial bearing and manner of anyone I knew, had joined the U.S. Army as a new immigrant en route to becoming a citizen. I drew conclusions from this incident about the reliability of assumptions about individuals based on their appearances and demeanors.

Later, during the war, Harris was sent to Edmonton, Canada, to work on the Alcan Highway, a great project that I would like to travel some day; I would think of Harris with affection while doing so.

I have a clear memory of being downstairs in Grandma's old-fashioned hardware store and being given a small box of nails of assorted sizes to sort out—probably nails that had spilled in the process of weighing them out by the pound for customers. That was a wonderful task; it occupied me and made me feel that I was "working" and doing something useful. The desire to be useful has animated me throughout life. When I feel that a chunk of my life has been a waste, it is because I think that what I have been doing is not useful to anyone—that the nails I've sorted have never been sold and nailed into a piece of construction.

Frequently there were fire engines with screaming sirens rushing uptown on busy West Market Street in front of the store and bell-clanging ambulances scaring me as they pushed through traffic to and from St. Barnabas Hospital further downtown. Every clanging or screaming passage evoked images of street accidents, fires, blood, pain, and death. But though the ambulances and fire engines scared me, they did not *seriously* scare me; the images did not preoccupy me or carry over into other moments.

As a kid I had pretty strong nerves. I didn't get nightmares from the clangings and the images they conjured up of broken bodies from auto wrecks; or from (a few examples of incidents I'll tell you about later) the drowned boy in the park lake when I was 10 or 11, or from the burning of the Morro Castle a mile or so offshore from where we were staying, or the attempted homosexual seduction when I was five or so, or even from the not unreasonable fear that the family would soon be without any means of support and indigent. Of course, in adolescence, I worried plenty about our potential indigence, but I was not traumatized; my daytime consciousness was not dominated by these matters, and I didn't wake up at night screaming. Nor was I scarred later in life by these incidents, so far as I can tell.

I think that my basic nature is not full of fears—a gift for which anyone should be grateful, as I am. Lest I mislead you with too sunny a view of my life though, please note that through most of my life since I left Newark, I have been much more afraid of other people, especially people who have any power over me, than are most other people I know. Of course you'll hear more about that later.

Later in life my nerves became less strong, and when they enter my zone of attention, the images of people's deformities, mortal sicknesses, and death now disturb me greatly. I turn away from these thoughts and those of ethnic holocausts as quickly as I can, and I worry that I will not handle such an event well if (when) it occurs close to me. I am horrified now at the knowledge (which my Aunt Ruth and Aunt Anna told me of recently) that next to the frame wooden building of Grandma's hardware store were kept steel drums of kerosene. Even worse, inside the store were drums of linseed oil, turpentine, and other flammables to be sold by the quart or gallon. All these a stray match could have ignited and in an instant made the building into a flaming pyre.

Looking around our 1996 kitchen, I am astonished at the differences in convenience—and even more so, differences in safety—from our kitchen in Newark and my grandmothers' kitchens on West Market Street and High Street. I seriously scalded a large part of my arm by yanking a pot of boiling water off Grandma Goodie's stove; now we draw almost-boiling water from a dispenser (that I never would have bought if it had not been in place when we moved in, but that I have come to love) and then bring it to a boil in a closed microwave, almost eliminating the chance of a child getting scalded. The food processor slices and dices vegetables in a jiffy, greatly reducing preparation time and obviating the big knives that were always a danger to children. The electric toaster is much safer than making toast the old way on the stove or oven. And so it goes through operation after operation in the kitchen. I am puzzled how so many people cannot be aware of how much better-off we are in so many ways. Maybe if people were more aware of these differences, they would be more grateful for what they have, and thereby improve their moods.

Our world nowadays presents us with many fewer hazards due to litter, too. Cut feet from broken glass on the beach, in the grass, and on the street were common when I was a child; lifeguards seemed to spend half their work time with their first-aid kits (including iodine, bandages, and scissors), and no one questioned their credentials or sued them for malpractice. Today's cans and plastic bottles, together with a higher level of civic cleanliness, surely have greatly reduced such injuries, just as industrial injuries have sharply declined in rich countries such as the U.S. And of course the dangers consequent on injury were much greater when I was a child; before the wonder drugs against infection became common around World War II, it was not unusual to die of such an infection.

Some accidents could happen in any era, though. About age four, I went fishing at Bradley Beach, maybe with Harris Solman. One of my first casts of the line put the hook neatly through my ear lobe. The doctor was stumped about how to get it out, short of cutting it out. My father, in one of his finest moments, fetched a pair of wire-cutting pliers and neatly cut the shank of the hook; end of problem. This event left me the memory of the doctor whose higher education may have prevented him from arriving at this simple solution; "educated incapacity" is the common term. Early on I learned about the frequent lack of association between credentials and skills.

Very heavily garbed nuns occasionally came into the hardware store. They told Grandma or the clerk what they wanted. Payment was refused, which the nuns seemed to take for granted. I understood that they were religious persons and of a religion different from mine.

Events such as the nuns shopping and Grandma's family living over the hardware store gave me the sense that business is a very human endeavor, influenced heavily by human discretion and emotions, rather than a monolithic rule-based institution such as the army or a government-based bureaucracy.

I was very fond of Katie, a middle-aged, heavily shaped Polish woman who came to wash the clothes and do the heavy cleaning once a week or so. Her English was broken, and her manner was that of a peasant in the Old Country, but her maternal manner was unmistakable.

When one of Katie's kids got married, the parents threw a traditional Polish wedding, inevitably at savings-destroying expense. I heard that the wedding party lasted three days. I remember a huge bare wedding hall full of young people dancing and older people standing around chatting. For years, that scene constituted my vision of a wedding.

The fact that we were well-enough off to afford to hire someone to clean our apartment was one of the elements that gave me the impression that we were in the better-off class in the late 1930s. Later, in Millburn, we were not able to afford such help.

Mother's social attitudes were such that, with respect to Katie, mother was the lady of the big house. (Never mind that our apartment was a modest lower-middle-class flat.) And I suppose that attitude was nurtured by the fact that mother then did not have a job; there was no possibility for her to treat the relationship as a division of labor—one goes out to do some sort of office work, and another comes in to do some sort of cleaning work.

My parents owned two little houses at the Jersey shore in Bradley Beach that my father had bought as an investment before he was married in 1927. My parents rented out the front and back of each house for the summer. We went there for weekends in the spring to get them ready to rent and in the fall to clean up; during the summer we sweltered in the city (without air conditioning, of course) with the rest of the neighborhood.

I enjoyed the old windup phonograph in Bradley which had records of famous comedians, such as Scotch-accented Harry Lauder. The houses had been electrified but had been originally fitted with gaslight, and the old gas jets had been wired.

During the renting season I suffered with my parents the suspense of each potential renter deciding whether to take either the front of one of the two houses, or a back apartment, or neither, agonizing as my parents would discuss whether to lower the price as the renting season got late with our still having vacancies. In the city, however, I was somehow ashamed that we were "rich" enough to be in the "landlord" class, which seemed to put us a slight cut economically above the neighbors in Newark.

Feet enter into many memories of Bradley Beach—the hot sidewalk under bare feet going to the beach, with the alternative of walking in the sparse grass and taking a chance of cutting your feet on the broken glass that was everywhere. The boardwalk made of very rough planks full of huge splinters that could gouge a foot. The pleasantness of putting my feet on the wet sand near the water. The heat of the hot sand burning my soles at midday, digging my toes into the wet sand, wondering if I would touch a crab.

If I could draw, I could render in perfect detail from my mind's eye how the old ladies—many of them fat and with loose skin as so many more old people looked then compared to now—hanging with one hand onto the ropes leading into the water in the protected area, and with the other hand splashing water onto their necks and bosoms, saying "it's a mechaiyah." *Mechaiyah* is Yiddish for "a great pleasure". (It was only many years later that I realized that it came from the Hebrew "me-ha-yeh" which means "it makes life." That meaning is indeed lovely.)

Revisiting Bradley Beach a few years ago when giving a talk in a nearby town, I found that everything had been made better. The houses had been improved. And the lawns were much, much better kept: they actually had grass on them, and there were flowers planted, in contrast to the barren dirt of the late 1930s. Indeed, humans generally tend to make things better—not everywhere and all the time—but most of the times in most places.

We sold the houses in Bradley Beach during World War II because we had insufficient gasoline rations to get us there in spring and fall to rent and care for the property. And the price then was a pittance because renters also had trouble getting there during the war.

The Big Bear Supermarket on Elizabeth Avenue in Hillside was one of the first such stores in the U.S., or so I heard then. It was a great wonder: self-service and shopping carts, rather than a storekeeper picking each item off the shelf with a long squeeze stick as the other customers waited on the other side of the counter. The efficiency was obvious to my six-year-old eye; that is the sort of thing I've noticed all my life.

Newark was then a city of about half a million people, situated at the outer edge of the inner ring of the New York metropolitan area, separated from Manhattan by the Hudson River and a few miles of marshes and industrial areas. It was not very different from the New York City boroughs other than Manhattan. Its proximity to Manhattan has caused a problem for Newark since the riots of the 1960s, because the proximity kept Newark from being rebuilt. Whereas when I was a child, people would go downtown to the center of Newark to shop and for amusement; after the riots, people had New York available and hence there was less pressure for reconstruction.

There was still some high culture in Newark in the 1930s. Mother took me to see Paul Robeson play Othello at the Mosque Theatre and also to some symphony concerts. The concerts bored me, but I did not do my children a favor by not dragging them to such events; I think that these early impressions are worth having.

Mother also dragged me to shop at the downtown department stores from time to time, and I remember a very strong dislike for the entire shopping process. I always seemed to feel overheated by heavy clothes and a hot store, bored while Mother chose among this blouse or that one or that one or that one or that one…then waiting for a sales clerk to take the order, send the order, and the credit card whooshing away in the shining pneumatic tube to an office somewhere else, and from start to almost finish, the continuing uncertainty about how soon we'd get done and go home, so I could get back on the street. This dislike of shopping continues to this day, in part because I have so little interest in the difference in appearance between one object and another; shopping in hardware stores is the only shopping that I nearly enjoy.

As far back as I can remember Grumman Avenue in Newark, I was like a fish in water. I felt like a part of the group, never like an outsider. I may even have been somewhat pampered by the older kids and grown-ups. This certainly is the impression given by photograph Newark 1. I remember the big kid in the picture, Richie Zinn, being like an older brother to me—the last time in my life I had that experience. Memory tells me that there was a tribal-like arrangement in which the gang made allowances for various ages and physical capacities (I was the youngest), but I may be romanticizing.

There was always something to do on the street: roller skating, making and riding wooden vegetable-crate scooters mounted on used steel skate-wheels, pitching "picture cards" against the house wall in the alley (baseball and "The Horrors of War" series of cards; I still have a box of old war cards showing the "Horrors of War" in Spain and China), with the closest toss being the winner of all the cards tossed in that round; making and shooting little squares cut from shirt cardboards with rubber band guns carpentered from corners of apple crates; shooting hard, uncooked tapioca balls with pea shooters –metal tubes bought at the drug store for a nickel, I think; shooting slingshots made from bent wire clothes hangers, rubber bands, and pouches made of pieces of scrap leather or old inner tubes. There was a wonderful event called a "scatter," in which someone who had collected a lot of bottle caps or matchbooks or picture cards decided to give away the entire lot and, after calling a crowd together, dumped them all into the alley from a second-floor window or just from over his (I remember no hers) head; maybe this is akin to the Northwest Native American's potlatch.

Of course there was stickball in the street between parked cars, just the way you've seen in it in movies of Brooklyn and Queens, with a broomstick and red rubber ball. We sometimes played stickball with half a ball. The variety of curves that were possible with half a ball was extraordinary. We also played stoop ball, banging the stick ball or maybe a tennis ball against the points of the steps; the trick was to hit sharp line drives, or the occasional sweet home run across the street, with fielding and scoring rules much like baseball.

There were salvage expeditions with string, weight, and chewing gum to get the rubber balls out of the sewers after they rolled in, and sometimes we got someone big to lift up the manhole covers, though we somehow felt that that was illegal. Learning to ride the older kids' bikes; it was Mark Schupack (the spellings are guesses, of course), lean and dark, who let me try his. I made my first attempt, learning by supporting myself against the walls of the houses up and down the alley. There was kick-the-can—soccer with a soft drink or beer can and very sketchy rules; a treatise by a law professor on the subject of the evolution of the rules of kids' games like these would be enlightening; such a book must exist. Buying one or two cents' worth of candy at Throm's Drugstore at the corner of Grumman and Maple Avenues, and later, war and baseball cards with bubble gum, though I don't think I ever bought any new ones. Shoplifting a few cents worth of candy and bubble gum, I'm ashamed to say. Opening the fire hydrant in summer time for splash baths. My cousin Dan Goodstein recalls my neighborhood as having lots more kids than his own neighborhood about eight blocks away, near the Maple Avenue School where I was a pupil; the rents were a bit higher where he lived.

These games were left behind when we moved from Newark to Millburn at age nine. All my learning, my "human capital," had to be abandoned forever. And I may have been part of the last generation to play those particular games before they were replaced by I-don't-know-what.

These were typical city streets. The houses were two-story clapboard, one step up from the tenements in the neighborhoods that the Jews and Italians and Poles first lived in when they arrived in the city from abroad. But it was a huge step up in the perception of the residents, a jump in what the sociologists call "upward mobility." The only trees were the hardy maple trees, from which each year fell a bountiful harvest of flexible green branches-to-be that made terrific whips for kids to play with.

I don't remember any birds in Newark. There was some litter in the streets. And it surely wasn't pretty. But so what? For a kid age five or nine who had no special personal problems, it was a fine place to start life: enough (actually, too much) food, a roof and central heating for the winter, and lots of other kids around. Much more than that can lead to overly high expectations and hence dissatisfaction for the rest of your life.

The standard stores of the times were at the corner of Grumman and Maple Avenue, most of a long block away: fruits and vegetables, Throm's Drugstore, a barber and a beauty shop, a grocery store where women went shopping every day, and lots more. The kosher butcher shop was the most memorable: I can see the proprietor Mr. Kramer in his bloody apron laying a chunk of carcass onto his butcher block and whacking off cuts of meat with his chopping ax and knives. He occasionally wiped the blood from the block toward a bucket, but some always went onto the sawdust on the floor. It sounds gory in the telling, but it did not seem so then; it was just a fact of life.

An open question: Why do I—as do other autobiographers—tell you about the stores in the neighborhood where I grew up, and not about the stores in the neighborhoods where I have lived earlier as an adult, and most certainly not about the stores in the suburb of Washington where I live now? Is it that there is some historical interest in the scene then? Maybe. But I don't think that is the whole explanation. Is it that a description of the stores as they were in those days reveals something about the milieu that supposedly produced me, whereas the stores nowadays do not affect my life? Maybe again, but my life was no more affected by Mr. Kramer's butcher shop in 1935 or 1940 than by the meat counter at the local supermarket in 1996. This is puzzling. Maybe these descriptions are simply "local color" to enliven the autobiography, just as with any other story.

For a bigger shopping area, with bakeries and a delicatessen, we took the Number 8 or Number 48 bus to Bergen Street. The buses had a hand-operated door, so all entrances and exit were from the front (unless there was a conductor); how many times a day did the driver have to operate that heavy levered mechanism from his driver's seat, while making change and giving directions, as well as trying to drive in the clangorous traffic? The first electrically opened doors in the rear and front of buses were an astonishment to me when I first saw them after we moved to the suburbs.

In those days peddlers still shouted their wares on the city street, often from horse-drawn wagons. Fruits and vegetables and the purchase of old clothes were staples. The daily milkman still used a horse, who seemingly by himself moved and stopped as if he knew the route as well as the milkman himself.

When I was maybe five years old, I ran home crying to Mother that somebody had hit me, and I wanted her help. "Go out and fight your own battles," she said. That was the last time I asked her for help in my relationships with people. And I haven't asked many other people for help in battles since then. There are goods and bads in trying to fight your own battles. The good side is obvious. The bad side includes losing a lot of battles and feeling very alone. One simply cannot get through life effectively without knowing how to solicit and gain allies, even within a family. But I never learned how to do it.

When I was maybe six, Mother decided that I had perfect pitch. She would play a note on the piano and I could tell her the note, without having heard and identified other notes. Contrary to what I have read about this in casual accounts, this heralded no special aptitude in me for music. I think that the perfect pitch disappeared without notice some time thereafter.

Supposedly being endowed with some rare talent like perfect pitch did not impress me. I doubt that I ever told anyone about it, and my aunts do not remember the event, nor do I remember thinking about it again until adulthood. Maybe I never possessed it. More generally, I've never been terrifically impressed by myself; I have always assumed that whatever talents I have are not rare. But I am also not awed by others, either. I remember thinking that the graduate students at the University of Chicago—supposedly a very elite bunch—were nothing special. I have sometimes been surprised and disappointed at the low level of competence I have found. For example, soon after I arrived at the University of Illinois, I had a discussion with a textbook author about his subject. I was amazed to find that he kept no file of references to articles and books in his field. Nowadays I would not be at all surprised at this. (Indeed, my own habits have gotten looser as I've gotten older.)

Movies in Newark on Saturday afternoon were fun, though Mother discouraged my going. (To her, movies were déclassé—though not really lower-class—and I don't remember her ever attending one). (How I got my father's permission to go to a show and pay money on the Sabbath I don't know.) My most vivid memory is of Charlie Chaplin in *The Great Dictator*, performing a brilliant sketch with a huge balloon globe that he bounced in the air with various parts of his body, satirizing Hitler. Would that satire is enough to demolish tyrants; unfortunately, they are made of tougher stuff.

The movies meant thirteen part, cliff-hanging serials to induce you to come to the movies every week; irresistible, annoying chewy candy that you would get between your teeth and then would need many minutes to pick out, but would immediately eat more of; the free dishes on Monday night (come for six weeks and get a complete set). The movies were air conditioned in summer, the only place that I ever experienced that extraordinary device.

I mentioned the picture-card competition earlier. When I was six, seven, eight, and maybe nine years old, in the alley (that is, the driveway) we scaled the bubble gum cards against the house to see who could get closest, the winner getting all the cards played on each round. There were two styles of throwing: (a) holding the corner of the card between the second and third fingers or between thumb and forefinger and then scaling it, and (b) propelling it by bending it between the thumb and the index finger and using the spring of the bend, plus the thumb, to snap it forward. The latter was the "big kids'" way—sophisticated and macho. Little kids did it either way. I well remember experimenting to see which worked best for me and reflecting that the scaling method was more efficient, in considerable part because it was simpler—no moving parts—and did not depend on the snap of the card not decreasing as it got older. And I opted for it because of its efficiency despite its lower status.

That decision foreshadowed many decisions in my life—simplicity over sophistication, efficiency over style. I have always wanted to do well what I was doing, even when the choice was between doing the task skillfully or impressing other people. The interesting part about the picture-cards story is how clearly I remember making the decision on those grounds even at that young age.

In games, too, right up to the present, I like to win, but winning is usually less important than doing well. To win a squash game when the opponent errs on the last point, rather than my scoring a nice winning shot, leaves me unsatisfied. And playing in tournaments never mattered much to me. I don't yearn for the excitement of competing. And I almost never had the sense of competition against other students in school work.

One of the hurts of my life is that no one seems to notice that I do skillful work, competently and with care. I take great pride in doing so, even though it will not be noticed. Unfortunately, those who happen to read my writings seem to have other matters in mind, and the issue of skill gets overlooked. But a person who has plenty to eat should not complain about the desserts he or she does not get, so I do my best to think about this source of hurt as little as possible. (Writing an autobiography brings such matters to the forefront of one's attention, however.)

A neighbor on the other side of our alley in Newark bought one of the prewar Hudson automobiles with an electric gearshift mounted on the steering column, rather than the old polelike stick shift standing up through the floorboards. And the car had no foot clutch, I believe. Sitting in the front seat with him, parked in the alley, I asked him how the thing worked. I remember him twisting himself into a pretzel lifting up his right foot and making as if to move the lever with his foot. When I got the joke I laughed a lot. That's exactly the sort of nuttiness and slapstick comedy that has appealed to me all my life.

I went to Hebrew School twice a week in the afternoon after elementary school and on Saturday morning. Special school buses took us on weekdays to Temple Oheb Shalom (Love of Peace) downtown on High Street. (Indeed, the street goes up a hill.) When the bus was crowded and some kids had to stand, I and some other boys would clamber up from the seats into the luggage racks and lie there, very comfortably, chortling about our triumph over our predicament. The buses surely did not run on the Sabbath, so I don't know how I got to synagogue then. I also remember walking up the long hill at other times. My Aunt Anna taught at Oheb Shalom, so I felt protected there just as I did at summer camp when I was five and six and she was the arts-and-crafts counselor. I also remember competition to see who could read the Hebrew prayers the fastest, a competition I took to be a joke because it seemed to me so ridiculous a task to read letters without understanding. That's all I remember of Hebrew School.

All the people I knew on Grumman Avenue were Jews except for the Greek family that had a nice one-family home with a garden at the corner; they owned a restaurant and had a son, Jimmy-the—Greek, who was my age. Like other inner-city areas, it was a neighborhood of nicknames—the kid across the street, whose name made me laugh, was Bupkiss (Yiddish for "beans") Barnhart (I'm guessing at these spellings).

There was often loud vocal expression within families that the rest of the neighborhood would hear, especially through the open windows in summer. People hollered for their children and yelled at their mates and neighbors. Upstairs-downstairs quarrels about noise were common. My memories of communal life in Newark are much richer than my memories of the following years in Millburn even though my Newark period of consciousness was shorter and I had a less mature memory. There simply was a lot going on on Grumman Avenue, and there was less privacy. Mine was quite the same as the neighborhood a few blocks away that Philip Roth immortalized in *Portnoy's Complaint*; his description rings absolutely true to me.

Perhaps the most important impression I received from my environment as a child was that—despite the fact that we had what we needed—life is a struggle. I assumed that to make a life a person must claw his or her way against the impersonal natural environment. If you didn't take responsibility and ensure that you provided for the basis of life, the needs would not be provided. No safety net. No la dolce vita. Being "laid back" in the 1960s expression would only get you laid in the ground. The world has changed since then, and perhaps this world view is no longer appropriate. But it still applies to almost all the inhabitants of almost all of the poor countries of the world.

Many of the people who now (1996) live in the neighborhood in Newark where I lived as a kid until 1941 are classified as "in poverty." But on average their purchasing power surely is three to six times greater than that of the families who lived there when my family did. That is, it was then considered to be a gritty lower-middle-class neighborhood; now it is a "ghetto." How does one make sense of these economic facts and labels? (I leave out as irrelevant that it was Jewish then and black now).

This reminds me of the tale of the teacher who complained that the bottom half of the class "is still below average." The intellectual content of much of reformers' thought is exactly that of the teacher. And those reformers often dub as "conservative" or "non progressive" or "reactionary" anyone who points out that what the teacher laments must indeed always be so.

2

Newark 1937–1941: Old Enough for School

As I look back and try to recapture memories of school, I find that I remember almost nothing of information or ideas imparted in the classroom, or of the school routine. I find this very surprising, but Frank Lloyd Wright, in his autobiography, wrote that though he remembered a great deal from the rest of his childhood, "But—of the schooling itself? Not a thing can he remember . . . Trying to find traces of it in that growing experience ends in finding *none*. What became of it? Why did it contribute so little to this consciousness-of-existence that is 'the boy' [himself]? It seems purely negative and for that son it may not have been positively harmful" (1977, pp. 56, 57).

I also remember little of the routine of life outside of school. Rather, it is the bizarre and the outrageous and the ridiculous and the colorful that I remember clearly.

My first day in Maple Avenue School was in either first grade or kindergarten; I'm not even sure I went to kindergarten, and I would assume I didn't if Aunt Anna didn't say that I did. I remember the entire class being kept five minutes after the bell because we were noisy—and I was near tears. We lived at the farthest end of the school district; the border between Newark and Hillside ran just beyond our backyard. I remember being walked to and from school by a bigger kid at first and lining up outside the building before the doors were opened so that we could enter; some status attached to being in front of the line. But that's almost all I remember. Of what happened within the classrooms for four and a half years before we moved, I remember nothing.

The schoolyard was surrounded by a high wire fence to be sure that kids could not get in to play when school was out; that typified the thinking of city and school bureaucrats in that era. Nevertheless, sometimes the kids climbed over the fence, which was a bit dangerous. My cousin Danny and I did it—the school was near his house—but I guess that was a year or two after I had moved away, when we were bigger.

What does it tell about me that I remember the school playground and the fence around it and even the lineups at the door in the morning, but not a bit about the content of my classes?

The first "original" idea I remember was when I was perhaps six. On the way back from the Jersey shore we were caught one evening in bumper-to-bumper traffic of the sort that rarely exists any more. (A 45-mile trip could take four or five hours.) I suggested to my parents combining an auto and an airplane by putting wings on the car to escape the traffic. It is relevant that though this idea shows some imagination, it is not a *wild* imagination. It is a reasonable, feasible engineering response to the problem at hand. And one part of my imagination—perhaps its core—is that of an engineer who finds the better way of doing things.

Whenever I have looked back on that idea, however, even when I was young, I assumed that thousands of people—including kids my age—had probably had much the same idea because it was so obvious. I did not think of the event as special, and I doubt that my parents made much of it (if anything).

I remember little consciousness of self from that period, and no self-inspection. I didn't need to examine myself, because there did not seem to be personal problems to solve. It was only later, after we moved to Millburn at my age of nine and I did not fit in easily that I began to study myself. The aim of my self-study was to learn how I could be different in order to be more successful with other people. Of course the change may have been simply a function of age rather than of circumstances. But the complete break in the before-and-after nature of my memories persuades me that the change in environment had at least a considerable impact.

Dad owned a tiny business selling sal soda—also known as "washing soda"—for use as an industrial water softener. The business employed only my father and a half-time laborer, Willie, but it provided the family perhaps \$50-\$100 a week (say, \$500-\$1,000 in 1995 prices) during the Depression, and that was not something to be sneezed at.

National Crystal Company—it sounded rather grand—was located next to a railroad siding in Irvington, right near a drop-forge factory whose trip hammers banged incessantly. Dad's factory was four sideways concrete steps up from the railroad track, through a heavy tarpaper door that slid sideways, then onto rough wood tracks that barrels were rolled up and down. The main equipment was a crude mixing vat that combined water and the main input, potash; the technology was vintage 1830s (yes, 1830s), except that it was powered by an electric motor instead of an overhead belt powered by steam or water power. There was also an "office"—a walled-off desk and telephone with piles of burlap bags for seats, other than my father's desk chair; I don't imagine that many people entered that office. The entire establishment had no heat in the winter other than a kerosene stove in the office.

When I talked with my older relatives in the mid–1990s about their and my memories of the family, none of them had ever been to Dad's factory or knew where it was; it surely was too unprepossessing for my mother to want the relatives to see it with their own eyes.

My father and my uncle Israel (Si) Simon bought the business together about 1927. Mother was anxious for my father to leave my grandmother's profitable dairy business in which he had grown up, both because she wanted to separate him from his mother's dominating influence and because a retail store was déclassé, especially a store in a first-generation immigrant neighborhood as was Prince Street where the store was located.

Uncle Si had a degree in chemistry from Cornell University, so the nature of the business made sense. But after a couple of years he sold out to my father, maybe because he could see that the business could not support the two of them and he was newly married (or about to get married). There may also have been difficulty connected with his wife, with whom my mother never got along.

Besides potash the main input was my father's labor—shoveling the potash from the railroad cars (with which Willie helped or maybe did most), mixing the potash with water (and perhaps other materials), packing the crystals into wooden barrels, putting the barrels onto the truck, and so on.

Once about 1937 when he was rolling a barrel to the door, it slipped and fell on Dad's kneecap and broke it. This constituted a business and family crisis: How would the business be continued? Mother went down to the factory—undoubtedly hating it, for which one can't much blame her—and answered the phone. Just how production was managed for the weeks while Dad was out of action I don't know; probably he hired Willy for more hours a week and supervised him. It is hard for most people who have come to maturity in the last quarter of the twentieth century in the United States to understand the economic insecurity felt by earlier generations, always one misstep or accident away from economic disaster and then (at best) the charity of relatives.

There was a quasi-mythical "Mr. Fick" who was an executive for a large firm that Dad sold to, perhaps his biggest customer. He was spoken of with awe in the house because so much depended on him. Dad went to see him in New York about once a year. To me, Fick had the status of lord of the world; in fact, he probably was a very middle manager. But such is the point of view of a child not too high up in the economic pecking order.

One evening I overheard my father on the phone fixing prices with his competitor—an illegal practice, but in this case hardly a threat to the public welfare (which does not excuse it). There was one other sal soda firm in the New Jersey area, at the other end of Newark. I do not know the size of that firm, but from my parents' comments I'd guess it was about the same size as my father's business. And I remember my father's side of the worried phone conversation—we may have already moved to Millburn, in which case it would have been after June, 1941—in which he and the competitor agreed to hold prices at something above what would be a cutthroat level. Afterwards there were discussions between my father and my mother about whether the competitor would keep the agreement or not. (This is the stuff of industrial economics that gets lost in the equations we write.) I therefore was not surprised when I read Adam Smith saying that no matter how festive the occasion, business people inevitably fall into conversation about how jointly to get more out of their customers. That's why George Stigler's theory of polypoly, with its emphasis on firms making price-fixing agreements and cheating on them, resonated with me. (None of this is inconsistent with my belief that taken as a whole, the world of commerce induces people to act more honestly and cooperatively than does any other system of economics.)

The business ended in 1943 when my father was unable to get raw materials because of the war.

We were in someone's kitchen—maybe my grandmother's, because I remember Mother and several other people being there. I could not understand a word of the German being spoken in the speech being carried live and in full on the radio, though Mother translated some of it (she had been a star German student in high school for four years, helped along by her skimpy knowledge of Yiddish). Yet I knew that I was hearing someone in a frenzy; that's part of why the event left such a powerful impression. The speaker was Hitler and the year must have been 1938. All who were in the kitchen were scared to the bone by what he had to say about Jews, as well as about the possibility of war. This was the only time in my life when I have ever seen—or it would be better to say "felt"—a group of people so frightened to the core of their beings. I do not have memories of such fright from any part of World War II, even December 7, 1941. The fright in my family and many others resonated their horrible experiences in Europe during World War II.

In those days before air conditioning, people kept their windows open for ventilation on hot summer nights. And in the city some people did not have screens on the windows. In these circumstances operated the "fishing pole burglar." His modus operandi was to stick a pole with a hook through the windows of first-floor bedrooms, and fish for the pants that men customarily folded over a chair when disrobing. (It wasn't worth bothering for weary workingmen to hang work pants in the closet.) The burglar then hauled the catch outside, extracted the money from the wallet that was usually left in the pants, and left wallet and pants in the alley. This story was relevant for us because we lived on the first floor.

Why did this story stick in my seven—or eight-year-old memory when I have completely forgotten so many more important aspects of our lives? Again, it is the bizarre, the eccentric, that caught my attention.

Dad and I would take walks down to Weequahic Park, which in retrospect can be seen as a paradigm for American economic society. At one end the park then had a trotting racetrack where amateurs stabled and raced their horses; Dad loved to watch the races, and I think I enjoyed them, too. I have no idea whether such a track was unusual for American cities then. The park was well-kept, a result of cheap labor and the WPA, probably. And it was entirely safe.

At the other end, one day we wandered just beyond the boundaries of the park, across the border to Hillside, near railroad tracks. We were startled when we startled a couple of men squatting in a hobo "jungle"—homeless men on the move, probably riding the rails, making coffee there in the secluded wooded area. For all the talk about homeless people in the 1990s, there now is nothing like the hobos—millions of men, able not only in body but also in mind, who could find no jobs and therefore had no homes. And this was probably as late as 1938 or 1939.

As far back as memory carries me, my aunts Anna and Ruth used to refer to me laughingly as a "bonditt," with emphasis on the second syllable. That's Yiddish for "bandit," but in their mouths it had the connotation of being a cut-up and a tease. Even my mother used the word "bonditt" in an amused fashion, another reason I liked it. My Aunt Anna reminds me that when I was in bed with scarlet fever at age six and beginning to feel a bit better, I threw spitballs at the doctor. I always enjoyed being called "bonditt" by them because I knew that it was an affectionate term and because I enjoyed that portrait of myself. And I guess I still do. I like to stir things up a little bit just for the sake of some fun, though not the sort of stirring up that hurts people even if it seems irreverent. Rather, it's a bit like pulling the monster's tail. Along this line, I have always enjoyed minor practical jokes, such as tying people's shoes together under the table or (skirting the edge of decency and safety) giving somebody a hotfoot by sticking the end of one match into the crack between the sole and upper body of the shoe and then lighting its end. I suppose as I got older I knew that this might be a bit dangerous, and I wouldn't do it any more. To the extent that it is harmless, the idea still appeals to me, especially if the receiver of the hotfoot is a highly respectable, highly influential, powerful person.

Naturally, I see some things from the other side of the table now. In the second of my only two courses in economics, Jack Hirshleifer was teaching managerial economics to a class of about eight people and he insisted on occasionally using calculus even though that was not supposed to be part of the course. So when he did so, I—sitting almost across the table from him usually—would put my head down on the table and snore lightly in protest. To his credit, Jack—with whom over the years I have been in touch more than with almost any other teacher—never batted an eye at my protest. (It didn't seem to deter him from the calculus, either, however.) Now I reflect that maybe my development of a better way of teaching managerial economics—entirely without calculus and using spreadsheets instead, with much fuller understanding and much more practical application—may have had some connection to this early incident.

I have continued to enjoy pranks, no matter who plays them. I still take what I think is innocent pleasure in tapping a person on one shoulder as I pass behind the person to the other side to start the conversation; the person invariably turns to the side that is tapped, which creates a touch of confusion and amusement. I don't aim to annoy or discomfit people, but rather I just like to tease them into some reaction, to join me in a bit of play.

I enjoy hearing about get-back-at-the-bastards pranks, like the story my Uncle George Cooper (Aunt Helen's husband) told me when I was about thirteen years old. A Brooklyn apartment dweller—a chemist or pharmacist—had neighbors upstairs who banged heavily on the floor from time to time. In retaliation, the chemistry man threaded a tiny pipette needle through the floor. He then injected a bit of noxious gas into the air above whenever the banging on the floor became too much to take. The origin of the odor apparently remained unknown to the people upstairs. Whether it affected the banging I do not know.

It seems to me that the pranks suburban kids play nowadays are much less obnoxious or malicious than when I was a kid—pins in doorbells, turning off Christmas-tree lights when turning one off, turned them all off because they were in series, and so on. I never participated in the burning of a bag of dog turds before the front door of a nasty neighbor as you rang the bell and ran away, but I know that it was at least within my realm of possibilities.

Many kids may not get traumatized as easily as many adults worry that they can be. When I was perhaps six years old, the baby sitter—a scrawny young man S with a pronounced Adam's apple who was the son of one of Mother's longtime friends—asked me to perform oral sex on him. I clearly remember his sitting on the living room couch when this happened, as I was standing. I refused, either because of distaste, or an inborn sense that it was wrong, or both (or maybe those elements are much the same thing in this case). I'm sure that I had no prior knowledge of such matters. I told my mother, which suggests that there was at least some stretch of my life when there was personal talk between us. I never saw S again.

I doubt that I have thought of this incident ten times in my life, and

I think that this is the first time that I have related it. It certainly did not have a great effect on me (peace, you psychoanalytical arguers of the unconscious). But though I downplay the significance for me, the incident makes it easy for me to believe that such occurrences are more frequent than people used to think they were. (Or maybe this is an example of the power of a personal experience to influence one's judgment about aggregate frequencies.)

All my friends were boys rather than girls, aside from Cookie who lived upstairs next-door when we were both about two and who I have only heard about and do not remember. I wanted to learn how to do the things that boys did. This has been the pattern of my life. I have seldom had casual friends of the opposite sex. By the time I was ten or eleven, girls were as fascinating as movie stars to me, far too exciting for me to consort with casually. I could never engage in the kind of flirtation in word and touch that many high-school kids played with; just touching a girl was potential dynamite for me.

When I was in casual contact with females, as when I lived in International House at the University of Chicago for a year as a graduate student, sex rarely left my mind, even if it was entirely absent from the woman's mind; I don't think that I had a single woman friend with whom the possibility of sex did not lurk in my mind somewhere, which made social life very complicated. But I also never shared any of their female interests—neither in physical activities (such as cooking) nor in societal activities. Though in my early and middle adulthood, I reflected comfortably that there is a lot of the female in me—especially my interest in other people's inner lives and in my emotional ability—I now would guess that I was born unremittingly male, though the absence of sisters may also have contributed to my unease with them.

The most contemptuous expression I heard in the Navy or Marines was "He can't fuck or fight, all he can do is fart and holler." That fit with my view of manhood. And indeed, the things that have always been deepest in my inner nature are making love and continuing to struggle against whatever forces I think deserve to be struggled against, whether personal or impersonal or natural. It was a shock for me when I found that a great many people pride themselves on accommodating the dark forces rather than fighting them and that many men lose interest in sex not far into adulthood.

I am in many ways still the same person I was as a boy in Newark and then in Millburn. I have noticed three autobiographers—Herbert A. Simon (*Models of My Life*, New York: Basic Books, 1991), Alan Paton (*Towards the Mountain*, New York: Scribners, 1977), and Frank Lloyd Wright (*An Autobiography*, New York: Horizon Press, 1932/ 1977)—referring to themselves as "the boy," rather than "I," up to adulthood. Simon, if memory serves, says that this was because as an adult he felt a discontinuity between himself and what he was as a boy. I still make some of the same jokes, use some of the same gags, such as when walking with another person, especially my kids, reaching around to my left with my right foot (or vice versa) to kick my companion in the rear end without breaking stride and hopefully without detection, or (as I mentioned before) touching the person's right shoulder as I walk behind from his or her right to left so that he or she looks in puzzlement for the toucher in the other direction. Sure, my hopes and expectations have changed a lot. But many of my social fears are about as they were when I was thirteen or seventeen years old, and so are my interests in the offbeat and bizarre. My sympathies are still with the same classes of human beings—the struggling poor, the powerless, and those denied opportunity by circumstance. I still dislike elite practices and attitudes. So unlike them, I continue to use "I" rather than "he" when writing about me, from first memory to now. I have had no basic changes in ideology or religious belief or political outlook, either. Of course, I'm more skilled, but I'm pretty much the same person, just (!) older.

3

The Family I Come From

Bare facts first about my family of origin, so you'll know about whom I am talking.

My father, Philip Mordecai Simon, was born in 1895 to Jenny and Abraham Simon in Newark, New Jersey. His Hebrew name was Mordecai, and hence my religious name in Hebrew is Yehuda ben (son of) Mordecai. He was followed by brothers Israel (Si, 1898) and Benjamin (Ben, 1903), and a sister Helen (1900). Israel married Helen in 1929, and bore Barbara (1932) and a son Michael (1936) with whom I have become closer as the gap between our ages relative to our ages became smaller and as we began to talk more about his profession of philosophy. (He also got a law degree in mid-life and combined that knowledge and his interest in ethics with philosophy.)

Barbara may have been born with brain damage, because in childhood she was already unusual and after childhood she was never completely normal; Michael refers to her as "psychiatrically disabled" and says she was diagnosed as schizophrenic at age fourteen, at which time she was hospitalized for the first of several times; she has lived her life in a halfway house and her delusions have been controlled by medicines in recent decades, but she has progressed little beyond prepuberty in her physical and mental abilities.

I remember with shame Barbara's coming occasionally to parties as an adolescent and my being reluctant to perform such social duties as dancing with her because she was so clumsy (not that I was any great shakes as a dancer); she was a quintessential wallflower. My classmate Paul Shiman was much more noble than I in that regard.

Neither Dad's sister Helen (born 1905), who after World War II married George Cooper who had been a suitor years before, nor Ben, who in 1945 married Rose Popkin, had children. In the years before the end of her long life, in 1988, when our aunt Helen Cooper was in a nursing home, Michael was an almost-saintly nephew in visiting her regularly, watching over, and arranging for her needs; then as co-executor with me of her (small) estate, he pressed almost none of the difficulties upon me, her only other living relative. In 1995, at age ninety-five, Rose and her sister Gert had their first art show at a local library in Livingston, New Jersey.

My mother was born Mae Goodstein in 1900 to Fanie and Julius Goodstein in Newark, New Jersey. Following her were a brother Jacob (Jac) in 1905, and sisters Anna (Anne, 1909), Ruth (1910), and Carol (Carrie, 1912). Jac married Evelyn Tepperman and bore my cousins Judith (Judy, 1931) and twins Daniel (Dan, Danny, 1933) and Claire; I remained close to all three (though Judy died in 1984), in part because they lived near us except the three years or so when we moved to Millburn ahead of them. Among the three of them are ten children. Anne married Sam Johnes, and Ruth married Sidney Markowitz; neither had children though Sidney had a son Elias by a previous marriage; it was a devastating blow to Ruth when Elias turned out to be a psychopath who got into almost every form of difficulty and then died at an early age.

Carrie married Charles (Charley) Brodsky and had daughters Ellen (1940) and Joyce (1942), whom I always liked but never was close to because of differences in age, sex, and geography; they lived in Newark until they were grown. All my cousins are fine people who have lived productive lives and have produced children among whom there has been a happy lack of the troubles of social pathology.

I joke that I am the illegitimate son of a married Jewish couple in Northern New Jersey. "Illegitimate" has nothing to do with the family, but rather with my feelings. I don't feel I have any claim on others to do anything for me, even that which is sanctioned by the informal rules. For example, I haven't asked from a department head or dean even a nickel of special travel or research funds since I came to the University of Maryland, and no research help and maybe funds for two or three trips in the near 20 years at the University of Illinois. Even first-year assistant professors feel justified in asking for such financial support and routinely get some travel paid for. (I once asked Dean Rudy Lamone for $200 for assistance paying for computer programming, and he graciously proffered it, but I never took the money.) Why? Simply because I just don't feel comfortable asking. Instead, whoever wants me at a meeting pays, or I pay myself for travel and other expenses, including all petty (and most not-so-petty research expenses). I feel somehow that the bosses will look at any request as illegitimate, and I will feel like some sort of thief trying to justify a request. So I don't bother.

Only once in my university work history have I opened a discussion with a department head or dean about my salary, and that was in the context of a general letter reviewing my situation after I had a stroke in 1989. My discomfort with such matters is so great that I would rather not even know what my and others' salaries are. Obviously this is an expensive peculiarity on my part.

My relationships with bosses of any kind have been my least competent type of relationship in life, except sometimes with Rita and the kids. I deal with it by avoiding contact with them as much as possible; I never met my first dean at the University of Illinois, College of Commerce during the three years he served. This surely reflects my relationship with my father, especially his disinterest in my welfare, his arbitrary exercise of authority over me, and the unreliability that he would do what he said he would do. More about him later.

But my reluctance to petition authorities also reflects my belief that I have no claim on the resources of the world around me, and that I'm damn lucky to get what I get. I know that this belief does not square with the mores and even rules of the organizations that I have worked for, but I cannot convert my abstract understanding into the affective thoughts that will get me to do what I need to do without seeming defensive and therefore ineffective. (Nowadays, my reluctance to ask also reflects the belief that people like me are quite well-off and therefore the world doesn't owe us anything more than we have—not even that.) This doesn't mean that on a few occasions over the decade I haven't raised hell with a bureaucrat—not my boss—if I feel that I have the law on my side, but in such a situation, there is no element of request or petition.

Our relevant family history begins with the immigration to this country of my grandparents on the Goodstein side from Austria and from the Pale of Poland on the Simon side. Everything from earlier ancestors that influenced my development was carried by those four grandparents, in the sense that all relevant previous history was embodied in them. Knowing about the parents and grandparents of my grandparents would not help me or you to understand me, I think.

I also doubt that knowing the personal characteristics of even my grandparents would tell much about the person I am. More generally, I doubt there are extended family influences through genetics or the family's own ways that heavily influence an individual's development. Similarities of physique, energy, and the like probably are transmitted reasonably well, but traits of character, I think, are transmitted hardly at all. The conventional nineteenth century English autobiographies that make much of the "family line" never seem convincing to me. But this is a matter that in future years surely will be put to systematic empirical test.

"Simon" had been something like "Sczymschak" before officials sheared the Yiddish-, Polish-, Italian-, what-have-you speakers of their long, unspellable handles at Ellis Island. Others of my grandfather's family turned (or had turned) their Sczymschak into "Solomon." On my mother's side, my cousin Judy's daughter Naomi has collected much of the genealogy, so our children are remarkably well fixed in this regard.

Once, Earl Browder, former head of the U.S. Communist Party, told me that he came from a very old family; he could trace their history back more than 400 years in America and England, he said—to the Mayflower. My first ridiculous thought was that it is a rare "new" family indeed that should be thought to have sprung full-blown from biological zero within the past few generations; but of course he did not intend that, and I should not make sport at his expense, even silently. I replied, "My family traces our history back about three thousand years." I can't remember whether I got a laugh out of him; probably not.

I speculate that Jews are less interested in their own genealogy than are many others because Jews' imaginations are rooted in events very long ago rather than in events a few hundred years back.

My Grandfather Goodstein died in 1916 when my mother was sixteen years old, and my Grandfather Simon died when I was two or three, so neither of them mattered in my growing up. As I look ahead to grandfatherhood, I have no secondhand experience to draw upon to learn how to act. (Nor is it a role that will come naturally to me.) My Grandma Goodstein's history and her contemporary presence meant much more to me than that of my Grandma Simon. One reason is that

Grandma Goody seemed healthy, pleasant, and clean, whereas Grandma Simon always seemed ill—something about a "drain" that was in her, though whether this was temporary or permanent I don't know; whether she was really ill, and how much she simply took on the role for effect, is not known to me or to any other relatives I've quizzed. She was a dark eminence—made dark by Mother's strong dislike for and distrust of her and by the dark clothes she always wore as she sat almost all the time in her favorite rocking chair in the gloomy house on High Street where she lived.

Grandma Simon's house always seemed to me almost haunted—a dark, Gothic place where all the furnishings seemed not to have been moved for half a century. My Aunt Helen lived there almost like the living dead, and when she married George Cooper and he moved into the house, it was as if he were moving into a cemetery. It was a very kind thing, and I think a great sacrifice by George, to be willing to move in with Grandma in order to be married to Helen, whom he had been in love with many years before, but married only after the war.

The effect was heightened by the three spinsters who lived in the adjoining house, who ventured forth in their aged Packard. Grandma almost never left her rocking chair, though sometimes she went into the antiquated kitchen to make a cup of tea.

Dad said that among his (and therefore my) ancestors were both the Baal Shem Tov (literally, Master of the Good Name) of the first half of the eighteenth century in Poland and the Gaon (genius) of Vilna of the second half of the eighteenth century. This is quite a parlay, as the horse players say, because the two great religious leaders were on exactly the opposite sides of the fence in the age-old struggle between mysticism and legalistic talmudic exegesis; the Baal Shem Tov was the founder of the mystical Hasidism movement that stressed feeling more than learning, and the Vilna Gaon—a great Polish Talmudic scholar—and his Mitnagdim ("Againsters") fought Hasidism bitterly; maybe Dad was simply laying off his bets against each other to cover all possibilities.

I know of no evidence that Dad possessed for this line of descent, and he may even have been jesting by making outrageous statements that he did not expect anyone to take seriously—something that I do and that sometimes drives Rita crazy if she believes me for a little while. But Dad repeated this statement often enough that I think he expected to be taken seriously. Distinguishing between my father's fact and fiction was relatively easy, because very little of what he said that was interesting was also factual. Here may well lie roots of my skepticism of authoritative pronouncements and conventional opinions.

Dad quit high school around the end of his junior year, ostensibly because he was needed in Grandma's store. And that event was made to sound like the tragedy of the talented boy who was deprived of the opportunity for higher education. But the story never rang wholly true to me. The two brothers—Israel ("Iz" or "Si") and Ben—and Helen all went on after high school, and Si and Ben went away to school at Cornell and Michigan, so money was not the constraint; indeed, Grandma's store was a great flourishing success. Of course, Grandma may well have needed Dad and pressured him to drop out of school. But I don't think that Dad ever had much interest in studying anything; I never knew him to do so. So he may have welcomed the "need" to quit.

A less elevated connection—though one that proves nothing except the location of the neighborhood where he grew up—was that the young men he ran with as a boy included the major bootlegging figures of New Jersey in the 1920s. Among them was Longie Zwillman, the top dog among the New Jersey clan of the Meyer Lansky bunch that were a major component of mob operations in the U.S. for many decades. (In the book *Lansky* by Hank Messick [New York: Berkeley, 1971]), Zwillman has the largest number of citations other than Joe Adonis, Vincent Alo, Albert Anastasia, Al Capone, Anthony Carfano, Frank Costello, Vito Genovese, Jake Lansky, Lucky Luciano, Bugsy Siegel, and Franklin Roosevelt—most of the foregoing names known even today among those who have watched an occasional late movie or episode of *Eliot Ness*. (Who else but a professor would give you supporting evidence like this?)

In 1927, Zwillman once asked Dad if he could borrow Dad's new Studebaker car to move a load of hooch. I believe that Dad found an excuse to fob him off, perhaps that he was getting ready to take the car and his new bride on a transcontinental honeymoon.

That honeymoon was perhaps the high point of their marriage. It included numerous thrilling escapades such as auto breakdowns while traversing a country that was still not fully paved across the continent; a visit to Yellowstone National Park, from which we still have the souvenir chunk of rock shaped like a sphinx that they illicitly took with them (not exactly the crime of the century); and an episode in which Dad drove onto the hard beach of southern California and decided to wash the car's wheels in the surf. The right side done, he turned to do the left side, but got stuck. The car was soon inundated, and a picture exists of Mother being carried overhead from the car by some local surfers. That was very close to disaster, with everything they owned for the trip in the car.

The greatest source of pride for Mother was having been valedictorian of her class in high school. I heard about the achievement often. But even when very young, I was neither abashed by it—I never felt I had to compare myself to it—nor was I all that impressed with it. It always seemed a slightly sad honor that something that happened in high school was the high point of Mother's life. And I always had reservations about the valedictorian type; in my high-school experience, drones were too much given to careful detailed work for my taste and too much mistake-avoiding, which seemed to me antithetical to creating things.

As did almost everyone else, I greatly respected Mother, and felt affectionate and protective toward her. But the distance at which she kept me (and others) worked to diminish any passion I might have felt toward her.

Let Mother tell you about herself in a memo she wrote to Rita about her friends, who were such a large and successful part of her life:

> Feb. 17, 1983
>
> I have been very fortunate in having friends who have been a source of companionship, inspiration and comfort over the major portion of my life.
>
> I was born in Newark, N.J., in the Italian quarter of the city. Most of the families in the area were recent immigrants who spoke English poorly, if at all. There were only a few non-Italian residents. Among the latter were four or five Jewish families who operated the stores in the neighborhood. In this small group was the Starr family who had three small daughters, Jean, Blanche and Mathilda. Jean was a little older than I and Blanche was a little younger while Mathilda was the youngest. Occasionally I was taken to the Starr home to play with these children and Jean and Blanche have been my friends since then. Jean now lives in California but visits me whenever she is in the East. We also exchange letters when something of special interest occurs. Blanche lives a few miles from my home and we see each other. Our husbands had some common interests and so there has been an unbroken relationship to this day.
>
> Sophie Goodman Klein, who died only one year ago, was also an early childhood friend from the time I was eight years old when we moved to a well integrated neighborhood. Here we both mingled with Jewish, Italian, Greek, German and Irish children. We all played jacks, jumped rope, skipped, visited each other's

homes and sampled various ethnic foods. We also learned to listen to our Italian neighbors play on the harp and violin as they were professional musicians. We walked to school together and Sophie and I went to Hebrew school together. At about age 13 Sophie's family moved to another section of the city but we visited and kept in contact. Sophie married earlier than I did but we communicated and visited. She was widowed when her son was three years old and Sophie had many problems to contend with. At each crisis she turned to me for comfort and help. When I faced a crisis before my husband died it was Sophie who came to stay with me.

Shortly after I graduated from High School at age 16 I joined the Chavoth Zionist Society. Here I met boys and girls who were 2 or 3 years older than myself but was very comfortable with them. Here I met Ida Greenberg Cowen and Hannah Malovany Horowitz. They are still my friends. Ida and I have enjoyed a deep understanding since then. We freely share experiences and confidences. It was with Ida that I went to theatre, concerts and operas in New York regularly. Whenever I went on vacations we communicated regularly. When there were romances we exchanged reports on experiences. Years later when Ida traveled abroad for 2 years I was in charge of her financial affairs and was responsible for sub-letting her apartment. Phil and I were helpful in many other ways. We are still in touch regularly and see each other whenever possible.

My friendship with Hannah Horowitz originated at the same time as Ida's. We were interested in Zionism and went to lectures and community events. Rob, Hannah's husband and Phil, my husband, enjoyed each other's company [when] we exchanged visits. We took an interest in each other's families and achievements. We still exchange views on personal and community affairs and problems as well as personal problems.

Frances Cohen Solman became my friend a little later, but it was not until we both married that our friendship and that of our husbands really developed. We were very helpful to each other in innumerable ways and visited together often. Before my son was born it was Frances who drove me a long distance to the doctor's office for regular visits. When Frances' husband was injured in an automobile accident we were helpful and supportive for a long time. And so it has been through out the years until the present, in times of crisis and joy.

When I was about 21 years old I met Helen Gordon Gartenlaub. Helen was not interested in Zionism or golf or some of my other interests, but we did enjoy each other's company as she was jolly and rather happy-go-lucky. After we were both married we continued to visit together and took an interest in each other's family. Of recent years we have not been in close contact but whenever we do get together there is great understanding and exchange of experiences.

My friendship with Birdie Benjamin dates from the time her son Donald and my son Julian were 6 years old. We all socialized together. The sons still are friends and so are the mothers. We exchange experiences and confidences. We have visited and played golf and picnicked together. We have been helpful to each other whenever and however it has been possible up to the present time.

Before I was married I was a member of the newly formed Junior Hadassah. In this group I met Ann Greenberg Klein. I never was very intimate with Ann but we did enjoy meeting each other and discussing events. Over the years our paths went in different directions but within the past 10 years she has been living in Millburn where I live. We have resumed our relationship and work together with great understanding and rapport. There is a solidity in our friendship that seems to stem from our earlier friendship. It is easy to close the gap caused by the many years we were not in contact, as there is an openness and depth in our relationship which is not readily created with friends of more recent years.

Over the span of years I have had other friends such as Rose Baskin and Rose Wolfson, and a few others, but because of death or moving the duration of the friendship was not continued.

I now count Esther August as a valuable friend. I have known Esther also since Junior Hadassah days but only during the last 20 or so years has it been my pleasure to have her as a friend. Esther is always ready to be helpful to me in many ways. We share similar interests in a current events group and other community affairs as we live in the same town. Our husbands also were compatible and had good rapport.

For the past two years Mollie Fiedel has been a good friend and companion. I regret not having known her earlier as we are both interested in arranging programs for a Retirees Club, and enjoy each other's company.

Mother and Rita had a wonderful relationship even though it was rather formal.

Mother herself was not a great producer of creative ideas, as my Aunt Ruth confirms. But I do remember Mother's urging Dad to try to break out of the narrow industrial market that permitted him only a small profit margin and instead to sell sal soda as washing soda to the consumer, packaging it in a fashion similar to what the large firm Arm and Hammer did and still does. She probably underestimated the extent and difficulty of the marketing needed for this, though, which almost surely made the project infeasible for Dad.

To use an interesting word, Mother was "cultivated." She was not wild, and she was not "natural"; rather, she worked on herself. She had a correct accent with no slang or ghetto or street expressions, though she did use Yiddish expressions sometimes. She used words like "Cheers" and "Bravo," which led Rita to refer to Mother as "Scotch Presbyterian"; indeed, when young she played golf when few women did so, undoubtedly because it was the cultivated thing to do; certainly it was not because she cared about sports or was good at them. And she and her friends bought books of poetry and read them together; I still have some fine editions of poetry that were hers and some classic novels.

I was a dutiful son when I was grown. But I fear that I was insufficiently attentive to Mother when she grew old and after Dad died; though we spoke on the phone, I did not visit her enough. And I may have urged more on her than she was capable of. The phrase "Don't tell a person how to walk until you have stood in his or her moccasins" came home to me with force when mother had a walking ailment, and I urged her to change how she was standing and to use a treadmill. A walking therapist heard me urge some movement on mother that mother said she could not make, and the therapist gently instructed me with the moccasins phrase.

Once we went to a restaurant and I urged her to walk in a certain way on the way out. She tried so hard that she passed out, greatly scaring me and the rest of the family as I had to carry her to the car. She was all right, but I suffered (and still suffer) from remorse due to my insufficient sympathy for her age and lack of physical abilities.

My family were all staunch union people. It was an article of faith that unions are good for the working person, and anyone who is not in favor of strong unions getting as much power as possible must be against the working person and a tool of the bosses. I was a member of the Newark, N.J., local of Teamsters, Chauffeurs, Warehousemen, and Brewery Workers when I held a "temporary book" one summer, working at Krueger Brewery making about $2.80 per hour at a time when the minimum wage was $1 and I was worth just the minimum wage in a non-union market. And Rita and I even joined the professors' union at the University of Illinois and quit only late in the 1970s. Though I think that bargaining for wages is not a good idea for the society as a whole, or even for the workers in the industry in the long run (the disaster that befell the U.S. auto industry in the 1970s was largely due to the union's activities with the complicity of the auto companies in the 1950s and 1960s), I still believe that unions have an important role in many other issues, such as safety and arbitrary dismissal; they provide some counterbalancing power on behalf of the workers in their struggles with the owners.

Throughout their entire lives the Goodstein girls and their brother Jac were wonderful in their mutual support, trust, and affection. There was some quiet, lasting bitterness, but there were no continuing quarrels that I knew or know of, a great achievement, though it had some costs.

One of the costs of the absence of quarrels that was a characteristic of the Goodsteins that they themselves comment about: the lack of intimate talk among them. They did not talk about their feelings or their private activities with each other, or perhaps with others. Late in life Aunt Ruth has talked about her life with me and said she enjoyed the talking. But when I ask her now for details about the family she warns me against "digging too deep," not because there are any family skeletons but because the ordinary facts might make me unhappy; she is not convinced when I tell her that I enjoy talking of private lives and I feel privileged when someone shares some of his or her life with me.

When I read others' autobiographies, I wonder about their accuracy when they describe their antipathies toward one parent or another. But, negative as it is, I'd guess that my view of my father is more benign than the attitude toward him held by any of my other relatives, except Mother and perhaps Aunt Helen, Dad's sister. For my mother's sisters and brother, Dad was an affliction that they did their best to help Mother to bear.

In person, both Mom and Dad were quite the opposite of many of the maxims they urged. Mother was fond of saying that if you have nothing good to say of a person it is better to say nothing at all, though I've forgotten the exact language of the maxim. I must have been forty years old before I recognized that she was no less hard on her fellow human beings (though perhaps no harder on them, either) than the average person; it is surprising how much one's impressions can be formed by what people say rather than what they do. And she led me to believe in a humility that she very much did not practice; her self-pride, together with her sense of rectitude, was perhaps her strongest feature, and not an unpleasant one. There was not the slightest note of being a victim in her demeanor except occasionally when my father was especially unreasonable.

When I made some inquiries in the past few years, some interesting inquiries have been made of me in return. The hottest question came from my aunts and from Uncle Charley (the husband of Carrie Goodstein Brodsky, now dead). They wanted to know how my father made a living. They knew that he had "some kind of a factory" prior to World War II, but none had ever been there—not surprisingly, as I mentioned, given its appearance and my mother's attitudes. And they had even less information about him after World War II. They asked me how we supported ourselves, and I reminded them of Mother's working. I did learn one interesting item: Mom and Dad did not contribute to supporting Grandma Goody in her late years, and Charley speculated that this must have humiliated Mother.

All the family conspired to save Mother—whom all respected greatly—from embarrassment and humiliation from my father; not asking questions of her was one part of that support.

These were the words that I spoke at the unveiling of Mother's tombstone on the anniversary of her death, after reading *Proverbs 31,* the poem spoken on Friday night about a "woman of valor" (Eshet Chayil).

> The period between Mother's death and this unveiling has given us time and perspective to reflect on what she meant to each of us. And the fact that the family, with Uncle Sidney rather than a congregational rabbi, is conducting this unveiling moves us to active thought about Mother and her life.
>
> I will not talk about Mother herself. The words spoken at her funeral were good ones, and they are enough. But the time since her death has brought home to me time and again that Mother is remembered by many people, and she is remembered well, as she deserved. An amazing number of letters and cards came, with thoughtful and emotional words, from an extraordinary variety of friends and relatives. People spoke about the influence that mother had had upon them, and the ways that she helped them. Mother had a kindling power, and she evoked a most unusual respect in those who knew her. And she had a peculiar ability to bring out the best in people. All spoke about how grateful they were to have known Mother. And here I shall mention the gratitude for having known Mother and for having shared her life that is felt by her brother and sisters, her grandchildren, her daughter-in-law, and her son.
>
> Sometimes the prayer book is the best wisdom of all. The Eshet Chayil with which the unveiling traditionally concludes, and which was Uncle Sidney's inspired choice to begin with, is exactly right for Mother. She was indeed a woman of valor. We miss her greatly, we think of her often and well, and she will influence our thoughts and our lives forever.

At Dad's funeral, neither I nor anyone else, except the Rabbi, had anything to say; indeed, there was no one there except my mother, Rita, maybe our kids, and maybe one or two other relatives. The Rabbi, who had never met Dad, just kept saying, over and over, "He was a good man," and I thought to myself, that is exactly what he was not. I probably would not have gone to the funeral if Mom were not still alive. I'm faintly ashamed to say that for many years he had meant no more to me than he meant to anyone else other than Mother—just about nothing. My ability to separate myself from him emotionally once I had decided that there was nothing there—about age twelve—disconcerted the few people I told about it, and perhaps disconcerted me a bit, too. But this cool behavior saved me a lot of the pain that the children of other unpleasant fathers suffer because they do not cut loose emotionally from a bad connection.

Does one ever know well what someone, or a group, thinks of you? I feel surer of what my Aunts Ruth and Anna thought about me than anyone else; they doted on me, and they were the only ones in the world. Why them? I don't know. They say it is because I was active and "bright." I would guess, rather, that one first likes another person for some undefined and (as of 1996) unknowable attracting qualities, and then attributes praiseworthy qualities to the liked person.

What did my parents think of me? I don't know. Even though I was their only child, despite their own uncertain economic future and my possible assistance later on, and despite my mother's dissatisfaction with what my father's occupational life had brought them, I was surprisingly unimportant in their lives, I think. Or at least I certainly had absolutely none of that feeling that I was the center of their universe, as many other only children have. I don't think that they saw me as a salvation, economically or otherwise; for my father to do so would have meant according me an importance of which he probably was not capable.

I think that the nature of my relationship to my parents derived from their relationship to each other. My mother focused her attention on my father. And my father focused his attention upon himself. So I had plenty of space to grow up by myself. It never even occurred to me that one of my parents would come to watch me play in a sports contest; when I went to about half of Judith's high-school basketball games I thought that that was quite a lot, perhaps because of my own experience, while she thought that it was only a little, perhaps because some other parents went to everyone of their kids' games. Nor did either Mom or Dad show much interest in any of my activities for their own sakes, though Mother thought that getting good grades and being an Eagle Scout would be good things because of their credential value. Nor did they share with me such concerns as being popular in high school. Mother focused on my future capacity to make a good living; Dad did not enter my world except when I did something that annoyed him.

Money was a big thing in the family. As every family that tries to economize knows, saving money can be expensive. I had a stamp collection and I wanted to buy some standard plastic hinges to mount the stamps in stamp books. My father instructed me to save money by cutting into strips old gummed labels from various sources and use them instead. But when I came to trade or sell some stamps several years later, I found that the gum would not peel off and the stamps were mainly ruined from a collector's point of view. That's the cost of saving imprudently.

I remember many hours sitting on the window box in my bedroom in front of a little desk that Judith has now, working on homework or my stamp collection. Occasionally I'd turn around and stare out the back window at the pleasant backyard, the squirrels, the huge oaks, and the birds. The solitude was often pleasant, but I also was often lonely. I felt I lacked the company of brothers or sisters. It never occurred to me to seek the company of my parents, or that I yearned for parental company. This is one of the many things I learned about the past from writing this volume. It seems to me as if our ignorance about our own lives at the time we are living them dwarfs our knowledge at that time.

Dad was the urban Jewish equivalent of a Georgia redneck with respect to race. I am not very critical of this. I am sure it was some combination of ignorance and the desire to feel better than somebody else when there aren't too many people you can feel better than on objective grounds. But there is a world of difference between condescension or contempt and denying someone a job or killing them.

I remember mother referring to Eleanor Roosevelt as being "so democratic." I thought that meant that mother thought that Eleanor Roosevelt gave no external signs of her social superiority, which I think mother also aspired to do, and perhaps successfully. Her attitude towards race relations came out of the same mold, I think. She got to be very good friends with Lee van Horn when they worked together in the insurance office, and they visited with each other at home. I think her ideals went in this direction, too. But it would be amazing if, in that era, mother had a very different concept of full equality.

Goodness knows I am as unblind to race as is everyone else in U.S. society, though I think that that awareness does not predispose me to negative attitudes; indeed, I have always "rooted" for blacks to do well as if they were my own—in sports, from Joe Louis to Jackie Robinson to Arthur Ashe; in literature, Native Son, etc.; in politics, Ralph Bunche, ...And I certainly am one of a very very tiny number of people who thinks that once the facts shake out well enough, there will be found to be no more intelligence differential between blacks and whites than between immigrants from various parts of Europe, differences which I think nobody claims any more. Of course there are many pieces of evidence against us at the moment, but I am simply making a best guess about the outcome when vastly more evidence is accumulated. (Clearly this is one of the most difficult topics for social science to make sense of.)

Perhaps the most important characteristic of growing up as an only child, as I did, without everyday casual interaction with other families, such as next-door neighbors or relatives close by, is that one has very few models of life among which to choose and few kinds of interactions in which one can practice one's skills dealing with people. Also, there are few sources of judgments of oneself which one can weigh and compare in such a circumstance. Hence one's parents may have an unusually strong effect even if they are not especially strong-minded people or even if one is not especially close to them.

When I was a child and I brought home a report card or a report of some success—for example, gaining a Boy Scout merit badge for bird-watching or whatever—Mother would say, "That's very nice. But you can do better"; never "That's terrific; let's celebrate."

For example, I would guess that my mother's expressed attitude toward me that there was always more I could do, and that it always could be done better, enters heavily into my lifelong pattern of working hard for long hours and never sitting back and basking in the pleasure of a good job well done; this probably also is the source of my not thinking myself to be a fine fellow and of not taking considerable pride in those pieces of work that I do—their quality and quantity—or in rewarding myself handsomely for such accomplishments with vacations, parties, and self-congratulation, but rather being perennially dissatisfied with what I have done, judging it to be illegitimate (that is, I should be doing something else), ill-chosen as a subject of my attention, poorly presented, and the like. (All the while I can also be entirely convinced that the work itself is sound in execution and correct in conclusion, even though I know that others already disagree or will disagree in the future. This is the sort of apparent contradiction that makes any person's mind such a fascinating object of inquiry and of autobiography.)

On the other hand, I cannot explain my worry throughout my adult life about not completing tasks, and about my writings not getting published, by any reference to my parents. Neither of them was a great worrier. I cannot even find an explanation in this behavior being the *opposite* of my parents ("The same fire that hardens the egg melts the butter"). So I do not want to push too far my attribution to the enhanced influence of the parents when there are no siblings or other adults or children in constant close proximity.

One of the results of the paucity of models to imitate and of persons with whom to practice interactions may be that one is more likely to invent one's own patterns of life. This may especially be true if one does not have the closeness with one or another parent that John Stuart Mill had with his father, for example, as is described in his autobiography.

Though Mother told me that they had no more children because they worried about being able to provide for more, Aunt Ruth was surprised when I told her that. She—and also Rita—though it might have been because she thought she was too old; standards were different then, and she was thirty-two years old when I was born. But in any case, having no brothers or sisters did not make me feel more valuable to them, but rather the opposite; I had the idea that if they considered having me a good thing, it would be natural to have more such good things. Indeed, I was always surprised that my parents expressed no worry over the precariousness of life when mortality was even more significant than now and they had but one child; this worried me on their behalf when I was in the Navy. And I'm sure that this was a consideration for me when we decided to have three children (rather than fewer). I also considered the "portfolio" effect of the bad luck people have with children—falling prey to drugs, pathology, parent hate, and the like. ("Worse than a serpent's bite is an ungrateful child.")

I have searched back for memories of celebrations and happy moments. I remember few. This is not to say that my parents were glum, but rather I remember little joy. My bar mitzvah was a happy day. So undoubtedly was the day we moved into our new house in Millburn. But when else? I do not remember toasts to any successes, though Mother certainly celebrated my acceptance to college (though the Navy ROTC scholarship was a mixed blessing even though it entailed going to Harvard). The fact of the country being at war certainly moderated joyfulness for all, but I refer to the years after the war ended, as well.

I think Mother made birthday cakes. Indeed, her food was one of the most pleasant parts of life. She was a good cook, and her pies and cakes—especially her patented cheese cake, made inside a steel frame that I still have—were delicious, and we all enjoyed them, as good a part of our lives as there was.

***

True, you can't choose your relatives. But one can imagine. My choices in relatives: William James as my father, Hayek as my uncle,

Milton Friedman as my older brother, Theodore Schultz as my thesis adviser, and David Hume as my idol. This is a bit short on mothers and sisters, I know. Maybe George Sand as my sister? I know too little about her.

4

Millburn I: Until High School, 1941–1945

People who have suffered badly from boredom say that it is one of the worst of afflictions. Solitary confinement in prison is essentially a painfully boring situation; there are no outside stimuli to excite a person. Giving us the means to lessen boredom surely is one of the great benefits of modern communications for many people, especially the bedridden.

My only experience of extended boredom was when I was nine and we moved to Millburn just as the summer vacation began. There were no kids in the neighborhood that summer, and I did not know anyone elsewhere in town. I remember just sitting on the curbstone and occasionally saying to my mother, "I ain't got nuttin' to do." (Chances are she admonished me not to say "ain't".)

Mother would tell me to go to the very nice town park half a mile away where there was a lake to swim in, four tennis courts, a baseball diamond, and other facilities. So I might walk over to the park, but I never knew how to meet anybody there, and therefore I usually aimlessly wandered around and came home. (I did learn to play horseshoes at the park, at least. But I made no friends that would carry over from the park.)

I suffered a bit of boredom aboard ship in the Navy after we had been out at sea for many days on a long cruise. But by then I had short-story writing to occupy my time and a variety of books that I wanted to study, including calculus and biology preparation for medical school. And the routine at sea of "four on, eight off"—that is, four hours on watch out of every twelve, around the clock, every day of the week, in addition to the regular workday from 8 A.M. to 4 P.M. five days a week, left little time for boredom. (The bad part of routine at sea was the little time left for sleep. I have a very low threshold for sleep deprivation, though my physical pain threshold is generally high. So I suffered from the routine at sea.)

Since that first summer in Millburn, I have spent more hours wishing that the conditions would enable me to get bored than I have in the grip of boredom.

Often on the Sabbath I get up in the morning, pick up a book, read half a page, look out the window for an hour, read another half page, look out the window for another hour, and so on, until it is midday. There are so many exciting things to think about and to ponder, it seems. It is a great benefit of being interested in basic questions like relativity, probability, calculus, and other such subjects that one can continue plumbing deeper and deeper and perhaps never touch bottom. This unending source of interest is one of the great lucky aspects of my life.

We moved to Millburn, a New Jersey suburb a few miles north of Newark, in the summer of 1941. The move produced a crack in my life, though not an earthquake. I never again felt like an insider. The picture of the gang in Newark with me as the littlest kid in the center was my last such experience.

Though I had no brothers or sisters, I do not remember wishing for siblings until we lived in Millburn. But then the phrases "my sister," and especially "my brother," became for me the sweetest words in the English language.

There was a tree nursery at the end of the block. The nursery seemed as huge as a jungle to us kids. (As an adult I am shocked at how small an area it covers—about large enough for two sets of two houses back-to-back.) In our game, "tribe war," one of our favorite stratagems was to dig an "Ethiopian elephant pitfall trap"—a pit in the path covered with slight sticks and grass for concealment—and then lead the other tribe of two or three boys through the path, in hopes that one would fall into the pit (all the way up to one knee. We never worried about spraining joints or breaking bones, of course.)

Those elephant traps are my image of pitfalls in thinking that all of us too often fall into inadvertently. It is in these ways that the growing-up period seems present with me now, more than the kind of stuff that Freud talked about.

It seems to me that the range of games that we played was wider than the range of games kids play today. Of course this may be due to my having experienced games in two dissimilar areas—the inner city and suburbs. The previous chapter mentioned some of what we did in Newark. In the suburbs, we could play hockey on the mill pond, and we could play skating games such as snap the whip, which was exciting and could get to be scary for the kid at the end of the whip, but we didn't think much about the danger. The lawns in Millburn made possible knife-handling games for which there was no place in the inner city, mostly involving throws into the turf. I liked them because there was room to practice and learn—starting from the simplest toss from the palm of the hand one-half revolution up and down and into the dirt, then from the back of the hand half a revolution. Then the tosses evolved over the head and behind the back, and various other gyrations resembling a diving competition. Of course the rules were very intricate and relatively well agreed on, though it must have been very different from neighborhood to neighborhood.

We also practiced throwing the jackknives into trees. I acquired a small skill in that, not huge. Also, we practiced throwing hatchets at large trees, imitating the Indians; very poor rate of success. Trees were excellent targets for snowballs, though.

I also practiced placekicking in football, hoping to find a role for myself. Because you need someone to hold the ball for you, which gets tiresome, I tried to learn drop-kicking, the way it was done by Jim Thorpe (America's most famous athlete when I was a boy). But when Jim Thorpe played, the ball was rounder and therefore much easier to drop-kick.

The skill I could never seem to acquire was whistling with my fingers at the corners of my mouth; I just saw my grown son Daniel do it, and I was amazed. Will I get him to teach me? I am also looking for somebody to teach me how to ride a unicycle. (David was going out with a woman horse-riding trainer, and I asked him to ask her if she could teach me how to ride a unicycle because I don't own a horse. For some reason, that didn't seem logical to anybody besides me.)

Bikes in Millburn were another endless source of the leader games. I was seldom the leader, but often a pretty good follower.

We threw at each other anything that could be thrown, crab apples, snowballs of course, usually mud balls.

Now after much procrastination I'll write about an incident that I've never told anyone about, and that I'm still very reluctant to tell about. First the facts:

The first fall after I was in Millburn, Dick Steive, Eddie Mehm, and I were fooling around on somebody's lawn. Dick and Eddie were both Catholic—I heard what sounded like "Sarosalima" so often that until adulthood I never knew that it meant "St. Rose of Lima." the name of their church. And they knew nothing of Judaism. Upon learning that I was Jewish, the two of them began to construct a ten-year-old's image of a heathen and bizarre churchlike synagogue. "The altar is a toilet," I remember, and the rest went with it.

These were good-natured kids. These were not kids filled with religious hate whom it would be sensible for me to fear. Dick and I were good friends for years. (Eddie moved away soon.) They were just fooling around. But they had the usual prejudices of ignorance.

The most interesting part is why I have tried so hard to close out this memory, and why it still bothers me so much. I am not twitchy about anti-Jewish sentiment in this country; I believe that we are now living in the most golden Golden Age of Judaism. I think that the "Never again" view that a killer anti-Semitism lurks beneath the surface of other peoples, the mentality of many Israelis and the U.S. Jewish Defense League, is a costly error in judgment. (But I do believe that Israel should speak softly but carry a big stick, as Teddy Roosevelt put it.) I don't worry about Jewish cultural-religious survival; I figure that if Judaism has had enough of value to stay around for three millennia, it has the staying power to persist in the future, and if it lacks the ingredients to persist on its own, then let it disappear (but I'm quite sure it won't).

Yet I cannot discount that this memory has affected me, simply because it is still so tender with me. And if this little thing affects me, how much tougher it must be for others such as blacks in the U.S. who really have faced (and still face) severe discrimination?

Maybe it is just that this incident feels so *embarrassing*—embarrassing to me on my own behalf, and embarrassing to me on their behalf. Maybe this is like kids teasing you because you are fat, or short, or stinky, or a teacher's pet; one could remember such an incident with painful embarrassment, too.

I have often wondered whether the workings of my mind now would be very different if we had not moved from Newark and I had not been made an outsider by events. It is entirely possible that the basic processes are much less affected by social and emotional circumstances than the Freudian school convinced us they are, though I am not ready to conclude that there really could be such a sharp break between that period and the next eight years in Millburn without affecting me substantially.

After we left Newark, I never went back to my neighborhood there. I doubt that I ever even asked Mother to go back to visit. (Asking my father would not even have occurred to me; I have no memory of ever asking him to undertake an expedition with me, and the only times we went out together, such as for a bike ride, it was initiated by him.) I did not feel that I had any rights to have my desires fulfilled by others.

I had not wanted to move to Millburn, and my parents had made the concession of promising me a dog and a bike when we got to Millburn, two things I had asked for earlier. They delivered on that promise, and I think I felt that I had received everything that was coming to me, and it did not occur to me to ask to be taken back; that would have interfered with people's (my mother's) work. The fact that much she did around the house—like dusting every day—was easy to forgo never occurred to me until she had to go to work a few years later when Dad closed his business, and miraculously, the house seemed none the dirtier for being dusted only once a week.

My scrapbook for "Social Science" for the 1942–1943 school year at South Mountain School—which my mother saved for me, one of the many loving acts of conservation on her part—is interesting largely because it reveals just how ordinary I was. The books I read for book reports, mostly chosen by myself from the library or from birthday gifts, were decidedly run-of-the-mill. In order, in the scrapbook, they were *Knights of the Sea: A Story of Stephen Decatur*, for which I received a grade of A; *Sentries of the Sea* by Floherty, grade B, (Writing B+); *Submarines* by Herbert Zim, grade A (writing B); *Alexander Hamilton* by Smertenko; *Historic Ships* by Rupert Holland, illustrated by De V Lee, grade B-; *Skywinder Mystery*, grade B; *Man Without a Country* by Everett Hale, with notes and questions by George Ross, grade A; *Mutiny at Midnight* by Stackpole, grade A+; *The House Where George Washington Slept, Klondike Partner* by Edward Sabin, grade A+; *Our Gmen*, grade B+; *Coast Guard Cadets* by Kensil Bell, grade A; *Buffalo Bill* by Shannon Garst, grade A+; *Duke Decides* by John R. Tunis, grade A.

By far the most interesting report was about *Man Without a Country*, which was assigned, I believe. This is what I wrote:

Man Without a Country
by Everett Hale

Philip Nolan was a fine young man and this story about him is stirring. He was a lieutenant in the army when Aaron Burr made his first dashing expedition down to New Orleans. Nolan met Burr and was fascinated with him. When Burr gave him permission to write to him, Nolan was delighted and although he did write he never received an answer. As you may know Burr killed Hamilton in a duel and was then regarded as an anarchist. Later on when Burr was tried Nolan was tried with him and was convicted. When asked if he had anything to say he said this: D—n the United States. May I never hear her name again.

This sentence changed the whole life of Philip Nolan. The Judge decreed that Nolan should have his wish. He was put aboard a warship, although he was allowed the run of the ship no one could talk of home in his presence.

Philip Nolan lived fifty six years this way. He was on many differents [*sic*] ships.

Through all this when Philip Nolan died he had these words on his lips. "God Bless America."

Nov. 6, 1942

The report for *Man Without a Country* seems to me now to be quite competent, but it is revealing in how ordinary it is. There is absolutely nothing in it that reveals a mind that is unusual, eccentric, creative, amusing, or insightful.

Most of the Social Science scrapbook is about Greek and Roman mythology. A turn-of-the-millennium reader in the U.S. might consider that material to indicate more "rigorous" schooling when I was young than now. I'm not so sure that that is a sound conclusion. What is so valuable about memorizing or knowing the names of the Greek deities—the nine muses who were daughters of Jupiter and Memory, including Thalia, who was in charge of comedy, and her eight sisters? Would we not have been better-off learning about famous explorers, or scientists, or even political leaders? Or even, famous baseball players? Just because the Greek and Roman material is "classical," does that mean it is worth learning?

And another question about this material: Why is it acceptable to teach about Greek and Roman religion but not about contemporary religion? Why stories of the Greek and Roman gods and not bible stories? I would have been much more enriched by reading the Old

Testament than by the stuff we did read, and Christians (or now, Muslims) would have no problem with it, either. Reading the New Testament is touchier, undoubtedly making many Jews and Muslims uncomfortable, but that could be considered separately.

Looking through the scrapbook, I find the names and faces of all my classmates—listed as members of various "committees" for our study of mythology—are familiar to me know. The teacher, however, is not named in the scrapbook, and I have no memory of either her face or her name. It has been this way all my life; authority has not been interesting to me except as a force of nature that I have had to deal with, like the weather. I did not look to my parents or to other adults (my aunts Ruth and Anna were the exceptions) for either affection or instruction. In contrast, my contemporaries were full of interest for me, and I cared intensely about my relationships with them. This stance I take to be related to my egalitarianism, and my discomfort with hierarchical society.

I do remember one (and only one) encounter with my first teacher at South Mountain School, 1941–1942. When I volunteered an answer without being called on, she gently took me aside after the period was over and instructed me to raise my hand and wait for her to call my name before speaking. I slunk away in shame, seldom raised my hand, never again volunteered without raising my hand, and thereafter tried to sit toward the back of the class when there was any choice.

About that age, at the Silbers' house when I baby-sat for Joan and Ralph, I read a vignette in the *Reader's Digest*, about a girl who applied to a fancy women's college such as Smith. In those days a questionnaire was sent to the parents of prospective students that included the query, "Is your daughter a leader?" The parent replied, "No, but she is an excellent follower." The college admitted the girl, saying, "We expect 599 leaders in the incoming class. It will be nice to have at least one good follower." I identified with the girl who was the follower.

When I tell Rita that I was a very ordinary child, she responds with "But you did X," as if my saying now that I was ordinary then is just an adult conceit, adopted now for effect. My remembering that *Reader's Digest* story so vividly all these years seems to me evidence that I was indeed very ordinary in at least one aspect of my behavior. If there was anything unusual about me, it was that I recognized how not-unusual I was.

At several places in the book reports, the teacher corrected me to use "which" in the sorts of places in my current writing that [sic] copy editors cross out "which" and insert "that," on the grounds that "which" is *wrong*. How things do change, especially when they don't matter a damn.

Listening to a professor of music play at a memorial service for Rita's friend Irene Lorenczi in 1995 reminded me of reading the remark that "the past of every aging, third chair violinist at the symphony is a small boy [small girl] giving a recital with dreams of becoming the next Paganini." I'm lucky, I feel, that never when I was a child did I have grand dreams of achievement in any field—not in academics, or in any performance art, or in social life, or in athletics. Of course, I harbored the dream that somehow I would discover or grow into some great athletic talent in some sport, but I was fully cognizant that the probability of that was about the same as the probability of being hit by lightning. And I never felt different, unlike a very large proportion of adolescents and young adults. (I remember asking nine people in Chicago in 1958 whether they felt different as adolescents, and everyone at the table said he or she did).

Part of the reason I never felt different was that I always had an acute statistical sense that the probability of my being special in any particular way had to be extraordinarily small, given the very large number of human beings and the very little experience I had to compare myself to. And this was indeed realistic. Of course, I carried this too far. When I met Walter Primeaux at the University of Mississippi and recognized that he was a talented economist, I thought that there must be many more like him who were stuck away at third-rate places just by happenstance. I later found out that the number of cases like Walter is far smaller than I imagined.

I started school in January in Newark and had completed four and a half years when we moved. But Millburn only started classes once a year, so it was either go ahead or go back half a year. I went ahead into fifth grade, and the small jump made no difference academically, but it moved me a bit behind physically. Though I can't remember where I stood with my class in Newark—probably just average—I felt myself a bit smaller than most of my Millburn class. In fact, I was probably at least average and probably considerably better than average athletically, but from then on I felt as if I were always chasing the pack by a bit, even if I wasn't; if I had stayed in Newark it probably would not have been that way. Because I focused on physical rather than mental competitions with others, this change mattered.

Furthermore, the school class played soccer rather than football, so in my first sports season in Millburn I was out of things during physical education; learning to use one's feet with a soccer ball takes longer, in my experience, than most other kinds of skills. And I was never speedy afoot; my strengths have always been accuracy of hand and eye, and speed of hand. This was more reason to feel that I was behind others. Those of you for whom athletics have not been important in your lives may be puzzled by the stress I put on this side of my child's life. I believe that this emphasis fairly reflects sports' importance in my sense of myself and in my pecking order relationship to the "significant others" (that's a pun on modern-day bureaucratic-demographic jargon) of my social life.

I always thought of myself as being essentially similar to most other people—which may in itself be a little unusual for an adolescent. I also never paid much attention to being good in school, and even then I put little value on being school-smart or "clever." I just thought it was one dimension of a person among many, and not a particularly important dimension. I would have swapped being 25 percent less school-smart for being a 20 percent better athlete or 25 percent more attractive to girls.

Later, when I was in the advertising business, I thought that I was on reasonably safe ground in assuming that my reactions to a product or advertisement would be representative of other peoples', because of my being a fairly average person in fundamental ways.

Reading the autobiography of Herbert Simon (not a relative), *Models Of My Life* (New York: Basic Books, 1991), I am struck by how different I am from him. One point is relevant here: He wrote (page 17) about how

> the boy [H. Simon] saw himself as different from his friends. His left-handedness, his brightness, and his color-blindness set him a little apart.
>
> One of the differences was that the boy was conscious of being a Jew . . .

Like many or most adolescents, I did my best not to seem different. If boys carried school books in the hand with the arms hanging at one's sides, without a bag or briefcase, that's how I carried my books—in contrast to girls who carried them in their arms in front of where their bosom was or would soon be. If no one wore a hat no matter how icy or wet it was, I also limited myself to ear muffs. I was always a fashion follower rather than a leader (as I was not a leader in anything). I never was super-good at the game of being perfectly turned out. At college it would have been very expensive to dress like the fashionable preppies, besides requiring more attention to grooming than I was willing to devote to it—and I guess I did not want to be identified with the preppies, either, even if it had been possible, which it was not. When I came home and heard Joe and Sol (the latter later called "Joe", too), a couple of Jewish Yalies from a nearby suburb, talking about the right kinds of socks and garters, I could only make a bit of fun of them behind their backs. (Recently I have read of research that claims that the most attractive faces are those that are most average. If true, it jibes with the urge to conform in appearance.)

Of course, not feeling different or particularly gifted can be something of a problem if it keeps you from stretching yourself to your maximum reach.

The only way in which I thought of myself as being different—actually marginal, rather than different, as were many other of my classmates who were marginal, too—was not being part of the gilded central social group in the school. Other kids who shared this with me were boys who were a bit poor, or shy, or socially awkward, or obnoxious, or ugly, or who had parents who were disreputable, or themselves were disreputable by (say) drinking or getting thrown out of school. But this included about 80 percent of the boys.

In fact I was not distinguishably different from lots of other kids, except perhaps for bringing home a bike-basket load of books from the library fairly regularly. The boys on the block razzed me good-naturedly about being a bookworm, but I didn't take it seriously because I was out playing with them as long as there was action to be found. And my best friend Mort read many of the same books—John R. Tunis, etc.

I can't remember either Mom or Dad hugging me when I was young, except when we had not seen each other for a long time—when I had been away at camp or at college. In contrast, I have an enormous appetite for pressing the flesh of those close to me. I laugh when I see a bumper sticker that says "Have you hugged your kid today?" I think it should read "Did your kid let you hug him or her today?" It was a great day for me—he was thirty years old when it happened—that David, who is the most diffident of the kids in this way, hugged me back hard when we first saw each other at Christopher Waaler's wedding on Cape Cod in June, 1995. And I loved to jostle and fool around pushing back and forth with the kids; I still do. Whether my hunger for hugging and for making love is a result of my parents's behavior, or is congenital, or both, I can't know.

The closest times between Dad and me were when he would ask me to go for a bike ride with him. (He had been an enthusiast of bicycles since the six-day races at the Newark Velodrome when he was a kid at the turn of the century, and he still had a bike he bought from a famous racer; it had wooden rims and was a thing of beauty, but it had no brakes, because a six-day race required none; this meant that riding it in the street was more than a touch hazardous. Dad kept the bike until the 1960s, and then in a fit of housecleaning he put it in front of the house with the trash. Half an hour later he changed his mind and went out to retrieve it, but it was gone. I'd have liked to have had it, along with my great-grandfather's penny-farthing with the big front wheel and little back wheel Dad left for me and that I, Judith, and Daniel sometimes ride.)

The bike ride I remember best is when we went to gather wild watercress in a stream in some woods off Millburn Avenue, now the site of a department store. When we stopped our bikes on the dirt path next to the creek, I blundered into a hornet's nest. Dad did just the right thing. He took off a sweater and vigorously swatted the hornets away. I admired his decision and coolness.

A later time when I also admired him was when I was just about to leave for the plane to fly to the West Coast for my first midshipman cruise after freshman year at college. When I tried to put a new white covering on my cap, the inner springlike flat plastic liner flipped out and away, and even though we were in the kitchen of my parents' house, the bugger couldn't be found; sounds impossible, but so it was. I was in a panic about appearing out of uniform and looking ridiculous to boot. Dad went downstairs and found a piece of metal junk that he fashioned into an adequate substitute retainer, and all was well. I was grateful for his ingenuity.

***

World War II broke out half a year after we moved to Millburn. It had little immediate effect on us, except that my Uncle Ben, a dentist, soon enlisted.

There was a vacant lot next door to us, and we planted a Victory Garden there. Raising tomatoes, cucumbers, and other vegetables was fun. To get beanpoles, my father and I went to the woods about a mile away, and cut some. This put me in business, in partnership with another kid. We cut the poles, brought them to our street on a kid's utility wagon, and sold them by the dozen to neighbors. It never occurred to us to sell them at houses closer to the woods to reduce our transportation "costs." It's amazing what kids don't think of for marketing. They set up lemonade stands in front of their homes even on the quietest streets rather than take the stands to busy streets nearby.

I also shoveled snow in the winter for neighbors—a heavy snow was a windfall (ha!) for me and other kids. And I cut lawns with a hand mower. (In India in the 1970s, I was fascinated by watching an adult Indian male driving a goat harnessed to a hand mower cutting the vast lawn of the fanciest hotel in New Delhi. They probably did as much work in a week as an American working at a fancy hotel would cut in an hour. The difference in work patterns, capital, and knowledge exemplify the economic difference between a poor country and a rich country and explain why India was then poor and the U.S. rich at a given time. There is more to it, of course, especially the nature of their economic and legal institutions, but the effects of those institutions make themselves felt through the way work is done and goods produced.)

About 1942 or 1943, National Crystal Company shut down for war-induced lack of raw material. For the rest of his life, my father worked only for two periods of about 18 months each, until I could hire him part-time in 1961 when he was sixty-six years old. My mother would not allow him to take the jobs he could easily get during the war—such as driving a bus and working as a semi-skilled laborer in war industries—because of status considerations; his not working on the Sabbath was mostly an excuse during the war, because there were jobs galore. My mother then went to work as an office manager, and the wolf lurked behind the door thereafter. Ensuring the future economic well-being of my parents became a constant element in my thinking for the next 25 years.

From reading others' autobiographies, one gets a checklist of topics to cover. Alan Paton talked much about the moral and religious lessons his parents taught, leading me to inquire about my own experience.

My parents did not deliver a great deal of moral instruction, which may have influenced me (Rita must have gotten the same impulse from other sources) to say little and hope that our children would learn by observation or by some other primitive process. My father offered such practical maxims as "You catch more flies with honey than with vinegar," but he himself set forth no honey and caught nothing whatsoever. His specialty was to say "No," and I can still hear my mother saying in Yiddish (the language I supposedly and mostly did not understand) "Luzzim"—let him—about some minor freedom that I wanted to exert, perhaps playing ball on the Sabbath. He was still using the same no-saying routine to establish his importance when he vetoed a party for his and Mother's fiftieth anniversary on the basis of some ridiculous objection. (Early on I became a connoisseur of phony objections.)

I don't remember much in the way of moral lessons. I remember Mother enjoining me that there should be "No histrionics" whenever I expressed any emotions. She eliminated in me any expressions of protest toward her or any other authority, and she led me to believe that certain kinds of fights were illegitimate; Rita and I never had a fight of any kind before we got married. (The past is not always the best predictor of the future.) But I can't say that Mother inhibited my inner life in any way. Though I may display less negative emotion publicly than do most people (I have no such inhibition about the display of love and appreciation), and I discipline myself not to allow anger to show because I fear that it will bring on bad repercussions, I am at least as emotional—both positively and negatively—as anyone else I know closely. That probably came with me at birth.

Mother liked fancy words like "histrionics." She also used "emote," and "emulate"—as in her injunctions that I try to do the same as the virtuous, respectful, and diligent kids in the family or neighborhood. On the outside I followed her instructions about being respectful, but inside I never quite believed in the legitimacy of the reign of older folks or in their infallibility. I would never urge that one *doubt* authority; I would allow authority to have the presumption of being right but would urge one to keep an eye open, anyway. The Russian proverb that Ronald Reagan brought to the American public—Trust, but verify—had it about right, I think. Anarchy no, prudence yes.

It is quite amazing how important stuff can enter into your brain at an early age, affect your life importantly, and yet you never know that it is there. It was only when I was sixty-three years old that I remembered this important fact about my mother: sometime before I was ten, I was told that she had a weak heart. This implied that I was never to cause her too much emotional hassle for fear that her heart would give way. The fact of the matter is that she was strong as a horse. I never knew of her heart being said by a doctor to be the slightest bit weak until she died at the age of eighty-six. I only remembered this fact when I mused about Rita continuing to say that she could not ride a bicycle long after she had learned to do so and the entire family had seen her ride unassisted around a parking lot behind the infirmary at the University of Illinois. Remembering this reminded me that my mother did not drive a car during my memory, though she had learned to drive in the late 1920s. Mother drove for the last time when she drove into a ditch. And the reason given for her not driving again was that she was supposedly too nervous. While it is true that one would not call my mother a serene woman, she had an emotional constitution to go with her physical constitution—wrought iron.

Perhaps all this enters into why I particularly appreciate Rita's having started exercising in her forties—I was sure that she would quit soon, but she has continued without pause and with increasing intensity up to the date of writing. She delights in her physical well-being and strength, and I do, too.

Women criticize men for their macho attitude toward life, implying that they insist on being seen as strong. This viewpoint of women undoubtedly reflects some reality. The mirror image is that men criticize women for wanting to be seen as frail; similarly, this view truly has some elements of reality to it—or at least I so believe in my daily life, as a result of my experiences with my mother.

***

A deep, dark secret that I have mentioned to no more than ten people (including my children) since I was fourteen years old: I was an Eagle Scout by that early age. (The award card I just looked at says November, 1946, having joined right after my birthday in February, 1944), a result of hard work and liking to learn the Scout skills. I delighted especially in the nature-study merit-badge learning. I loved building footbridges over streams using only vines and tree limbs, and I was proud of my skill at making fires with flint and steel or Indian-style with bow-and-drill and tinder. Typically, I considered the achievement no big deal, and I was embarrassed about it.

The summer when I was twelve years old, I went to Boy Scout Camp Ken-Etiwa-Pec for six weeks. We bunked according to the "council" we were from, I believe; in any case the other seven boys in my tent were also from Millburn. They all had been to camp together the previous summer, were all older by a year than I was, and all were white Protestants, so it was natural enough that I would be singled out for hazing. The problem was that I didn't know how to respond.

At first there were a few minor staples of camp life—for example, "short-sheeting," wherein one sheet is removed and the other is doubled so that the prospective sleeper jams a leg against the fold—but they made me feel like the outsider that I was. Then I caught wind of their next plan. It was rumored that if you put a boy's hand in a pan of water when he is sleeping, he will urinate in the bed. So it was natural to try that on the new boy—me.

I was sleeping in the upper of a double bunk bed when I was awakened by a kid on the ladder with his head poked above my bed with a basin in his hand. I kicked out, knocked the basin out of his hand clattering to the floor and the kid sidewise to the ground, though without harm to him. I then leaped to the floor and a confrontation ensued. Somewhere along the line, I grabbed a penknife, but I don't think it ever got opened. I can't remember anything else of what happened—it feels as if my memory is trying to protect me from embarrassment—until I challenged them all to fight with fists, one by one. The ensuing result was rather funny: All seven begged off, one by one, on assorted grounds. The only excuse I remember specifically was a kid who could certainly have handled me easily at a normal time—they all could, probably, all being older and bigger than I—but he said that the braces on his teeth precluded him from fighting lest he damage those expensive items.

My berserk demeanor—and it was that—had frightened the others, as berserkness does.

But worse was to come. I had no idea how to bridge the gulf between the others and me. And I was sure that the tale of my berserkness was common knowledge. And I walked around with my fists clenching and unclenching, fitting the crazy-person role I had fallen into.

That fist-clenching behavior has given me some sympathy for, and perhaps some insight, into people who act in bizarre ways, whose dysfunction you are sure they must understand, but whose ways they continue nevertheless.

Unfortunately, I had never learned how to handle an attack of any kind with cajolery, jest, appeal to reason, or any of the other soft arts, or even with curses, denunciations, satire, or any other verbal weapons. I did not know how to appeal to authority for help or justice, and there was no counselor for the tent. All I knew to do was to fight, and not with my mouth but rather with my hands.

Despite this, camp was an interesting experience. We washed our bodies and clothes with frigid cold water, because that's all there was. The northern New Jersey country was very rough, and we built bridges over streams with vines and branches. I was lured into fighting a match for the camp boxing show against Ralph, about my size; we circled the ring, occasionally waving a huge padded glove against the other fellow but doing no damage; it was apparent that neither of us was anxious to get hit.

All of us were fascinated by Mr. Lambly, the middle-aged caretaker who stayed at the camp all winter to make repairs and keep an eye on things. Supposedly there were weeks when he was out of touch with all other persons due to snows and poor transportation; there was only a dirt road to the camp, and if memory serves, there was no telephone. We thought him a Western mountain man—trapper, hunter, army scout, Daniel Boone.

I quit the Scouts when I was either still 14 or shortly thereafter because it was wartime and there was no scoutmaster or other adult regularly present; there was an adult committee, but the members were far in the background. As the "ranking" scout in my troop, I was responsible for planning and running the weekly meetings, organizing trips for competitions with other troops, and so on. I did not like bossing other people around, especially kids older than me. One of the parts I hated most was marching the kids around the gym at South Mountain School where we met. I could not stand thinking that they were resentful of my putting myself over them. So I left scouting. My attitudes toward bossing people around have remained much the same since then, and caused me some problem in the Navy; more about that later.

This was the list of my "accomplishments" prepared in my mothers' neat typing as part of my application for promotion to Eagle Scout:

> JULIAN SIMON
> Troop 12
> Millburn, N. J.
> Activities outside of Scouting:
> School:
> Vice President of Chess Club
> Vice President of Mathematics Club
> Member of championship sandlot Baseball Team
> Participated in intra-mural Basketball
> On Honor Roll
> Other Activities:
> Attend Hebrew School
> Former president of Y. S. H. C. Club [the youth club at the synagogue]
> Present chairman of refreshment committee of Y. S. H. C.
> Member of an orchestra at Y. M. H. A. [Jewish equivalent of YMCA] of Newark
> On Special Services Committee of Newark Youth Council of Y. M. H. A.
> Winner of Tennis Tournament—Summer 1946
> Hobbies:
> Collecting Stamps
> Collecting Match Covers
> Repairing broken Fountain Pens
> Making tricky repairs on sports equipment
> Dog
> Collecting miscellaneous articles

During the war, Larry Wortzel and I collected newspaper around South Mountain Estates in a little red wagon. We then stored it at home until we had enough for a carful. Our parents cooperated with us, and we then took the waste paper for sale at the Fandango Paper Mill at the south end of South Mountain Estates. During the war there was a market for waste paper, and it was a patriotic duty as well, so we felt particularly good about that business.

As I look back, it seems that I gravitated toward such business opportunities as a kid.

The events of most of our childhoods probably included events and conditions that, if we were to think about them now, might scare us in retrospect. For example, when I was perhaps ten or eleven or twelve years old, a high school student of perhaps sixteen years old—call him H—often hung around when we played. He was clearly very strange. He showed us things like how to bend someone's finger in a way that hurt, and he would demonstrate chokeholds. He was reputed to know some ju jitsu, but I doubt that he did. He was oddly formed, with a huge Adam's apple, a thin frame, very unathletic, and always dressed in a suit and tie. We casually referred to him as a "pervert." In fact he did later live some kind of a life of perversion, I was told, until he suffered an early death involved with his life style. But he never scared us very much, perhaps because there was always a bunch of us when he was around, and we felt safety in those numbers.

If as a parent we were to know that such a person was hanging around one of our kids, we would take alarm, investigate, and perhaps call the police. And properly so, because we sometimes read in the newspapers of tragedies arising in such situations. But in most cases, the normal kids pass these events unharmed and consider them as casually as a hurricane or an ice storm.

I sympathize with people born with such twisted drives, because I know the power of the desires they experience from the power of the normal desire that I experience, and I can imagine how difficult it is for them to live with their desires unsatisfied; I thank heaven that my own drives are normal. Yet these people are frightening to a parent or grandparent, and it is confusing to know what to do about them.

Let's end the chapter on a happier note. A long-snouted dog sticking its head out of the rear window of a car, ears pushed back by the rushing wind, epitomizes curiosity for me. Sparky, my dog, was once so curious that as we were bowling down the road at about 35 miles an hour, he jumped clear out the window on to the shoulder of the road, perhaps chasing a rabbit. We did then what seemed natural: We picked up poor bleeding Sparky, took him home, put him on a mat with food and water, and hoped that he would recover from his cuts and bruises. Unlike today, the idea of taking him to a veterinarian was entirely unheard of. It is hard for me to get used to Judith's taking her dogs to the vet and receiving a very hefty doctor bill when the dog is sick.

5

Millburn II: Until High School, 1941–1945

Mother said that I was "college material," which is about as complimentary and as personal (non-"material") as she would get. Nevertheless, she worried that because I did not have a focused interest in any subject, I would—as she imagined was the case with Dad—never achieve a solid, reliable way to make a living. And she felt it necessary to ensure that I always had a backup occupation that I could practice.

She had read about the famous showman Billy Rose, who had started life by learning shorthand, and by becoming a whiz at it, had started up the ladder of life. (I admired Rose because he had gotten his hands on the famous swimmer Eleanor Holm, even though she was a foot taller than he was, and married her). So she decided that I should "emulate" (one of her favorite words) Billy Rose, and she contacted Miss Rose (no connection) de Sessa, who taught shorthand at the high school, and arranged that I should have private lessons with her.

I remember that we got through a single lesson on a summer day, sitting on the glider on our wonderful outside porch (so valuable in the absence of air conditioning). Indeed, I remember that single lesson, and even what she said, more than almost all high school classes together. And I knew that I wanted no part of shorthand. This was one argument I won with my parents, probably because my father was not involved. (He probably was glad not to spend the money, anyway.)

The wonderfully funny book *Anything Can Happen* by George and Helen Waite Papashvily (1940) is one of my all-time favorites. George was an immigrant from Georgia in the then-Soviet Union to the United

States. He tells how his parents arranged for his economic security. They apprenticed him to a maker of ornamental whiphandles. And in case the market for ornamental whiphandles should falter, they also arranged for him to learn another trade. This was the outcome:

> We went to an employment agency. Conveniently, the man spoke Russian. He gave Zurabeg ticket right away to start in Russian restaurant as first cook.
>
> "Now, your friend? What can you do?" he asked me.
>
> "I," I said, "am a worker in decorative leathers particularly specializing in the ornamenting of crop handles according to the traditional designs."
>
> "My God!" the man said. "This is the U.S.A. No horses. Automobiles. What else can you do?"
>
> Fortunately my father was a man of great foresight and I have two trades. His idea was that in the days when a man starves with one, by the other he may eat.
>
> "I am also," I said, "a swordmaker. Short blades or long; daggers with or without chasing; hunting knives, plain or ornamental; tempering, fitting, pointing—" I took my certificate of successful completion of apprenticeship out of my *chemidon*. (p.5)

From that failure of planning, one can learn one of the fundamental rules of investing your money, a rule the proof of which has consumed so much of the Latin and Greek alphabets for formulas that those languages stand in danger of depletion. (In fact, there is no more danger of that than that the human race will "run out" of copper or energy, and the operative principle is not very different. Of course that seems ridiculous to you, but much of my life has been devoted to making that statement plausible. More about that later.) Anyway, when you diversify, make sure that your investments are unrelated to each other with respect to various seasonal and long-run trends. That's easier said than done, I know, but believe me, this advice is by itself worth more than the price of this book; so from here on, it's all gravy; you can now just pitch the book without a sense of waste.

Nowadays a knowledge of shorthand is about as valuable as a knowledge of wagon-wheel repair; this fact is worth a bit of reflection, along with the fate of the large supply of steel pen nibs that I scoured up in the 1960s, when I was afraid that my favorite brand would disappear.

Helen Demarest, my part-time secretary, is a whiz at shorthand, and sometimes we both enjoy my dictating a letter. But the exercise is a luxury. Of course, with a command of shorthand when I started out, I might indeed have placed my foot firmly on the ladder and gotten a good start on what my Mother would have considered a proper life. Next time, maybe I'll do better.

Whenever I rue my having worked on many research topics, undoubtedly to the detriment of all (though sometimes also to the benefit of them), I think about Mother's worry that I would never concentrate on anything and therefore never amount to anything. "Just like my father," I think—a distasteful thought given that I think he was such a useless person, taken as a whole.

People sometimes ask children what do you want to be when you grow up. I have never once thought about what I want to "be." Rather, I have only thought about what I want to *do*. I wanted to learn how to jump my bike high enough to clear curbs. I desperately wanted to learn how to make a good catcher's throw to second base, but alas, my arm was never strong, and that's a tough throw for a little kid. I wanted to learn to make radios, but a razor-blade radio (the blade works like a crystal or a transistor) was my top achievement. I wanted to learn how to make friends effectively and how to get girls; I was in grad school before I felt comfortable about those abilities, and I never felt that I was among the gifted. Nor was it because I had learned anything about how to do those things, I think. The conditions I lived in were different.

The war had little effect on our daily lives. Sure, sugar and meat were rationed, but my parents would not have been in position to buy a new car even if they had been available. The gas and tire rationing did make it impossible for people to drive back and forth to the Jersey shore, and therefore rents fell and my parents had to sell the houses there. And Dad was forced out of business. There were stars in the windows of families with sons in the service, but there were no deaths that I remember. Still, it was a day in the park compared to the experiences of people in Europe or the Far East.

Victory in Europe was a great relief, though tempered by the continuing war with Japan. Victory over Japan was a great easing of the heart, even for a thirteen year old. I never even considered the possibility that dropping the atom bomb was not the correct military and moral decision, and I have never doubted it a bit. Somewhere in the Talmud, it says that if a wild beast comes to kill you, kill it first, and I think the same is true of a human beast. Sure, there are times of overwhelming domination when showing mercy is fairly safe and therefore appropriate, but the war with Japan was not even close to that criterion, from what I know now. I have contempt for those who have never endangered their own lives in defense of others yet are quick to spend the lives of others within the group that nurtured them and to which they still swear fealty, for the sake of some abstract virtue.

The only time that I have experienced the feeling of public celebrity, or its opposite, was when I was in the seventh grade and I won a schoolwide junior high spelling contest—the only thing I have ever won in my life (I haven't competed for many things publicly). The rest of that day, the next day, and who knows how long thereafter, I remember walking around school imagining that the kids were saying to each other, "There goes Julian Simon who just won the spelling championship." Celebrities must walk around with that feeling all the time. It is obviously intoxicating, at least for a while. But I can imagine the intoxication wearing off quite rapidly, at least for me, and the annoyance of not being able to do anything anonymously would be a terrible burden.

I can also imagine how it feels to be notorious—a person accused of some crime or scandal who walks around feeling exactly the opposite—there goes XXX with the scarlet letter on his or her forehead. It must be at least as devastating as positive celebrity is intoxicating.

A television camera has the power to intoxicate in similar fashion. In 1964, when the local television station interviewed me about an article of mine on smoking, cancer and advertising for seven minutes, I was so entranced by the red light on the camera that I was sure that not more than 30 seconds had passed when the seven minutes was over. Since then I have not felt any of the same intoxication from television. After that first appearance, even national network shows have seemed to me simply another daily chore to be gotten done. I feel no exultation at all. I simply wonder whether it is time well spent in getting across some message I want to tell the public.

I first learned to say "Do you want to bet?" as part of an argument about facts when talking to my father. He would say outrageously wrong things in an authoritative fashion and refuse to hear any questions. There really was nothing that I could say except "Do you want to bet?" I also learned early on that this is not an attractive thing to most people, partly because it seems confrontational, and partly because they don't like to be called to account for what they are saying.

There were a fair number of boys on my block of South Mountain Road, plus a girl down the street who played with us sometimes; she was reputed to be a quarter Native American Indian, which explained her being a tomboy, of course. Dick Steive and Eddie Mehm were my age, and there were several guys a couple years older with whom I played football and baseball in the quiet street that was very unlike the busy auto-lined streets in Newark. The houses had garages, so there were few cars parked and hence more room to play in the street. Though I was part of whatever group there was, and there were other kids who did not play sports and go on adventures with us, I never felt part of a gang the way I did in Newark. ("Gang" then had no negative connotation in that context.)

An overweight boy, D, lived a few houses away, and he seemed very effeminate; his corpulent mother sat out-front all day, and he sat with her a lot. I'm told he lived and died as a homosexual; his early effeminacy was an accurate predictor in his case, I guess. The only feeling I had about him was pity for his not enjoying the life of an average kid.

(A reader of an early draft said that the previous paragraph is not—in that term of the 1990s—"politically correct." Therefore I'll expand on the remark. I would bet that recent research showing that homosexuality has some genetic basis is confirmed. I'd also guess—a testable hypothesis—that antipathy by heterosexuals toward homosexual acts and what is seen as homosexual life style also has some genetic basis. Attitudes toward homosexuals may be malleable nevertheless. My attitudes were greatly affected by the deaths from AIDS of philosopher Bill Bartley and environmental biologist Bill Havender, both of whom I respected and liked greatly, and whose courage I admired. Their personal styles were not distinguishable as homosexual. This sort of change in attitude may be one of the few positive effects of the AIDS epidemic.)

Up the street lived a family whose daughter, B, was in my class. She, like her parents, seemed deficient of basic intelligence, truly "retarded." The house was very dilapidated, unlike the rest of the neighborhood, and I wondered how such incapable people could make a living and maintain a household.

As I look back now and mention some of them as above, there seems to have been a wider variety of kids on the block than would be average, even though this part of Millburn was very homogeneous—white with Anglo-Saxon, Dutch, and German last names, all native English speakers, and two-parent couples with children not yet grown. We were the first Jews on the block. For that reason, it was a quarter century or more before Mother and Mrs. Heiss next-door became "Mae" and "Alma," though they got along very well; this degree of formality did not exist among the other families who were there when we arrived, I believe.

Around the corner on Wyoming Avenue was an open lot with a tree on which we hung a basketball rim. Of course the rim had no net most of the time. And the ground under the tree grew mushy in spring when the icy earth melted. In that season, we lugged buckets of ashes from the furnaces that heated our houses—which contained many small solid pieces of grit—to the lot, and then stamped then into the ground to firm it up and make it playable. Of course the small bits caused many unpredictable bounces when dribbling, but hey, it was immeasurably better than no basketball at all, wasn't it?

(The ashes remind me of how waste disposal problems decline at some level of technical advancement. Gas and oil heat eliminated every householder's chore of every night shoveling the coal that was stored in the basement—a hell of a lot better than heating by wood—and then taking out the buckets of ashes. Also eliminated was a huge proportion of the total household waste.)

The tree helped us perfect our skills in giving an opponent the hip when jumping for rebounds; mashing the other guy into the tree was part of the maneuver. Of course this was not my specialty, being neither tall nor wide nor springy of foot. But I did what I could because—what choice was there?

The basket was next door to the Rosenthals' house. The important Rosenthals were, of course, Howie—a year or two older than me, stocky and strong—and Jerry, a year younger, with glasses that caused him to be called "Four-eyes" but which probably toughened him into the excellent competitor that he was in every sport.

After Dad stopped working, we may have been the least secure family on the block economically except for the family up the street that I mentioned above, though of course there may well have been others who also lived in private desperation. One never knows, just as my parents' families knew no details of our economic situation. (But my mother's family did infer our lack of income from such matters as my parents' not contributing to the support of Grandma, which Uncle Charley Brodsky told me about in 1995.)

(In the course of that conversation, Charley said to me in a half-hearted way, "I had respect for your father." I said, "About what? I'd like to hear some nice things about Dad." Charley replied, "I don't want to get into that." "Into what?" I asked, very puzzled. He changed the subject. I pressed him, for the first time in my life, to please explain. But he stonewalled, as he was good at doing. In fact, Charley had limitless contempt for Dad, which he expressed by never tangling with Dad but instead simply laughing him off with a patronizing smile. Charley was an extremely amiable and charming fellow, and he could pull that off very well.)

I still could not tell Charley the full story. When Dad closed National Crystal Company, the war was on, and anyone with both arms and at least one leg could get a job in war industry, driving a bus, and the like; there even were plenty of jobs in retail sales where one arm was enough. Dad was only forty-seven or forty-eight years old (born in 1895), so there was no age problem. But he did not work for quite a while. After maybe a year, he took a job as a coffee roaster for a New York firm; he had roasted coffee in his mother's retail store on Prince Street. Every morning he left the house with his briefcase just as all the other commuters on their way to jobs in the financial and banking districts in New York, but instead of work papers, Dad had his lunch in his briefcase. That job lasted less than a year; I don't know why it ended.

Dad did nothing more until after the war ended. Why did he not work despite their very difficult financial straits? Mother was working by then, but that was not much of a cushion. Not working on the Sabbath was not the cause, though he said it was; during the war, Dad could have made arrangements to work on Sunday. The reason he did not take a job as, say, a bus driver was that my mother thought such work was below him. I lay this at my mother's door. If she had not taken the line that my father was too good for such a job, I believe that he would have taken one. If we had not moved from Newark, where many or most of the neighbors were blue-collar or menial workers, there would have been less of a social problem for mother. (And part of the reason for moving from Newark to Millburn was to elevate our social status.)

In his autobiography, *A Dreamer's Journey* (1949), Morris Cohen wrote about the human costs of the need for status:

> When, therefore, my grandparents came to Theodosia, they had very little money left. As it was unfitting for the dignity of my uncle Elyeh, who was a scholar and a shochet (a ritual slaughterer of animals), to have his father work as a tailor, the two old people had to pack up their scant belongings and go to Kishenev where my

> uncle Yankel lived as a fairly prosperous tailor. Their remaining years constituted a sorrow's crown of sorrows, for my grandmother could not get along well with her daughter-in-law. And after the death of my grandfather, my grandmother was reported to have committed suicide. (p. 58.)

From this destructive attitude of "being too good" to do some work flows (I believe) my hate of "front," of putting appearance before substance, of allowing status to detract from more important elements. (Of course I have erred in letting this tendency go too far, but that's another story.) Though I am always wary of being too sure of such explanations, I tie my dislike of elitism to this aspect of my parents' lives. More and more I see how powerful a force is "I'm better than you, our group is better than your group." It explains the willingness of people to believe arguments about the low IQs of various groups (Jews and Italians and Poles in the past, Hispanics and blacks now), and combined with the innate dislike of foreigners, it explains the arguments used against immigrants.

Adam Smith said that it is the desire for "honor" that is the fundamental human motivation. When I first read this I thought that he meant the high estimation of one's peers as a reward for good work. But maybe he had something less admirable in mind—simply the desire for status and accolades whether or not in connection with real achievement. That is, a hereditary ruler could receive "honor" in this way. If Smith meant the latter, then he is referring to the quality that was an issue when my father could not take a job as a bus driver.

After the war, when rationing of various commodities had ended and it was again possible to start a new business, my mother's Uncle Nat Friedman (brother of her mother), who had been a grass seed salesman for many years, had a fight with his employer and decided to go into business for himself. He got financing from his nephew, Abe Friedman, who owned a small chain of hardware stores (the connection still going back to Grandma Goodie and her 100 square foot store in 1900). He needed an "inside man" to take care of the production, while he, the "outside man" made the sales; that was the classic organizational set-up for a business then. Dad was doing nothing, so he was recruited as the inside man and was given 5 percent of the stock, so that he would feel like an owner. Around our house there was much hope for this business.

Producing grass seed was a matter of buying 100 pound sacks of fescue, blue grass and other species, hauling them to the second floor of a little bare building in a neglected part of Newark, then mixing the contents in a mixer to the proper proportions. The seed was then transferred to weighing machines that dropped the seed to the floor below. At the bottom of each weighing machine was a funnel.

The machine operator suspended below the funnel a cloth bag holding ten, five, or two pounds, then pulled a lever that allowed the weighed amount to fall into the bag. The bags were then stacked, and batch by batch, each bag was closed with a wire that had loops at each end which were pulled with a revolving screw device with a hook at the end, so that the wire was twisted until tight. (I've still got one of those tools, and I show it to my classes.)

Dad hired workers from the state employment service, but at the wages he paid, he got mainly drifters who were unreliable; many were alcoholics who would stay around for just one day's pay. He also hired me and got me to recruit some of my friends, including at least Herbie Bagdon. The work was miserable, however. Not only was it monotonous, but the air in the work room was full of the dust from the dry seeds. We wore filters over our noses and mouths, but, especially for me who had hay fever, it was a mess of spit and snot and sweat. Enough said about that. This is another example of the kind of work that has been automated since then, and no one should cry about the loss.

After 18 months the business failed, probably in 1947. That was Dad's last work until he came to work with me in 1961 in the mail-order business.

Granville Hicks began his autobiography with the memorable phrase "I was a good boy." I was a rather good boy. I didn't get thrown out of class. I didn't skip school, even after-school Hebrew School. I delivered a respectable Bar Mitzvah speech. I never felt the need or the urge to be rebellious publicly or within the family, or to act differently in public, perhaps because I sensed that there was something irregular and irreverent within me. (More about this later.) Perhaps my most radical act was being best friends with Mort, who was a rebel and seemed to some to be a bad kid. But the fact is that *most* boys and girls were "good"; there were few who were even mildly delinquent.

I wasn't *such* a good boy that we didn't set the lot next-door on fire when roasting potatoes in the ground and have the fire engines have to come. Nor so good that I didn't participate in the to-us-hilarious cruelties that drove an English teacher frantic and then out of her job—the concerted rattling of lunch bags, and the conspiracy to move the movable desks (with our sitting in them) inch-by-inch toward the front of the room, pinning the teacher against her desk, and then upon her command to retreat, moving the desks against the back wall amidst much screaming as mock "I'm getting killed." I suppose Miss M was not well-equipped to teach, but that hardly excuses us of adolescent insensitivity and cruelty in which, though not a leader, I was a blooded miscreant.

I was never asked by the teacher to run an errand within the school or had bestowed on me any of the other marks of the "teacher's pet" or the goody-goody. Essentially, I was just another kid. And the idea of tattling to the teacher about another student was so much against my personal code of honor that the thought of doing so never even crossed my mind; the act evoked my profound contempt and loathing when someone did it.

One of the topics I am tempted to omit out of embarrassment is an IQ test that I took when I was about six years old. Probably in early adolescence I came across a newspaper clipping around the house from years before that said I had a high test score (I won't say what score it gave). But I never believed the entire business meant anything, and I have never told anyone about it except maybe Rita. I was shocked recently when she told me that the children knew about this and that the story came from my aunts, but on inquiry, they say my aunts did not tell them.

When our children were growing up, I refused to learn the results of the aptitude tests they were given at school, because I did not want to develop expectations for their performances. I always said to them that it is what a person produces that matters, and that success in any endeavor is likely to be more a matter of hard work than inborn talents; talents are worthless without the capacity to work. And I have studied the IQ literature in a semiprofessional way, finding little to convince me of the great importance of measured IQ. I also have delighted in coming across examples such as the best electronics technician on our ship whose test score was too low to go to ET school and had to learn on his own. All this fits with my distaste for aristocracy, elitism, and special treatment for particular classes of people.

My overwhelming memory of school is of being horribly bored. I hated coming back to school in the fall for that reason. I met this problem in a variety of ways. I read novels under the partly open cover of my desk, probably with teachers' connivance. I'd write notes to other kids. I'd stare out the window. I'd watch the clock, and I hated an eighth-grade classroom where there was no clock. (There was a windup alarm clock that on several occasions we set to go off sometime during the class, and once even stuck it into a closet where the teacher could not easily see it to turn it off; the class conspired that no one mentioned the absence of the clock to the teacher. My visual memory of that classroom and of the closet is sharper than almost any other image of junior high school.) But mostly I just fidgeted.

I dislike the idea of splitting children into several tracks according to how well they do in school. This aversion is part of my general aversion to elitism, and I believe that the social and psychological effects are very deleterious. I also would not be happy about my kids going to a private school. On the other hand, my painful boredom in school supports the views of those who argue that students should be "challenged."

Maybe a good system would be to have all the kids study together but to let kids leave the class and play after they master the required material for the hour. That would reduce the amount of boredom, give an incentive to work hard on the material, and allow the teacher to give more time at the end of class to children who need more attention. Of course public-school teachers and administration would never accept such a system.

The most important idea I acquired in Millburn was a vision of society as including in's and out's, majority and minorities (Jews and Catholics), also the awareness of war and possible world catastrophe.

6

High School Years in Millburn

In high school there was nothing I was outstandingly good at—not art, not music, not athletics, not science, not telling jokes (typically, I wanted badly to be an excellent joke teller, but was middling at it), not rowdiness, not popularity (middling again, despite my fondest dreams). I was above average in schoolwork, but no superstar.

The qualities that let me achieve whatever I have achieved have been a plethora of new ideas, sound judgment that has kept me from going off the rails and believing in nutty ideas, a variety of skills with no big holes in my intellectual armamentarium, discipline, and the ability to hang in there for a long period of time, plus independence of mind. The main characteristics that have kept me from achieving more are—independence. The very independence that was crucial in achieving whatever I have achieved was also crucial in keeping those achievements from having the impact they might have had because of my inability to function as a well-connected, well-socialized member of the scientific community, which so many have pointed out is very much a social activity. I probably even would have been better off if I was a disruptive and obnoxious person, rather than just independent.

On our last day as high-school juniors, a bunch of us got to arguing about who could throw his history book over a low roof of the building, and we began to settle the argument in the most natural way. Before the winner had been declared, Pop Toan, our likable chemistry teacher, came by and admonished us that we were ruining the books. As a punishment he required each of us to mend ten books broken at the spine with some smelly glue cooked up in the chemistry lab.

The repair process worked well, but it was slow going with the broad-bladed stick that we were given—like the tongue depressors doctors once used. It occurred to me that it would be much easier to do the work with a turkey-basting syringe, squirting the liquid stuff down the spine. So I tried my mother's baster (without her permission), and it indeed worked well, especially when I diluted the glue to make it less viscous. Thereupon I went to the principal and asked if he would like the rest of the school's broken books fixed—for eight cents each—during the summer. Amazingly, he agreed. At a cheap price the school got the broken books repaired, and I made what was then a lot of money per hour.

Because my father was not then working, it seemed to me that this could make a good business for him with other school systems. Even more amazing, my father agreed to try. He succeeded in getting a contract with a couple of schools the next year, but unfortunately, he did not have enough entrepreneurial energy to push the matter further and let it drop. This incident constitutes my first mature creative idea, and my first attempt to carry the idea into the realm of the operative and the useful.

Earlier ,when my cousin Danny and I were thirteen years old, we bought a set of stencils for painting house numbers on curbstones. We then set out to try our fortune knocking on doors. We had just reached our fifth prospective customer when a police car swooped down on us and the officer asked if we had a license. We knew nothing about licenses (which were free), so after being hauled to the police station, we made the proper arrangements and were back on the street the next day. That was my first personal experience with the law and regulations. (I admit I now can see the point of such licensing.) Our enterprise turned out to be pretty profitable. It baffles me why so few young people engage in such businesses nowadays.

There were a few several-sport star athletes—Don and Bill. Phil Norwine awed me with his multiple talents in art, music, and writing; he wrote much of the senior yearbook. (For "Seen doing" under my name he wrote "Finding an easier way," an amazingly perceptive remark about my life.)

There were some contests I couldn't bring myself to play. At lunch, one game went like this: someone would take a tea spoon and put perhaps a bit of bread on it and pass it to the next guy. The second guy would load on another piece of food—maybe a pea—and pass it along. Some of the stuff was greasy and awful; butter would stick to the spoon and hence was a good thing to add. The spoon's journey continued until, when a guy would put on his mite, a bit of the stuff fell off the spoon. And the loser then had to eat everything on the spoon. Not for me.

From time to time, some boy would try to entice another to put his face close to some dish in front of him by saying it smelled bad, and then an accomplice—or the enticer himself—would quickly push the enticee's face into the food. The practical joke (a strange term for a mischievous prank) never seemed to work. But one day Bob R was sitting next to me, and after he finished his sandwiches he brought a cream pie from the sales line. I innocently asked him if it smelled all right, and when he bent his head to check, I snapped his head right into it.

Bob got up and with great dignity stalked off to the boy's washroom with cream pie all over his face, followed by a couple of other guys looking to foment a fight. Suddenly I was afraid of the results of my success. I feared that the other guys would stir Bob up and he would come back and take a swing at me. Not only did I not want to get into a fight with him because he was bigger and an athlete, but I would be battling outraged righteousness while being handicapped by feeling penitent for embarrassing him. Happily, Bob simply came back, sat down, and ignored me. It was a couple of days before we were back to amiability.

After I got to high school, I played ball and had friends from elsewhere in town, but there also was a special connection to Jewish kids. This was surely due in part to our feeling that we were not homogeneous members of the town society; for example, we assumed that non-Jewish parents would not be thrilled to have their daughters go out with us. (David, Judith, and Daniel felt none of this when growing up in the 1970s in Urbana, Illinois.)

My first date was a hay ride. For those who are mercifully unacquainted with this hilarious social activity, it consists of a horse-drawn wagon loaded with hay on top of which people sit, usually on a crisp October evening at the time of the year when the farmers have finished their harvest and are ready to make merry. The group sings old corny favorites ("Take Me Out to the Ball Game"), gossips (something I never learned to do), engages (if you are the confident and daring type) in a bit of light physical contact (not rising to the actual level of the magnificent Navy phrase "playing grabass" that is applied to any insignificant activity, as in "He's just playing grabass about shipping over again [re-enlisting]"). And of course, throwing hay. Lots of hay.

My date that Friday evening was Jean H, a pleasant young classmate but with whom this was strictly a minuetlike engagement, probably brokered by some chain of intermediate parties ending with a formal well-programmed invitation by me followed by a well-programmed acceptance by her.

Within minutes aboard the hayrack, I remembered that I suffered from hay fever. Within half an hour, I had run out of anything on which to blow my nose. And my eyes were so runny, half-closed, and itchy that I could hardly see. Luckily, everyone around me was having such a good time, and the air was so filled with hay that my miseries went unobserved (I assumed).

But that was not bad enough. I had to urinate. Then badly. Then more and more badly. Luckily, a stop for hot chocolate was not long ahead. I bore the affliction—because what choice had I? Finally we stopped. I looked for toilet facilities. And looked. No facilities. Before I had time to find a place to skulk away to, it was back on the wagon. Omigod. The bodily and mental sensations are so painful in retrospect that the rest of life since then seems like nothing but a waltz. Finally the end of the ride. Walk Jean home rapidly. Flying good-bye at the door, not even a passing thought of a kiss. Down her hilly street at breakneck speed (luckily I did not trip and break my neck). Into some bushes. Ohhhhhhhhhhhhhhh.

Then the embarrassment. What did she think when I bid her the lightning good-bye and ran off, with the thinnest of excuse? What did she tell her friends? What will she and they be thinking when I see them at school on Monday? Ohhhhhhhhhhhh.

Maybe somehow Jean will happen to read this and, with the wisdom of maturity, absolve me of my gauche behavior. But I'm still too embarrassed to send her a draft of these pages.

When people wonder whether years past were better days than now, I reflect back to the hay ride and to working in the grass seed factory. When Doc Silverstein prescribed the new antihistamine tablets for mother (perhaps soon after World War II), they seemed like a miracle. And they could have prevented the worst of my miseries with hay fever. Nowadays people take them for granted, for allergies or for the symptoms of a cold. What other evidence would be persuasive that life really is better now?

Let's quickly leave the hay ride and pass to some sociology. Like most high-school classes, probably, there was a central ring of the insiders—the interlocking group of those who had some entrance qualifications by excelling in sports, academics, school activities, popularity, beauty, or social grace—the "leaders." There were some who were retarded, ugly, delinquent, strange, or otherwise beyond the pale. Then there was a larger number of kids who were okay but undistinguished; I was part of that group. It would be interesting to classify the kids into these groups and estimate the percentages in several high schools in similar (and maybe dissimilar) areas to see if the patterns are similar.

I was among the top 10 percent of the school-smart kids. That was higher than my athletic ranking (which I then underestimated greatly, however). I was maybe the best tennis player in my class, and played both singles and doubles on the tennis team. Pablo Eisenberg, who played at Wimbledon, was a class behind me, but he seldom if ever played on the high-school team; the results would have been ridiculous. I was ashamed of playing this nonmacho sport and seldom mentioned it to anyone. (More generally, my attitude in life usually has been: If I do it, it isn't worth doing. This fits with my perception of being illegitimate.)

I had most of the skills to be an excellent point guard in basketball; I was a terrific passer, enjoying passing almost as much as shooting, and I was also an excellent shooter. But my personality intervened, something I did not recognize at the time. I did not have the force to get others to accept me in that boss position; instead, someone else brought the ball down the court and managed the offense. Unlike a lot of other kids, I did not think myself better than I was, which made it harder to tell the other kids to let me do the job. I also was not a great dribbler; this I could have done something about if I had practiced, one of my few shortcomings in sports, due to insufficient practice. Lacking any coaching—an observation I am a bit surprised to find myself making—and never discovering this by myself or hearing it from another kid or reading it in a book, I never learned to dribble with my head up. If I had become a terrific dribbler, I might have overcome the shortcoming in force of personality.

In my senior year I was the last boy cut from the high-school basketball team that vied for the state championship in our size division; being cut was one of the more painful moments in my life. True retribution and sweet vengeance came to me in an intramural basketball league game. The coaches had a team, and my team was playing them. My shooting got hot; I couldn't miss. So the coaches moved basketball Coach Frank Focht to cover me. I got even hotter; everything I threw at the basket went in—running one-handers, jump shots, even hook shots. I scored 26 points while playing less than the 24 minutes of the contest. Sweet, sweet. As sweet as it comes in life. (It would have been sweeter if Coach Focht had invited me onto the team. But miracles don't happen anymore.)

Some parents—especially those with finished basements—permitted their kids to hold parties with low lights, close dancing, and the fevered, totally preoccupying, fantastic fantasy-laden desire for the opposite sex. The Jewish kids mostly had their own group, inviting Jewish kids from the adjoining suburbs, but sometimes we went to parties with the non-Jewish kids.

God, how little one knows, especially those of us who were inhibited by the belief that we should not exert pressure on other people. For example, there was the problem of getting an erection when dancing. What to do? "Press it against 'em. Let 'em feel it," counseled Marvin Fish. But what about if the result was that you came in your pants? What about the ensuing embarrassment? Clearly this sort of thing could not happen in a traditional Arab or Jewish society in North Africa, for example, and many youths might be less afflicted by such doubts in various communities in the 1990s.

At various times in my life, I have taken some astonishingly foolish and dangerous risks of various kinds—physical, occupational, and social. But I generally tend to be prudent, even if what I think of as a danger to prudently avoid is preposterous. For example, one fragment of the understanding of the law of marriage among my high—school friends was that if a boy told a girl "I love you," and later wanted to break up with her (or never even start a long-term relationship, the girl's father could sue the boy for breach of promise, even in the absence of sexual intercourse). So even in those moments of passionate embrace (all clothes on), when my emotions or hopes would have spontaneously led me to utter that golden phrase, and even though I had some doubts about the correctness of the legal opinion I had received from my legal counselor sitting around in someone's basement or the locker room, I refrained, lest I found myself dragged into court and entered into a shotgun marriage before high-school graduation.

My high-school class had a few boys who were known to be very smart. That is, they got good grades and answered teachers' questions well. They were very much "straight arrows." Paul Shimon was a cut above everyone else in scholarship. He was one of the 40 Westinghouse Talent Search Award winners in the U.S., and when we took Sunday morning Hebrew lessons together from Rabbi Gruenewald, no matter how hard I worked on the homework during the week, Paul did his at the last minute and scored better than I; this is the only academic competition of any kind that I remember in high school, surely because it was one-to-one.

Not being first or best in anything, or even close to it, did not bother me. Indeed, I did not even think about my lack of distinction, except maybe once when I scored well in a language aptitude test, and I reflected that I did *well* at many things even though not *best* at anything. This assessment of myself was part of what led me to decide, after I got out of the Navy, that I would go into business, where I thought that being good at a lot of things would be particularly advantageous.

In academics I was quite uncompetitive; in fact, I may have tried to avoid seeming to be a "brain." It didn't matter much (though some) where I placed in academic competition as long as I thought I did well. Later, it was much the same as an adult playing sports, though others saw and still see me as a tough competitor; I just want to do my best and do it well, as in judo and squash; there was little pleasure in winning a tight squash game by a fluke or by my opponent making an error on the last shot.

My only self-study in high school, except for sports, was a book on electronics and the Scout merit badges. I experienced extreme difficulty in learning the electronics, and I compared this difficulty to what seemed like great ease in learning the same material that I attributed to Paul Shiman, who had recommended the book to me. I still struggle, as when for decades, I tried to learn to understand special relativity, spending years of Sabbaths reading Einstein's book for the "high-school graduate." (Only in 1996 did Herman Bondi's book and very different approach strip the scales from my eyes.) Only later did I find out that most physicists don't understand relativity either, though they can manipulate the equations; ask them why speeds don't sum at very high speeds and almost none can answer you in an intelligible way, though they think they understand. Finding something difficult to understand is now a great pleasure for me, and I feel myself understanding new difficult topics all the way down to their roots, almost too easily because of the tools I can now wield, especially the operational definition (about which more later).

Rita asked me (in 1995) what prizes I had won in high school. I snorted. "I never won any, I don't remember thinking about winning any prizes, and I don't even remember if there were any prizes," I said. "I wasn't even elected to Hi-Y," I added.

Rita didn't know what Hi-Y is because the high school she went to was mostly Jewish, and Hi-Y is connected to the Young Men's Christian Association (YMCA). But my not being Christian had nothing to do with my nonelection; other Jews were elected. Anyone who excelled in any aspect of school activities—academics, sports, whatever—was elected. The class yearbook shows that of the 163 members of my graduating class, there were about 30 senior boys (35 total members of the club) and about 50 girls; that adds to a total of about 50 percent of the graduating class being elected to these clubs. There surely was no student ranked academically nearly as high as I was—eighth out of the 163—and not many with an athletic letter, who was not elected. So why wasn't I elected? It's not because I'm obnoxious, because I'm not; I was then and am now a reasonably pleasant, reasonably friendly person who does not do ugly things to other people, and mostly likes other people. I can only guess at the reason(s), because I certainly never asked anyone in the electing body to tell me; such a question was unthinkable to me then, and still is. My only specific guess is that I hung around with Mort, and he was not very respectable. More likely is just that I'm not the sort of person you elect to anything; that is, there is something intangible about my personality or way of life that makes people not want to elect me, have me serve on committees (except to punish me for not doing enough of such work), and so on. Maybe my irreverence for institutions and authorities makes me seem like not a good citizen. Maybe you, sweet reader, can explain it to *me* after knowing me through this book.

Did not being elected to Hi-Y hurt? Of course. Was it devastating?

No. How would I feel if one of my kids were in that position? Miserable; much worse than I felt for myself.

Nothing that I did or said in my early years showed signs of radical or strikingly imaginative thinking. I was not exotic in thought or deed. I conformed to the rest of the kids in dress and behavior to the very best of my ability. I do not remember writing anything striking in high school, and I never joined the newspaper or other writing groups. My main deviation from orthodoxy was occasional irreverence. I just was not completely "sincere" in my attitudes toward institutions and groups. I never felt fully committed to the system and its authorities. I considered many things ridiculous that they took seriously. I did not immerse myself in and completely identify with any group except perhaps for sports teams. To the extent that I had eccentric thoughts, I tried to hide them, and probably did so very successfully.

A trivial but telling example: When the English teacher required us to write sentences with new vocabulary words in them, I'd put two, three, or more words into the same sentence. The teacher would object. I never could understand the basis for the objection, and therefore I would scuffle lightly—but only lightly—with the teacher about it; I'd argue a bit, not vehemently or impolitely, but usually unsuccessfully.

As Phil Norwine memorialized me in our yearbook, I was always looking for an easier way of doing things. It's easy to get that impulse confused with the impulse to slough off work and slide through, but my aim was never to avoid work in general; rather, the impulse is almost an esthetic one; it comes from the same source as the desire to reduce cost and increase efficiency in any context.

I was always looking for a way to excel in sports. I tried all sports, all positions, all techniques. In baseball, when I thought that my future was as a second baseman, I practiced throwing like an infielder, and as a catcher when my chances of playing that position were my best chance. I read books on sports and studied the technical pictures. (I was actually a better athlete than I then thought I was.) In my twenties and thirties, I studied how to improve my judo. Even in my forties, fifties, and sixties, I studied my squash and even now my racquetball. I never had a coach, though by the time I was mature I was aware how much a coach or a *sensei* (teacher) could help one in judo.

The same propensities for study in hopes of improvement have carried over to my intellectual work. In school and other formal situations, it never seemed satisfactory to me to go along with the group just because I was told to do so. I would go along because of the sanctions for not doing so and because I did not want to seem rebellious or temperamental. Though I went along, belief that the teacher was right did not follow.

To put it differently: I did not believe something I heard just because I was told it by an authority. Perhaps that is the reason religious belief never took hold in me, like a failed inoculation. I remember arguing to Mort on a long walk home from a dance in Short Hills, about midnight on Millburn Avenue, that religious belief and institutions had positive social effects and that he should not condemn the institutions out of sheer rebellion.

Aside from the chess club and sports, I participated in no activities in high school, especially not any school politics. The last political activity in my life was being elected a figurehead president of the synagogue youth club when I was thirteen years old. Mort maneuvered the election among the 15 or so members as a device to get our hands on the club treasury, so we could use it for sports equipment instead of "cultural" activities. This was the last elective office in my lifetime.

You may notice that I have not mentioned any teachers or other adult having had a strong influence on me, nor have I said that someone was a "role model." (This phrase, like some others in the book, is in quotes because it is a current cliché and I use it because it has meaning to many people. But I feel uncomfortable with it because it is not a long-standing element of our language, and I'm not sure what it will mean to people in the future, if anything.) I never had a close relationship with an adult wherein I either fashioned myself in the image of the other person or the adult was a trusted advisor to me. I once read a study asserting that every chief executive officer of a major U.S. firm in the sample had had a patron who helped advance his (her) career. There never was such a person in my life. This is probably due to some combination of my not seeking out adults to be surrogate parents, uncles, and aunts—that is, patrons—and of their not seeking me out, either, because I seemed very independent or because I was not very lovable. My wariness with anyone who has had authority over me surely has mattered, too.

Regrettably, I had no propensity to ask for help or advice from teachers or other elders, simply because I did not have the sort of close relationship with any of them that would engender this. And I did not ask much advice from my friends, either, out of shyness or embarrassment. I lived rather independently of parents, though of course I lived with them and they supported me. So I thought a lot of foolish thoughts about life and how to live it for lack of the wisdom of others. This pattern has continued too much throughout my life.

The pattern continues now as then: People seldom spontaneously offer to help me, even when what I am doing accords with their beliefs and desires. Nor am I good at inducing them to help even when I ask. Peter Bruce says that the explanation is my apparent independence and my seeming not to need their help. This makes sense, because as a point of pride I have tried not to seem as if I needed help.

A theme that recurs in these chapters on my adolescence is my concern about people liking me. Of course, this troubles many adolescents, but I think I was bothered more than most. I had no strong talent for attracting people.

I lacked brothers and sisters with whom to practice human relationships, from whom to get advice, and in whom to confide. And I did not stand confidently on a firm base of securely warm and accepting relationships with my parents. I never learned how to reach out to make new friends; I was reluctant to, even when Mother urged me to do so, because I was embarrassed. I thought that overtures would be received badly and would be a counter-productive sign of need.

About my future, the over-riding question that I addressed was: Would I be able to find a reliable and satisfying way to make a living, one that would enable me to provide for my parents as well as for a family of my own? This surely was not atypical then; lots of people worried about the same matter, probably more than now (because there was more objective reason to worry about it than now).

The summer after (I think) my junior year in high school, I worked at a summer camp in the ice cream and convenience store (what is known in the Navy as the "gedunk stand," the etymology of which I don't know; the *Naval Terms Encyclopedia* by John V. Noel, Jr. and Edward L. Beach doesn't even list it). The job was long hours and not much pay, but a lot of fun shooting the breeze with the campers and other staff who came in. The closeness of the sexes in this free environment drove me nuts, especially the noises at night when the older male staff in my eight-person dormitory—including "older men" such as a sophomore in college—smuggled their girl friends into their beds for who-knows-what. Oh those sounds. It was probably much less serious than I imagined, but the stimulus to my ears was such that the imagination could not have been exceeded.

I enjoyed playing tennis with Gennifer x, who was at the top of the collegiate women's standings. Her brother had been U.S. national champion, I think. We played pretty evenly.

One night my work partner and I were awakened not long after going to sleep by our boss Sam Schmukler (I may not have the spelling right, but believe me, that's how it was pronounced). He was a thick-bodied, florid man with jowls and a heavy beard who wore high leather boots, of whom we were not fond. He dragged us out of bed and over to the store and made us look inside the cash register. It was empty! We then remembered: We had forgotten to take the $37 day's receipts that were in the register to his office as we were supposed to. Now what had happened to the money? What would happen to us? After scaring us about the consequences, Mr. Schmukler finally told us that he had taken the money from the register to teach us a lesson. "If it happens again I'll send you fellows home," he warned. Good job, Mr. Schmukler. You did indeed shake us up. We didn't do it again. (And screw you, you son of a bitch.)

My awareness of the concept of probability and of probabilistic calculations was heightened when, in high school, we played poker and bet on the school's football and basketball games. I became convinced that the odds usually were heavily tilted toward "our" (Millburn High School) team winning, just as at another school the odds would be tilted in favor of the home school. But after once betting on the other team to take advantage of the favorable odds, I realized that it was bad social practice, and I thereafter refrained despite the tempting opportunity. I also remember being aware of the connection between people's hopes, their false optimism, and their overvaluing the chances of our team winning.

I also became aware of the hazards of gambling through Mort's father, who I knew was often on the run from bookies to whom he owed money. I heard the story that he twice lost his butcher shop gambling in back of the synagogue on the high holidays.

It must be confessed that I found Mort's father entertaining. He was full of such instructional one-line jokes as: The only way to make money following horses is with a shovel. And, you can't fight city hall, but you can shit on the steps and run away. But when I commented to Mort that his father amused me, he tellingly replied, "Yes, but he's not your father." That reply has often recurred in my thoughts. Mother's chosen profession for me was to be an actuary. I'm not sure how she came to this decision, but I think she believed that actuarial work is somewhat similar to the accounting that she herself had practiced and into which her younger brother Jac had gone with great success, but she felt that being an actuary was more stylish than accounting.

This was a very ironic choice in light of my later history.

On the one hand, my slight knowledge of actuarial work suggests that much of it consists of highly routine calculations of insurance rates based on large bodies of mortality, health, and accident data, with little role for creative ideas; to that extent, actuaries are mostly calculators, and actuarial education consists in large part of courses in highly technical formal mathematics of probability. On the other hand, the work that actuaries can do at their best—making estimates of probabilities that require much knowledge of the world and good judgment, such as shipping insurance rates in war zones, and of estimates that a movie star's legs will not be damaged during the next five years, the sort of thing that Lloyds of London does a lot of—is of great interest to me, and I would have enjoyed it. In my work on resampling statistics and Monte Carlo methods for estimating probabilities, I have come to argue that actuaries could jettison almost entirely the conventional analytic machinery that they employ; instead, they would be better-off with the simulation methods that I urge upon them. Quite a turn of events.

I never had sympathy for communism or even socialism. The saying has it that such a person lacks heart just as a person who does not eventually abandon such a sympathy lacks head. My opposition to communism stemmed from the same source as many people's attachment to it: I thought of it as a regime that increased the power of the powerful and therefore oppressed the powerless. And I had a self-interest motive: I remember joking in high school that if the commies took over, I would be the first guy they would put up against the wall and shoot, not because I was dangerously rebellious but simply because I am irreverent concerning institutions and authorities. Totalitarian regimes cannot tolerate irreverence, I assumed.

Being irreverent does not mean that I was disrespectful of people generally. I don't know the origin; I do not remember parental teaching on the matter, and maybe propensities like irreverence are partly congenital. It also has been true throughout my life that I have seldom been publicly contemptuous of anyone except the great. I have never written that anyone has been stupid except for a few figures, such as John Maynard Keynes, reputed to be the cleverest man in England, and Paul Samuelson, the first American Nobel prizewinner in economics; I used such a term for them because both men were harmfully wrong in their contemporary analyses and their consequent forecasts for the future (especially about such matters as future scarcities of natural resources such as food and oil), because they arrogantly relied on their supposedly superior intellects and therefore scanted on the examination of the available evidence. I am respectful of everyone who has some reliable knowledge to pass on to me, whether it be the refrigerator repair man about his specialty (I've never seen a repairwoman), a chemist, or the garbage collector relating the most efficient pattern of collection.

Short Hills, the town next to Millburn, was at that time completely without Jews and of course (heaven forbid even the thought) blacks. This purity was accomplished by means of legal devices ("restrictive covenants") in the sale transactions. When biking or taking the train to practice with the tennis team at the Short Hills Club at the center of the town, I felt as if I were an invader, subject to banishment by the police. This was nothing in comparison, of course, but later on it gave me an insight into how blacks might feel in South Africa or the South of the U.S.

One day during the high-school summer that I drove a taxi, I had a fare from the train station to deep in Short Hills—which was terribly hard to navigate because there were no street signs; this device was adopted to make strangers even less likely to venture in. I passed a large estate where it seemed that the house was being knocked down, so I stopped and entered. In what had been the living room I saw a man with a sledge hammer smashing a fresco on the wall. That was one of those moments when life makes the same impression upon you that great art does.

I took three years of mechanical drawing in high school. It was a total waste of time. First, I had no intention of becoming an engineer; conventional wisdom among Jews was that Jews had no chance of getting jobs as engineers, and hence business was known as "Jewish engineering." Second, the course was useless, consisting only of copying engineering drawings from a book of plate models. The teacher was seldom there, and a good deal of our time was spent goofing around. Goodness knows what atrocious decision-making and lack of good counsel led me to choose this instead of auto mechanics, metal shop, wood shop, or even cooking. But I did take away two good things: (1) a very modest ability to write in block letters, and (2) a story that the children liked. The request "Tell us the smashed sandwich story" is one of my happiest memories of them when growing up.

Unfortunately, I cannot remember the principals in the event, so if any of you guys read this, and I've got it wrong, please forgive me.

One day Ben was looking over Adam's shoulder at a plate Adam was drawing, and accidentally leaned on Adam's lunch. Adam pretended to be outraged, went over to Ben's desk and banged his hand on Ben's lunch. Ben then went back to Adam's desk and put his elbow on Adam's lunch, mashing an apple, from the sound of it. Adam then went over to the desk of Charlie, an innocent bystander who had made the mistake of laughing, grabbed Charlie's lunch and pitched it to Don at the back of the room. Don stood aside and let it hit the back wall. Charlie, no longer an innocent bystander, grabbed Don's brown bag, put it on the floor, and stomped on it. By this time, secondary action of various ingenious kinds was taking place elsewhere in the room, culminating in most sandwiches having been taken from bags and balanced on the bottom edge of wooden desks with tops that opened with a hinge. The top of the desk was then firmly pressed downwards to produce remarkable deformations in the sandwich.

I can see it all now, with marvelous clarity. And I now realize that it was at that moment that there began the ominous decline in American morality and Western civilization that continues to this very moment, and that threatens the very future of the planet.

Needless to say, we bought our lunches in the cafeteria that day, with an unusually cooperative system of communal loans among us for those who lacked the necessary cash. (Question: why did the Jews have to eat unleavened matzoh when they exited Egypt? Answer: Because they could not raise the dough for bread.)

If the kids heard the smashed-sandwich story once, they heard it ten times. Daniel reminded me of it as I was writing this chapter, which is how it happens to be remembered here.

When my father said that he would not allow me to drive the family car when I was old enough to have a license, Larry Wortzel and I bought for $25 an old convertible that didn't run, and we had it hauled into the lot next door. It was probably unrepairable in that condition—burned out cylinders or transmission trouble. Eventually it got hauled out in the same shape it got hauled in. As I got closer to license time, I told my father that if he would not let me drive, I would buy a car with my own money. Spending family money was even worse than the alternative, and therefore I did get to drive the wonderful old 1935 Chrysler Airflow. Regrettably, on one early trip with my parents in the car, I was slightly hit from behind, perhaps because I had not signaled properly, leaving unfortunate damage on the car.

Getting drivers' licenses was a very big thing, of course.

It created a new social role for some boys—being part of the fast-driving culture. There was lots of talk about the best way to take curves—slow in, fast out—and about the gains from double-clutching the cars with manual gear shifts (most of them). And there were some like Don, whose minor popularity depended on usually having his fancy family car at his disposal for wild rides. Miraculously, there was never a death in my class from driving accidents due to fast vehicles and inexperienced drivers.

Speaking of Don, his family had an antiques store. We used to tease him that the antiques were created by buying new furniture and then throwing the pieces down the cellar stairs to age them. I hope that we were wrong.

Gerry Dale and I spent occasional afternoons together at my house or elsewhere. He was (and is) an excellent athlete who, though only five feet eleven inches tall, came in third in the state high jump. Gerry lived at the farthest end of the school district, next to a golf course and caddied there. Once a golfer threw Gerry a discarded iron, and Gerry began to play with it. He soon became pretty good. There was a complication, however: The club was right-handed and Gerry was left-handed and swung a baseball bat that way. So he began to play cross-handed. Nothing could look more awkward. But Gerry became a good player, soon actually shooting in the 70s. When I saw him at our 35th or 40th class reunion, I asked him what he was shooting in golf. "In the good 70s," he said. "Are you still playing cross-handed?" "Of course." "Why did you never change?" "It's more fun that way." He told me that he is not the only skilled cross-handed golfer, however.

I learned to shoot a .22 rifle in Ben Merrick's cellar. He had set up a range and was a top guy in the high-school rifle team—a really good shot. Though I was not a crack shot, acquaintance with the shooting tool was one more skill I enjoyed learning, and it served me well when I was with the Marines.

When I was not playing basketball on our dirt court with the tree-hung rim, I was playing on Warren Gray's asphalt driveway with an "official" basketball hoop on a stand, with even a net. Sometimes the only black boy around, Billy Hines—he was one year behind me in school—played with us. Billy's family was poor and lived in an old house near the railroad station—the only house around and hence not in anybody else's neighborhood. I never asked Billy how his family came to live in Millburn; I didn't think much about race relations, and the subject was managed in such a way as not to arise in conversation. True to all stereotypes, when late in high school Billy grew beyond being an undersized kid, he became a terrific basketball player.

I did not look forward to the Jewish High Holydays, except for one event that was a high point of each year. It occurred during the Jewish New Year, Rosh Hashanah. The elders of the synagogue sold the Torah-reading ceremonial roles in an auction that was marvelous comic relief to the serious High Holyday mood. The auction took place in Yiddish, a bit of an anomaly in suburban, mostly non-Jewish Millburn. The auctioneer went through a spiel for each honor, as the bidders bid and the kibitzers whispered in the pews wonderful commentary about each bidder. For example, about Jack B: "That goniff [thief]. He makes money selling black market sugar [this was in the middle of World War II], and then he thinks he makes it right by giving a few bucks to the shul [synagogue]. He thinks he's a big macher [doer] when he goes up to the Torah first."

I take pleasure nowadays in noticing how various experiences in the long-ago past enter into the mosaic of my thought. I built on the auction of the aliyot in this idea in a letter to newspapers:

> Virginia, Maryland, and the District of Columbia, and the other states could pick up a nice piece of change for their universities or other worthy causes using the principle that public honor can be sold to people at zero supply cost. For example, Spanish kings made a good business of selling titles. Lordships are commonly auctioned in England nowadays; not long ago, plain Harold Hobbs of Sussex became Lord of the Manor of Plegden Commons, a title dating back to the Middle Ages, by bidding 9,000 English pounds at a public auction. And when I was a child, some Jewish synagogues sold the torah ceremony roles in an auction on the

first day of Rosh Hashanah that was marvelous comic relief to the serious High Holiday mood.

The states and the District could auction off the numbered license plates. Number 1 goes to the person who bids the biggest donation, number 2 to the next biggest, and so on. Give the governor (or mayor) and other muck-a-mucks plates that say "GOVERNOR" (or "GUV"), "MAYOR," "COUNCIL," and so on. The outgoing politicians can have "EX-GUV" and the like.

The auction might be held on television, call-in style. A celebrity from government or sports or entertainment could MC the show. And it might be held at the convention center. Anyone who wants to come might have to pledge $25.00 or so even if not a winning bidder. And it might be billed as the millionaires' charity bash.

Something for nothing? Yes, Virginia, there really is a free lunch sometimes. But whether officialdom and bureaucracy can stir themselves to prepare the lunch for us is another matter. How about it, you energetic and imaginative politicians? And the first state that pulls this off will probably get the credit for pioneering a freebie benefit program that the other states in the Union will follow.

I couldn't even get the letter published, let alone get the idea going.

7

My Mind as a Young Person

If my life is diagramed as if it were a tree of probabilities—what's called a "stochastic branching process" by mathematicians—the probabilities for my engaging in unusual behavior probably became larger and larger as I grew older. Of course, the probabilities of any given kind of behavior are what is known as "path dependent," and probably increasingly so. That is, the older you are, the greater the chance that what you will be in the future is influenced by what you were in the past. My paths diverged further and further from the average, rather than converging toward the average, as I grew older; I have become less and less socialized with time, rather than more socialized. Maybe this just reflects the general tendency to get more quirky as you get older, but I think that it is much more than that with me.

I started out supernormal. Rereading now my essays written in high school and freshman college English, they seem remarkably banal and trite. My development was just the opposite of the autistic Australian woman, Donna Williams, who—in one of the most amazing of all autobiographies, and indeed, of all lives—tells us how she had to build a "normal" life absolutely from scratch. She had to laboriously understand and create the simplest elements that we take for granted in our everyday life. An example is the touching behavior when one person shakes hands with another. This was frightening and repulsive to her from her first awareness, and she had gradually to build a tolerance for it.

One of the constants of my life has been my doodle. I draw a semicircle at the corner of the page of the pad that I am writing on—usually the right-hand top corner is first, then the left top corner. Then

I draw rays to it from the corner tip, usually first bisecting it and then slicing it into smaller, symmetrical pieces. I may add additional semi-circles and additional rays. This doodle has never had any meaning to me. Yet I find myself drawing it over and over again, if not irresistibly, certainly consistently.

Do I draw this figure now simply because I began to draw it earlier? Does it have no more meaning than that it was a spontaneous accident once and then persevered simply by habit and the continuation of the past?

Another constant in my life is that when I wake up in the morning or from a nap, I look at the top of a closet or of a window and imagine a straight object or projectile going across its top, usually from the middle of the room to the edge of the room, though sometimes from one side to the other. Sometimes I imagine a measuring stick going across the tops of two windows, and I wonder whether the tops are indeed at the same level and parallel. It is as if I am a surveyor and I am "surveying" for straight lines—at the top of the window frames, across the radiators, etc.

The object may be a long, thin strip of metal or wood. It may also be a narrow beam of light—in recent years a laser. Perhaps most commonly, it is a .22-caliber bullet. If a bullet, I imagine a block of wood against the wall to absorb the bullet so that it will not damage the wall.

When I nap in a room with a peaked ceiling, as I do on the third floor of our house in Chevy Chase, I imagine the projectile or object following the peak, testing whether the peak is indeed flat and level. And I imagine the triangular block of wood at the end of the peak to absorb the projectile.

What does this mean? I haven't got a clue. Yet I have done it for at least 50 of my 65 years. Clever Freudians would come up with convincing explanations, but I'll bet that some of those explanations are mutually contradictory. And I doubt that any of them would make sense to me. I'd guess that this is an abstract, perhaps genetically-based, esthetic, akin to the esthetic of mathematicians and of the cave painters in Europe whose art was much the same for fully 60,000 years—from 100,000 years ago to 40,000 years ago or so. Those people felt the urge to draw animals. The Egyptians felt the urge to draw people. I would guess that it is the commonality of the impulse that we should marvel at, rather than any differences.

(Again and again, I am impressed by the similarity of human behavior in the aggregate over long stretches of the history of our species and across the entire range of human societies, from the most "primitive" to the most "developed" economically, even though as individuals we vary greatly from one to another. In statistician's terms, the differences within groups are much greater than the differences between groups; the statistical distributions from group to group of most of the traits I have observed overlap greatly. Consider the existence everywhere of the taboo against incest, the omnipresence of gossip, and the enjoyment of bathing, for three casual examples.)

As with the doodle, I often wonder what in me is due to nature and what is due to nurture (leaving aside the complication of the interaction of nature and nurture). For example, to what extent is my joy in the thinking that I do (as I am right now) inborn, and how much is it due to the circumstances in which I was raised—an only child without outlet for casual talk? To what extent is my unusual degree of nonassociation with formal or informal groups a result of the particular parents that I had and of the move from swimming in the water like a fish in Newark to being an outsider in Millburn? I suppose it will be many years before social scientists can answer questions like this with any surety.

I do not enjoy controlling myself or situations (though this does not imply being beyond control or in chaos). I enjoy free, uncontrolled floating in social conversations, and especially when making love; I like best to abandon control so as to feel myself floating freely on the tides of the interpersonal currents. I delight in those glorious moments when we are in resonance like a tuned electronic circuit, with the impulses flowing through the circuit ever faster and ever more effortlessly. (An electronics engineer will understand the analogy.) My romantic attitude toward such spontaneity, however, has sometimes been unhelpful at those moments in life when someone *must* take control in order that events will go forward well.

Just as I did not like bossing around the Boy Scout troop so much that I quit so early, when I was fourteen years old (Chapter 4), I have not liked controlling the behavior of others. And I feel no need to be in control of situations or even of myself. I usually prefer that the other person drive, and I drive only out of duty, to share the burden; I figure that the other person is probably a better driver than I am, anyway. (I rate myself no better than an average driver, and maybe worse than average, in contrast to the fascinating studies showing that in all countries 80 percent of the people polled say that they are better-than-average drivers.)

Part of the Boy Scout meeting every week was a marching drill, full of "forward march," "left turn, right turn," the command for reversing line of march, as well as some standing drill. Having to lead this marching was another of the reasons that I left the Scouts. I considered the whole matter ridiculous, because I saw no connection between this militarylike activity and the rest of scouting. Nevertheless, I went along with it as long as I stayed in the Scouts.

Even as a midshipman, I could not see the point of the marching in close-order drill. When I asked some Navy instructor the purpose of it, the answer was that it is excellent practice to teach military people to respond to orders instantaneously. On reflection, I could see some possible rationale for European armies at the beginning of the nineteenth century, but I could see little reason for it nowadays, and certainly none whatsoever for the Navy. Nevertheless, I did not demur against drill. On the other hand, I could not be reverent toward it, and I would make private jokes about it. That was typical of my inner and outer life when young.

Naturally enough, a group is not going to choose as its leader someone who is not reverent toward the activities to be led. I think the marching may be a good example of my reactions to many of the other aspects of small groups in larger institutions in which I have been involved.

When I read delightful Tom-Sawyer-and-Huck-Finn autobiographies—the book by Dan Rather, the famous television anchorman, is one such—I ransack my memory for delicious memories of childhood like those that I read there. But I find few of them after leaving Newark. I strongly suspect that the typical adult recollection of such adventures is seen through very rosy lenses and airbrushes away the realistic rough details. Nevertheless, I find few such memories that I delight in. Father and sulkies in Weequaic Park. He'd come with me to sandlot baseball in Millburn on Saturday because it was free. But Mother took me to my only major league baseball game. Other Millburn kids and I went to Knothole Club Newark Bears games in the days of Tommy Henrich.

The earliest reading that I remember fascinating me was *The Swiss Family Robinson*. It is (in my memory) the account of a shipwrecked family on a deserted island who built a tree house for protection and executed many ingenious projects to create a safe and satisfying life, without any civilized assistance except the tools they brought with them. This exemplifies my lifelong fascination with useful, challenging feats that improve the lives of oneself and others.

Also exciting to me were the adventures of Richard Halliburton, who in the early part of this century swam rivers and bays and experienced other great adventures. And I devoured the baseball stories of John Tunis. Mort and I used to trade our library copies and talk about them.

I held the usual stereotypes, as do most of us. It is probably inborn to be exceedingly aware of, and perhaps hostile toward, those who are different from us in any distinctive manner, and we quickly construct often faulty generalizations that fit our predispositions. For example, on behalf of a trade association in 1962, I interviewed a young man with an Armenian name for a job as an economist. I asked him what he most wanted to do in life. I was startled when he said he wanted to be a professional baseball player, a pitcher. My stereotype was that Armenians hung around Fresno, California, getting mellow on cheap wine and reciting the lines of William Saroyan plays. My personal acquaintance with Aram Mardirosian in my NROTC unit made no dent in this stereotype because I somehow had never thought of Aram as an Armenian.

But stereotypes can change, and one can come to enjoy those who are different from us. Charlie Quick was a law professor at the University of Illinois and a friend of Rita's and then of mine since she and he worked together on the Jury Project at the University of Chicago in the 1950s. To me, Charlie was almost a dead ringer for my father, except a bit darker—Charlie was "black" by standard definition but not very dark—and a bit rounder. When I commented on this similarity to someone, the reply was "But he's black." Though skin color was just one of many elements of similarity and difference, it completely dominated the comparison for my interlocutor. Such is the power of race in the United States in the second half of the 20th century. (For blacks it is probably exactly the same in reverse.)

Kay Redfield Jamison writes in her autobiography *An Unquiet Mind* about being partly in the "world of tradition," or in other "worlds." This kind of description can be efficient in drawing a shorthand picture of an entire milieu. But neither then nor now do I think in such large abstractions about this "world" or that one. Even Newark and Millburn, so very different, never seemed *representative* to me of larger collections of similar places. Maybe this is another illustration of the concrete nature of my thinking.

Opposition to communism was an element in my youthful mentality (see Chapter 6), not because I was rebellious but because I was (and am) irreverent toward institutions and authorities; hence I feared the consequences for me of a totalitarian system. Another element was my prankishness, as in Aunt Anna's story about throwing spitballs at the doctor when I was recovering from scarlet fever at age six. Of course much of the rest of the chapters in this book describe (whether they truly reveal or not, you will have to judge) the nature of my mind, its processes and its substantive contents.

I regret how unable I was when young to express to others my needs and desires. I could not tell the other kids that I wanted a longer turn in the batting cage. I could not make explicit in words to young women my desire for sexual closeness, leaving it to spontaneous mutuality for the encounter to happen. I could not ask for help at camp when I felt embattled by the other kids in the bunk. I hope that my sons were not as shy as I was (I am sure that Judith was not, though she says that she is indeed very shy in some social matters.) And I have not been good at expunging and preventing regrets; I still kick myself for some of my most inadequate moments in helping myself, as I kick myself for my inadequacies in helping others.

One must be lucky to survive without tragedy one's youthful errors of judgment and values. When I worked in the "ethical" (prescription) drug advertising agency, I thought that the only tests of a drug advertisement were how much it sold and whether it was legal, not whether it was essentially truthful. When I was in the Navy I thought that I could drive when drunk—and I mean legally drunk and worse. Once I had an accident when the other driver, who was entirely at fault, was very very drunk, and I was only *very* drunk. Wow.

Mort told me that he felt he was different than others and more creative, until he met a copywriter named Casey who worked at the famed advertising agency Doyle, Dane, Bernbach. On the other hand, I never felt different or creative until I found the first major improvement in understanding of the concept of causality since the pathcleansing achievement of David Hume, when I was about thirty-three years old. Even then I was tentative about that belief and thought that my discovery was a one-time thing.

8

On the Job as a Kid

When I was in sixth grade, the teacher asked me if I would like to do some clerical work for a man who lived across from the school. I don't know whether she picked me because she thought I was neat and reliable or she perceived that money was short in our family—which would have been fairly rare in that solid middle-class neighborhood. I went to the man's house, and he gave me a small notebook in which to draw lines on each page, perhaps for purposes of keeping a budget.

I did the work—well enough, I suppose, but I was not artistic, and I doubt that it was quite a first-class job. When I brought back the completed work, the man first paid me and then asked what nationality my parents were.

"My parents were both born in Newark," I said.

"What was the nationality of your grandparents?"

"My father's parents came from Poland, and my mother's parents came from Austria," I said.

"But what was their nationality?" he pressed me. At that point it became clear to me to that he wanted to confirm the fact that I was Jewish. So I said that my father's parents were Polish Jews and my mother's parents were Austrian Jews. He rested.

When I was fourteen years old—the legal age to work—I started to caddy at a golf course in Maplewood. The pay was $1 per bag per round; carrying double was a windfall, but some of the bags were heavy enough that a "loop" with a double was tough on a skinny fourteen year old. Getting a loop meant lying around for hours on the grass near the caddy shack until the caddymaster picked you. He first gave loops to professional caddies and to his favorites, despite the supposed order of first-come-first-served, on the grounds that the golfers had asked for those caddies. I sensed that the system was unfair, and I was of course never one of the favorites, but I was never stirred to huge anger; I just figured that that was the way the world was.

I burned a bit at the many players who treated the caddies badly. If a player missed an easy putt, the caddy often got blamed—for not standing perfectly still or not holding the flag motionless above the cup. It was perfectly clear to me that it was in the nature of these men (and occasionally women), who were surely the pillars of their churches and communities and most dignified and courteous as neighbors, to treat the caddies like dirt. It would not be a wonder if research found that those people who are not members of the "club" have a less benign view of human nature than insiders, whom the powers-that-be have good reasons to treat well.

I never could have been comfortable as a member of a country club, because I always looked at them with a caddy's eye. In 1994, Ed Crane, who founded the Cato Institute and whom I greatly respect and enjoy, was "roasted"—the fashionable fete of the 1980s and 1990s—at the Chevy Chase Country Club, a block from our house. When Rita and I arrived at the main staircase and shook hands with Ed, it was natural for me to ask: "I seem to be lost. Which way is the caddy shack?"

The golf club where I caddied had no Jewish members, of course; the idea that it should have black members was so outlandish that I never even heard it mentioned. One of the members was the ex-Jewish father of one of my classmates, who had converted the family to Protestant Christianity. My Jewish friends at school assumed that this was just to advance the father's work life. We might have been wrong, of course; perhaps the reason was the belief or the desire to unburden the children of Jewishness, but we never considered these possibilities. This conversion induced our contempt; my personal contempt may even have extended to the son, a perfectly nice fellow (though a goody-goody) with whom I never got friendly.

I admired the legendary caddy on the golf course where I worked who got fed up with some duffer tormenting him and simply dumped the clubs into the stream at the water hole and kept going; of course he did not work there again.

Classmate Norman Corwin then aspired to be a pharmacist (as did Larry Wortzel), and he worked at the Whelan drugstore at the central crossroads of town. I heard from him of an opening, so after school my junior year I worked there stocking shelves, doing odd jobs, and serving customers with cigarettes, cosmetics, and other nondrug products.

Part of my early instruction was how to sell threesomes of condoms: Grasp the package under the overturned hand and give it to the (invariably male) customer palm down. The incredible strength of the demand for contraceptives, even in the face of the trade being against the law—"sold only for the prevention of disease," the package then said—has always made me a bit dubious about the need for high-powered methods to promote condoms to people in poor countries who supposedly "really" want them.

Larry Wortzel worked in his father's drug store, so he could be freer in his behavior than we Whelan employees. When a customer asked for three condoms, Larry's joking response to those he thought could stand it was: "Buy a box of twelve and stay all night."

9

College

Harvard was the only good college that admitted me in 1949; Yale, Princeton, and several others turned me down. I passed the Navy ROTC written test and then the physical exam. ("Overbite [of the teeth]; Non-disqualifying defect" was the only mark against me; I was proud of the eye test showing 20–20 vision). Some process of joint determination between Harvard and the Navy then put me into the NROTC unit at Harvard; if Harvard had not agreed to accept me in that category, the Navy would have found another university for me among the 50 or so that had NROTC units.

My parents had not wanted me to take the NROTC test; in those years, any voluntary association with the military just wasn't the thing to do for a Jewish boy trying to make his way in the world, they judged. This attitude was a residue of stories about how the Czarist Russian army conscripted young Jewish boys and kept some for 25 years. But my father was not working in those years, and my parents obviously would have been hard put to find any money to pay for college expenses, even the little I would need above the tuition scholarship that Harvard would have given me if I had not taken the NROTC scholarship. Furthermore, a certain amount of glamour attached to the Navy scholarship. I told Mom and Dad, my service obligation would only be between 15 months and two years. (How wrong that proved to be!)

The summer before college I was reluctant to tell people where I was headed, because Harvard then had an effete reputation. One reason it didn't seem very muscular was because of its famously weak football team. Out of such trivial and subtle wisps of knowledge our judgments are formed.

I also was reluctant to mention Harvard because its aura tended to separate me from fellows and maybe girls and (the dominant feeling about mentioning Harvard later in life) make me seem part of the privileged class (as indeed I was). Neither hard work nor suffering accounted for my good fortune; just plain luck. (On the other hand, I never felt guilty about this good luck, the way some middle-class whites have felt and still feel guilty toward blacks and about their family-bestowed affluence. I have, however, felt guilty about my lack of awareness or recognition of the plight of blacks in the country during my adolescence and twenties, and I should have made some contribution of effort, no matter how slight.)

After a train ride from Newark to Boston and a subway to Harvard Square, I emerged from the underground station, lugging my two heavy leather suitcases. I set forth across Harvard Yard—I heard the Boston-accented "Haavud Yaad"—from the mouth of the man from whom I received directions to my dorm, Stoughton Hall. That was one of the moments in life when one feels a true beginning. I was leaving the life of a dependent child and entering self-supporting adulthood, entirely responsible for my own fate—and already beginning to feel responsible for my parents' economic future.

Freshman year was exactly the experiences (plural) that colleges want for their students. I lived in four-century-old Stoughton, with rope ladders as fire escapes. I was put into a room with Malcolm Rivkin, another Jewish boy (just chance?) from Hyde Park, just outside of Boston proper, and we got along reasonably well. My intellectual horizons expanded at breakneck speed. The bull sessions in Stoughton were a mind-opener. Many of the fellows—especially those who had gone to private preparatory schools (half the class) had an awesome knowledge of literature, and my sense of being ignorant set me to reading some classics. (I took very few literature courses and certainly did not major in literature, because I felt that reading great books is recreation, not work, and one would not obtain a marketable skill in those majors.)

There were a few fellows who would hang around other people's rooms forever as a way of avoiding going to their own rooms to study. One such fellow was from Mississippi. Once I mentioned that my ancestry is one-eighth black. That did the job; he didn't come in again, though he certainly was never unpleasant or distant to me in other people's rooms.

The Navy required us to take introductory physics, which I would not have done otherwise. It probably was the single most valuable course I ever took. I tried hard to get our kids to take physics in college. Rita and I made a list of requirements for our kids, figuring that we respected our own judgment as much as that of university curriculum committees; the list included one course each in computers, physics and/or general engineering, world history, music, art history, Judaic studies, and maybe something else. Our kids bitched a bit about the extra requirements, and they dodged a few of them (especially engineering or physics), but they mostly went along without too much protest; they may even have respected our judgment, too.

In addition to the dormitory groups, the fellows (I'm still not ready to say "men") in the NROTC unit constituted another group I was part of. Being in the Navy unit while at school and on summer cruises was perhaps the high point in my life with respect to institutional membership; I thought then and still think that the other 30 Holloway Plan scholarship students constituted the single best bunch of men I have ever met, by far. I was proud of the unit and the other fellows, and our summer cruises as a unit brought us close together.

Like many boys from small public high schools, I was at first worried about whether I could make the grade at Harvard. It was a blessing for me that on the first NROTC quiz after a few weeks that I was near the top grade. I knew that the quiz was more like high school than college in content, and the subject matter in that introductory course was trivial. It did at least signal that the other guys "put their pants on one leg at a time, too," a phrase I have always found meaningful; my worry diminished (though I seldom or never did that well again in college).

The standard course load at Harvard was four courses each semester. Our Navy ROTC courses counted for a standard one point each, and I thought that those courses did not contribute very much to my education; I thought of them as "Mickey Mouse" or "gut" courses, in the slang of the day. (The term "gut" puzzles me now.) In retrospect, however, though the material on navigation may not have been worth much to me in civilian life, I learned a lot more valuable material than I thought I did from our engineering, world law, and world history courses.

After freshmen year, students were distributed among the "houses"—then seven residential colleges around which college life revolved, modeled somewhat after the system at Oxford and Cambridge. Each pair or triplet or quartet of freshmen who wished to room together made application and gave a list of their preferences among houses and were interviewed by their (I think) first and second choices. Only perhaps five or ten percent of freshmen did not receive appointments and were instead relegated to Claverly Hall for a semester to wait for openings in the spring. Mal Rivkin and I were so relegated. Naturally there was a stigma attached, as there is to the nonselected in any such process. One of our classmates who was given to cutting remarks then—and still was at the Twenty-Fifth Class Reunion—referred to me (and surely to others there) as the "Claverly klutz." It is one of the very few nasty jibes I remember in my life (though there surely were plenty that I don't remember).

Of course we went to football games, especially in Cambridge. When I worked with the college radio station (which transmitted mostly classical music electronically to all dorm rooms using the duct system of the university as its "cable"), I served the public-address announcer as spotter of which players did what and then wrote up and delivered a summary of the game on the radio station. I often wondered how many (or how few) people were listening.

One weekend five of us went to Princeton for the game in the parents' car of one of the fellows who lived nearby. We left Friday afternoon and stopped at my parents' house in Millburn to sleep the night. We arrived after Mother and Dad had gone to bed, so I apportioned the four others to two couches and a double bed, and I thought I provided coverings. Before going to sleep, I came in to check on the two in the double bed and saw them shivering comically beneath a bedspread with large crocheted holes in it; they did not want to bother anyone by asking for a blanket.

After the game, at a boozy party at one of the Princeton clubs, one of the guys I was with—Dick Lionetti, the center for the basketball team, about 6'5" and hefty—was set upon by some smaller Princeton type who insisted on trying to pick a fight with Lionetti. (That often happens to big guys.) After good-naturedly trying to discourage the Princeton fellow for a while, Lionetti finally went outside with him into the alley. The rest of us followed as spectators, of course. But Lionetti kept talking to him, and the Princeton guy got a better look at Lionetti. Eventually Lionetti convinced the Princeton guy to buy him an ice-cream bar. That was the peak performance of statesmanship seen in my lifetime. (It also speaks for being able to make clear to your opponent that you are well-armed and are not running a bluff.)

The Navy would pay my tuition fee for a fifth course, so I took one each semester. This did not constitute an overwhelming burden, especially because I did not have an outside job, as many students did. (The Navy money took care of my needs.)

As was the case with high school, I remember almost nothing of the ideas and information I read and heard in lecture in college courses. In my freshman year, psychologist Gordon Allport said, when speaking of human development, that "The same fire that hardens the egg melts the butter." I've quoted that line a hundred times; it probably caught my attention because of its paradoxical nature. I learned a great deal about the nature and the practice of science in the sophomore laboratory course in experimental psychology, and I learned about operational definitions. I learned much factual material in courses in psychology, but I can't tie particular learning to particular courses. I learned lots of interesting practical stuff about propulsion and mechanical engineering in the Naval Science classes, much more valuable than I thought at the time; I rather looked down at the extent of the challenge the Naval Science courses offered.

When I went to college I was anxious to study some philosophy, because I believed that the great thinkers of history had conveyed to us knowledge that would help us conduct our lives well. My first course in the subject was not a systematic survey but rather a gallop through Western thought of recent centuries. I enjoyed it and did much of the extensive reading. Though I benefited from reading some of the philosophy of science, much of the rest that I read in a survey course either conveyed nothing meaningful to me or seemed to me obscurantist nonsense. Most especially, the pompously unreadable school of German philosophy following after Hegel seemed to me to be as close to a purposeful fraud on the public as one could get without running afoul of the law; pure nonsense, I concluded. This did nothing to diminish my underlying skepticism. (And when much later, I read John Locke and David Hume saying much the same about the bulk of philosophers, I knew that there was foundation for my doubts.)

The exam for the course was my last of five, and I therefore let slide my cramming for it. Then the night before the exam, I could not find my class notes, which were unusually important in that course.

A philosophy major upstairs lent me his notebook for a few hours, but it didn't seem to help much. I then had the inspiration to ask him to teach me some impressive-sounding German words that I could insert into my exam essays. He did so. The next day, for the first and last time in my life, I B.S.ed on an exam.

The result? During my first three semesters I had not received a single A for a course, perhaps because I never addressed myself to getting grades as a game, or because I could never write an exam answer that was squarely on the beaten track. This time I got an A, and my philosophy major friend upstairs, who had been doing very well in all his classes and understood the material thoroughly, got a C. Lest one put the incident down to the inadequacies of a third-rate institution, this happened at Harvard College.

I took a course on politics and history with McGeorge Bundy. All agreed he was "brilliant" for the first half or two-thirds of a class. After that, he ran out of prepared material and improvised worthless time-fillers. Years later, when he was one of the "best and the brightest" in the U.S. government during the Vietnam era and then leaped spectacularly from the springboard of failed policies to the presidency of the Ford Foundation, the pieces all seemed to fit well together. That foundation has been amazingly consistent in giving money to brilliant ideas that turn out to be inconsistent with the facts and often socially harmful. Once more it is the bizarre that I remember from my college education (Bundy's behavior) rather than the curricular education.

I can remember going up to the lectern of one instructor or another after lectures, maybe once every few weeks on the average, and thanking him or her for a very good lecture. I wish a student would do that to me once in a while. Surprisingly, in retrospect, no lecturer ever stopped me and asked my name, what I was studying, and so on. I make sure to do that when someone congratulates me on a lecture or talk anywhere. Maybe my college teachers were just more blasé about their excellence than I am. Or maybe I'm unusually curious about others, or just polite.

From a course with John L. Sweeney, curator of the Poetry Room at the undergraduate library, I took away one of the key guides to scholarly life. No matter how empty or foolish was a comment in this small class in a basic survey of great literature, Sweeney could somehow extract a valuable grain of thought and focus the class on that. The tactic is exactly the opposite from most of the communal life of the academic, wherein the object is to find the fatal flaw in the material being presented, thereby proving that the critic is more clever than the presenter. Of course this is destructive of a communal creative spirit, by focusing on the worthless rather than the worthwhile.

If someone should ever ask about me: Did Simon appreciate the finer things in life? I hope someone will answer: He appreciated what Sweeney taught by his practice and cherished it. Like so many lessons, this one is most likely to be learned from observation rather than from preaching. (Yet here I am preaching it. Inconsistency, inconsistency.)

I was a major in the Psychology Department. This was a bit peculiar, because most psychological study at Harvard had some years before been merged with sociology and anthropology (I think) into a department called Social Relations. Only laboratory experimental work on behavioral and physiological psychology was left in the Psychology Department.

I opted to major in experimental psychology because I liked the idea of doing laboratory experiments. It seemed much more solid science to me than did the clinical and survey-oriented psychology work done in Social Relations. I'm not sure how I acquired this view; probably it came from the elementary course in psychology taught by Edwin Boring.

Perhaps my first independent professional action began when I was troubled by the wind that usually blew through the tennis courts down by the river. I was just playing tennis casually, or maybe for the Kirkland House intramural team; I had never considered myself good enough even to try out for the varsity because I knew that people like Art French, also from Millburn-Short Hills, was on that team and was much better than I; he was a prep school star. (Actually, with some decent coaching from a college coach—I had never had any personal instruction—I probably could have been a passable college player, even in the Ivy League where the level of play was pretty fair. And as I write this at age sixty-three, I'll bet I could win a combined all-racquets tournament—racquetball, squash, tennis, and ping pong—among the members of my college class).

At some tennis courts I had played at in high school, there had been canvas sheets hung on the metal chainlink fences, with little crescent-moon slits in them, which I assumed were wind shields. I therefore suggested to (I think) the House sports committee that we ask for such sheets to be installed. Someone had the sense to ask me if there was reason to believe the canvas worked, and when I said I had no evidence, I was empowered to act as a committee of one to find out.

I learned that there was a faculty member who taught aeronautical engineering, one Richard von Mises, and I made an appointment to consult him. He turned out to be a Viennese immigrant about whom the story was told, (true or not; with the passage of time I can write recklessly without checking the veracity of the tale) that he had lived in sin with a woman for decades, ostensibly his housekeeper. When he arrived at Harvard, social pressure caused them to marry; they then divorced and parted soon thereafter. I drew a lesson from that story, true or not.

Von Mises opined that the canvas would not help. At best it would direct the air above the courts and cause eddies on the court that might well be no better than direct breezes and might be worse because of the irregularity. Report then delivered; suggestion canceled.

Mises came again into my later life twice. The NROTC had a system wherein we supposedly returned all our texts to a repository from which we drew books for our upcoming courses, if available there, and we were not discouraged from taking books that would be useful "outside reading" for courses, a rule that some of us interpreted broadly. We could also borrow books for summer cruises, as I remember. I saw *Positivism* by R. von Mises on the long waist-level table, and triggered by a stray remark in the philosophy course, I picked up the book and borrowed it for the summer. Scandalously, I delayed returning it after the summer until it slipped imperceptibly into my personal collection (a not infrequent event with NROTC students and the book repository, I should be ashamed to say; no records were kept).

When I got around to reading it some time later—after college, while I was in the fleet—*Positivism* greatly influenced my thinking, perhaps because Mises was not doctrinaire and was eclectic and tolerant to the point of not considering poetry and religion simply metaphysical nonsense, as did some Vienna Circle Positivists. It was the best and most influential philosophy book I had read until then. (More about this when I discuss the concept of causality.)

R. von Mises later reappeared when I worked on statistics, in his main scholarly role as the father of very influential views on probability. Some of his technical work, and perhaps especially the invention of the concept of a sample space, may be very valuable. But his frequentist concept of probability strikes me as trying to argue that half the loaf is the entire loaf, and it is as unnecessary as it is misleading. More later about an operational-definition view of probability that resolves all philosophical problems connected with probability.

R. von Mises' brother Ludwig also showed up in my life, as the man that Hayek referred to as his mentor. Though Ludwig von Mises may have had a large influence on Hayek, especially L. von Mises' enormously valuable criticism of socialism as inevitably flawed because it has no price system to transmit signals and knowledge through the economy, I think Hayek gave von Mises too much credit; he did not demur when I offered that view to him. In the end, Hayek's work is much more important than that of the antiempirical von Mises, in my opinion. (But then, I consider Hayek the most important intellectual figure in the twentieth century outside the physical sciences, following on David Hume and William James, a remark I'll repeat elsewhere in this book.)

One of the most painful failures of my life was being turned down a second time for election to the editorial board of the Harvard student newspaper, *The Crimson*. It was only in my junior year that I decided to try out for the paper, which was considered very late by the staff, and this made me feel different from most applicants, and ashamed. I also felt troubled that I was a member of the radio station staff, a competitor organization of sorts, and I felt like a bit of a traitor (though now I'm sure that no one even noticed). I had mostly lost interest in the radio station. I wanted to write editorials—and I wanted access to the Saturday night parties at the *Crimson*.

I wrote regular weekly submissions, deposited them in a box at the newspaper office, then picked up the corrected copy when I deposited the next one. I furtively sneaked in and out like a thief (which I felt myself to be) when making these transactions, lest I run into either a staff member whom I knew or a member of the radio station passing on the street. I don't think that I was ever more than ten feet into that building after the initial organization meeting, and I never met with any of the staff members who were correcting my work—the full stupidity of which I did not much realize.

What was I so ashamed of? There is no reasonable explanation. But I'm ashamed in many aspects of my life that are perfectly decent and moral—my sense of shame is entirely with respect to what I think others will think, despite my own belief that what I'm doing is blameless. Another complication was that my roommate was a member of the editorial board, and I felt that this was "unfair" in a positive way. (It actually proved to be a disadvantage, in all likelihood.)

Still another difficulty: I was then under the impression that people should write only about things they know about, and therefore I never wrote about national or international affairs. In my ignorance, I assumed that other people who were writing about these subjects *did* have some solid knowledge. Hence, I confined myself to writing about college topics.

It still distresses me to find that the editorial gatekeepers of the media pay so little attention to distinguishing between those people who know what they are talking about and those who do not. A person's track record should throw *some* light on the person's knowledge. But the newspapers continue to consult for their news columns, and print in their editorial opinions and columns, the comments of people who have been wrong across the board for decades. The failure rates of such pundits seems not to affect their credibility at all (I'll name some of these people in later pages.)

I began the "competition," as it was known, with an editorial about the dingy quality of the box lunches that students were given when they spent the day at a science laboratory. That first try was a terrific success, actually being *published* (unusual for a "competition") under the title "Box Lunch Blues." From there on, it was downhill. That was the only editorial I got published.

I failed in the first competition to make the newspaper. My failure was probably due to some other factors also, such as my assuming that the written work was all that mattered and there was no need to get to know the people on the editorial staff.

I was invited to compete again the following semester. Then I failed again the next semester. On the same day that I got word of being turned down for that second competition, I found out that our affair was being ended by the girl with whom I was desperately in love and who was my first sex partner (don't ask for details, please; it is still too painful); she broke off with me. That day my parents arrived to visit for a day, an event that had only happened once before during college.

I remember feeling during dinner—I had not told my parents a word of my troubles, of course—as if I were frozen in a block of ice, struggling to carry off the evening in a manner that nothing would show. If my parents did discern how miserable I felt, neither of them mentioned it or asked any questions.

I learned how difficult an elementary or high-school teacher's job is when, in my junior year at Harvard, I taught Sunday school for 90 minutes to a small group of very young children in a town a long bus ride north of Boston. The floating attendance was about five to eight children, and the pay was $10 per week—plenty of spending money for the week, including laundry. My main goal was to give the five-, six-, and seven-year-old children a positive feeling toward Judaism. This required that I project my personality for a full hour and a half, tell stories, and—with the kids—dance and sing. Half the kids were seeing child psychologists, I remember, and I was not allowed to apply any discipline, not even "Please sit over there in the corner." This work was so exhausting that I would stay home Saturday night to get a good night's sleep.

Harvard has an unusual institution of "final clubs" and "waiting clubs." If one is elected to a waiting club, one can then join a final club. But once one has joined one final club, one may not join another. The X club was quite different from all the other final clubs because it had no clubhouse. Its activities were mainly getting together once a month to drink beer and sing songs, and organizing coed weekend parties that aspired to Saturnalia but that regrettably did not reach it; drinking beer and champagne on Sunday morning with Saturday night's hangover was about the most licentious it got.

I quit before my senior year, which was a bit complex because one is committed to a final club through one's bachelor's degree. The gimmick we used was that I would probably receive my degree at midyear because I had already taken enough courses (less one) to graduate in three years. Groucho Marx's remark that any club that would elect me I wouldn't want to join may apply here, I regret to say. I felt and feel that I was ungrateful to those who elected me—especially John Rutter, whom I had known at the radio station (another institution I left after a couple of years) and who had proposed me for the club—especially because I think that I was the first Jew elected to the club.

The bachelor's honors thesis I did in my senior year was the first professional work of my life. It was a very important experience for me, and it certainly was the most exciting and rewarding part of my undergraduate (or graduate) education. The thesis-writing process was a model for what I believe education can be. I benefited from it so much that I volunteered to teach the senior honor's course at the University of Illinois as soon as I found out that my friend Jim Heins, who usually taught it, would not be teaching it in 1971. It has given me the best experiences of my teaching career.

The work started when senior thesis advisor William Verplank showed me a pack of cards, started laying them down one by one, and asked me to guess the pattern. He told me that this was an experiment in concept formation. There wasn't much more discussion before I went away with a pack of cards and an agenda to discover how concept formation occurred in situations like this one.

I spent much of the year devising experiments, trying them on my classmates, and then devising new experiments. Eventually I generalized that people behaved in one or the other broad ways—either gradually improving their accuracy until they had the rule correct, or making no progress for a long while and then suddenly finding the rule. Eventually, I generated a theory for why I observed what I did. Then I devised more experiments to test the theory.

It was exciting to me to realize that I was not just a consumer of knowledge but also a producer of it—and that I had mastered a corner of the world of knowledge better than any other person had up to that time.

The thesis-advising experience was like much else in my life, however. I ended up with no adviser or mentor because Professor Verplank, with whom I began, and who posed the problems I worked on, went on leave the second semester of my senior year. I was too naive to realize that personal relationships matter in the outcome of almost any work except farming, and I assumed that disinterested intelligent faculty members would read and then grade the thesis after I submitted it. With hindsight in light of my university experience, I imagine that only one person read the thesis, and that person probably saw no familiar landmarks in what I had written, but saw a lot of experimental work, and after ten or 15 minutes scanning, gave it a cursory *cum laude*, the basic passing grade for theses. However, even though the work was not received particularly well by others, I was convinced of its value and that my own judgment of it was more sound than those of others who put a grade on it.

Looking toward my later professional work: John Ziman and others emphasize the extent to which science is a social endeavor. Human interactions are a crucial ingredient in advancing a given line of work to success. But for a variety of reasons (an important one being that I have worked on many topics and shifted from one to another), it has not been possible to operate within a single broad network of other scholars—economic historians, for example, or demographers, let alone the more narrow networks that matter a lot.

I wrote an article about the thesis study a year or two later, while I was in the Navy, and sent it to a top psychology journal. But the editor and referee—obviously assuming that I was a Ph.D. (the editor addressed me as "Dr.")—saw in the article only that I was entirely ignorant about the proper format for an article; they assailed me unmercifully for the sloppy style of my references and for my imperfect citation of the literature. That was the end of that. There was no serious editorial inquiry into whether the subject was important, the ideas original, and the experimental work competent. All this was a forerunner of the reactions to my work for the rest of my life, though my deviations from standards were less superficial later on. I put the article away and did not send it out again. However, I still was convinced of the validity of the work. I'm not sure where that confidence came from, but that also foreshadowed the rest of my work life.

My experience trying to publish the fundamental idea in the thesis foreshadows (and maybe "shadow" is the ominously correct word) the central struggle of my entire life. It has been mainly an unsuccessful struggle, as such struggles are fated to be, with a few wildly lucky successes in my case—more than a person has reason to expect. The nature of this struggle, which you will find played out in the various chapters describing my work, is perhaps the most instructive material in this book.

In the late 1980s, when I read Jerome Bruner's autobiography, I found some ideas akin to my thesis, so I sent it to him. At that time I received the only good word I had received about it. That was some solace, but not much; in some ways I would have felt better concluding that the work was not of value than that it was of value but that the intrinsic value came to naught because it never was published.

The education I got at Harvard was valuable not because of the excellence of the teachers, but because of the curriculum. Most important, it provided me with a map of the domain of knowledge. The curriculum required some study of literature, and hence I learned that there was literature both in other languages as well as in English, and in English both from England and from the U.S., classics as well as moderns, to be studied as individual literatures and comparatively.

The curriculum required some study of science, which was fine, though the one course that I took—in physics—excellent as it was, left biology and astronomy and the fundamental outlook of scientists unillumined, because it left my knowledge that of a high schooler (like religion for so many is the knowledge of a twelve-year-old Sunday school student).

The curriculum provided for a broad survey of knowledge, a deeper concentration in a single subject, and a thesis on a single topic of discovery; this is the perfect recipe, in my view, to lay the groundwork of learning for an educated person.

The broad survey of knowledge fits an expression I have long been fond of: If you don't know where you're going, any road will do. I'd amend this to: And traveling many roads is best. None of us is sure where we are going in life, and I was less sure than most, so a broad education fit me well.

Leo Rosten, in his *Giant Book of Laughter* (p. 43), reports seeing in an antique shop window: "If you don't know what you want, we have it." That's a pretty good slogan for a liberal arts university, too. Additionally, some *kinds* of roads are better than others—picturesque, close to the countryside, passing through a variety of places.

The common intellectual idiom was that of literature, whereas later at the University of Chicago, the common idiom was that of the social sciences. The most important single idea I took away with me was that of the operational definition. Here I was lucky to have majored in psychology, because that field, more than any other, has been forced by its subject matter to take advantage of this idea that was at the heart of Einstein's discovery.

I had little social consciousness and zero political consciousness, as measured by how I spent my time. I did not do volunteer work tutoring young kids or any other such activities administered by Phillips Brooks House. I never went to a political meeting, though out of curiosity I probably would have gone to a meeting of the communist John Reed Club, but I was afraid that this might get back to the Navy and be misinterpreted. What were then known as panty raids caught my fancy, not protest marches (if there were any; I don't even know). One balmy spring evening, enough students were drawn outside by the lovely weather that the spark of mass action somehow was struck and caught, and soon hundreds of men began to surge toward Radcliffe College shouting "Panties, panties." Along the route I saw a kerosene lantern marking street construction, and I picked it up and lifted it over my head. Suddenly I found myself leading the mob. It was an extraordinary feeling of intoxication—the sheer sense of power, I suppose—that I have never had again in my life, never wanted, and desperately do not want now.

Though I recognized certain constraints at Harvard due to being Jewish (or at least non-upper-class Jewish)—not entering engineering, not being considered for certain clubs at Harvard, knowing that many non-Jewish girls would not want to date me let alone marry me—I did not feel handicapped. Perhaps this is because I had the advantage of knowing how much better off I was—despite any constraints I faced—than most of my parents' generation who could not get a college education and enter the professions that their natural abilities and interests might have fitted them for. This was even more true for my grandparents' generation, especially people like Grandma Goodie, who had no schooling at all (though in fact she may have realized her abilities quite well in the hardware store).

In thinking about my future I dismissed the possibility of becoming an academic because I did not think that I was particularly well-equipped for doing research. Throughout my college career I could not help but be impressed with the students who were academic shooting stars—the straight-A types (I never got an A until my sophomore year, and that was a perverse freak event, as mentioned above), the junior Phi Beta Kappas (I did not make Phi Beta Kappa at all), those who were taking far-advanced courses in physics and math, and those who had some other marks of brilliance bestowed on them by others. I assumed that they were capable of intellectual feats of scholarship that were beyond me—deeper, faster, and more voluminous. I thought that to do good research required the same qualities that would lead me to excel as a student in college—to be Phi Beta Kappa, graduate summa cum laude, and all that. I therefore figured that it did not make sense for me to aspire to an academic career because it would be people like those shooting stars who would be setting the pace, and I would be consigning myself to mediocrity. It wasn't the status of mediocrity that bothered me, but rather that my work itself would be mediocre and hence not very valuable. So I turned my attention to finding an occupation that would give greater play to the talents I did possess—mostly the broadness of my abilities, as I saw the matter.

I assessed that I had a considerable competence in a wide variety of activities, but no great strength in any of them—and certainly not in understanding and advancing scientific theory. Nor was there any teacher who might have suggested that I had a future as a researcher/scholar. Later, partly as a result of my experiences in the Navy, I added institutional reasons why being a professor would not work well for me.

10

College Summers and Midshipman Cruises

Navy life began for me as a midshipman during three college summers. They were very good cruises, extraordinary eyeopeners for a kid who had never been outside New Jersey except for summer camp in nearby Pennsylvania as a six year old, to Washington for a few days during World War II, and to Boston for college.

The flight from Newark to San Francisco was my first time in an airplane, and, of course, I was excited. It was an all-day flight, with fueling stops at Chicago and Denver. It was my first inkling of how huge the United States is and also how empty of people almost all of it was and still is. (Indeed, aside from metropolitan areas and along rivers and the sea, it is becoming even emptier.)

The 1950 cruise was to Hawaii aboard the cruiser *St. Paul.* We lived in the same quarters as enlisted men, stowed all our personal gear in the same half-lockers, tied our clothes with the same tie-ties (small precut pieces of string), ate the same chow, and used the same "heads" (toilets). The enlisted-men's head facilities for defecation were two long planks placed over a trough through which coursed sea water (to save fresh water), and you sat where there was a space next to whomever was there. My sensibilities never coarsened to the point at which I did not mind this. Compared with many public "facilities" in China as of the late 1980s, our midshipman heads were the Ritz.

We ate as did the crew, carrying trays through the mess lines. That could be tricky when the ship was rolling, though a cruiser was very stable compared to small vessels such as destroyers (on which I later served). There was great social pressure not to be a "screw-up" and drop your tray, no matter what.

We learned to love such breakfast delicacies as "shit on a shingle"—chopped beef in barbecue sauce on toast. And when we went for day trips—also during the next summer when we were at Norfolk learning landing operations and we were in small boats all day—we took along sandwiches with such specialties as "horsecock with mustard" or mayonnaise—that is, a species of light-colored bologna with bread and a spread. It must be obvious that one of the charms of the Navy for me was the picturesque language.

We were given classes on all the various kinds of equipment aboard this very large ship, and we got to try everything, from being cox'n (coxswain) for the small boats to steering the ship as helmsman. College had already taught us the differences between professors and high-school teachers; now the lectures by the enlisted men taught us the difference between professors and artisans as teachers. The talks were usually very narrow in scope, very detailed, and without relationship to the rest of the ship. I had no doubt that many of these same enlisted men could have learned very well to be professors, but their narrowly focused talks were the result of their backgrounds and situations, I thought.

We quickly learned a dozen ways to hide away to catch a bit of extra sleep; at sea, one is always sleep-deprived due to standing watches around the clock (which we did, along with the ship's company) plus putting in a full work day five days and a half a day on Saturday. One could sometimes duck a lecture and sneak under the decking of a storage compartment that held canvas, or behind the racks (bunks) that were triced up during the day so that supposedly no one could bed down for sleep in the regular sleeping places. Some of the places we napped were dangerous; danger is never far away aboard a warship full of equipment arranged so that there is barely an extra inch of unused space.

We learned to parrot Navy talk and even to make jokes with the jargon. Learning to mimic the in-language is an important part of the process of becoming a respected member of any group, and there was enormous pressure on us to "shape up" as quickly and as completely as possible. I've only recently learned how important this sort of conformity is to being "regular" and therefore an integral part of any group; I notice this in the perfectly regular, expensive pinstriped suits of the big-time corporate lawyers one sees on television, testifying before Congress about one thing or another. These are serious people—not as serious of mien as high Mafiosi or the members of the Soviet presidium when the USSR was still in business, but still they are not people who fool around in undignified fashion; even their jokes are dignified. Sometimes I find myself trying to play that sort of role for a while, but eventually I break up and make a bit of fun of the entire affair—not good, not good.

The cruise was marred only by the outbreak of the Korean War as we were outbound. This caused consternation among the enlisted men who were due to end their hitches soon but were immediately "extended." Our own periods of service were also extended from the 18 months or two years we signed up for, to three years. (When we got back to Harvard we were required to sign new agreements with the Navy.) Almost everyone else signed without much murmur, but one other fellow and I explored our alternatives. We found that if we did not sign, we would lose our scholarships. Harvard said it would give me some money, and I could get a part-time job, which would be enough. But I was told that the draft board would be instructed by the Navy to draft me immediately, so I had little choice in the end but to sign, as did the other fellow.

Entering port in Hawaii was very exciting. "Join the Navy and See the World" is a powerful appeal to young men. The first things we saw were graceful aloha dancers on the quay and a sign on a truck: "Edible Garbage." That stumped us until we realized that the subject was edibility by pigs, not by us.

A minor curiosity of the 1950 cruise later became an example in one of my writings. One cause of misconceptions about natural resources and of the belief that they are limited and exhaustible is not understanding that the supply of a resource depends upon where, when, and how. This cruise experience when the rapid provision of air was in short supply points up the matter.

The usual enlisted quarters then were three bunks high and 40 or 50 bunks per compartment. The ships were not air-conditioned in those days, aside from the few compartments that had sensitive electronics gear in them. (People were assumed to be less fragile than equipment.) When we were in hot climes, the sun would beat down all day and heat the steel ships so much that the sleeping compartments sometimes were near 90 degrees. You had to sleep with your arms above your head so that the area from your armpits down your sides would get a little bit of circulation.

The ventilation system in the compartment consisted of air blowers in the engine room with outlets at the ends of casings in the compartments. To be situated reasonably near the blower outlet was unbelievably good luck. For a few of those who were not near the ends of the blowers but near whom the casings passed, there was an opportunity to increase the flow of air by punching a small hole in the casing. This was totally contrary to regulations, of course, and meant that there was less air to go to others. Yet we were so desperate for a bid of wind that some men would make the holes anyway, sometimes causing fights.

So even air is not an inexhaustible resource under particular circumstances. On the other hand, as people learn how to make air conditioning more cheaply, and as the spaces that we live in increase in size, cool air comes to be in greater and greater supply.

And so it is with every natural resource.

I'll tell you my one bad memory of the 1950 cruise in the context of a tragic event that occurred in 1996: The Chief of Naval Operations, Admiral Michael Boorda, killed himself in connection with the press interrogating him about whether he was wearing a decoration—two "V" for combat in Vietnam ribbons—to which he was not entitled. In the aftermath, there was much discussion about whether or not he really was entitled to wear them; his ship had been in the combat zone and had fired on the enemy, but had not itself been shot at. Boorda had immediately stopped wearing the V's a year before, when he had heard informally that someone had raised a question about senior officers wearing unauthorized decorations. He left a suicide note saying that no one would believe that he had made an honest mistake. Boorda was a particularly interesting person because he not only had not gone to Annapolis, but rather had started as an enlisted man and been commissioned from the ranks—the first CNO to have done so. By all accounts, he continued to keep close ties to the enlisted ranks and to care for their interests.

Many writers say that they could not believe that Boorda killed himself only about the decorations; there must be more to it than that they said. Some referred to him as a "disturbed" person simply because of these events, though there was not any evidence that he was anything other than a remarkably effective, decent, and balanced person in his work and personal lives.

Not long after we left Hawaii on our way back to Long Beach, there was a locker inspection. The inspecting officer—probably a midshipman about to enter the senior class—found a stick of chewing gum in my locker. This was a crime punishable almost by death in shipboard regulations because of gum's capacity to gum up the works.

I was astonished. I could not remember putting the gum in my locker, and I said to him, "It can't be mine. I never chew gum," which was true (though I'm sure I chewed once in a great while). "Another fellow stowed some stuff in the locker the other day when he was in a hurry and his own locker was already closed," which was true; getting a combination lock open in a hurry was tricky, and we'd sometimes help out one another in such fashion. The inspecting midshipman looked at me queerly, but simply passed on with the several other midshipman in his inspecting entourage.

Later I remembered: I had indeed brought the gum aboard; I had been holding it for a girl I had met at a dance at the famous Punahou School that had arranged an event for us. I was mortified. (Notice the relationship of "mortified" to "death.") I was sure that the guys whose lockers were right next to me heard all this and assumed that I was lying and told the others. I felt as if my honor was lost forever; I did not want to face anyone. I was indeed mortified, and I doubt that I have ever been able to tell this story to anyone.

I'm not saying that someone like Boorda or me cannot tell lies, even rotten lies for the worst of purposes. I am saying that people like me—and I would guess Boorda—cannot tell lies *with impunity*, just shrugging it off if we get caught, as many others can, including many in public life. Shrugging off getting caught in lies is so common that many journalists assume it is true of all persons and are convinced that no one has a deep emotional fidelity to the truth just because it is the truth. "Why are you saying this?" a journalist will often ask of someone who writes to challenge a wrong scientific position that is entering into public policy. If you answer, "Because I'd like the truth to be known, and I get some satisfaction out of trying to have it so," the journalist will often look at you in disbelief. "Come on," he or she may say. "What's your real motive?"

From my own experience, it is not difficult for me to imagine that Boorda might indeed prefer death to living while everyone he knew and cared about would read in the newspapers that he was a cheat.

One of the pleasant features of our summer cruises was the wide range of experiences the Navy gave us. We got to ride in most types of vehicles known to humanity at that time, whether on the sea (landing craft of every description), the air (dirigibles, airplanes of various kinds), and land (jeeps, tanks). Many hours and days were a waste of time educationally, but the company of the NROTC guys was so good that we were never bored. While I was a bit closer to some than to others—for example, I roomed with Tom Clarke and Aris Demetrios my senior year—almost everybody was comfortable with almost everyone else, so I won't even bother mentioning other names. That was the best experience of large-scale camaraderie of my life.

The second "cruise," in 1951, consisted of three weeks learning about amphibious operations at Little Creek, Virginia, and three weeks learning about Navy air operations at Pensacola, Florida. Liberty—free hours off base—after work and weekends clearly was not very interesting in those places, so we stayed around the bases a lot. Perhaps the most interesting event of the summer concerned Aram Mardirosian, a member of our unit.

Aram reported a day late because he had had to fly to California to visit his sick mother, and he was delayed on return by a plane strike. He went to the USO, which handles these emergencies for service people, and they told him that he would have no problem with being absent without leave. But he omitted to read the fine print on his orders, which required that he telephone the base. Therefore, upon reporting, he was told that he was being given 149 demerits, and 150 would get him thrown out of the unit, and he would lose his scholarship. That is, the slightest additional slip during the summer and he was out on his ear.

Aram was a hero. So as to avoid the possibility of a mis-made bed in the morning, he slept on the wooden table in the middle of our room instead of sleeping in his rack (bed). The guys in the unit supported him however we could. By the second half of the cruise he was appointed the head midshipman (whatever it was called) and he made it through the summer intact. He told me recently that this was one of the great events of his life.

It is interesting to reflect, however, that he and we accepted the matter just as the Navy handed it out. There were no protests by him or by us that the punishment was unfair or too harsh—which I now believe it was. Would men do differently nowadays? Someone in Aram's position would probably rush out and hire a lawyer.

The third summer, 1952, we shipped out to Europe and the Mediterranean. Our first port was Cherbourg. As we came into port, a couple of the guys from the unit and I were able to stand atop the highest deck on the ship—thirteen decks high, if memory serves. The very height magnified the size of this huge battleship, perhaps the most majestic warship ever built. I had the sense of returning to our roots, the continent from which most or all of us had sprung. The Navy band on the main deck began to play as we entered the harbor, making the event even more emotional, emphasizing the young power of the New World of which this ship and we were the representatives. This feeling was heightened when we saw the quay at Cherbourg, still unrepaired from the bad damage of World War II. I am stirred again as I now relive the moment.

We had the opportunity to take a three-day trip to Paris, and most of us did so. We stayed in a hotel wherein we were at first puzzled and then wildly amused by the bidets in the bathrooms. We saw all the standard sights of the city and flirted with young American girls we saw, but my bunch of guys got nowhere with them.

My cousin Jerry Cohen had spent the previous year in Lyon, France. Upon inquiry through family channels, he suggested that a Paris tavern called *Lapin Agile* would be fun for us to visit. So five or six of us took off on foot to find it, though none of us (and especially not I) knew a word of French. I had the name and address written on a slip of paper, and when we first were in doubt about the way, I stopped a woman and read the name off the paper: "La pin a gile." She looked at me and said: "Monsieur?" and hurried on. So we tried a man and got a similarly poor result. The third person, a man, took the paper and began to laugh uproariously. *Lapin agile* means *agile rabbit*. As I read it phonetically, it came out *agile penis*. After a moment, he composed himself and explained the situation to us in broken English; he got us started in the right direction. *Lapin Agile* was indeed a pleasant, picturesque place, where people came to sing folk songs and drink wine.

Of course I worked summers after returning from cruises. As I look back, the idea of simply doing nothing or just vacationing for more than a week or so was not even thinkable.

One summer, I worked loading trucks at a beer can factory in Union, New Jersey, and I still have some flat sheets of cans before they were cut and pressed into shape; they make a nice decoration, like an Andy Warhol painting. That work was the worst I have ever done. The boxes had to be stacked eleven high, and they came to us in twos, threes, or fours. So you had to keep doing arithmetic all the time your were working. It was much worse than most manual labor because you could not even daydream. That is, it was drudge work with the mind as well as with the body. That's as bad as it gets in industrial civilization, aside from tasks that are dangerous or dirty. Work at a job like that for a day, and you will no longer wonder whether automation and robotization that eliminates such work is a good thing.

I learned a bit about unions. Anyone who showed up at a meeting of this mobster-dominated union (it was a local of the Teamsters, Chauffeurs, Warehousemen, and Brewery Workers) and had anything controversial to say risked getting his head busted by goons. And the union would protect you against the company no matter what you did—up to a point. For example, we were instructed that if you were seen throwing a case of beer out the window into the yard intending to take it home later, the union would protect you. If you were seen picking up a case in the yard but had not been seen throwing it out the window, you were okay. But if you were seen both throwing it out and picking it up, the union would not protect you.

I worked the 4:00 P.M.–12:00 P.M. and the 12:00 P.M.–8:00 A.M. shifts one time or another; the day shift was reserved for "permanent book holders." On these shifts there was a tank containing cold beers, and you could drink what you liked as long as you did your job. It was always tempting to have a few to make the time go faster. But it seemed harder to get through a shift when a bit tipsy, so I would not have any until the last hour or so. Then it was pleasant to ride the bus home "three sheets to the wind," as it is known in the Navy, especially Friday morning, watching the other riders on their ways to work while you could look forward to the weekend off.

I played a lot of golf with Paul Friedmann that summer, with whom I had played a lot of chess in high school.

Nick Volk and I made two long overland trips together after midshipmen cruises. We had a glorious time hitchhiking from San Francisco to Salt Lake City, where we and a third friend picked up a car that needed driving across the country. We did all the national parks and had a spectacular time.

The next summer, we hitchhiked together from Pensacola to New Orleans and stayed at the YMCA with the worst indoor collection of mosquitoes I have ever seen. We were reduced to sleeping on the floor, and even that was a misery. We then hitchhiked north (in our uniforms) and had the usual time full of small adventures—interesting people, a variety of places and sights, and a remarkable feeling of being free and young. Nick was a good person to hitchhike with because he was spectacularly good-looking in a blond way.

11

In the Fleet

Immediately after graduation from college, the men in our NROTC unit were commissioned as ensigns. There was a ceremony, probably at the same time as graduation, but I remember that commissioning even less than I remember graduation. Life as a naval officer started with three weeks of playing pool and drinking Heineken beer at the Officers' Club at Guantanamo Bay, Cuba ("Gitmo" to Navy people), plus ineffectually trying to learn to man a tiny one-person sailboat. I was waiting for my ship, the destroyer *Samuel B. Roberts*, DD823, to come into port, when I would join the ship's company.

There also was plenty of time at Gitmo to go into nearby Cuban towns for dinner and drinks and try my two years of high-school Spanish with the menu. *Pollo con arroz*, chicken with rice, was delicious. I did not eat the *langusta*, the local lobster, because I still forswore shellfish because it is unkosher, though by then this forbearance had become a distaste rather than a religious prohibition that I earlier had obeyed out of respect for my parents (an example of how socialized a person I am in my knee-jerk reactions).

Gitmo was much in the news in the 1990s as a place where Cuban refugees are (as of 1996) interned by the U.S. government. That interning of the refugees rouses me to fury when I see the scenes on the Spanish-language television station. It would improve the lives of everyone and harm almost no one if those people were simply allowed to enter the U.S. freely. Most would be met by relatives who would take care of them, find jobs (as they quickly would, often through the relatives), and produce output whose value would be income for the immigrant families. Instead, they are held within steel fences doing nothing, the kids losing school time, and the adults wasting their work time and becoming more bitter day by day. This story is repeated in Hong Kong with the Vietnamese escapees and by other peoples elsewhere in the world. Yet, when my research shows that there are economic benefits and few costs of allowing these people their freedom from these pens and giving them immigration visas, I am assailed as an enemy of humanity. Peculiar.

The displacement of our "tin can," the *Roberts*, was 2250 tons, and it was about 300 feet long. My first job aboard the *Roberts* was as a division officer (something like a platoon leader in the army) in the deck force. There are two such divisions aboard a destroyer, and together they are responsible for the external appearance of the ship, the maintenance of the hull, plus all the gear and arrangements for the ship's boats, lines, and so on. My job was to be in charge of all the work done by the 2nd division as well as the work lives of its men.

A great benefit of going into the service as an officer after college is that the responsibility is immediately enormous. In most first jobs in civilian life, nothing you may do for months or years will have a major impact on the enterprise or upon human beings. But a destroyer division officer has great power to decide matters that fundamentally affect the lives of his (nowadays, or her) men (and women): when they get to go on liberty and leave (liberty is short-term—an evening or a day, whereas leave is like a multi-day vacation), whether they go before captain's mast for punishment, whom they work for and with, and much much more. Most college graduates have hardly had responsibility for their own lives, let alone for others. So this responsibility was awesome for me and probably for most other young officers.

After a few months the "First Lieutenant"—that's a job title and not a rank, the title for the officer in charge of the two deck divisions—was transferred. I was made First Lieutenant, a job I loved. Soon after I took over as First Lieutenant, we went into dry dock in Boston, during the cold winter months. The ship was to undergo renovation and maintenance, and my job was mainly to get her perfectly shipshape and looking spankingly well kept.

Chief Boatswain's Mate Charles Peart (Boatswain is pronounced "bosun"), who worked with me when I was First Lieutenant, weighed about 130 pounds dripping wet, and probably was a high school dropout. But he was as keen mentally, and as powerful morally and in personality, as any officer or man aboard ship. Standard Navy joke:

"The only thing dumber than a dumb gunner's mate is a smart bosun's mate." But Peart was as wise as any man aboard ship.

(A note on how mathematicians think: The gunner's mate-bosun's mate joke has the same logical form as the expression: Professor X went from university Y to university Z and improved the average quality of both of them. It also has somewhat the same form as Simpson's Paradox in statistics.)

Our two divisions were responsible for getting the decks, sides, and seamanship gear shipshape for the major inspection following a period in the shipyard. Peart told me that the divisions were grossly undermanned; we did not have sufficient men in the deck gang to do all of the chipping and repainting of the decks that needed to be done before we left dry dock. I did not recognize that fact fully, nor did I know how to argue for more resources. I think that I told this to the executive officer, but it never occurred to me to "fight" for more men; even if Peart or someone else had advised me to, I would not have had any idea how to do so. I have an unforceful personality, and I have no skill in such interpersonal tussles. I never believe that I am armed with righteousness so that I can claim injustice, partly because I can see the other person's position—that there are other and perhaps better claimants for the resources—than mine. I always feel that I am somehow illegitimate in asking for what may be simply better treatment than other people get. All this makes me quite ineffective on a committee or in any other such deliberative body. This in turn is one reason why I don't like to be involved in group decision-making, especially when the group is making decisions that affect me personally. Whenever I muse about serving as a department head or dean at the university, I think that I would be a washout in those jobs because "fighting for your people" is a big part of the work.

The result of our being undermanned was a poor inspection grade, followed by my painful firing from a job which I liked very much. By firing me the captain could show he was taking action to remedy the defect. I later used this incident to make the point in my how-to-think book that a sensible manager learns how to fight for resources to meet goals or to point out that the goals cannot be met with existing resources.

Navy ships are interesting vessels. I found the efficiency devices fascinating—for example, how the same fresh water is used again and again in the boilers and turbines, and the manner in which the last bit of energy is extracted from the steam that powers the turbines. The redundancy of the systems aboard ship is very instructive; for every mechanical or communication system there is at least one backup system to reduce the chances of being disabled by enemy action in wartime. For example, the telephones used for much of the ship's communications are powered only by the sound of the speaker's voice, needing no additional electricity supply.

The Navy bureaucracy also is interesting. It is commonly referred to as a system designed by geniuses to be operated by idiots. That's a good way to design almost any system—so that it can operate as automatically as possible.

Life at sea is frequently exciting, and it has a real-life aspect to it that the army does not have. Moving a ship from place to place, and performing the duties a Navy ship performs, is mostly not make-believe or just practice (except for gunnery drills). Some of it is scary, like fueling at sea in bad weather, where you are only one wrong turn of the wheel by the helmsman away from a collision.

One of our too real duties was "plane guard"—that is, following astern of an aircraft carrier as planes take off and land. Carrier pilots ply the most difficult trade I know of—the most dangerous and the scariest. One black night we were the plane guard, and a plane with three men aboard missed the landing and plunged into the sea. We did not see anything immediately, and we did not know if they survived. By the time our ship turned around to go back for them, we were perhaps a great distance from where they went into the sea. We put boats into the water, but still no sign of the fliers. Then we saw a flare in the distance, and everyone aboard ship cheered as the boats moved toward the flare—but we did not find them. Then another flare, and another failure to find the fliers in the pitch-black night. Another flare, and another. Finally one of our boats found them—after their very last flare. If they had not been found then, they might well have been lost for good. When the boat brought them alongside and they came up the ladder, I felt myself looking into the faces of three men who had come back from death; that was what we seemed to see in their expressions. When we transferred them by "high line" to the carrier the next day, everyone on both ships was happy.

I felt comfortable with em's (enlisted men), though some other officers did not. All I my life I have identified and felt more solidarity with the buck private in the rear rank than with his sergeant, more with the sharecropping peasant than with the landowner, more with the last team in the league than with the first, more with the caddies than with the golfers whose bags we carried. Of course, as a kid, I was a fan of the Brooklyn Dodgers ("Dem Bums"), before they were World Champions, and not a fan of the regal New York Yankees. Because of Navy rules and of the wisdom in those rules, I could not step over the boundary and be a buddy of enlisted men; I had to keep the appropriate distance. But I respected many em's for their knowledge and for the fact that they were guys like me, different simply in not having had the good chances by background to have the Navy send them to college, or to have the particular twist of mind to have made them as good in school learning as I was.

This attitude is part and parcel of my dislike of elites.

Perhaps partly for this reason, it inevitably fell to my lot to be appointed defense counsel, serving as the ship's defense counsel at captain's mast and lesser courts-martial for sailors accused of minor offenses. Any defense lawyer's job is antiestablishment in its fundamental nature. I liked the job, and no one else wanted it. I doubt if I would have felt as comfortable being "trial counsel" (prosecution) representing the establishment. I did not realize that I was supposed to act my part in a court-martial drama whose script was informally written in the wardroom over coffee. Giving one man a spirited defense that got him off on appeal to higher authority got me in trouble because it was a black mark for the ship. My stupidity about organizational realities like this has persisted throughout my life.

I handled lots of captain's mast offenses (the fourth and lowest level of court-martial), such as a man being out of uniform, or sleeping on watch, or minor insubordination. I even acquired something of a regular clientele among the "fuckups". One of these was Soper (not his real name, which bore the same relationship to its Hebrew origins as Soper does to So-faer, a writer). Soper was a pimply Jewish kid who always seemed to be slightly out of uniform or at the wrong place at the wrong time. He sought me out to defend him on several occasions, though his division officer might ordinarily have served in that capacity, probably because he thought that the bond of our both being Jews would get him some extra help from me. (He also sought me out after he got a telegram that his mother had died and he wanted to fly home on emergency leave, but we were in the port of Bahrein and the bastard Bahreinis wouldn't let him ashore because he was Jewish, despite the circumstances, no matter how much the ship protested.)

Speaking of being Jewish aboard ship, I conducted high holiday services for perhaps five of us, using as a lectern one of the old analog computers in the Fire Control Center (i.e., the place from which the firing of the guns is controlled). I didn't think of myself as having much Jewish learning, but what I had was more than anyone else had.

Perhaps my most interesting case as defense counsel was that of Pack, a petty officer who was accused of selling some old pieces of junk over the side to "bumboats" (small, junklike boats) in Hong Kong in exchange for a pair of boots. The official rumor was that the Communist Chinese were surreptitiously buying and collecting these pieces of old equipment and constructing warships of them. (Really! You say no one could believe such nonsense? Think again.)

A special court-martial trial was held, and I presented as complete a defense as I could assemble, focusing on the absence of good evidence that Pack had done what he was charged with.

After the defense's case was complete, the trial counsel (prosecutor) Charlie S., made his closing speech, which I can quote word-for-word. Red in the face with anger, he said to the three-officer court, "I know he's guilty. You guys know he's guilty. Even Simon knows he's guilty. Find him guilty." And he sat down.

They found him guilty.

We filed an appeal and Pack got off.

The captain came down on me like a ton of bricks for filing the appeal. (But see the end of the chapter for the great benefit that flowed to me because the captain was down on me.) Stupid me for not even knowing that. But it probably would not have made any difference if I had known. Even more stupid, but I'm proud of this stupidity.

One of the less-pleasant aspects of shipboard life for me was that the "stewards" mostly dated from preintegration days during and after World War II and were all Southern blacks who cooked our meals for us in their own style. This meant that every vegetable dish from string beans to mashed potatoes came drowned in bacon grease or accompanied by tiny chunks of bacon; fancy round pieces of prime steak were encircled by strips of bacon, and the stink of bacon pervaded every meal. The first short story I had written in college was about the reaction of a Jewish young man who ate his first piece of nonkosher meat—not even pork, just beef—in the Navy, and how he almost gagged on it. (A couple of my friends give me enormous pleasure by remembering the story on occasion.) Then it was not just non-kosher beef or chicken, but pig! I ate a lot of bread and peanut butter from the galley; probably very good from a cholesterol point of view, I suppose, but not very enjoyable.

One day the men were chipping paint on the main deck by hand with the usual paint-chipping hammers—hydraulic or electric chippers would do the job too quickly, and not sop up enough of the men's time. I passed by L., a stolid seaman (the equivalent of a private first class in the army) who never caused any problems and always pulled his weight. I watched him for a moment and said something like, "You do good work, Jones." A few months later we were in the same bar ashore, and we fell into light conversation. After a few minutes he recalled my comment to him and said, "That's the only nice thing that a petty officer or officer has said to me in the two years I've been in the Navy."

The boss of L. and the other men in his gang was boatswain's mate second class R., a hard, surly, obstinate, nasty man—heavyset, with tough looks to match his personality. In R.'s division were two Italian kids from Brooklyn, A. and P., below middle height and not powerfully built, but excellent athletes—a shortstop-second baseman combination—and good workers. One of them bore the name of perhaps the most famous Mafia "family" in New York. R. used to ride them hard about one thing or another. One night A. and P. were in the same bar as R., and R. made a slighting remark to P. P. hit R. with one blow and broke R.'s jaw. Because it was ashore and off-duty, P. was committing no Navy crime. The next day the entire ship celebrated. Sometimes good triumphs over evil.

Unrelated: a few months later the other kid, A., came to me with a request for Special Liberty. I had heard many remarkable reasons for Special Liberty, many of them transparently preposterous, which I turned down. A. had returned from New York the night before and had stowed five pounds of Italian salami in a locker at the train station, and had forgotten it there. It was not just that he wanted to get the salami, but he was afraid it would soon be stinking up the entire station. He got his Special Liberty.

Over the winter we were in dry dock in Boston, which was good duty. Fellow officer and Harvard classmate Gerry Freed and I rented a tiny apartment ashore because it was almost impossible to live aboard ship in dry dock during cold weather.

Before putting to sea after an extended period in port, such as dry dock, a key "evolution" (Navy language for an activity) is securing gear that might come loose when rolling and pitching at sea, and that might have been stowed loosely during the period in port. But though you try hard, you always don't catch lots of stuff. As soon as the ship would meet the first swells, you could hear minor crashing sounds all over the ship as overlooked items fell from their harbor stowage and hit the deck—hopefully not hitting you in the head on the way. (This is what flight attendants warn you of in airplanes.) This illustrates the difference between engineering analysis of a problem (that is, theory) and field test (that is, actual experimentation). No matter how good your analysis is, you are likely to omit some important items; only actual experimentation can test the system.

The best part of my years in the Navy was the close relationship to awesome nature. I loved the sunsets and sunrises at sea, the flying fish in tropical waters, the driving rain and high waves, too, even at the cost of going without sit-down meals. I had the extraordinary experience of being aboard our small ship near the eye of a killer typhoon—the same spot near the Philippines where three U.S. destroyers foundered and sank in World War II, with the loss of 778 lives, a story told marvelously well by C. Raymond Calhoun (who was captain of a destroyer that survived) in *Typhoon: The Other Enemy*. That typhoon certainly was one of the great events of my life. Luckily we had time to get well-ballasted (that is, to make sure the fuel tanks were full of either oil or water, so as to reduce the center of gravity) whereas the ships that went down were low on fuel and not well-ballasted. There is no more compelling evidence of the awesome power of nature than a typhoon. One wave smashed our steel post office compartment on the main deck and another sent depth charges rolling back and forth on the fantail until they went overboard, to our huge relief. Afterwards we had to get repairs in port.

I have many such pleasant memories of the cruises, but some of my memories are painful and bitter. Being fired from the job as First Lieutenant that I loved, because the ship failed the deck inspection after being in dry dock, and then being dumped into an engineering job about which I knew nothing was no fun. It was no pleasure to be put "in hack" (that is, confined to my stateroom as punishment) because the ship came right when it should have come left, when I was in CIC (Combat Information Center), and it was the officer of the deck who was responsible.

If memory serves, this is what happened: We were steaming through a very large number of small fishing boats, hundreds. There were so many that they were not reported when seen on the radar scopes, because there were always so many of them. The daylight visibility was good, and the Officer of the Deck simply weaved his way through them. But the OOD took action with respect to one of them—perhaps starting to turn in such manner as to get too close to another ship—which made the ship look bad and embarrassed the captain. The captain took his usual action—punish someone for supposedly not doing his job, against the captain's orders. The logical person would have been Jim L. But Jim was the captain's protégé and look-alike. So the captain turned to the next candidate for punishment—the CIC officer, which was me.

My letter to the Captain on the latter issue, which got me out of hack in a hurry, still reads well.

16 September 1954

From: Commanding Officer, U.S.S. SAMUEL B. ROBERTS (DD–823)
To: Ensign Julian L. SIMON, 519573/1100, U.S. Navy
Subj.: Improper performance of duty—Imposition of disciplinary punishment
Ref.: (a) Uniform Code of Military Justice, Article 15
(B) U.S. Navy Regulations 1948, Article 1405

1. On the morning of 16 September 1954 while on watch as CIC Watch Officer, your neglect to report any of eleven (11) radar contacts in the vicinity of the ship to the bridge, thereby placing the ship in an extremely embarrassing position, is considered to be improper performance of duty.
2. You are hereby suspended from all duties except during General Quarters and restricted to the limits of the ship for a period of two (2) weeks.
3. Your attention is directed to reference (a) and (b).
4. You are advised of your right to appeal in accordance with paragraph 134, MCM, 1951. You are directed to reply without delay, through official channels, and to state therein the date of receipt of this communication and any appeal you may desire to make.
5. A copy of this letter will be attached to your next fitness report.

Copy to:
BUPERS
Service Jacket

R. H. WHITE

18 September 1954

From: Ensign Julian L. SIMON, 519573/1100, U. S. Navy
To: Commanding Officer, U.S.S. SAMUEL B. ROBERTS (DD–823)
Subj.: Improper performance of duty—Imposition of disciplinary punishment

Ref: (a) Uniform Code of Military Justice, Article 15
(b) Uniform Code of Military Justice, Article 31
(c) Manual of Courts-Martial, Paragraph 133
(d) Manual of Courts-Martial, Paragraph 134
(e) Letter from Commanding Officer, USS Samuel B. Roberts, to Ensign Julian L. Simon, 16 September 1954, Serial: 483

1. Receipt of reference ( ) on 16 September 1954 is noted.
2. I appeal from this punishment on the basis that the procedure specified in reference (c) was not followed, to the substantial prejudice of my rights. Specifically, no copy of an accusation was furnished to me in accordance with reference (c); no warning of self-incrimination, consistent with reference (d) was given to me before I was asked by the Commanding Officer for a report on what had happened; I was given no opportunity to bring forth the testimony of witnesses; no mast was held; and I had no chance to prove the following facts and circumstances in defense, mitigation, and extenuation, all of which I believe to be true:

a. Throughout the approximately 1–12 hours which I stood the CIC watch, the surface search radar operators were on RD3, and an RDNS of two years CIC experience and sufficiently qualified to be nominated for the RD3 advancement test. The latter man had the surface scope for most of the 1–12 hours and up until the time of my relief. He was awake, and at least sufficiently attentive to the scope to intermittently provide me with ranges and bearings to navigational points for purposes of plotting the ship's position. Also present in CIC were the watch supervisor, an RD3 nominated for RD2, and the leading radarman, as RD1.

   None of these people ever informed me that the ship had any radar contacts.
b. At the beginning of this cruise I had carefully instructed all watch supervisors, including the supervisor on watch the morning of 16 September, that I desired to be informed of all contacts, tactical signals, and other occurrences during my watch in CIC.
c. Although visibility from the bridge was good, and many if not all the contacts—including the one that embarrassed the ship—were held visually, the bridge watch never asked CIC for information on any contact, or notified CIC that there were any contacts.
d. No contacts were reported by other ships in the formation via voice radio. Normally all contacts are reported when discovered on the CI Net.

J. L. Simon

Shipboard closeness breeds strong emotions, of course. I had liked my first captain, P. J. Brownlow, but he left in dry dock. I then despised Captain White and Executive Officer Loudermilk as human beings for a variety of shipboard actions in addition to those involving me; the pair are among the less noble people that I have been forced to get to know well over my lifetime.

Unfortunately I am cursed with a memory that is biased in favor of remembering the bad more than the good. This makes me remember the sorry parts of my Navy three years more vividly than I should, probably.

Navy life was full of exciting events, surely much more so than the army. A few memories at random (and only a few, because these stories tell little about why my life developed as it did, which is my main mission in this book).

I drew the assignment one day as shore patrol officer in the Dominican Republic. Shore patrol basically is police duty with respect to the ship's people ashore, plus any other Navy personnel. We were given a list of whorehouses that were off-limits, and we toured that hot, flat city of wide boulevards in a jeep—myself plus one or two petty officers. We'd go from joint to joint and halfheartedly roust out any of our men whom we would see. I can't say that my heart was in this work, and I was not anxious to find our people. We were told, of course, that all the houses were hotbeds of disease, and our men did acquire cases of gonorrhea fairly regularly, but they were cured reasonably easily with sulfa drugs (though I suppose with some risk of sterility), and I never heard of any syphilis; AIDS was, of course, not yet in our part of the world. Whatever else it was, shore patrol was an excellent way to see a city that the tour buses do not show you—all the neighborhoods and not just the tourist sites (of which I remember few in Santo Domingo, anyway.)

My last shore patrol assignment was the ship's coming-home party at a huge banquet hall in Boston. Tensions between men that had been kept bottled up aboard ship because of sanctions against fighting, and by the absence of liquor, were expected to come out at the party, and they did. But there were only a few one-on-one fisticuffs, and we avoided the major brawl that sometimes happens at such events, so we counted the occasion a shore patrol success.

While we were in Japan, I asked for and received three days of leave to go to Nikko, a famous mountain shrine site north of Tokyo, once upon a time the capital of Japan. I spent the day traveling by train, feasting on the wonderful snacks that I purchased through the train's window when the train was in a station; every snack seemed to be contained in a beautifully made wooden box that was then thrown away. I wondered at the economics of that packaging, but the esthetics of the package were very Japanese.

I enjoyed watching the Japanese travelers, many of whom I assumed were tourists, too. Every single male seemed to carry at least one fishing pole, and every family had at least one camera. Though Japan was still poor and still recovering from the war, the farms and towns were very well-ordered; this was surprising because World War II had only been over for about a decade.

Instead of a Western-type modern hotel, I lodged in a traditional Japanese hostel that was very lovely. I slept well.

In the morning I made a Pidgin English acquaintance with the lovely young chambermaid, Michiko. Then I spent the day seeing the sights of the hilly town whose sidewalks were being washed by the proprietors of the stores as I passed. I saw many of the shrines, with many handicapped war veterans in white clothes there serving to collect fees and donations. I also saw a very impressive huge Buddha.

When I returned for my second and last night in Nikko, I met Michiko again, and we became friendly. I took her out for a simple meal and a walk, and then—by implicit agreement—we returned to my room. After long preliminaries of sake, cigarettes, and talking as best we could, romance bloomed, and we soon got into bed.

Not long after we began to snuggle together, however, there was a great yelling in the hotel. Michiko was upset and made as if to leave the room to find out what had happened. I tried to persuade her to remain, but she insisted. After a brief time she returned and gestured to me to get dressed. "He die," she said to me. I indicated that that was undoubtedly very sad, but it was not of paramount importance to me; she was.

But Michiko said, "He Amelican." She got me dressed in a kimono and dragged me down from the second floor to a back room on the first floor where I saw candles on the floor, and within the large "U" framed by the candles was a recumbent male figure. A closer look showed crewcut hair and obvious signs that he had died in flagrante delicto. He had been with his regular Japanese girlfriend and expired from the ecstasy.

Michiko and the manager made it clear that, because I was an American, they expected me to do something about the tragedy. So I first specified that a policeman stand guard at the door, and one came. (Unfortunately that did not prevent the girlfriend and her parents from going into the room to arrange and cover the body properly.) I then began to try to contact the appropriate authorities.

I found from the dead man's papers that he was an army major, married with two children, who had been stationed at an R and R (rest and rehabilitation) facility for U.S. personnel in Nikko. The hotel manager got the Army manager on the phone, and I asked his assistance. He was not happy at being awakened late—it was about 12 P.M. by the time I finally reached him after much confusion and great difficulty with the long-distance telephone (the facility was outside of town). He told me that the major had already been transferred from his post in Nikko to an army camp elsewhere in Japan. He told me to contact them, and he went to bed.

Then came frustrating hours trying to reach the facility where he was going. All this time there was wailing and keening at the body, and I was desperate to get back together with Michiko. When I reached someone at the facility to which the major was en route, he told me that it was none of their business because he was not yet attached there; he had not reported in. When I asked for advice, he suggested calling the army special investigative department (SID).

Then more trouble reaching SID and finding someone who would take responsibility. To shorten the story, it was 6:30 A.M. before an officer arrived with an ambulance and took charge of the situation. Yes, you guessed it, it was too late for Michiko and me to get together. *Sayonara*.

My first published writing is almost (maybe the *only*) publication that I consider to be wrong, and that I am ashamed of. I went wrong because I relied on authorities and upon theory, rather than checking my speculation against reliable facts. It happened this way: I found it difficult to issue flat orders to enlisted men, especially those who were older than I, those who were experienced and knew what they were doing, and those who were surly about taking orders. I have never enjoyed telling other people what to do, as my experience as a Boy Scout showed. Instead of seeing this as a special characteristic of mine, I reflected back to my reading of David Riesman et al.'s *The Lonely Crowd* in college, a book that was then, and is still now, exceedingly fashionable both within and outside academia. I saw my own situation as a manifestation of the theory of Riesman et al. that there had been a transition in American personality from "inner directed" to "other directed." This would square with my being sensitive to the reactions of those being given the orders, hence making it more difficult for me to give orders.

So I wrote up my idea, sent it to The Naval Institute Proceedings and found myself having it accepted and published.

When the article appeared, there were congratulations. The editor wrote me that he had overheard General Maxwell Taylor, then head of the Joint Chiefs of Staff, talking about the article in the halls of the Pentagon. Very heady stuff for a young man of twenty-three.

Then I heard from the ship's Captain White—negatively. Why had I not submitted the article through the chain of command?

Taken aback, I responded that I assumed that there was no need to do so because the submission was within the Navy system, rather than outside. (In fact, the journal is nongovernmental, but leave that aside.) The captain did not push this further, perhaps because he was receiving congratulations about this achievement from one of the members of his crew.

There was much worse to come with the article itself. It is just plain wrong. Somewhat later I realized that what I had observed was one individual's experience, which I had simply projected on the world. There were no data to support Riesman's theory, and I had just bought their untested theory hook, line, and sinker.

Being on the subway in Tokyo was particularly strange because an American male of average height was then six inches taller than the next tallest person in the car. (The increase of about half a foot in height of the Japanese within a generation or so is an astonishing testament to the effect of nutrition.) Watching the official pushers pack people in so the car doors could close was a sight.

On the platform on one occasion, a group of Japanese students came over to practice their English. After a while, they began to harangue me about the racism toward blacks in the U.S. I agreed that the prejudice was terrible, but I asked them about their views of the Koreans in Japan. They said the Koreans were inferior. I asked what made them think the Koreans were inferior.

"They smell," the students said.

"That's what they say about Negroes in the United States," I said.

"But the Koreans really smell," they replied.

I have told that story many times as evidence that racism is everywhere. The only variation is in the identity of the group being discriminated against.

"Join the Navy and See the World" had been the Navy's recruiting pitch in the past and one that I urged the Navy to adopt again in a marketing scheme I published in *The Navy Times*. For me it was just that. Seeing the world was more than interesting and fun: the impressions and knowledge I gained in going literally around the world and on separate trips near and far have been very important to me in my professional life.

For example, my work on population economics has dealt with the relationship of both knowledge and population density to economic growth. The ship's visit to Hong Kong is the basis for the following observations I have made in several popular publications, including the second edition of *The Ultimate Resource*:

Check for yourself: Fly over Hong Kong—just a few decades ago a place seemingly without prospects because of insoluble resource problems—and you will marvel at the astounding collection of modern high-rise apartments and office buildings. Take a ride on its excellent, smooth-flowing highways for an hour or two, and you will realize that a very dense concentration of human beings does not prevent comfortable existence and exciting economic expansion—as long as the economic system gives individuals the freedom to exercise their talents and to take advantage of opportunities. The experience of Singapore demonstrates that Hong Kong is not unique.
Two such examples do not prove the case, of course. But these dramatic illustrations are backed by the evidence from the aggregate sample of countries, and hence do not mislead us.

Hong Kong is a special thrill for me because I first saw it in 1955, when I went ashore from a U.S. Navy destroyer. At the time, I felt great pity for the thousands who slept every night on the sidewalks or on small boats. It then seemed clear to me, as it must have to almost any observer, that it would be impossible for Hong Kong to surmount its problems—huge masses of impoverished people without jobs, total lack of exploitable natural resources, more refugees pouring across the border each day. And Singapore, which our ship also visited in 1955, was then more marked by the street peddlers of colored waters for every disease on earth and for the famous fantasia park, Tiger Balm Gardens (Tiger Balm being some sort of salve), than it was for the appurtenances of a well-developed commercial and financial center. Upon returning to Hong Kong in 1983, I saw bustling crowds of healthy, vital people full of hope and energy. No cause for pity then.

At sea one Saturday or Sunday in still air and perfectly calm water in (probably) the Persian Gulf, I sat on the ship's fantail to enjoy the feeling of a breeze caused by the ship's motion. I noticed that I did not enjoy nearly as much as did the other officers just sitting around in the wardroom hour after hour, over the omnipresent Navy coffee and cigarettes, just shooting the bull about the ship's affairs, the liberty we had visited most recently, and shotguns or fishing rods. Indeed, as I thought about it, the conversations I enjoyed were those concerning some common project in which I was engaged with the other person or some other business we had together. This theme recurs in the story of my life and may be important in understanding my relationship to others with whom I work or live. (In later life, I noticed that I most enjoy intimate conversations about the personal lives of the other person and myself; they are the most exciting intercourse between me and others, except for sex.)

Noticing my lack of enjoyment in this pursuit, that for most other people is a fundamental pleasure, was perhaps the first time in my life that I considered myself different than most other people in any way. It is significant that the point of difference was not that I had some special virtue—stronger, handsomer, more clever, the possessor of more artistic talent, or of better character than others—but simply a propensity to live my daily life in a particular way, or the lack of a propensity for a type of human contact.

I first came to understand deep in my mind the principle of variability in sampling and how the lack of understanding it leads to error from our tours abroad. When the men aboard ship exchanged observations about the European ports at which we called, after every port, there were some men who said it was the greatest place ever, whereas others said it was the worst. Nor was this simply the tendencies of some to criticize and others to praise, because the same man might have a very good experience in one port and then a very bad one in the next, or vice versa. The obvious explanation was that a person could have only a very limited amount of experience in a given port, and the luck of the draw might therefore influence whether the overall impression was positive or negative.

Once in a great while it is possible to teach the broad public an abstract idea with drama. The U.S. Navy has a perennial problem with the citizens of port cities who resent the negative aspects of the Navy presence and do not appreciate the positive aspects—especially the economic contribution, which is very hard to make convincing. When I was in the Navy, the services still paid enlisted personnel in cash every two weeks. The Navy would, from time to time in Norfolk, Virginia (and I assume elsewhere, too), pay only in two-dollar bills on a Friday. The diffusion of this money into the local economy was unmistakable to all.

Sometimes being an undesired person has advantages. And so it was with me and my assignment in the Navy. Two other newly commissioned NROTC officers came aboard ship at about the same time I did. The Bureau of Personnel (BuPers) specified that one would remain aboard for 18 months, one for (I think) 27 months, and one for 36 months. Captain White desired me the least of the three, and therefore I left the ship after a little more than the stipulated 18 months, which suited me just fine. I had probably learned most of what I would learn from shipboard experience. I hated the work schedule of always being sleep-deprived when at sea, and my having been fired from a job I loved and given a job that had no interest to me was still painful and embarrassing. My friendships were less close during the period aboard ship than in any other period of my life before or after. So I was happy to move on to my next assignment, attached to the Marines at Camp Lejeune, North Carolina.

12

Troopin' and Stompin' with the Girenes

After the *Samuel B. Roberts* (DD823), my next Navy billet was as a battalion Naval Gunfire Liaison Officer—NGLO—attached to the Marines at Camp Lejeune, North Carolina. As with all other billets not connected directly with ships and sea duty, this was a poor assignment for anyone who wanted to make a career in the Navy. But it was fine for me.

The job of an NGLO is to go ashore in a landing boat with the first waves of an amphibious force and send instructions by radio to the ships offshore about where to aim the cannon fire that the ships are shooting to support the troops, and then to determine how to correct the aim after the first shots land. This is very similar to the job of an army artillery spotting team with respect to cannons and mortars ashore.

My stint at troopin' and stompin'—that is, making like an infantryman—with the Girenes (shorthand slang for G.I., government issue, Marines)—began with two months of training at the Naval Justice School in Newport, Rhode Island. That was nice, because Newport is a pleasant place that I knew as the home port of the Roberts, and I appreciated the opportunity to gain some knowledge that I could take with me into civilian life. The purpose of my having been sent to Naval Justice School was that I would have the secondary job of serving as my battalion's legal officer.

Learning about the law—the Uniform Code of Military Justice—especially the procedure, was interesting, though we were taught the material in rather a cookbook fashion. After the school was completed, I reported to the Second Bat Eighth—that is, the Second Marine Battalion of the Eighth Marine Regiment—at Camp Lejeune.

Within the first two days at Lejeune, I got an emergency call that one of our men had been killed in a knife fight, and it was my task to "investigate." It turned out that my investigation was not for the purpose of finding out who killed John; that was already known, and the two men who did it were already in jail. Rather, my job was to determine whether John was officially "in the line of duty" when killed—that is, conducting himself lawfully, even though off-duty—so that his parents would receive the $10,000 payment the government was obligated to pay in such cases.

The murder took place at a "juke joint"—a rural tavern—in Burgaw County, North Carolina, 40 miles from Lejeune. The first task was to view the body in the morgue. It was a heartbreaking sight—a small but muscular, beautifully formed body with two huge rents in the chest, one all the way through to the chest cavity.

The Marine clerk in our battalion legal office and I took a jeep up to Burgaw County and found the sheriff. He then took us to the juke joint and explained what happened. The young Marine had a girlfriend in the tiny community, and he was with her in the juke joint when one of the local toughs picked a fight with him over the girl. The Marine went outside for what he thought would be a fist fight, but an accomplice grabbed and held him while the tough knifed him to death. The sheriff took us to witnesses who confirmed that story, but the sheriff had to interpret for us; the local dialect was so thick that we could not understand the speakers. For example, one of the killer's neighbors told us something that sounded like "He vey mane boy. He cut to tree head for dis." Translated it was "He is a very mean boy. He had cut [knifed] two or three other people before this."

The young Marine had indeed been in the line of duty, we ascertained, and the $10,000 was paid to his parents.

The poverty and backwardness of the area are hard to describe or imagine nowadays. The all-black school stopped at eighth grade and was only in session about five months a year. The houses were ramshackle in the extreme. To me they smelled sickeningly of pork grease, I suppose, and maybe collard greens. The two killers, who we met in jail but had little to say, could hardly write their names.

The trip to Burgaw County was a great education. I have not returned to see whether all is different now or not. It could be that the older folks are still living in much the same old ways.

Rita and I visited the Yucatán village of Chan Kom in 1992 and then again with Daniel in 1995. (Chan Kom had been studied by Robert Redfield in 1937.) The village still looked very much as it did in the pictures in Redfield's book. People slept in the same sort of hammocks and used the same primitive tortilla flour-making machines that they did in the 1930s. Farm animals—pigs, cows, and poultry—were still kept in backyard pens. Electrification was the main change we could see. The young people had either moved away or commuted to jobs in the nearby tourist city of Cancún. That's the pattern of economic development in much of the world; if you look just at the villages, you miss the central developments in the process of progress. It may be much the same in Burgaw County.

Within a few more days of my reporting to my battalion, the major, who was the battalion executive officer, called me in and asked, "Are you going with us tomorrow, Simon?"

"Going where, sir?" I asked.

"On our annual 26-mile hike," he said.

"I have no equipment yet, Major. I don't even have boots," I said, thinking fast.

"We can get you some down at Small Stores (or whatever the store is called in the Corps)," he said. So with sinking heart I hied myself down to the store. Glory of glories, the store was closed for inventory, so I reported back to the exec.

"They're closed for inventory," I told him. "Of course I would have been pleased to go otherwise," I imprudently added.

He picked up the phone, dialed, and said, "Sergeant, this is the exec. Lt. Simon is on his way down there. Please fix him up with whatever he needs for the hike tomorrow." He then turned to me and said, "We'll look forward to seeing you in the morning, Simon."

I saluted weakly and went back to my office.

I knew that I was in trouble. I was not in fit physical condition, having been aboard ship for more than 18 months. And worse, new boots can be intolerable until they are broken in. I had the sense to go to a physician to ask what to do about my feet. He said he had no idea, but referred me to the Chief Medical Corpsman. "Doc" was the right man. He gave me some tincture of benzoine and told me to paint it on all the places on my feet that might rub, to form a hard lacquer-like layer before starting. And he referred me to the Gunnery Sergeant.

"Gunny" gave me another tip: "After you put on your boots in the morning, stand in a bucket of water until the leather gets wet and swells. Then when it dries it will dry to the shape of your feet." Brilliant advice by both of these petty officers—knowledge that an MD did not have, of course, because one doesn't die of sore feet.

We took off early in the morning. I'll make a short story of the never-ending long day. By the halfway point, 11 miles, I was in big trouble. Much competitive joking back and forth about the toughness of the Navy and the Marines. By 17 miles, I was in agony and would have quit (as many others did, to be picked up by a truck), except that I felt like I was the representative of the entire Navy in front of this girene battalion, and I personally would be judged on this for a long time. Not much strength left for joking. By the time it was over, I couldn't have made another step. My thighs were so sore that I could hardly walk for days, longer even than my feet took to recover. But it was all worth it.

The annual week at the rifle range was fun. I "dry snapped" aiming the M–1 Garand rifle without bullets, then proceeded to shoot. I affected that I was not able to insert the clip of bullets myself—a complex movement in which the spring can hurt your thumb if you don't do it right. But I could shoot pretty well, perhaps because I had done a fair amount of shooting in Ben Merrick's basement range in high school. By the end of the week, I had qualified as Sharpshooter, the second rank.

I also went to the pistol range, and I fired the huge .45 caliber pistol. I was pleased to qualify as Marksman, the top rank, and the second highest score in the battalion. It didn't take too much skill to do well because the .45 is so big and heavy and clumsy that one is lucky to hit the target at all.

I also noticed that many of the veteran sergeants shot the pistol very poorly. They anticipated the heavy kick and jerked the pistol before the trigger was pulled, which ruined the shot. Furthermore, it seemed that their shooting did not improve with more years' practice, and maybe got worse.

My second piece of scientific work emerged from that experience. I describe it in the following letter to Professor Verplanck.

H and S Company
First Battalion, Eighth Marines
Second Division
Camp Lejeune, North Carolina

11 October 1955

Dr. W. S. Verplanck
Department of Psychology
Harvard University
Cambridge, Massachusetts
Dear Dr. Verplanck:

Despite the tutelage of the noted applied experimental psychologist of New London, W. S. Verplanck, the Navy has seen fit to utilize my services as a line officer, and has now attached me to the Marines.

Nevertheless, I am now engaged in some experimentation which might prove interesting from the standpoint of both the Marine Corps and psychology. A little long range advice from you, who have probably fooled with something similar, might help avoid some snags and pitfalls.

Here's the skinny—despite inflated propaganda claims, Marine Corps marksmanship is not overly good, and the pistol shooting is abominable, as I discovered when I went out to the range several weeks ago. Many veteran officers and staff NCO's, as well as less experienced men who carry the .45, did very poorly. Many could not hit the big 1 1/2 by 1 1/2' (approximate) target five out of ten shots at 25 yards.

I got to think [*sic*] about this failure. The most important cause seems to be jerking the trigger rather than squeezing it, anticipating the kick of the explosion. All who fire know how necessary it is to "hold `em in and squeeze," but they never develop the habit.

It occurred to me that with a simple training device and a small amount of practice we might build a habit pattern of squeezing, as well as instill confidence in the men that they can really shoot straight, a confidence they do not now have. They have done poorly for so many years they believe the weapon is beyond their abilities to control.

Here is a brief description of the simple gadget: It starts at the bottom with a solid tripod support. Above this, at adjustable height, rides a metal sheet with holes bored in it, and a strip of miniature targets placed above the holes. The targets are 1/25 the size of the range targets, since the eye will be one yard from the miniatures.

A service .45 is fitted with a narrow aluminum rod projecting from the bore about five inches. When the sights are dead on the target the rod is exactly in the order of the hole.

The rod will make a complete electrical circuit when it touches the side of the hole, ringing a bell in series. Simply, the idea is that the shooter can practice squeezing and firing an empty pistol with instant knowledge when he pulls off the line of aim.

An auxiliary gadget similar to a doctor's office height-measurer on a swivel will be used to obtain proper target height for the individual subject. He will take his stance, the experimenter will swing the bar to his eye level, and then fix the target at the same level.

The accompanying sketch may make all this clearer.

Here at Lejeune I work with an infantry battalion and my superiors saw possible merit and utility in the scheme, but since I had neither shop facilities nor the necessary authority to experiment on a large scale I lugged the idea over to the Naval Medical Field Research Laboratory on the Base and discussed it with the psychologist—a clinician who is only somewhat interested and somewhat grounded in experimental problems—but who was glad to help implement and test the gadget under Naval Medical Field Research Laboratory's aegis. The shop engineer was likewise helpful.

But partly because I am more familiar with Marine Corps organization and the pistol problem, as well as the sort of experimental testing the gadget needs to verify its worth, I cannot dump the problem in the Naval Medical Field Research Laboratory's lap and call it a job.

This is roughly the experimental setup I had in mind: Presently, Marines who fire a pistol shoot a .22 pistol twenty shots a day five days in the week, preceding the trip to the range. This firing takes approximately half an hour of a man's time per day. (I should point out now that training time is not as much of an obstacle here as in the Navy). They fire for qualification after three more days of practice on the .45 range during the following week. A battalion goes to the range one week per year, and depending on the function of the outfit, 10% to 100% fire the pistol. One fourth of the pistol shooters who did not shoot expert or sharpshooter the past year in a battalion, picked alphabetically, would follow the above regimen, and constitute one control group.

A second control group, selected similarly, would be given instruction and would "snap-in" with empty .45's at field targets a half hour per day for one week instead of shooting .22's.

A third group would spend half an hour per day at the training device for five days preceding the qualification week, sticking the rod on the gun through a single hole, the same hole each day. They would get instruction and would have the scores recorded of the number of times they succeed in squeezing off the shot (just an empty hammer of course) without hitting the side of the hole and ringing the bell. The hole would be large enough so that the gun could be pointed as far out on the target as the 7-ring. If a man shoots seven or better each time he will fire better than a sharpshooter on the range. A hole this large will also allow for normal sway of the pistol arm but not for bucking or jerking which cause a man to miss the target completely.

The fourth group would hold the rod in a hole relatively as large as the five ring the first day, six ring the second, seven ring the third, eight ring the fourth, and nine ring (bulls eye) the fifth. Their bell-rings would also be scored by the instructor as experiments.

Validation would be accomplished by comparing scores on qualification day at the range the following week.

As I see it, the questions this experiment must answer are two: First, will practice on the training device, in the amount and manner we give it, improve scores on the training device? Second, will this improvement, if it occurs, transfer to the range firing and boost scores there?

The problems: To simulate present time intervals spent on the .22 range we will not be able to distribute the practice as much as I would guess would be advisable in learning a motor skill of this type. On the device we cannot simulate the effects of the cartridge explosion, anticipation and apprehension of which may cause all the trouble. It may not actually be humanly possible to avoid this fear, although I strongly think it can easily be trained out of the subjects. The pistol weight and balance will be slightly different—though only very slightly—from a service pistol. The shooter must assume his original position in an uncommon way; he must shove his pistol forward to reach its firing position rather than lowering a bent elbow.

Naturally, there are bugs in the machine and in the experimental design that we will work out as we run pilot studies. But can you give me: (1) A few selected references on allied motor skill training. There are few journals here, but the Naval Medical Field Research Laboratory can get microfilm copies of almost anything. (2) Any comments or observations of your own derived from similar work. Any help we can get here will be greatly appreciated, because there is no one here who is sophisticated psychologically or experimentally (including the clinician and me). I hope all goes well with you and the laboratory, and that the book is growing.

Sincerely,
J. L. SIMON
LTJG USN

JLS:ds

Just as with my senior thesis work, I never found a place to publish that work—not recreational shooting journals, or outdoors magazines, or anyplace. How about it, editors? You can have it cheap. (Indeed, I'll pay you to publish it, another theme that has often arisen in my professional life.)

My research life has followed a trajectory almost exactly the opposite of Einstein's. At age sixteen, he started thinking about the nature of light, imagining what he would see if he were atop a light beam, and he continued thinking about this question until his great discovery of special relativity. At a slightly older age than he was doing such grand theory, I was doing empirical research on human feet and shoes, trying to understand the causes of chafing and blisters. Of course, my senior research thesis was on a large topic, concept formation. And I grappled with the philosophical problem of causality in my thirties, though it was only much later that I devoted a large part of my time to the philosophical-practical issues of statistical inference. The fact that I would address such earthy noncosmic utilitarian questions is informative, I believe. It is certainly a reflection of the promiscuous curiosity that my mother warned me about and that I swore off in a Cambridge bookstore when we were in Boston Navy Yard; as I looked at books in one section after another, I mentally put big X's across all the sections except medicine (a career I was then considering), psychology, and literature. I was happy to work on issues that aroused my curiosity and that seemed as if the answers might be immediately useful to some individuals. This propensity to work on "targets of opportunity" as they were called in gunnery, continued into my research life later. If there had been important alternatives that would have forced me to decide between the earthy topics and cosmic work, the situation would have been different. Time and energy seldom seemed like difficult constraints to overcome, because I would work on a wide variety of studies in my "spare" time.

Even the largest and most abstract issues I worked on, such as resampling statistics and causality, arose for me almost by accident, rather than by choice, as we shall see later. Perhaps if I had hooked up with a great researcher early on, I might have addressed a menu of great questions in a "rational" manner. I doubt that even an accidental meeting could have hooked me up with such a major figure as an advisor.

This was not all bad; if I had followed a well-focused plan I would not have allowed myself to drift into some of the most important work I've done. Nor is it necessarily bad to start with the simple, earthy questions. One is not likely to make huge time-wasting and career-deforming blunders that way, and one learns one's craft well in such manner.

This general theme will recur again and again throughout the book.

Work as Battalion Legal Officer was often interesting. An example was a young private who had stayed 31 days over leave because his wife was unhappy. The exec asked for a recommendation for what should be done about him. Nowadays, he might simply be discharged administratively, I judge from the newspapers. If memory serves, in those days the only options (because he was absent for more than 30 days) were (1) a bad conduct discharge (very bad for future employment to have on one's record) and (2) a general court martial (the most serious kind) that would surely send him to the brig for a long time. Either way, it was a heavy punishment for a scared, confused young kid.

I strongly recommended against the general court-martial and suggested that we invoke higher-up legal help to see if there was some loophole to get the kid out of the service on better terms.

Such cases could break one's heart. Society is more flexible and compassionate nowadays in these situations, which I consider all to the good. Whether a general trend toward lesser punishments exists in the service, I do not know, and I do not know whether that would be a good thing across the board; we may go too far in letting people get away with just a rap on the knuckles for offenses that deserve serious punishment, and there may be too much opportunity for fancy lawyering and appeals. The genius of the common-law system (which I admire and thrill to, down deep in my bones, as one of the great evolved inventions of humankind, and in particular, the English) is its determination of each case separately, on its own merits rather than on the basis of generalities; a flexible law system in the service aids in that.

I enjoyed friends at Lejeune. Ted Brown was a lawyer from Detroit who intended to be governor of that state. Jim Jones was a Ph.D. psychologist with whom I talked of many things and who continued the pistol work after I left Lejeune. Very regrettably, I lost track of both of them, but maybe somehow they will hear of being mentioned in this book and will get in touch with me. (One of the best parts of having your name in the newspapers is that old friends call or write.)

Despite the popular macho impression of Marines, the single officers in my BOQ (Bachelor Officers' Quarters) seemed to me to be pussycats rather than tigers in their off hours. After work, it was a few drinks at the Officers' Club and early to bed. Weekends it was two or three movies at the several theatres on the base, plus washing the car once or even twice. I didn't even see much athletics. To stay in shape and to tire myself out, I'd put on heavy boots and go out and run many miles on the asphalt base roads. Nowadays, when every step I jog is a hassle due to age and asthma and when three or four miles is a big deal, I remember the effortlessness with which I ran then, and my annoyance that it took such a long time to get a decent workout and be tired.

Unlike shipboard life in a navy, life in a peacetime army is as humdrum an existence as any I know of, especially for a bachelor officer in an isolated base. Unlike working in business, there is very little work pressure. The after-work drinks stretched seamlessly into dinner at the same table—a steak of some variety or roast beef—and then after coffee and perhaps another drink, back to the BOQ. With increasing frequency, I excused myself from drinks to go to my quarters to read my book on developmental biology to prepare for medical school. The other young officers found this hard to understand. "There's plenty of time to do that when you get to med school," they said. This was a second time in my life when I considered that I might be different from most other people. I seemed more impelled to acquire knowledge, though in this case not for the sheer pleasure of it—I took very little pleasure in the biology—but because I was ambitious to use my time productively and to increase my knowledge—my human capital, as economists have come to say.

The concept that "Ontogeny recapitulates phylogeny"—that is, the fetus passes through stages akin to a hierarchy of species from simple to complex—caught my interest. But I never learned an explanation for this fact. Writing this now provokes me to seek an explanation.

Charley Bove, another naval officer, and I took off for weekends a few times to Virginia Beach, Myrtle Beach, and the like. Aside from that, Lejeune was dull as dishwater; the only women were a few nurses I'd meet in the mess hall at breakfast or lunch. So when I heard that a cruise to Europe was scheduled for the First Bat Eighth, I looked around for a married officer who might want to swap with me so as to stay home with his wife (few had kids yet).

I found a swap, and we tentatively made proper arrangements. But there was a problem: If I were to leave the service after three years, the time would be up before the cruise was over. If I were to stay in the Navy (as NROTC officers were invited to do), there would be no issue. I therefore was asked if I intended to stay in or get out. I replied that I had not made up my mind yet. Though I suppose there was still some tiny uncertainty in my mind, in truth I had pretty much decided to get out. It was a safe lie because no one could check on the contents of my mind, and I doubt that I had ever written to anyone that I had decided. I was not proud of this afterwards. But it was a hell of a good cruise.

I got a kick out of "troopin' and stompin'" with the girenes. It was fun to dress in camouflage-colored fatigues, make an amphibious landing, and then go off for maneuvers into the boondocks ("boondocks" is Philippine Tagalog for mountains, but in the Navy it means the woods or rural areas) for maneuvers. In the summer in the swamps of Lejeune, the mosquitoes and the rubber air mattresses were devilishly uncomfortable at night, but that was part of the game (and it *was* all a game in peacetime, and hence I could never take it seriously, unlike shipboard work). In Sardinia (I think that was where we practiced when we were in the Mediterranean), nasty loose rocks and sprained ankles from climbing the hillsides were the problems, as I remember.

During war games (a phrase that bothered me even then) while I was in charge of my Naval Gunfire Liaison group, I informally learned all of Marine doctrine that the second lieutenant platoon commanders said was necessary at any level from platoon to regiment: "Two up, one back (two units on the line, one in reserve); take the high ground; and give the troops a hot meal." With those principles in mind, they said, one is prepared to command the entire Corps.

During amphibious landings, my group and I went ashore in the second wave of boats—which was bound to be a superdangerous place to be in any real war situation. I didn't relish the thought, but war was not on the horizon, so I did not worry.

The Mediterranean cruise was sheer heaven. Unlike ship's company (and unlike my previous time aboard the *Roberts*) I did not stand watches, and I had no duties in connection with the operation of the ship. That meant that I could sleep whenever I liked, read, work on my correspondence course in calculus (that I kept flunking), shoot the breeze in the wardroom, and get ready to go on liberty (or recover from the liberty we had just been on). None of that struggle of coming back late at night or early in the morning from the "beach" (the port city), getting only a couple of hours sleep, then having to struggle through a watch, having a cigarette that made it twice as difficult to keep my eyes open and causing me to swear I'd not make that mistake again when the same situation recurred, somehow manage to finish the watch, maybe a little sleep, go back to work, and on and on. Being a passenger instead was delicious.

When floating around the Med, the Marine officers (and I) received briefings on the armies of the various countries. About the Israeli army it was said—and this was early 1956, mind you, before Israel had ever fought a full-scale war other than its raggedy War of Independence in 1948—that the Israelis had a policy that no one would be left behind on the battlefield, alive or dead. The briefing officer said this with evident admiration, because it was like the boasts of the Marines, and it therefore impressed me; he, as most Marine officers, had had battle experience in the Korean War then only recently ended. His comment turned out to be sound military intelligence.

The fleet spent some time off the coast of Lebanon in the midst of a period of heightened tension, but our preparations happily were unnecessary.

There was plenty of time to play poker aboard ship, not just nickel ante but also at least one big game involving serious money; one could win or lose $500 or a month's pay in an evening. Of course I played, and I won money, but one did not flaunt winning unless onewere a great fool and cared much more about ego than money. As always, difficult situations arose.

One night, we were playing regular five-card draw poker. I had a fairly high three-of-a-kind, and the only player opposing me was F, the ship's doctor who was not a very good player and given to bluffing (though I usually tried to pay no attention to such psychological aspects of the game). On the last round, he bet $80 (a pretty fair sum at 1956 prices). Should I call or fold? I pondered and pondered. Then from T—a Marine aviator (a "flyboy") who had dropped from the game because he had lost a bunch of money and who was then sitting behind F and watching the game—came what could have well been a hand sign, maybe two fingers flashed twice. Was that what it meant? And if so, was it a truthful sign? Now what to do? It immediately flashed through my head that T owed me $100 on a poker IOU. I pondered more. I decided that I had to act as if I had seen no sign. And I decided that I would have called the bet with no sign. So I called. The doctor had two pairs. So I won.

I shared an office with the chaplain, a Catholic priest I liked a lot and with whom I talked intimately about some of our common cases—the kids who consulted me as battalion legal officer and consulted him as chaplain or priest. "Padre, I'd like to talk to you about a problem," I said.

"Who is it about?" he asked.

"About me." He looked a bit surprised.

"What's the story?"

I told him the story, partly because I was in a quandary about what to do and partly because I wanted to get on record about this event lest it jump up and bite me later. After we talked about it, we jointly decided that I would continue as if nothing had happened and wait to see if the flyboy said anything to me and whether he paid me what he owed. After all, I had no proof of anything, and I could not be at all sure of what had transpired. So I could not say anything to T or to Doctor F.

Then I asked the priest his thoughts about the game itself and whether it was getting out of hand.

"If I was a Protestant, I'd have the game shut down because I'd believe gambling is evil and also against shipboard regulations," he said. "But as a Catholic, the question is not so cut-and-dried. I ask whether the situation really is bad for the ship and the men. If it's harmless nickels and dimes, unlike the Protestants I have no reason to condemn it. But this game may be a different matter."

We agreed to talk more about the game later. Then came informal news on the grapevine about last night's enlisted men's big poker game. They played in a compartment deep in the ship, and they dogged down (tightened) the eight "dogs" (handle closers) on the door so that if an officer would approach, there would be plenty of time to get the money off the table before the officer could undog the hatch, get in, and maybe break up the game.

The compartment contained a portable fire extinguisher, and someone triggered it inadvertently. The foam (I assume that is what was emitted) began to fill the compartment dangerously. But the dogs were so tight that the men were almost unable to open the door; if so, they would all have died. At the last second, they succeeded in opening the hatch and escaping.

This news reinforced the outcome of my game. Together the chaplain and I agreed that the games had to stop. Luckily there was reason to stop both at the same time, so the enlisted men would have no grievance. The chaplain went to the ship's executive officer and told him the story. The word went out that the games had to stop. I was sorry to lose the entertainment, the poker practice, and the money, but it had to be. I spent the time studying my biology text on the development of the human embryo, a subject I expected to learn in medical school.

After I left the ship I sent the doctor a check for $80 with a noncommittal note such as "I think I owe you this."

I continued to wrestle with the problem of what to do for a living when I got out. The most important occupational knowledge I gained in my years in the service was that I would not thrive and be fulfilled as an employee of a large bureaucratic institution. I knew that it would cramp and throttle my natural inclinations. I considered that I had no special talents but was reasonably good at many things. I considered my parents' economic needs. I thought in passing about getting a merchant marine officer's license so that I could make a living and yet have plenty of time to write fiction, which I had continued to do while in the Navy. But medical school seemed the best bet. It would guarantee me a good living. It was a respected profession (yes, I thought of that). It would be socially useful. When I asked myself if I "enjoyed helping people," to answer that standard question on medical school applications, I remembered being the officer of the deck in port and enjoying solving minor problems of various sorts to ease people's assorted difficulties, so I figured this was not too far from medicine.

13

Working in the Advertising Business

After I got out of the Navy, I spent the summer in Cambridge taking a course in organic chemistry to complete my qualifications for entering medical school in the fall. Most of the other 200 students also were premeds, many of them from Harvard, taking the course during the summer so that they would not have to do so during the school year.

There were two hours of classes and six hours of laboratory work every day—forty hours a week, plus lots of homework. I remember nothing of the course content, except something about carbon molecules being a ring of carbon atoms and the story of Friedrich August Kekule, the father of organic chemistry. One night in a dream he saw a snake with its tail in its mouth. This gave him the idea that the structure of benzene is six atoms of carbon arranged in a ring, which turned out to be what the *Encyclopedia Britannica* calls the "most brilliant piece of prediction [ever made in] organic chemistry."

The most interesting thing I learned was a by-product of the course. The instructor put tough competitive pressure on the students to produce large yields in their lab experiments, which were then weighed. The tension in the laboratory rose so palpably that it became obvious that students would eventually begin to cheat. I passed on that observation to a lab assistant, but nothing was changed, and the pressure continued. Two-thirds through the course, the cheating began, and then the system broke down completely. The wholesale cheating was not due mainly to the characters of the students, but rather to the structure of the system. This was an important lesson to me: Focus on the structure of the social system, and its incentives.

Indeed, sometimes the only difference is whether the society calls an activity legal and ethical or illegal and despicable. In the United States, a supermarket manager wins profit and praise for stocking delicacies and supplying them to customers who desire them and are willing to pay a handsome price. In the old Soviet Union the outcome was different, as this incident shows: In the mid–1980s, the director of Moscow's Gastronom No. 1—a grocery store that sells gourmet foods to the elite—was put to death for selling delicacies like black caviar and wild boar out the back door. In the U. S., he could use the front door and he would get a bonus for his initiative.

All through the summer I wrestled with the decision about whether to go to medical school. More and more I felt that I would be ending some important freedom in my life if I went. I had an image of passing through an arched gate to medical school and medicine and my brain becoming ossified and turning to stone. Perhaps it was what I imagined what courses such as anatomy, with all its memorization, would be like. Perhaps it was my impression of an endless line of patients waiting for me to diagnose increasingly repetitive diseases. I worried whether the burden of reading to stay on top of an ever-growing profession would demand an unacceptable amount of free time.

There was still another difficulty: I had an intuitively based belief that people should not take medical drugs except when the need to do so is clear-cut and strong. I feared that that view would cause me to be badly-adjusted to the medical profession, which at that time dispensed drugs quite freely, as if drugs have only direct effects on a given disease and no side effects except those already known—and especially, assuming that there are no indirect or delayed side effects in the far future.

In the same vein, it has always seemed to me foolish and dangerous hubris for biologists and chemists to believe that they have been able to isolate everything important in food in the form of a few elements: specific vitamins, minerals, and such. Even now when I read on the V–8 tomato juice can, "drink your vegetables," it seems to me that the advertisement is likely to be wrong, and there must be some things in the fresh tomato and other fresh vegetables that have been left out of the V–8 juice—roughage, if nothing else.

One basis of my view about medical drugs was experiments showing that rats and babies choose their diets wisely from a cafeteria of possibilities. Another element was Walter Cannon's notion of "the wisdom of the body." I had always been very impressed with his book of that name, and it seemed ridiculous to me that physicians could know the full effects of the chemicals they put into human bodies as therapy. To corroborate this, my maternal grandmother's face was faintly blue when I knew her. I had heard that this was due to a physician prescribing the drug Argyrol to her on a steady basis many decades earlier; only later had it emerged that Argyrol had delayed negative effects, of which her facial discoloration was one symptom. So I had somehow come to the belief that tampering with a complex system that we still understand so little was inherently dangerous. (It surprises me that I had somehow grasped from this happening the general idea of possible lagged effects when I was perhaps nine or twelve years old; this now seems to me a very sophisticated idea, as I see the most sensible of adults take antidepressant and other psychiatric drugs on a semipermanent basis without concern about possible delayed effects.)

Medical practice nowadays is closer to this view. And the ecologists' conception of nature is similar to this conception of the human body, if I understand the ecologists correctly. They believe that we ought not to make changes in the existing natural order, unless there is pressing reason to do so and unless our knowledge of the likely consequences is extensive, because so many undesirable effects may be indirectly caused by a particular alteration.

Is this an argument against any intervention in human as well as nonhuman matters? This charge has been brought against such writers as Hume, Smith, and Hayek. I do not think that it is accurate, however. This view does imply that we should study the existing state of affairs very closely before changing it, to check for complex relationships that have heretofore escaped our notice. That is, we should find out why the fence was put up before we take it down, in Robert Frost's words. But knowledge need not be perfect, and never can be. When we are satisfied that we understand the system as best we can, then we should proceed to make changes. This point of view differs from a more interventionist point of view only in emphasis, not in logic. I do not, however, share a more extreme noninterventionist, antigrowth point of view with those ecologists who are so convinced that any alteration might knock our whole system out of whack, which would then induce a series of changes to compensate, which would then have even worse effects, and so on, until the whole system comes apart or explodes; this was the viewpoint that underlies the famous book *Silent Spring* by Rachel Carson (1962, esp. pp. 16, 17, 18, 22). Interestingly, many persons who espouse the latter view with respect to natural systems are very ready to intervene in human systems.

Between the summer of 1956, when I finally wrote to Tufts Medical School asking for a one-year leave of absence, until I was almost sixty-two years old, I never regretted not going to medical school. Then it occurred to me that I might have found my way to epidemiology had I gone to medical school, which probably would have been the best of all vocations for me. Not only am I particularly well-suited by inclination and mental capacity for the work in epidemiology, but work in that field also would have enabled me to write to a wider public. I might even have learned some economics along the way.

As an epidemiologist, there would have been relatively little problem getting the results of my work published, even if the work would have been done the simplest possible way, without flourish, as I like to work.

By the time I had finished the summer course in organic chemistry, I decided at least to postpone going to medical school; the atrocious learning experience of the summer—even though I had achieved the mandatory grade of B—may have tipped the balance. I wrote to Tufts Medical School and obtained a one-year leave of absence.

Then I had to ponder what to do next. For a time, I lived with my parents in Millburn, which enabled me to commute to New York.

Going into business was the obvious option; indeed, no other possibility even came to mind. The short-run sequence of events is unclear to me—whether I first did other jobs and then thought about the advertising business or vice versa. In any case, within a month I decided to look for a job in the advertising business—simply because Mort was working in an advertising agency in New York, and hence that industry was slightly familiar to me at second hand (on such thin wisps of knowledge are founded so many of our decisions), and because I could imagine myself being a copywriter.

I went to an employment agency and obtained some leads to a variety of occupations. My first job was as a technical writer for a New York firm that supplied manuals to accompany mechanical devices sold to the military services. After a week of that, I quit; it was very dull, and I could see absolutely no future in it.

The next Monday, I went to work for Prudential Insurance Company, whose buildings were famous landmarks in Newark and whose solidity has been their trademark there and logo was "The Rock of Gibraltar," which later became "A Piece of the Rock." I was hired to be a cost accountant. I was immediately given a phone, a list of phone numbers, pen and paper, and perhaps a typewriter, and assigned to check various expenditures with various persons and departments. The identical sort of work was done by a battery of perhaps 20 people to the left and right of me. Every morning at 10:17 A.M (here my memory is exact), a bell rang above our area and all 20 of us rose and walked out for our coffee break. At 10:32 A.M., we all returned—leaving the coffee cups behind so there was no chance of spillage at our workplaces. In the afternoon, there was another such break, the exact time of which I have mercifully forgotten. Regimented practices like this happily have disappeared from American business.

By Thursday, I was already fed up with being a cost accountant for Prudential, and I handed in my resignation. The vice president who had hired me—also a Harvard graduate, he had rushed to tell me—called me in. He exhibited shock at my hasty decision and told me what a bright future there was for me with Prudential. I said, "Thank you very much, but . . . " I was quickly gone from there, carrying only the memories of the coffee breaks and of the football-field-size room taking up an entire upstairs floor with dozens of huge punched-card calculating machines and millions of punched cards filed in neat racks. The room's silence was broken only by operators scurrying back and forth from one machine to another, fanning cards to cut static electricity before inserting them in the machines and programming control boards with innumerable varied lengths of wires with plugs on each end. Nowadays one personal computer probably can do all the operations and store all the information that was contained in that huge room.

The next job was selling the *Encyclopedia Britannica*. During this time, I prepared a sales letter that I sent out to about a hundred advertising agencies and media organizations. The text of the letter was as follows:

20 South Mountain Road
Millburn, New Jersey

Dear Sir:

Johnson O'Connor's Human Engineering Laboratory has found a common thread among most top-drawer marketing men; they score high in tests of inductive reasoning and contact personality, so-so in accounting aptitude, low in three dimensional visualization, and through the roof of the scale in creative imagination. Chances are that the best—and happiest—people in your sales promotion, advertising, and allied departments fill this psychological bill. So do I.

Of course, potential alone never earned a red cent. You demand drive and proven ability before you could hire a young man like me even as a trainee. Out of hand you will have to believe that I'm hell-bent on a successful career in marketing. But you won't have to take it on faith that I can produce fine copy and scads of fresh ideas for you, or that I am at home with research methods and statistics.

I'd like to show you an article I sold to the *Navy Times* that outlined a revolutionary (for the Navy) promotion campaign for re-enlistment, based on my evaluation of the market. A month later the paper printed a request that readers send no more letters pro or con.

The changes I made in WHRB's plug-writing boosted our sales of time 30% in a year. The audience research I directed graphed a big rise in sponsor identification, laughter, and spending.

Kid-stuff businesses like peddling bean poles and painting curbstone house-numbers started earning my fare to college when I was still in knickers. I'm glad I have this instinct, because a marketing man without it is like a high-wire artist with a faulty sense of balance.

In the accompanying resume you'll note my strong background in the physical and medical sciences. With it comes confidence to handle the plethora of new and improved products introduced to the public every day.

I should appreciate an opportunity to tell you more about myself, and how I can help your organization. You may reach me by phone at South Orange 2–6495, or by dropping the enclosed post card into the mail.

Sincerely,
Julian L. Simon

Most readers will despise the style in which that personal sales letter is written. It embarrasses me a bit, as do some of the things I say about myself. But the formula with which the letter is written is a good one: (1) Get the reader's attention; (2) Promise the reader he or she will be better off if he or she buys your product and explain exactly how he or she will benefit; (3) Provide evidence to make your claims believable; and (4) Make it easy for the reader to order the product. The advertising style has the immense advantage that it has (or should have) one objective only: To make a sale. No artistic or other values should matter. No other kind of writing is so single-minded, and writing an autobiography is quite the opposite: it has the most diffuse aims of any kind of writing. My style shifts in this book as I shift from one aim to another.

Back when I was still in the Navy and on watch aboard ship, about 5 A.M. one morning, while we were cruising around the world, I got to thinking about how we went from port to port and it was always a problem when shopping to do currency conversions in your head without making drastic errors. When looking at some of the slide-rule-type equipment either on the bridge or in CIC (Combat Intelligence Center)—it awes me to think that the age of computers has made slide rules so obsolete that even engineers don't even know what they are nowadays—it occurred to me that one could make a circular slide rule and mark it in such fashion that it would be easy to make automatic currency conversions. After getting out of the Navy and living in New York, I decided to try to sell the idea as an advertising promotion. It occurred to me that a currency trading firm such as Deak and Company (now Deak-Pereira) could use it as a cheap and useful giveaway. So I decided to try to sell the idea to Deak.

I was convinced that I would not be good at selling the idea myself, partly because I did not know how to sell (I had forgotten my experience selling advertising for WHRB at Harvard) and partly because I have always believed (rightly) that I am not persuasive in person. So I enlisted my childhood friend Don Benjamin as a partner; Donald was then a successful salesman of printing. We got a prototype made, and we went together to meet the head of Deak.

Donald made a terrific pitch. Mr. Deak (I believe it was he) was rather positive to the idea. But ultimately he decided against it.

Thinking that I could get some useful advice, I went to New York University and found a professor of marketing and offered to pay him a consulting fee. After one consulting session, I realized that he knew even less about practical marketing than I did, and this assessment of typical marketing professors did not change much when I later became one and got to know many other professors. He did, however, get interested enough in the device so that he bought the rights from us for perhaps $1000 and went out to market it himself—ultimately without success, I think. A funny twist to the story.

After a month of selling *Britannica*—which I was about to quit, anyway, because I could not stomach it any more—I found a job as an advertising copywriter. I would not take the usual entry-level advertising-agency job in the mail room, from which one was supposed to act the bright young man and charm one's way into some more elevated position. So I went to work for an "ethical" (i.e. prescription) drug agency, William Douglas McAdams, then owned in part or wholly by

Arthur Sackler, much later famous as the donor of the Sackler Library and collections at the Smithsonian in Washington. I got $80 a week and went to work in a group headed by Gil Totten.

Gil taught me that when you are stumped about what to write, you should ask yourself: What am I trying to say? I have broadened this lesson into many other aspects of my work life. When I am stumped in the preliminary phases of a research project, I ask: What am I trying to find out? And when I am exploring a new technique in statistical inference, or a practical problem in inference, I ask: What is the question we seek to answer? And I pass this lesson on to students both in class and when working with them individually.

It is curious that though I have no memories of learning anything specific in high school and little more than two phrases from college—Gordon Allport's "The same fire that hardens the egg melts the butter," and Anna Freud's "When the child misbehaves, smack him and then tell him you love him"—and though I have no memories of any other person teaching me a lesson one-on-one in school or sports, I have a sharp memory of this lesson that Gil taught me.

Another lesson Gil taught me was that, relative to our competitors, "When they whisper, we scream; when they scream, we whisper." This was taught in connection with a full-page ad with nothing but white space plus a small box in the middle with type giving our central message in a sentence or two.

Another scream-whisper lesson I took from advertising: One of the great pioneers of mail order, where testing the results of ads is everything, wrote: Test for differences that scream, not differences that whisper. I have repeated this lesson many times when discussing research with people; look for research situations and variables where the effects don't just whisper and require fancy statistical treatment to determine if they exist at all, but rather scream so loud that even a simple table of results is enough to prove their existence and importance.

At McAdams, I urged that we do some simple market research on a couple of our products. Even though I had no experience myself, I was astonished to find that no research was being done at the agency. I suggested a few lines of approach. I guess the social science researcher was just born in me.

This was the era of one and maybe two (for others, even more) martinis for lunch. It would take an hour and a half afterwards to overcome the lassitude induced by the booze and lunch. The drinking was supposedly because of the heavy stress of the business. But I never felt any stress at all, let alone heavy stress.

I shared an office with Alan Levenstein, later an author of at least one Broadway musical comedy. The art director in our group, from whom I also learned a lot, was Joe Phelan.

Many of the martini-at-lunch crowd had the attitude that doing advertising was a personal sell-out. This was heard especially from the would-be novelists who made a living writing copy and the would-be painters who worked in the art department. I never bought into this self-hate about advertising. And I respected Joe Phelan's very businesslike approach to advertising design; he accepted that his job was to help copy sell goods, and he never thought of himself as too good for that; he did his own drawings at home on his own time, as I remember. And Joe never tried to sneak artiness into the ads as some of the art-director types did. I learned a lot about advertising artwork from Joe, as I did about copy from Gil.

Around this time, there appeared several books with themes like that of *The Hidden Persuaders* by Vance Packard that warned of the enormous power of "Madison Avenue" to propagandize and influence people's buying and their ways of life. Academics such as Harvard economist John Kenneth Galbraith frequently wrote about the power of advertising over people as if it can have the powers of a Svengali. Clearly, these people had never attempted to actually convince people to buy a commercial product with advertising; if they had, they would have known how difficult it is to do so.

Prescription drug advertisements also do not have Svengali power over doctors. This does not imply that the sanction of law is unnecessary to keep advertisements honest. At the turn of the century, snake oil could literally be sold as a cure for cancer. In the 1950s, we relied on the flimsiest of medical studies to make strong unwarranted claims. We knew that the seven cases in an uncontrolled experiment published by a country doctor in a Mississippi medical journal were paid for by a drug company and were almost worthless evidence. If a drug had no therapeutic effect—as with a tranquilizer I worked on—we hollered to high heavens about how it had no side effects.

Why did we do it? We thought we were in a game and never gave ethics a thought. Thank goodness I left the business before a thalidomide case resulted from my work.

I lived in a fourth-floor walk-up rent-controlled apartment that I sublet. It was filthy and ugly, with the bathtub in the living room. There also was a tiny alcove called the bedroom. But it was *my own apartment*, a very exciting idea for me. And a place to *bring women*! For a time, I shared it with Tom Hexner, a close friend from Harvard, but it was too small for both of us to be comfortable.

I wish that I were good about sentimentalizing the past, both because it would give this book a warmer feeling and more rose-colored visage, but even more important, because I would look back with more pleasure. If I were that way, I'd write about how "we used to go to Lewinson Stadium for the concerts in the summer night," and such. Well, I did go to several such concerts, but the autobiographical "used to" suggests a much more patterned and frequent activity. Though the concerts were enjoyable, they did not have the extraordinary ambience of never-never land. I don't want to give a description that is pinched of spirit, but I don't want to exaggerate. My life did not resemble the *gemutlich* fraternity-house-on-Saturday-night beer ads on television, but neither does almost anyone else's. Let's just say that the year was a good one, with many good moments, occasional loneliness, no tragedies, no major hurts.

I made some good friends in the agency, including Edith Rosoff, though these friends I mostly did not keep up with after leaving New York. And I had a very pleasant, though never serious, affair with D who worked there; she was entertaining and pleasant. To our dismay, though, she became pregnant. That was the era before legal abortion. It is hard nowadays to grasp the fear and panic accompanying the search for an illegal abortion. Eventually we found through the grapevine a doctor in northern New Jersey who (it later was revealed in the newspapers) was very famous and very prolific. Luckily I could come up with the $400. I remember with shame not accompanying D when she went for the abortion; I did not realize the importance of doing so, and D was too brave about it, so I let the fact of an "important" meeting keep me from going with her.

I have always been against making abortion a crime. Illegality increases the medical dangers of abortion and keeps some women from having abortions who want to do so. Furthermore, the politics of abortion are terrible in themselves and a great waste, because they sop up energy that might otherwise go into fighting coercive population control. But D's and my experience certainly helped me to feel pain when people do choose to abort.

About five months after I started work at McAdams, I got a call from Stanley Greenfield, who was the advertising promotion director at Ziff-Davis, the publishers of many magazines on such subjects as photography, boating, and flying. Stan asked me to come over for an interview. He had received my sales letter half a year earlier and kept it in his desk until he called. After our meeting, he offered me a job at double my McAdams salary to do advertising promotion—that is, to prepare the various written sales devices used by Ziff-Davis to help advertisers sell their wares.

About this time I decided that I would not go to medical school but instead would continue in business. I concluded that I ought to go back to school to learn my chosen profession, so I enrolled for a night accounting course at NYU. It was pretty mechanical stuff, and I learned the basics. But I was dead tired after a day's work. I found that it made sense to come to class, put my head down on the desk in the hot room, and doze for the first ten minutes rather than desperately try to keep my eyes open and absorb nothing. (All learning concerning sleep is important to me.)

After a class I noticed a poster advertising a $2000 Sears Roebuck Foundation Fellowship to the University of Chicago to study for the MBA degree. My instructor in accounting said that though he didn't know anything about the U of C's business school, he did know that the economics department was excellent (which was, in fact, not very relevant, though I didn't know that then). So Chicago seemed pretty good; I was apprehensive only about whether there were plenty of young women in Chicago, as there obviously were in New York.

Each year McAdams gave a one-year scholarship to a staff member to study a subject that would improve his or her skills. So I applied to go to the University of Chicago to study business. The head man, Arthur Sackler, asked that I come to see him. I was told in advance that he was a master manipulator of people, which worried me, though I have learned since then that my general skepticism usually serves me pretty well in such circumstances.

Sackler tried to persuade me to stay at McAdams for a few more years before going to study. I then told him that I had an offer from Ziff-Davis. But McAdams turned me down for the scholarship, offered me something of a raise (but less than Ziff-Davis would pay), betting that I would stay at McAdams. Instead, I went to Ziff-Davis, telling Stan Greenfield in advance about the Chicago possibility, which would depend upon getting the Sears Roebuck scholarship.

At Ziff-Davis I worked with Herb Hutt. Every morning we went to the coffee machine, and I bought Herb his coffee. Every afternoon we went to the coffee machine, and Herb bought me my coffee. That system was immeasurably more enjoyable than our buying our own coffees. When I got to Urbana in 1963, I would frequently have coffee with M, but M insisted that we buy our own coffees; I never could understand his reluctance to treat and be treated.

One of the very few times that a complaint ever did me any good was with respect to my application to the University of Chicago. The application asked what you would accept—scholarship, research assistantship, or some other category. I checked only "scholarship." There came back a letter saying I had been awarded a research assistantship. In fact, a research assistantship might have been better for me in the long run, but let that go. I thereby wrote to the University of Chicago in some dudgeon and said that I had indicated that the only thing that I would accept would be the scholarship, and they had not even done me the courtesy of telling me I had been rejected for it. By return mail, there came a letter from the University of Chicago, saying I had been awarded the fellowship. What probably had happened is that one of the persons they had earlier awarded it to had turned it down, and my letter happened to be in the right place at the right time.

Knowing what goes on behind the scenes in some selection processes is as bad as seeing what goes on in the kitchens of some restaurants. Consider another case of having a piece of paper be in the right place at the right time. This is how I became one of *Fortune's 150 Great Minds of the 1990s*. I had sent some material to an editor who was working on a story about immigration. He had not been able to use the material that he intended to, and his next job was to prepare the list of the 150 greatest. There was my stuff sitting on his desk, so he simply scooped it up, put it in a category that he called "immigration," and away we went. If he had used the material for the previous article, I would not have wound up on that list. The process by which I got to be one of the 25 smartest people in Washington, according to *The Washingtonian* magazine, was hardly more elegant. The writer of the story was trying to be a little bit countercultural and carefully avoided the people who usually get selected for this kind of thing, he told me.

I never have been ambitious for positions or honor. Once, in my fifties, I was together with a precocious fellow of twenty-four who was also giving testimony before a government panel on population. I asked him what he wanted to do in the long run. "Be Secretary of State," he said. I burst into laughter. "When I was your age my ambition was to make love to Elizabeth Taylor," I said.

When I was near to leaving Ziff-Davis to go to the University of Chicago, I told Stan Greenfield that I wanted to write an article on making home brew for a mass magazine, and I asked for his advice on how to sell it. He immediately picked up the phone, dialed the phone number of *Esquire*, and asked for the famous features editor there. When the *Esquire* editor came on the line, Stan said, "Tom [or whatever], this is Stan Greenfield over at Ziff-Davis," just like they were old buddies. He then pitched the idea for my article. The editor wasn't interested, but Stan gave it a good ride.

After he put down the phone, I asked Stan: "How do you know Tom?" "I don't know him," he said. I'd never seen that kind of commercial chutzpah before. I still don't think I could pull it off.

There was not the slightest trace of social consciousness or activism in me at this time. My aim was to construct a prosperous and interesting life for myself, my parents, and the family I hoped to have.

14

Chicago and the University of Chicago: I

Through a notice I posted at Columbia University, I found a rider to Chicago—Yoram Barzel, an Israeli who was going to study economics. Yoram is a wonderful economist and a pleasant companion, but at that time his English was such a struggle to understand that we talked very little on the trip, which I regretted then because I needed conversation to make the driving of my old clunker pass more quickly, and which I regret now because it would have been interesting talk.

The trip was most memorable when passing Gary, Indiana, as we neared Chicago. The large number of huge smokestacks at the steel mills that were pouring totally black smoke into the sky were awesome signs of the country's industrial might. The environmentalists had not yet conveyed the message that the particulates in that smoke kill people, as they do, and hence the sight did not induce an unpleasant reaction in me.

When I got to Chicago I went to see the dean of admissions to arrange my schedule. Jeff Metcalf was an amiable fellow who, it soon came out, had been in the Marines during World War II, so we had the girenes in common. He took me to the Commons for a cup of coffee and casual conversation. I was a bit older than most of the new MBA students, and for that reason, I think, as well as my voiced desire to get on with my work life, Jeff gave me course credit for some questionable prior experiences. My work in advertising exempted me from the introductory marketing course, and (I kid you not) my high-school classes in mechanical drawing sufficed to exempt me from the course in Production (perhaps because Jeff thought there was little or nothing to be gained from that course). This is the sort of spot where the writing of autobiography gets dicey, however; I am going entirely on my memory about this encounter, and I may be quite wrong, but it would be most difficult to check on the incident; the other person is most unlikely to remember many of the conversations that happened to stick in one's memory. Yet this incident may redound to Jeff's discredit in the eyes of some. (And it reflects no credit on me; after all, I accepted the credits.)

The first semester I went to a seminar in advertising put on by the longtime great editor of *Advertising Age*, Sid Bernstein. Through his good offices I found part-time work as a "consultant," analyzing the advertising for Chicago's famous Carson Pirie Scott Department Store. I found that their advertising was quite inconsistent in its underlying theme and the overall impressions of the store. When I asked the top managers what kind of a store they thought Carsons to be, there was absolutely no agreement among them and also no knowledge among them of how much they all disagreed on this. Finding the common theme and orienting the advertising around that theme promised to increase the sales potential of the store as a whole. In many business situations, analyzing the nature of your customers and of your products can be an effective tactic.

I took the required course in microeconomics with Jack Hirshleifer, and a good and challenging course it was. Then I took a course with him in managerial economics, and a course in economic forecasting with a wonderful elderly skilled teacher, Garfield Cox, the kind of industry-by-industry analysis that is no longer taught in universities but still is the heart of economic forecasting even though now it is mostly embodied in large econometric simulation models. This was all the education in economics that I ever had, before or after. (I also had courses in finance that adduced many concepts that derived or pertained to economics, but the subject matter was very specialized.)

In his autobiography, James Buchanan mentioned a couple of times that he was *not* "born an economist." Despite the paucity of courses I took, I soon realized that I *was* born an economist because I felt so comfortable with the economic way of looking at economic issues. The Smithian framework of the hidden hand (first stated clearly by Mandeville, though Shakespeare mentioned the behavior of the bees, which was Mandeville's metaphor for a self-organizing society) seemed obvious to me once I read about it, and it seemed natural to me to do a cost-benefit study of everything. The notion of allocation and trade-offs made perfect sense.

Incidentally, Garfield Cox had formerly been dean of the school and was said to have saved it from oblivion at the hands of Robert Hutchins, the famous president of the University of Chicago who was a great devotee of classics. Faculties of business were much looked down at in those days. It seems that just as Hutchins was about to abolish the school, an old friend of Cox's showed up on campus—Albert Schweitzer. Hutchins figured that a friend of Schweitzer's could not be all bad or just a professional drone; maybe there was something in the study of business after all. So the execution was stayed. Whether the story was true or not I do not know, but it fit Cox beautifully. Now the School of Business is one of the University of Chicago's crown jewels from all points of view.

The ruling paradigm in the University of Chicago's Economics Department and School of Business considered business people to be rational self-maximizers. It was clear to me that this was nonsense, based on my own experience in the advertising business. This idea came to a sharp point years later in an interchange with Milton Friedman about airline oversales. If I had indeed assumed that airline industry executives were rational self-maximizers, I could never have put forth the scheme that I did.

My second excruciatingly painful love affair—this one unconsummated—occurred at this time. A friend had given me A's name and phone number, so I called not long after reaching Chicago. She was a remarkably un-everyday sort of person, a bit fey and unrooted in the world of work (she was an artist), but fascinating. I believe that the source of her fascination was that because she lacked a strong ego herself, she reflected a man's ego and magnified it, making the man feel as if he were the most extraordinary person in the world. Whatever the reasons, I fell hard. But she always kept me at arm's length. In truth, I had reservations about her; her way of life and her thinking were so different from mine that I found it hard to imagine being comfortably married to her.

After a month or so, she explained why she kept me at arm's length: She had an ongoing relationship, and of course he was the other most fascinating man in the world — good-looking, the youngest full professor a famous university had ever made, etc. But she did not reveal his identity. When I went to Jimmy's on 55th Street (the hard-core hangout for the university crowd) to drown my sorrows, I met a guy I knew and told him my sad story. By chance he identified who A was talking about. That only made the matter worse because he was in fact the choice catch she described him to be.

Not long thereafter, D, a close friend of mine, told me of meeting A and of being fascinated by her. I told him of my speculations about her psychological nature and warned him of the likely painful end. And it happened to him just that way. Few of us can resist the drug of having our egos so magnified, even when told of the likely cost.

One of A's friends was a woman folk-singer M who had originally been Polish, had had a tumultuous life during World War II (though only in a refugee camp and never in a concentration camp), and then had been aboard the famous ship *Exodus* that had attempted to go to then-Palestine but had been turned away by the British and forced to wander the Mediterranean. A had connections to a newspaper Sunday supplement and wanted to have a story written about M. She asked me to do the writing, and I was glad to do so, both because the story was interesting and also because I wanted to help M; the fact that M was a very attractive woman and I lusted after her (though I never even dated her) had nothing to do with my decision, of course. (You don't believe that? What more can I say?). The article eventually appeared signed only "Anonymous" because M decided that she did not want her name used. Some time afterwards, she killed herself from the inability to shake the pain of memories of her experiences.

The first year at the University of Chicago is the only time in my life that I have felt like a prince or even a warmly-welcomed member of the institution. The Sears Roebuck Foundation Fellowship gave me some cachet, my background as an ex-Navy officer provided a bit of glamour, the experience in business allowed me to seem a bit worldly, and the School of Business was desperate at the time for good students; it had already accumulated lots of money and a world-class faculty, but a good student body takes longer to acquire. All that ended with a crash that I'll tell you about later. (Suspense suspense.)

Even though at that time the University of Chicago was almost surely the best possible place to study business—except perhaps for Harvard Business School with its case study work—I was not exactly dazzled by the course of instruction and the professors. In a class on investment, I wrote a term paper on the appropriate discount factor pointing out that it could not be deduced by any objective means but rather had to depend upon the needs of the decision-makers. The instructor gave it a "C" in response to my apparent simple ignorance of what was being taught (foreshadowing so much of my experience as a scholar).

In that paper I included a poem from Omar Khayam about the virtues of a wide range of choices. The allusion was not a success—a problem of the "right" style that was to recur throughout my work life (and still does). Because of writing for magazines and advertising, I aimed to be interesting and illuminating, but the allusion was too casual. Indeed, after being socialized to technical writing over the decades, such an allusion would not sound right to my eye and ear, either. Nothing in the style issue pertains to doing tight technical work—meaningful and parsimonious theory, good data, sharp and clear analysis. I demand that as much as anyone. It is strictly a matter of the in-groupness of the prose—like using Navy slang in the Navy.

A second characteristic problem of mine that surfaced in that paper is my offering a multiplicity of answers, the choice depending upon circumstance. Professionals and technicians want a single answer, and no desire to argue which is better. My general strategy: Try both and see if there is any difference in results; don't waste energy and brain cells arguing if the arguments do not imply different answers and behavior. This is unwelcome to all. (So why don't I change my ways? That's like asking a religious zealot to give up his or her religion.)

The same professor got into my life in a different and also unpleasant way. His wife took a job as my administrative secretary on the research project that I supervised for my Ph.D. thesis. He was also on my thesis committee. For motives that I can afterward only guess were jealousy, he inquired closely into the details of the research design—even though it had not been presented formally—and announced that if I went forward with the design as I had it, he would block my Ph.D.

As usual in my life, after I rethought the matter several times, I concluded what I was doing was sound and appealed the matter to my thesis supervisor, Jim Lorie. He was wise enough to ease the other professor off my committee on the grounds of having a conflict of interest, and the design went forward as I originally had it, in a satisfactory manner.

Almost never subsequently in my life has such a satisfactory conclusion been reached between me and authorities when they have had any control over me. This reinforced my belief that I could not work in a university and be a professor. My assessments of universities or other large institutions with respect to my own involvement certainly were correct, but things worked out much better than I ever expected when I finally decided to become a professor, simply because the structure of universities is loose enough to enable one to get along satisfactorily and do one's own work, even if you have to pay some price for this in salary and other perquisites.

While I still advise anyone who feels that he or she has many options in terms of his or her own abilities as well as desires to seek another occupation and not to be influenced by the apparent comfortable life style of the professoriate. For anyone who is burning with a desire to do research and to write and feels she or he would simply wither on the vine doing anything else, American universities certainly provide a wonderful environment of freedom where you can make a decent living and have most of your time to do the work that you want to do. As to the company there, early on I contrasted advertising people with university people. The advertising people are full of imagination and often are a lot of fun, but they frustrated me with the lack of discipline and depth in their thought. University professors tend to be more disciplined in their thought (at least in their own professions), but there isn't much imagination or fun about them, on the whole. They also take themselves more seriously than advertising people.

This incident is worth mentioning in a professional autobiography because what I have done professionally and how I have done it, have been greatly affected by my relationships to the organizational structures within which I existed—both the university structure and the structure of the professions. One reason I never seriously considered being a professor was that I assumed I would not flourish in a go-along-to-get-along structure, where making allies and having a winning personality would be crucial. (On the latter, a key reason for my going into mail order rather than some other business is that I believed that I am not good at selling to and negotiating with other people, except on paper.)

One sometime-benefit of my studying business is that I did not study economics and thereby avoided getting socialized into the mindset of the field. One example: I was not terribly surprised when the Nobel laureate John Hicks stated in the 1990s that the core of the

Keynesian formal analysis that he himself invented—the IS/LM figure—is faulty, and that the two curves do not belong on the same page. This led me to think about the drawbacks of studying a subject. Usually one thinks about people becoming socialized into the language and concepts of a field and becoming limited thereby. I think that the mechanism is a bit different. If one studies a field and takes examinations in it, one swears to the validity of the content. In my own case, I never saw the IS/LM curve until the early 1970s at a brown bag lunch talk, and my reaction was that the diagram simply did not make sense. Unlike everyone else at the talk, I had never had a course in macroeconomics, and therefore I had never had to pull the forelock in subservience to IS/LM in order to pass a course. Therefore I had no allegiance to it, as other people did.

None of us has the brains and guts to challenge all the concepts that are presented in a graduate course that are not satisfactorily clear to us. Never learning a faulty concept is better than learning it and having to discover that it is faulty.

My first couple of years at Chicago were the gay bachelorhood that one imagines for young men: lots of noisy parties to which I'd bring my Spanish wineskin full of some cheap vintage; lots of women; some very good talk with friends like Marc Galanter, a lawyer then teaching social science, and Cesar Grana, a sociologist; considerable bar time at Jimmy's; and a lot of study.

I lodged at International House, which was a delight for me because of the day-to-day company of women at meals in the cafeteria. I never formed liaisons with any of my acquaintances there, but I did become close friends with Rochelle Simon (no relation), and she later introduced me to Betty Glad. There was an Indian woman to whom I was much attracted, but she wore a sari, and I somehow felt that this was a hands-off signal, indicating that the hanky-panky I had in mind was not acceptable in her culture; here as mostly, the regrets of my youth are for omissions rather than commissions.

International House had strict rules about guests in the rooms. Also at International were several fellows studying business, too—Australian David Johnson (now the top man at Campbell Foods and one of the most respected businessmen in the U.S.), Canadian and former Czech Kristian Palda (when he escaped from Czechoslovakia in 1956, he reached Milan, stood in a public square where there is a famous statue, and rubbed the statue's genitals for luck, and then was immediately recognized by one of his father's business acquaintances who gave him a bit of economic first aid), and Ian Whiting (who as a nineteen year old had commanded a platoon in the guerrilla war in Malaysia). Together (actually, only three of us at a time), we moved into an apartment starting the next semester.

Rochelle told Betty Glad and me about each other, and we were very attracted to each other on our first date. Betty is one of the few women I refer to in the book whom I call here by name; I do so because, though breaking up is never happy, and the uncertainty about whether one might marry is not a great joy, almost everything else I remember of my time with Betty was lovely. Betty left tangible marks on my professional life. One of her stories about being an airline stewardess—with that job, and opting for the late-at-night flights that other stewardesses never wanted, so she could study for her Ph.D. in political science—was the kernel and inspiration for my idea for the airline oversales auction (the volunteer plan) discussed in Chapter 00. My attempts to explain the Normal (Gaussian) distribution to Betty by way of a visualized simulated model of little balls was a trigger to my later discovery of resampling—Monte Carlo simulation in statistics—as a general method for tackling problems in statistical inference.

Our romance was long-distance for a year when she taught at Mount Holyoke, but then she came back for a summer during which we lived together—in an apartment I injudiciously sublet on the floor of a building without air conditioning. God, it was hot at night; no wonder the apartment's possessors wanted to sublet it. But Betty and I had a good time aside from my having comments on the way she did lots of things, even chopping meat, which were easy to construe as criticism. I learned that every idea is an implicit criticism, and therefore every suggestion must be framed carefully—and still usually comes as unwelcome to most people.

In the end, I guess that I just was not ready to get married, and Betty had a job in New York while I had to remain in Chicago, so parting was inevitable though difficult.

One New Year's Eve I was out on the street about 1:30 A.M. with my date and another couple, slightly intoxicated. As we started to cross the street, a big, black Cadillac slithered in front of us into the crosswalk, very impolitely. As we stepped around the back, I smacked the big fin with the palm of my hand. No sooner did I do this than the two back doors opened, and a couple of men started to get out. I saw a bulge under the coat shoulder of one, and with an astonishing survival sense, I started to run at half a pace down Fifty-Sixth Street toward the lake. One of the hoods started to follow me, and I increased my pace. He shouted, "Come on back and fight." I said, "Run awhile after me, and then we'll fight." And I took off some more down the street. After another half a block, I turned and saw that he had started to return to the car. I prudently waited until the car had gone, and returned to my friends. If this was not the Chicago mob, then I must have been in Boston, and it was the Boston mob.

15

The University of Chicago: II

I thrashed around looking for a thesis topic. First I wanted to do experimental research on risk, having in mind the pioneering work by psychologists Frederick Mosteller and Sidney Siegel in the 1940s that I had read about as an undergraduate in experimental psychology; that topic was deemed by the faculty not appropriate for a Ph.D. in business, however. (As of 1996, for two decades, this sort of work has been considered one of the most exciting and important of fields—and of course the University of Chicago Graduate School of Business has been one of its major centers.) Then I thought to start my own business, and in the course of doing so, develop a case study of the new enterprise; that was deemed insufficiently "scientific."

About then, someone suggested I talk to Lester Telser about an idea he had for studying advertising budgets; I consulted him and did a bit of the reading he suggested in agricultural economics, but I did not see the connection, and I let the matter drop; showing better sense, my apartment-mate Kris Palda picked up on the idea and it was (with considerable reason) one of the two national prize-winning theses in business the next year and the backbone of Kris's oeuvre for many years. (I remember this when I think about the students or colleagues who do not see the value of research suggestions I make to them.)

The most interesting nonstarter for a thesis topic was my proposal to study the ability of multivariate econometric techniques (especially discriminant analysis) to predict the winners of horse races. One faculty member suggested that the topic might be appropriate in a school of animal husbandry but not in the School of Business. Thinking this simply a prejudice (though in retrospect I can see his logic), I made an appointment to see Milton Friedman in the Department of Economics because of his long-ago work on lotteries, but alas, he, too, was not in favor.

While waiting to see Friedman, I sat in an anteroom where there were graduate students banging on old style Monroe calculators hour after hour—exactly the sort of dog work I wished to avoid in doing a thesis. One of the students was an Australian, and like so many Aussies, he was nuts about horseracing. So I told him of my proposed work to pass the time.

The next day, as I was walking down the long corridor in the Social Science Building, I saw the Aussie coming toward me. I did not turn my head to greet him, but as we passed I said out of the corner of my mouth in a conspiratorial whisper, "The seventh race is fixed for Flossie" and I kept going. Then after five paces, I turned around to see the effect of my joke. I saw a man standing in open-mouthed amazement looking at me—somebody who was not the Aussie. No wonder the fellow was amazed.

When I told this story at a lunch at the Hoover Institution, 25 years later, Friedman laughed the loudest of anyone. This sort of nonsense is the salt of my life.

About the same time, I noticed "Unconditional Guarantee" on a can of aerated whip cream. I sent the empty can back to the maker with a note saying, "Your product gave me a very poor shave. Please return my purchase price." I did not hear from them. No laughs at that end, I guess.

Jim Lorie, who had been my advisor since I arrived at the University of Chicago, put me in touch with Herman Fussler, the director of the university library system. Herman had obtained a grant of about $75,000—big money, then—to study patterns of use of the University of Chicago's libraries, with an eye to what could be learned about storing the least-used books in cheaper storage facilities off campus. This would not have been a good subject for anyone who planned an academic career because the results of the study would be of interest only to persons in library science, or perhaps to students of operations research if fancy new techniques were used. Given that I had no aspirations to an academic career, the job seemed to make sense for me. Most attractive to me was that I would not have to spend hours and hours doing such dog work as banging on those Monroe calculators hour after hour, but could instead hire people to do what needed to be done.

Herman hired me, and I then began to think through the design of what we would do. It soon became plain that almost all of the lines of investigation that were in the grant application were either inadequate or flawed, and I therefore had to design new methods. This was very challenging for me at the time, almost too difficult, and therefore it was not as enjoyable as it might have been a few years later when I had had more experience and could work with more facility; I still found my mind uncomfortably full of cobwebs that I kept trying to brush away, sometimes by taking a walk outside around the campus.

At the beginning of the Library Use Project, Herman and I talked at some length and had a few tussles about what should be done. On one occasion, he wanted a procedure that would produce two observations for some units, but only one for most, and counting all equally. I could not convince him that this was an error. So I suggested we talk to Jim Lorie as an "expert consultant," and after Herman explained his view and I explained mine, Jim said rather ironically, "You're saying that this would be double counting. That's a very serious charge." Despite the amiable irony, it was indeed double counting. This was awkward for both of us because I was only supposed to be a "student," whereas he was supposed to be the senior researcher.

After a while Herman must have decided that he would do best by simply trusting me, and we met on the average of once a month for an hour or so in his office, as I gave him a progress report. The distance between him and the work was not unwelcome to me.

We published the results of the various lines of work in a paper-bound preliminary report, which still reads very well, I think. I wrote all of it except a chapter on library management, which Herman wrote, though the authorship was "Fussler and Simon." The main analytic task was to predict how often a given volume in the stacks would be used in the future. It should not be surprising that after extensive investigation of many variables with complicated regressions, we found that the amount of use in the past—perhaps together with the age of the book and perhaps its language—would do as well as more complex formulations.

The year after the project was complete and I had left the university, Herman wanted to produce a bound book. I then told him that I thought I should be the senior author because most of the intellectual work—including the basic concepts of the research methods we used—was mine, as well as all the day-to-day work and almost all the writing. After getting the grant, his contribution had consisted mostly of the single hour a month that he spent listening to my explanations of what I was doing, plus a single chapter. But he said that he had gotten the grant and posed the general questions, and I should consider myself lucky that he put my name on the volume at all. I suppose that the canon of scholarly ethics would have me defer to him as senior author because he was older, because he was a faculty member, and because he had gotten the grant. If an outsider heard the story at that time, he or she would probably have assumed that this was just another uppity, deluded graduate student who put a higher value on his contribution than was really the case, and the graduate student would probably prove this by never doing anything again in his work life. In this case, Herman never did any further substantial scholarly work in his life to my knowledge, and he had done little or no empirical work before that. (He was, after all, a librarian rather than a researcher.) In light of that and of my research life afterwards, ex post facto an observer might well guess that I did indeed make the main intellectual contribution as well as mainly carry out the execution of the work.

Indeed, I saw no need for the new version and was not anxious to participate in it. I thought that the original version was fine and could simply be edited slightly and published as is. Furthermore, I was then in business and had no scholarly stake in another publication. I suggested that Herman undertake the work himself, since he apparently knew what he wanted done. It turned out, however, that he had to hire another person to do the subsequent work; Herman either lacked the inclination or (more likely) the understanding of the nature of the work of which he was the first-listed senior author to be able to carry it off.

After International House and then after living with various combinations of David Johnson, Kristian Palda, Ian Whiting, Ian Pontin and maybe someone else for a while in a big apartment on the edge of campus, I lived alone for three months in a third-floor apartment I sublet on Kimbark Avenue where thieves entered three times, twice successfully. One attempted theft occurred as I was just laying down to take a nap. As I heard the thief use a key to come in the door, I looked frantically around the alcove which contained my bed for something to attack him with. All I could find was a telephone. He heard me rustle around as I reached for the handset, and he ran out, leaving the door open. Afterwards I realized what a foolish and foolhardy move I had made, luckily aborted; the sensible thing, of course, would be to shout "Who's there?" and scare him off.

After maybe still another apartment or two—this was a period in which everyone seemed like a nomad—I moved to an apartment on 57th Street, where I lived for at least a year, a long time! While living there I swapped a big old car for a very small monkey—about 12 inches high. I thought that the monkey would be good company on my shoulder and would be fun with other people. But I found that making an accomplice of a monkey was not quite as easy as it sounds, and I sold him to someone else very quickly.

When I think about having the monkey, I think about Niels Bohr's phrase, paraphrased as: "A deep thought is one that both it and its opposite are both true." What's the logical connection to the monkey? I do not know.

While I was looking for a thesis topic, I had an all-encompassing idea for a complete philosophical worldview. The idea was that creativity is the source of all reward. With sufficient squeezing and interpretation—for example, that the joys of parenthood are a manifestation of the creative impulse in procreation—this constituted a logically consistent system (like the theoretical systems of physics and economics) where one can start off with one or a few basic propositions that are assumed true beyond question and where everything else can be deduced from the basic propositions. I put together a long typescript arguing this point of view. Fairly soon, I began to see how forced and contrived a structure it was, and I abandoned it. Since then I have never been attracted by grand schemes of life created by me or by anyone else.

Later, this system reminded me of a young man I heard describe himself as a prophet. I had gone to a lecture on prophecy at Hillel, at which the lecturer opened by defining a prophet as someone who declared himself to be a prophet, and then saying that of course there no longer are prophets. The young man to my right said, "Excuse me, that's wrong, I'm a prophet." The lecturer said, "Of course you're joking." The young man said, "I'm not joking at all. I say that I am a prophet, and by your definition that makes me one."

The young man went on to say that once you accept as true that

God handed down the first five books of the bible to Moses at Mount Sinai, everything else follows. In every sort of situation, one can then simply consult the system to decide how one should conduct life. I had fallen into one of the most seductive intellectual pitfalls of all. As to the lecture on prophecy, the lecturer and the prophet went back and forth a few times, and then the entire talk seemed to dissipate inconclusively, and the attendees left. It was a very unusual occurrence.

Having been hired on the university staff, I was eligible to join the faculty club. I did so and went there for dinner with a date one evening. But I found that when I was there, I got ice-cold and sweaty with anxiety, lest someone I know should see me and think that I was an impostor—being where I had no right to be. So I never went there again until in 1990, I gave a lecture at the University of Chicago and Jim Coleman arranged for me to stay there. I no longer felt like a complete pretender.

Despite the denial of permission to work on the horse races for a thesis, I later pursued the work nevertheless, during evenings, after work on the Library Use Project. One night when preparing punched cards in the large room that contained the old accounting machines, I met Rita, whom I had previously met once when a mutual friend suggested I consult her about something. This time something clicked. Within months we were engaged to be married. I lived for the last weeks I was in Chicago with Rita and her roommates Claire Friedland and Shirley Weinstein Kaplan; it is always a lot of fun to live with a girlfriend plus her girlfriends; all the overtones and undertones are pleasing. (Here I begin to be reticent, though nothing scandalous occurred.)

16

In and Out of the Mail-Order Business

While in Chicago I had decided that I was best suited for a business that did not require being effective in face-to-face personal interactions, because I assessed—and it was an accurate assessment—that I am not skilled at attaining my ends in personal negotiation with people. Why this is so is still somewhat a mystery to me; certainly it has much to do with my relationship with my father, but my fear of the outcome of such relationships also enters into the matter. If my own interests are not at stake, I do not have this fear and this belief in my ineffectiveness, at least to the same degree. I often enjoy casual meetings with people, and I have happy friendships. When I represent someone else, I do not feel like a blundering idiot, even if I have the conviction that my competence is no more than ordinary, or perhaps less than ordinary.

Along with my belief in my ineffectiveness in personally conducted business, I judged that I possessed some skill to sell successfully in writing; this pointed straight to the mail-order business. Another relevant element is that I like to make evaluational calculations of activities, and the mail-order business lends itself better to calculation—and to systematic testing—than does any other business.

After all the library project and thesis work was finished in February 1961, I left Chicago and moved in with my parents in Millburn, New Jersey, as I started to lay the groundwork for a mail-order business. Even for the few short months that I lived with my parents, I was not comfortable being around my father; I tried to smile and be noncommittal and simply ignore his ill-informed opinions about everything. living in my parents' house seemed inappropriate at twenty-nine years of age. Also, watching my parents' interaction was never pleasant—Mother doing her best to humor my father and to cover up for what he said and did. Toward me Mother was gracious, as always. In any case, we all got through the few months until Rita and I got married.

The first step in getting into the mail-order business was to decide what to sell. This was the beginning of the story as I tell it in *How to Start and Operate a Mail-Order Business*.

In the meantime, my parents' home served as a temporary base of operations. One of my first serious products was a service I called Flowers Every Friday, a delivery every Friday of a large bouquet of the flowers that were most abundant and attractive that week. The key to the business was to be able to supply lovely flowers cheaply by buying in quantity, packaging on a mass-production basis, and providing cheap delivery because of the proximity of customers to each other. From Yellow Pages collections in the library, I was able to find that there were some other similar businesses in other cities, which heartened me. In the two months that I offered the service, the business showed enough promise that it might have been a winner.

I offered a first-month trial deal and then found that the crucial continuation rate to the next month—showing consumer satisfaction—was high enough that the business might well have succeeded. I did not discover a crucial marketing device, however: I mailed letters first class, using criss-cross phone directories. It would have been vastly cheaper to distribute flyers to people's apartments, and that probably could have been arranged somehow; one way to do so would be to make initial sales in apartment houses by mail, and then when making deliveries, put leaflets under each door.

After I had read and learned something about flowers, I prepared the containers in Millburn, then went to the market in Manhattan long before breakfast on Friday mornings, divided the large lots into perhaps a dozen for each customer, and delivered the bouquets. Some customers were at home; others, I left in front of doors in plastic to keep them fresh. Occasionally a customer would strike up a conversation. Several asked me about my background and wondered that someone with a Ph.D. was delivering flowers. That did not seem at all strange to me, though in retrospect I suppose it was unusual, and that many Ph.D.'s might think such work below them.

A couple of other female customers expressed a more personal interest, but being an engaged man and very idealistic about such matters, I was hardly aware of the blandishments. Really!

I abandoned Flowers Every Friday because other opportunities that I was exploring seemed more promising. From a purely business point of view, that decision might well have been a mistake.

I also searched for businesses advertised for sale, and I found a mail-order sewing-materials business. This probably was a very good prospect. Perhaps the biggest thing that held me back, in addition to lack of capital, was my worry that I had no talent for selecting materials for sale. I had never had any interest in "fashion," or any artistic talents. Therefore, I figured that materials selection would be a problem for me. In fact, selection of patterns probably was quite routine, and one could rely on the recommendations of sellers, as the business's owner advised me. Again my lack of belief in my own talents constrained me.

Another opportunity that seemed to have real possibilities was to sell fancy coffee and tea. One advantage is that Dad knew a lot about coffee and enjoyed working with it. I bought a cheap packaging machine, found sources of supply, and advertised a sampler package in literary magazines. In subsequent years, others have developed exactly this product, both by mail and in retail stores. I continued this line in a low-key way until I left the mail-order business.

For a while I sold a booklet for $1 entitled "How to Make Your Will", and it was accompanied by blank will forms; the booklet was written by a lawyer, and the booklet was part of the great series of *Little Blue Books* sold by the millions in the 1920s and 1930s. But the Federal Trade Commission charged that this was against the law and effectively forced me to stop, on the grounds that I was dispensing legal advice without proper legal authority. In those days there were no public-interest law groups to assist citizens who were harassed by the government, and of course it would have been a piddling exercise to show that the First Amendment protects such an activity. The businessperson who is not long in pocket, and for whom an activity is not central to his or her business, simply has to cease the activity under those conditions; that's the tyranny of bureaucracy. Nowadays books and kits for will-making are sold routinely in bookstores, and nonlawyers freely dispense personal advice on the process without interference by the law.

When I was at Camp Lejeune, I had made home-brewed beer in my BOQ room; probably it was against some rule, but I never even thought about it then—in contrast to the situation aboard ship where liquor really was against all Navy rules and infractions were serious. At the end of my work with Ziff-Davis and then in Chicago, I wrote and published an article in the big-circulation magazine *Argosy* on how to make home brew, plus a bit of beer history and a few yarns. When I went into the mail-order business, I noticed firms selling instructions on how to make home brew in tiny classified ads in such magazines as *Popular Mechanics* and *Sports Afield.* So I got permission to use my material and ran a few trial ads. The results were good, so I got together a little catalog of materials for home-brewing—malt, hydrometer, bottle capper, and the like—and rolled out the campaign.

The results were excellent. But along came the government again. The law permitted people to make wine at home and seemed to permit people to make a limited quantity of beer as well. But the federal alcohol authorities—probably at the behest of the commercial brewers—carried on a sporadic campaign of harassment against the sellers of such books. They contacted the magazines and made vague, unspecified threats. There was not enough money in it for the magazines to worry about, so they would pull the ads for a while. But the regulators only hit a few magazines occasionally, and after a while the magazines would begin taking the ads again.

I decided to try to get the law clarified and contacted a classmate who was a lawyer in Washington. But the matter was too small potatoes for him and would have cost me a fortune. About this time I decided to become a professor, and hence I did not pursue the matter. A few years later, Congress passed a law making it clearly legal to make home brew, and the industry has thrived in a minor way since then, I see on my infrequent inspections of such magazines. Stores selling the ingredients and equipment can be found in many cities.

My foregoing criticism of regulators does not mean that I believe business should be without rules and unregulated; far from it. The story about the bad things we did in pharmaceutical advertising in the absence of satisfactory rules to ensure the full truth is one illustration of the need for sound regulation. But it is easy for legislators and regulators to exert too much control and unfair control over those in their power, not because the control aids the economy or protects individuals but rather because of the objective and subjective benefits of exercising power.

For the business, I rented a very large room in a wonderful old building in Hoboken, only a hundred yards from the terminus of the Delaware, Lackawanna, and Western commuter railroad that ran through Millburn, and of the Hudson Tubes that ran under the river to Manhattan. The purpose of setting up the business in that area was to provide employment to my parents, my long time goal. So the Hoboken location enabled my father (or my mother, if she were to have to come to the office) to get there easily on the Lackawanna, and it would be a quick commute for me when Rita and I moved to lower Manhattan, as we planned.

I found a serious poker game in New York that was congenial in both the companionship of the other players and in the size of the game. The appropriate size of a game that is not just an excuse for drinking beer is that you might win or lose a week's pay; much more than that can disturb your nerves so much that you will not play well, and much less than that makes the result sufficiently unimportant so that you will not concentrate hard enough.

Rita was not enthusiastic about my going out to play and leaving her alone for the evening. I came up with a scheme that brought her into the game and made it enough fun for her that she stopped reproaching me, even mildly, for playing. I kept a running account of my winnings and losings (the former greater than the latter) and promised her that when the sum grew large enough for a mink coat—symbol of affluence in the Brooklyn society in which she had been a child—we'd buy her one.

Great plan. But by the time I'd won enough, she realized that mink coats were not of great interest to her. So we postponed the purchase. And postponed it. But a few years after we moved to Champaign-Urbana, the moment came: A "Half-Price, Right-off-the-Truck Sale." So she bought one, and she gamely tried to enjoy it, but she had by then moved too far from the world she grew up in to take the coat out of the closet very often.

This incident typifies an important side to the way I related to people, which is often transmuted into my schemes of economic reform: Give people an incentive to do what you'd like them to do, rather than try to compel them or persuade them to do so. This is at the heart of all my auction schemes, such as the airlines oversale volunteer scheme. (See Chapter 00)

Though then and now I enjoy thinking about the strategic side of a business and conjuring up schemes for new products, new methods of production, and new ways to promote products, I didn't like the dealings side of business—making arrangements with printers and banks, hiring people, and the rest of the day-to-day management of business. Much of that work consists of tussling with people—the printer who promises to deliver the work on a given day but does not and lies about it again and again. Such relationships are too often a simple exercise of power and money: If you are a big customer, they'll treat you well; otherwise not. Or if you want your needs attended to, you may have to sweeten the pot in some straightforward or under-the-table fashion. You don't see the best side of people in those circumstances.

About December of 1961, I erred grievously. I ran an advertisement that was misleading, and because of a complaint from a competitor, I heard about it from the regulatory authorities. Even though I made good in such a fashion that no customer was damaged monetarily, I felt so guilty that I fell into a terrible depression that lasted for years; the entire story is told at length in Chapter 00. This was, of course, the most horrible period of my life, especially in the first days and weeks. Some internal events were so painful that it is still too painful to recount them. One example only: In the subway, several times I thought that someone was watching me on behalf of the police.

My feelings sharpened my sense of kinship with the have-nots. One day I walked past the main public library on 42nd Street, where there customarily were six or ten men with shoeshine kits. I watched as a policeman went down the line and told each one that he had to move. I felt the pain of poor men just trying to eke out a few honest dollars rather than take charity, whom the authorities would not permit to do so for the pettiest of reasons; that typifies too much of the relations of governments and individuals all over the world.

Twice a week I went to Hoboken where two part-time typists and my father were working. In considerable part because I so hated receiving complaints from customers—about the misleading ad or any other—I felt on the trip under the Hudson river as if I were in a slow descent into Hell. That hour was perhaps the worst sense of anticipation I've ever felt. Coming back in the evening, I felt as if I had been liberated from Devil's Island.

During one of my very grim months around the middle of 1962, I think, I picked up a secondhand copy of T. K. Quinn's book, *I Quit Giant Business*. He had been a superstar vice president of General Electric before World War II, but he came to believe that huge firms suppressed creativity and did too little to promote consumer welfare. So to everyone's amazement, he quit and thereafter did many fascinating and valuable things in and out of business. I felt that he was the kind of man I wanted to know and who might have much to tell me. So I called his office as early in the morning as business hours allowed. I was greatly distressed to hear his secretary tell he that he had died very recently.

My guilt over going astray from the truth and decency, together with the depression, greatly altered my values. My powerful need to be useful to others and to society at large arose in this period, a reaction of penance for my sin. So the relatively minor transgression resulted in that major transformation in my ethical life as well as my doing personal penance by punishing myself with a sense of sin for 13 years. This need did not manifest itself in my becoming a volunteer at a hospital, or reading to the blind, or coaching a Little League team; those activities certainly are wonderfully valuable. I felt that I had no special advantage in doing such things, and I wanted to use my own talents and skills as fully as possible. So my desire to be useful turned me to my professional work. Maybe this is just a cop-out for my being unwilling to do the hard, dirty work of being useful directly to people, one-to-one. I hope not; someone else can judge better than I can.

I began to read about the ethics of business, but I found little that would guide me or another businessperson about how one should behave in the variety of everyday situations that arise in business—neither specific advice nor more general theory. I therefore wrote an article on business ethics, having reviewed everything I could find that bore fundamentally on the subject. This led me to a proposal for research on the subject. The article concluded that the only sensible guide to business ethics is the set of values and judgments that one would use in personal ethics; that is, one ought to act in business in a fashion that satisfies you that you are doing the right thing as an individual.

My next work was a theory of how to make effective advertisements. While I was in the mail-order business, I puzzled long and hard how it could be that mail-order ads were usually small and full of type, whereas ads for national brands were usually the opposite. I remember sitting on our couch thinking through this question, and it led me to list the characteristics on which mail-order and other kinds of advertising might differ or be the same. This then led to a theory of the content of advertisements by which one could go from a checklist to the implied ideas, words, and type of advertisement. This paper was not the sort of thing that any journal would publish. Several years later, when I wrote *The Management of Advertising*, I included this paper. A perceptive critic wrote that many books that hold themselves out as research volumes are really texts, whereas mine purported to be a text but was really full of new research.

My life took a complete turn because of the act of writing. After a while, I decided I knew enough about the mail-order business to sell a correspondence course on the subject, given that there were two other courses on the market that were not very good, in my judgment, and courses had been sold successfully for decades. The title was *How to Start and Operate a Mail-Order Business*. I devoted the first two hours every day to writing it, and when it was almost complete, I realized that the time I had spent writing was the only part of my workday that I enjoyed or even found tolerable. This led me to wonder whether running a mail-order business was what I wanted to do. Indeed, all along I had never envisioned spending a life running a business but dreamed of being sufficiently successful in (say) ten years, so I would have enough capital to provide for my parents and nuclear family and could think about doing other things—perhaps being a publisher or entering another intellectual business that might be barely profitable.

When I left Chicago with the intention of going into business, my supervisor and friend Jim Lorie had suggested that if I ever wanted to change my life I should contact Joel Dean at Columbia University. Dean was the inventor of managerial economics as a field, and he had built a very profitable high-level economic consulting business. So one day I called Dean to ask if he'd like me to do some consulting. He immediately countered by asking me if I would give a lecture in his class that afternoon. I said "No, with regret," because I had some piece of routine business I had to take care of. But ten minutes later I reconsidered and decided to call him back. I remember the pounding of my heart as I tried to get his phone number, worrying that I would not reach him. In one of those turns of the lottery wheel that seem to affect one's life so much, I luckily caught him. Indeed, the entire matter was happenstance because he only came to Columbia one day a week and had taught halftime for years (which eventually led to the faculty ousting him).

I made notes for several hours, and then I lectured on the theory of mail-order operation. After I described the mode of operation for choosing in which media to advertise, Dean told the class and me that it is a complete analog to the concept of a ladder of investment opportunities that Dean had invented to handle capital budgeting, a field he pioneered. This impressed him, and he offered me a job working as a consultant at his home/office in Hastings-on-the-Hudson. Later I evolved from this specific theory for mail order a much more complex algorithm for the much more difficult problem of setting the overall advertising budget for firms that cannot trace the effects of individual advertisements as one can in mail order, as I'll describe in Chapter 00, and I also published the formalization of the theory for mail order.

I found this first teaching experience very exhilarating, as do so many others. As many others do, I projected that if I were to teach, each class would be as exhilarating as this first experience. It doesn't turn out exactly that way, though I am lucky enough that I still feel good about teaching much of the time and enjoy it considerably at least part of the time—though like all other professors, if given a choice of teaching a course or not teaching it, I'll choose to not teach. (In my case, it is because I am grateful for any additional time I can give to writing.)

Naturally enough, the idea then struck me that if I liked writing and research and teaching so much, I ought to do them for a living—which meant becoming a professor. And by an incredible stroke of good luck, I possessed a Ph.D. that I had never sought but that would now allow me to teach immediately. But I worried about the economic future of my parents if I became a professor. And I was not sure I had any talent for it, but it sure seemed to be better than the daily tasks of doing business, which I hated.

It is interesting to reflect on the benefits of the lack of huge success. If I had been enormously successful in creating a large and profitable business immediately in New York, it would have been much more difficult for me to leave it behind, or certainly much less likely that I would have done so. If I had remained in business there for say, ten years, it would have been unlikely that I could have embarked on the path that I found myself on, or one anything like it.

Similarly, if my early work on advertising had been extremely well-received by the marketing profession, rather than generally ignored, it would have been more difficult for me to turn to the entirely separate subject of population economics; the fact that when I would go into a library and see articles on advertising budgeting that did not refer to my work made me very happy to think I would not be reading those journals in the future and enduring that same pain.

And if I had somehow wound up with a huge grant to study incentive payments for people to have fewer children, though I hope I would have given it up; people find it hard to do that sort of thing. And if the research grant for an immigration panel that Rita and I worked so hard on had been funded in 1983, the demands of that project on my time would have been huge, and in retrospect, probably would not have been a good investment. And so it has gone with respect to so much of my work.

Perhaps this is an illustration of the ancient principle that George Ainsley makes so much of—that getting what you want is often the ticket to hell.

17

Urbana and the University of Illinois I: Starting 1963

Sometime in the summer and fall of 1962, I recognized that I am a scholar and writer by talents and at heart. Rita and I then decided that I should look for a university teaching job. It was extraordinary good luck that I already had a Ph.D., because, without it, I would have had to begin a degree program at that time, and I do not know whether I had the strength and courage to do so in that period of my life. Chapter 00 about my depression tells you how low in the mind I was, and it is not likely that I would have been able to plan such a long-drawn-out process; I lacked all hope.

Having earlier obtained the Ph.D. simply by happenstance is another of the fortunate twists of fate of which my life has been full. If the University of Chicago had not had a desperate need for warm bodies to fill the places in the Ph.D. program in 1960 and if I had not had a girlfriend to keep me in Chicago, I would never have gotten the degree; getting the degree was a luxury for me, for I had no intention of ever becoming a professor.

The question in 1962 was: What would I teach? Though my degree was more or less in managerial economics, I had no idea how to look for a job teaching in that subject. I would have liked to teach economics, but, though my thesis was very much an exercise in applied economics, I had no other credentials in that field; I had had only two or three economics courses in graduate school, depending on how you counted, and none as an undergraduate. Marketing seemed the best opportunity; I had practical experience in the field and had a field of concentration in the subject in my Ph.D. program.

I wrote to the University of Chicago placement office for leads, but inexplicably they only had two unattractive suggestions—a couple of tiny universities in the Southwest, I think. It is true that Chicago's towering reputation in business was still mostly in the future, but the paucity of leads is difficult to understand. Certainly I had done well there, aside from a failed oral exam and my choice of a thesis topic that was barely connected to business research; many people thought well of me. The lack of leads is probably best explained by my inability to ask for help effectively. I am always reluctant to do so, and I feel embarrassed about putting people to trouble on my personal account—even if it is their job to do so; I therefore ask weakly and not often enough.

I went to the annual meeting of the American Marketing Association in Pittsburgh and interviewed on the usual meat market. Only a few schools offered interviews. Two job offers eventuated: The Department of Marketing at the University of Buffalo and the Department of Advertising (in the College of Communications, i.e., journalism) at the University of Illinois. Illinois was by far the better university, and the Buffalo climate made us shiver. Our visit to Urbana-Champaign left Rita with a barren impression, but we felt that it was the clear choice. I was hired by the head of the ddvertising department, Charles Sandage, as an Assistant Professor.

One of the peculiarities of my job search was that having been in business seemed a liability to me rather than an asset. Rather than attributing to me valuable experience, interviewers apparently assumed that I wanted to become a professor because I had failed in business and therefore was defective. This seemed to me a peculiar way for academics to look at their own profession, but strange are the ways of human beings.

To go to Illinois meant Rita had to leave a good job in New York. Even before she found a position at Illinois we decided to move, simply because my situation was so desperate. Though such an act on her part was more expected by society then than now, her willingness to do so certainly showed a high degree of loyalty to and solidarity with me. Luckily, however, as soon as my job was arranged, she received a lovely offer from the famous psychologist Charles Osgood, who knew of her work and much respected it; he offered her a part-time appointment in the College of Communications' Institute of Communications. She also received an appointment in the Sociology Department.

Curiously, what starts as a pain often turns into a pleasure as habits and experience cause our tastes to change. When I was a student and afterwards as a beginner, I had to force myself to write. I had to struggle to remain in the chair for 15 minutes at a time; it was difficult to overmaster the urge to get up and move around and think of other things. But over the years I found that I could write for longer and longer stretches at a time, with less and less need to fight the urge to stop. At some point, there was no longer any need at all to force myself to write. Now there are times when I get so caught up in writing that I must force myself to stop in order to do other important things. I have read others describing the same personal history.

When Sandage recruited me in 1963, he told me of his dream for an advertising experiment "station" modeled on the agricultural experiment stations at land grant universities.

(The Morrow Plot at the University of Illinois was perhaps the first agricultural experiment station, and it was one of the places at the University of Illinois that made me most proud and that I always took visitors to see. I admired the decision of the state to spend lots of money to build a neighboring new library underground rather than a cheaper aboveground building that would block the sunlight onto Morrow Plot, thereby ending a century of valuable data.)

Sandage asked me during the interview if I'd be interested in working with him on getting an experimental station organized and running; he said it was a long-standing dream of his. I expressed some interest, though I told him that I had a book and other projects to finish before getting involved in anything else. I was less than perfectly candid. My interest was fainter than I expressed, and though my participation was not out of the question—a flow of interesting data always draws my attention—I was probably hedging somewhat about the administrative aspects of such an operation. And by the time he raised the matter a year or so later when I was teaching at the University of Illinois, my interests had shifted even further away from the technical analysis of advertising messages and more toward the economics of advertising. I believe that it was my disinterest in the "station" that led Sandage to want to get rid of me. Perhaps my lack of complete truthfulness —which he had no way of knowing for sure, of course—was some justification.

This incident causes me more shame than my not telling the Navy that I had pretty much decided to get out when I was dickering to get onto the Mediterranean cruise while I was attached to the Marines. Maybe this is because an identifiable individual is involved in this case—though perhaps this is the same moral blindness that allows people to steal from institutions even if they would not do so from individuals.

In his autobiography *Intimate Memoirs*, George Simenon talks frequently about his powerful need to express himself in writing every day. I have this need, too, as I first found out sometime during my years at the University of Illinois, and later it became even more pronounced. I sneak bits of writing like this paragraph, just as a cigarette addict sneaks a butt even when it is not permitted; we need our fixes. Even dictating some prose does not satisfy this need. People who don't have this need find it difficult to understand why people like us continue to go on working. (By the way, Simenon's book is surprisingly poor. It does not reveal much about him at all. And the love and sex affairs that are so fundamental to his life are merely set down as a list of encounters, with no fleshly detail or joy.)

In New York, I had talked to a high-priced psychiatrist four or five times about my depression, but never benefited from the conversations; my depression was unaffected, and the transactions annoyed me because I hated paying somebody so much to sit there being useless. The only thing I can remember is that I said it was difficult for me to think that by undertaking an academic career I would be forever forgoing the prospect of writing fiction, and he pushed me to say why writing fiction was so important to me; I could not say why, and thereafter the notion was less important.

In Illinois I went to the mental health clinic and hooked up with a graduate student in clinical psychology named Al Newman. We had a grand time talking together for an hour every week or so, though it didn't seem to affect the depression. But having a good time is, in itself, an excellent thing for a depressive. We both saw the funny side of things, including my depression, and Al was the kind of guy who ran for president some time later (really!—though I don't know that his candidacy was super-serious). More generally, my encounters with psychotherapy for the depression were never painful (except for the bill in New York) and often were enjoyable. I'm sure the old Freudians would say this was a sign that the therapy was not working—and maybe they would be right. Nothing else seemed to happen. (More about this in Chapter 00 on depression.)

While I said in the Preface that family relations was one of the aspects of my life that is too private for me to write about, I want to say something about our children, and this chapter seems the appropriate place to do it. First the facts: David, our oldest, was born on November 27, 1964. Judith arrived a year later on December 16, 1965. They were both born in Urbana. Daniel was born during our first stay in Jerusalem on March 27, 1968. He returned with us to Urbana in August 1968.

The emotions that I, like others, experience as a parent are quite unlike any others, and they deposit some of the most poignant memories in one's life. When Judith was perhaps ten years old, she had some peculiar symptoms in her knees. At the first consultation, her wonderful immigrant Irish pediatrician, Dr. Corbett, worried about some dread disease or another—a possible leukemia or bone problem. At the next appointment, the news was the best—no disease, just a false alarm. The relief I experienced when told about the negative x-ray and then walking out holding Judith was a primitive joy like no other; the air never smelled fresher, and the sky never looked bluer than at that moment.

Or the fear: One spring Saturday when Daniel was eight or nine, I was sitting on our second-floor porch overlooking Busey Avenue when David came running down the street and shouted, "Daniel had an accident." In panic, but trying to be calm, I asked him what had happened. He said he did not know. I rushed downstairs in the sandals I was wearing and ran two blocks following David. The feelings when finding Daniel sprawled out crying, with his back on the ground and blood coming from his mouth are indescribable; luckily, the damage to his mouth was temporary, and the teeth were reasonably repairable. I was so preoccupied with the accident that I did not find out until I got home that I had sprained an ankle in the process of running with the sandals flapping.

Another memory is the sense of being needed that goes along with protectiveness—for example, staying up all night with Judith when she had a very painful kidney infection at about the age of two. At intervals, I dozed while holding her in our favorite orange reclining chair when she slept, and I sang to her and walked around the room when she was awake.

Regrettably, telling stories about the kids now that they are older inevitably will make them feel that their privacy has been invaded, even if I somehow manage to get the story straight. That means I must forgo many such stories.

As far as their physiques, safety, character, personality and appearance go, we have been unbelievably lucky with our children.

They all grew up healthy, good-looking enough that they have no cause for resentment against the world for making them ugly and their lives harder thereby. They have had no disabilities that have kept them from doing well in school, and they have all had good enough work habits and discipline to enable them to make good livings. None of them has fallen into the pits of drugs or crime or violent antisocial behavior. How much more can parents ask? Perhaps especially because of this and other poignant moments, my heart goes out to those people who have not been so lucky.

Also, the children like each other and feel close to each other. This is something that both Rita and I desperately wanted for our kids. The words "my brother" or "my sister" were the sweetest words I knew as a child who yearned for an ally and a best friend in the family.

In my view—and Rita agrees with me—a huge proportion of the explanation for kids doing well or poorly in their endeavors can best be labeled as nothing but "chance." Those parents who have bad luck and their children fall into pitfalls take on too much if they accuse themselves of being responsible. And parents of children who have avoided the pitfalls and skipped from one peak to another similarly give themselves too much credit if they claim to be responsible. Yes, you can probably ruin kids if you really work at it. But worrying that your child enters into the right nursery school at the age of three is nonsense, I'm sure.

This view of the heavy role of chance fits with my general viewpoint on the happenings in life. Certainly, it's better to prefer a good education to a poor one. But who is to say that going to Harvard or MIT will provide better conditions with a high probability than will going to the University of Illinois or the University of Maryland or Central Arkansas University? The competence of the teachers and the excellence of the students are not the only elements that matter; for students who do not show obvious marks of academic excellence, the chance of being counseled and personally instructed by good teachers may be greater at less-grand universities.

One of the great things for us as a family was having the Waalers—parents Jack and Ginny, and sons Christopher, Luke, and Grant—

living next door from 1968 to 1980. Christopher is a bit younger than David, Grant a bit younger than Daniel, and Luke is between Grant and Christopher. They are a wonderfully decent and amiable family, and the six kids intermeshed like a television comedy show, constantly being in and out of each others' houses. So close were we that, for example, when one day Grant climbed up on the kitchen counter in our house to avail himself of our cookie jar, Ginny saw him when standing at her sink in her kitchen and banged on her window to get him to stop, so that he would not spoil his appetite for dinner. Grant and the others were as comfortable in our cookie jar as our kids.

Daniel remembered recently that when he was young, I said to the kids that some things were right and others were wrong in the inherent nature of the actions, and that this was different from what they were learning in school. When the kids were young, I trusted my instincts about when to tell them they were allowed to do something and when not; I did not spend a lot of time analyzing such decisions, and I felt confident in my decisions. But I lost confidence later, when they got to be eleven, twelve years old, and older. When one of the children would tell me that X's parents let X go somewhere we thought our kids should not go, I was conflicted and could be swayed by argument, especially when they got Rita on their side. And I think that Rita and I were less strict with the kids than we should have been; we (I) should have insisted that they finish doing the dishes before watching television or whatever, and we should have demanded more personal formal respect from them. I can't be at all sure that it affected the ways in which they grew up.

Speaking of washing dishes: I often said to the children that the aim in washing dishes is not to get the dishes clean but rather to dilute the dirt to an acceptable degree. This always put them in a tizzy. I pointed out that this is what one necessarily does in managing a swimming pool and in purifying a water supply. No amount of example or logic would budge them when they were young. They considered it downright immoral on my part that I did not cleave to the ideal of total purity. When I discuss the notion of "zero pollution" in *The Ultimate Resource*, I mention comparing the virtues of rinsing a dish from the faucet versus dipping it into a pan of rinse waster which fairly quickly is no longer pure.

Another interplay of personal experience and my work came when all of the Waaler and Simon kids were sitting on the second-floor porch overlooking Busey Avenue, and the subject of "overpopulation" came up. The Waaler kids were at first conventionally worried about this, because they had heard about it in grade school. I then asked each of them if our neighborhood had too many kids. They all answered "no." "Well, why then do you think that *other* neighborhoods have too many kids?" We then went through the same routine with pollution and the scarcity of natural resources. Later I used this dialog in my writings.

I tried to fit the parental response to the situation. When one of the kids would get obstreperous at the table—for example, David arguing vociferously—I considered that the matter did not call for punishment but did call for some intervention that would stop the activity. For such situations, I adopted the habit of simply saying, "Out! Twice around the block!" (or once, or five times or whatever). By the time a kid had finished a couple of times around the block a few minutes later, the mood had shifted and the logjam was broken.

One funny-to-me but painful to him memory is that I once sent David around the block ten times, intending that it be the short little block on which we lived. He took it to be the long block across the street from us, about three times as far around as the short block, and he continued running until he had finished quite awhile thereafter. He still throws this up to me as one of the worst pieces of my fatherhood, despite the fact that he now runs marathons.

When Judith consistently left her bike in the driveway, at risk of having it crushed by a car and also of forcing the driver to get out of the car to move it, after several warnings, I placed it about five feet high in the crotch of the little crab apple tree in the backyard. I figured that the effort involved in getting some help and then getting the bike down would serve as mild punishment and a bit of chastening, and also an indication of the cost of repeating the activity. She still feels to this day that this was unfair.

I reflect that if these are the worst things that my kids can find about my fathering—not lack of love, not lack of attention (except in Judith's case), not physical abuse, not disinterest in them as people—then I'm prepared to live with that record.

I enjoyed watching the development of the kids' analytic and creative thinking. I tried to prod them a bit, sometimes by trying to confuse them. For example, when we would go out for a walk when they were very young, I would point to a tree and ask, "Do you think that tree will be there tomorrow?" When they would answer, "Yes," I'd ask, "Why doesn't the tree fall?" or "Why does the tree stay up?" That's a tough question to answer. At first they usually wouldn't answer. After I pushed them, one might respond with something like, "Because it always has." And I'd tell them that that was quite a good answer.

Then I'd explain that there are two reasonable bases for predicting that the tree will be standing tomorrow. First and most compelling for most of us is that almost all trees continue standing from day-to-day, and this particular one has never fallen; hence, what has been observed in the past is likely to continue. This assessment requires no scientific knowledge of trees, yet it is a very functional way to approach most questions concerning the trees—such as whether to hang a clothesline from it, or whether to worry that it will fall on the house tonight. That is, we can predict the outcome in this case with a very high likelihood of being correct even though we do not utilize anything that would be called either science or statistical inference. (But what do you reply when your child says: "Why should I wear a seat belt? I've never been in an accident.")

A second possible basis for predicting that the tree will be standing is scientific analysis of the tree's condition—how the tree's weight is distributed, its sickness or health, and so on. Let's put aside this sort of scientific-engineering analysis for now.

The first basis for predicting that the tree will be standing tomorrow—sameness—is the most important heuristic device in all of knowledge-getting. It is often a weak heuristic; certainly the prediction about the tree would be better grounded (!) after a skilled forester examines the tree. But continuation alone might be a better heuristic in a particular case than an engineering-scientific analysis alone.

This heuristic appears more obvious if the child—or the adult—were to respond to the question about the tree with another question: Why should I expect it to *fall*? In the absence of some reason to expect change, it is quite reasonable to expect no change. This new question does not run away from the central question we have asked about the tree anymore than one avoids a probability estimate by estimating the complementary probability (that is, unity minus the probability sought); indeed, this is a very sound strategy in many situations.

I was delighted when one day, on a walk around the block, Judith said, "I think I've started to like thinking."

Once I asked Judith how many legs a dog has. She answered, "About five." I told her that that is a much closer guess than people make about most important quantities that we try to estimate.

One of my most successful devices was our giving the kids "option days" for not going to school. Like all kids, ours sometimes complained of being "sick" or just plain not wanting to go. The arguments Rita would have with them bothered me, so we crafted this policy: In first grade, the child could designate any five days as option days—no school with no argument. Then four days in second grade, and down to one and none. Once, when the teacher asked Daniel why he was not in school the previous day, he answered: "I took an option day." She was bewildered, of course.

Another successful device: Judith had interminable arguments with Rita about leaving the house on time. So we simply said to Judith: "OK, be late." She was never late, and the arguments were blessedly absent.

As to being dressed sufficiently warmly in the winter, the policy became: "If you're healthy—no sniffles or anything like that—you can wear anything you like; go in your underwear, if you want to." Our kids subsequently seemed as warmly dressed as any other kids.

The moral: Freedom is a wonderful thing. It's the best way to get people to act sensibly and an excellent device to prevent complaining about being abused by the system.

Rita disliked arbitrarily suppressing argument. I disliked wasteful back-and-forth bickering. At some point I would sometimes order: "Around the small block three times," or, "Around the big block twice." When the kid returned, we had a completely fresh start.

Perhaps the self-assurance I felt then is necessary and the absence of it, damaging. Later it was different; I lacked assurance then. I probably would have been a better father if, during my children's adolescent years, I had been more sure that I knew what I was doing and that my decisions were good ones. Instead, lack of confidence led me to indecision and weakness in the face of the kids' determined claim that Rita and I should have the same rules as other parents (except where our rules were more lenient, of course), and that the kids knew best what was good for them; this indecision and weakness on my part were, I now believe, unhelpful and unnecessarily painful. Even if I really did not know well what I was doing, it probably would have been better if I *thought* that I did and *acted* so.

One reason I have always thought it folly to try to plan and organize a child's life so as to attain a particular desired future is because I think that such organizing is likely to be ineffective; the role of chance dwarfs the impact of any planning, on average, I think. But the second reason for this belief is the classical philosophical problem—explored at great length by George Ainslie and immortalized in dozens of genie jokes, many of them obscene—that even if you get what you want, you are likely to be dismayed by what you get; the realized wish turns out to be very unpleasant. For example, even if your planning and organizing leads to the child having a remarkably successful life economically, the plethora of wealth may lead to great pains in the life of your child, and even perhaps more so in the lives of grandchildren. It would be bitter to sacrifice a great deal in the early years to attain as result in later years that which you wished you had not attained.

Occasionally I played serious poker in a game that usually included a few professors plus some others from around C-U. In a city that size, in which one could win or lose perhaps a week's earnings, it was not easy to get a game together. Ralph G, a retired farmer, was the winningest player over time—quiet, unflamboyant, careful, efficient. Upon Professor E's request, I brought her into the game, the only woman I'd ever heard of in such a game; she did pretty well, but she put off some of the players—because of her manner, rather than because of her sex. A beefy local trucker was a fairly regular "contributor" to the game (i.e., a loser), but not so much as to be a "fish" (a sure heavy loser due to not understanding the game well). We occasionally played in my cellar on Sunday afternoons. The scene was an eye opener for the kids. Once when Rita brought some soft drinks down to the basement, the trucker offered—half in jest, half serious, I think—to tip Rita a five dollar bill. She turned it down with perfect grace (showing the good breeding she acquired growing up with two uncles who were professional bookies).

The biggest fish was M, a professor in the social sciences who could not resist playing. He and his cigars were obnoxious, but he filled a seat and always lost; that was how the other players saw it.

M was also about as worthless as a professor as a human being could be. He taught a "theory" class that none of his students could understand, and his entire body of published work over about 20 years as a tenured professor was approximately one article and five book reviews (or so I was told by a member of his department).

Back to poker: I always waited for someone else to divide the poker pot when I won (or otherwise). Unlike many others, I have no need to *do* something, to be active or managing. I always wanted to avoid the possibility of making an error in my own favor, lest someone think I was cheating (typical thinking of someone who feels illegitimate and often ashamed, as I do).

I also was glad to leave the game because one of the regulars in the C-U game had a taste for playing with hoodlums; one of the occasional visitors to the game was boss of the rackets in the black (then Negro) end of town, and he later went to jail for a few years for a gang murder he was involved in. He was a very amiable and jovial fellow, of course, and a contributor to the game though not a fish; he just liked to dance too many dances, as the poker saying goes.

I notice that when I write about poker I shift to a style and attitude that fits the poker scene—the cynicism of phrases like "fish," the willingness to play with anyone who will fill a seat and make the game, and so on. I hope that the reader realizes that this style does not necessarily reveal my own attitudes about the situation, and I hope it is not necessary to make a lot of explicit moral comments in order that you understand what my judgments are. It's bad enough that I *behaved* as I did, being willing to take the money of willing suckers; I'm not exultant about that, but neither am I about to condemn those who do so.

During the three years I was at the College of Journalism, I was never in Dean Ted Peterson's office, though what I knew about him as a person was generally positive. (He was in our house once, though, because he and my good friend Jim Carey were close). Even more remarkable, during my first three years at the College of Commerce, I never met or shook hands with Dean Paul Green, and I assumed that he had no idea who I was; I was quite happy with that state of affairs, especially because I had not heard good things about him. When V was acting dean in 1967, he lost our family the opportunity to be in Israel for the Six Day War (those remarkable six days and their antecedents were the high point in the lives of many Israelis and of Americans who were there) because of bureaucratic timidity (the most benign assessment of his behavior); my request for a half-sabbatical was slightly late, and he refused to send it on because sending a late application might make the college look bad. When V later became the dean, I stayed as far away from him as possible; and in response to his frequent travel on college business, as much of it foreign as possible, when someone would ask me, "How is V doing?" I'd answer, "V is out of town." That was my petty, small-minded revenge on a man I considered a bungling, procrastinating, cover-your-ass administrator who was quite useless as a scholar, too. (V is catching the entire load of my manure that might just as well be delivered elsewhere as well; bad luck, V.) There might have been another dean between V and the time we left; my lack of memory of the matter, together with the above remarks, shows once again how my attitude toward authorities is to have as little as possible to do with them, out of fear that nothing good and perhaps something bad will emerge from any encounter with them, due to my personal ineptitude in such relationships.

One of the funny incidents of the racially polarized 1970s occurred as I was walking through the main corridor of the big library at the University of Illinois. A young black man was standing a couple of steps up the main set of steps, leaning against the banister and talking to a white woman. I kept looking at him as we walked past because he looked vaguely familiar. After a few moments, he bounded off the steps and with a wildly aggressive motion came over to me and said, "Something wrong?" in a very hostile tone.

Off the tip of my tongue I replied, "Don't we know each other from someplace?" His aggression collapsed like a pricked balloon.

The good and bad sides of small-city life: Mrs. G conducted the morning music programs on the local public radio station. She fancied herself very knowledgeable about the arts, and she loved to talk. On the chamber music hour from 11 to 12 a.m. that I loved greatly and looked forward to, she often droned on and on with her precious artsy comments while I was both anxious to hear the music and anxious not to hear her. Because hers was the only show in town, she had a monopoly, and people could not take their patronage elsewhere, which would eventually have toned her down or gotten her fired in a big city, and hence she continued unchecked. That's the *bad* part of living in a small place.

I found another person who felt the same way about the program. So together we called the station master—who was also a part-time faculty member—and arranged a meeting to talk with him about the Mrs. G situation. He fairly readily agreed to ask her to talk less. In a big city it would never occur to me to contact a station manager and then have coffee about the matter. That's the *good* part of living in a small place. But the fact that you *can* do something about it can sometimes be aggravation because you don't just accept the situation as beyond your control. That's another *bad* part of the small place.

By the second half of 1982, I was restless and anxious to leave Illinois. I wrote to the Hoover Institution to solicit a job, perhaps the first time I had ever done this and about the same time they were about to get in touch with me. I gave a talk at Hoover on my new theorizing and empirical work on immigration, and I knew that if the material passed that audience's scrutiny—it included Nobelists Milton Friedman and George Stigler and a host of other fine economists—I could consider the material sound. In fact, Friedman spotted a flaw in my procedure for estimating the costs of immigrants through the use of public capital such as schools and hospitals. It was not a fatal flaw, but forced me to go home and rework the theory and calculations, and it diminished somewhat the impact of the theory. This was the only time that I have presented material in print or to a seminar where someone has spotted a serious flaw—an incredibly lucky record.

It is quite amazing how often Milton Friedman has touched my thinking or my imagination, even though I've only been together with him on perhaps four occasions in my life, none for more than a half-hour (except for the seminar).

Did I get an offer of a job? I did not get the permanent offer I sought; among other things, I think I failed a test of ideological purity because I expressed the thought that if there is to be a corporate income tax—and I think it better that there be none—then that tax should be graduated to give large firms, especially conglomerates, an incentive to break themselves up into smaller units with less political power. This is an old idea, going back to the 1930s, but I rediscovered it, analyzed it, and worked out some of the procedures and implications.

18

Teaching at the University

The following definition of teaching is the most cynical joke I have ever heard: Throwing artificial pearls before real swine.

Ostensibly, my profession is that of university teacher—a professor. That's what the state legislature thinks I am being paid to do, and by most ways of reckoning, that is half the job for professors at institutions where I have taught: the University of Maryland, the University of Illinois, and Hebrew University in Jerusalem. Indeed, I have spent 60 (or in later years, only a blessed 30) hours a semester in the classroom, plus many more hours preparing for teaching, plus more hours grading, counseling students, and so on. (Here I do not mention university committees and other such activities, in part because I have done extraordinarily little of that.)

One would expect all this to have created a deposit of many thoughts and memories. In fact, I have few such memories, and I am only writing this chapter because I feel it necessary to do so in order to make this book complete. Nor is this extraordinary; in the autobiographies of other university professors, I also find little or nothing said about their teaching, except for their relationships with graduate students as part of their research.

This rather surprising situation reflects the apparently peculiar situation in American research wherein most of those who do most of the important research are ostensibly hired to do something else—that is, teach.

This situation naturally leads to calls for "rationalizing" the system by setting up institutions that enable researchers to spend all their time doing research. Yet the system does not move in that direction, in considerable part because the people who would be expected to want it that way—the research-emphasis professors—prefer the present system. I think they prefer it in considerable part because it gives them maximum freedom to choose what they want to work on, unlike the sorts of research institutions that the Soviet Union maintained, wherein the decisions about what to work on came from the top. That centralization of decision-making was disastrous for the freedom of thought necessary to produce great research.

There also is another reason for keeping the present system: the best researchers are the best teachers. Even if they are not the most interesting teachers (and they are at least as good, on average, studies seem to show), they have the most reliable information and the best grasp of the state of knowledge, and they are less likely to teach many of the fallacies and outmoded material often found in textbooks. Also, they are the best models for future researchers and the best people to guide student research, especially with respect to the crucial matter of how to choose topics for research.

This is not to say that most professors love teaching the way people love tennis or chess, or even the way many or most researchers love doing their research. Teaching is a way to earn a living in order to do research and write. If given the choice, I would take a very long sabbatical from teaching, though remaining at the university. And so would most other professors, including those who talk about how much they love to teach; just ask them sometime to teach an extra course without extra pay; the number of volunteers is vanishingly small. (And if you find any volunteers to teach my courses, let me know, though of course the system would not allow me to do that, on the principle that the value of a professor should not be measured by his or her output in terms of numbers of students taught or value-weighted amount of research, but rather by the amount of his or her input; that is, the amount of supposed sacrifice is too often the measure, rather than the value, to others of what the professor produces. Of course this sort of measurement is most prevalent among those who themselves supply a lot of hours at the office but would not fare well in output measures. The tailless dog praises taillessness, said the historian Collingwood.

Maybe there is more room in our system for the Max Planck Institute model in Germany, or our National Institute of Health. But I'll bet—and hope—that the present "irrational" system of the U.S. continues. (This is one more example of how commonsenseible "rational" analysis and social engineering often are inferior to the products of social evolution in conditions of considerable freedom.)

In our university system it is easy to see the waste—the worthless professors who manage to secure tenure and then never do any useful research; for them, teaching only two courses each semester is indeed a racket. It is this that the legislators have in mind when they want to double the teaching loads and remove tenure. The trouble with that strategy, however, is that the same system at the same university that supported the worthless poker-playing professor colleague mentioned in Chapter 00 (Illinois) also supported John Bardeen, the only double Nobel-winner in a single field who (with Walter Brattain and William Shockley) in 1948 invented the transistor. That device is a major basis of the transistorized electronics industry. If a person or a corporation were able to collect the money value of that invention in just a single year now, the net value of the goods made with that invention (a very rough calculation that involves the cost and value of similar products that would have been made with technology that did not follow from the transistor's discovery) is greater than the value of all the 3.2 billion ounces of gold that now exist in the world (a cube of 20 yards on a side), worth now perhaps 1.5 trillion (a thousand billion) 1996 dollars (thanks to Francis Curran for the information). It takes some wisdom for the legislature to realize that the price of getting rid of the system that harbors the racketeers is preventing the John Bardeens from making their contributions. One Bardeen might pay for the salaries of 10,000 racketeering professors.

Furthermore, the salary of (say) Bardeen, in the last year before he retired in the mid-1970s was $46,500, and in the year when the transistor was invented, he earned much less. (It is also interesting that he was paid less than some second-rate professors of finance and not much more than most professors in his own field of physics.) The difference between what society pays people like Bardeen, Shockley, and Brattain and the benefit we get from such people is a measure of the gain to the rest of us in our standard of living due to the advance in knowledge. This sort of observation is central to understanding the economics of population.

I learn a great deal from preparing lectures and from having my attention directed to subjects in such fashion that textbooks have resulted. Interaction with students (and with audiences at public lectures) has taught me what is not understood in what I say and has therefore improved my presentation and popular writings. But the number of new research ideas that have arisen in my interaction with students has been small.

I might have gained more in a substantive way from students if I had had the opportunity to teach a large number of first-class graduate students. But I have never been at an institution where I have had that opportunity. In the institutions in which I have taught, I have preferred to teach undergraduates and large classes of them, rather than graduate students, because there is a greater chance of someone picking up a valuable idea among 100 undergraduates than among ten graduate students; ordinary grad students too often seem interested only in what will help them pass their qualifying examinations. (On the other hand, casual conversations with groups of students sometimes are more interesting than with groups of faculty, because the students do not possess a stock of university and professional gossip that they can share, and therefore they must talk of substantive matters that are more interesting to me than faculty gossip.)

Among my teaching characteristics, the students grade me highest on student participation, because I try to induce the students to think of good responses to the questions I pose. I tell them that of all the sentences that are spoken in a classroom in an entire semester, the student is most likely to remember a sentence spoken by himself or herself. This raises a management problem of preventing a few students from occupying most of the participation time and having many not speak at all. I randomly choose people to deal with the latter problem. I try to deal with the heavy talker (there usually is only one, or at most, two) by using subtle gestures with my hands or by turning my back away to indicate that the student put down his or her hand, or not continue a remark. Usually this works fairly well. But one semester at Illinois there was a student so irrepressible and so obnoxious, that I finally asked him to leave the course. I thought the other students might resent this dictatorial move against a member of their "class." The reaction of the other students was: Why did you wait so long?

I tell myself that I may have been better-off by not working at a highest-ranked institution. At such a place, I inevitably would have spent more time with graduate and perhaps undergraduate students than I have, and that might not have been economical in terms of my life's time budget; but of course maybe I'm just kidding myself to avoid bemoaning my fate. (One clear advantage of being at a top institution would have been a prestigious letterhead, which can be helpful in getting work published and certainly is helpful in eliciting respectful treatment from the media, who rely very heavily on ascribed characteristics rather than the quality of work.)

I almost surely could never have had the benefits of creating a "school" of persons who worked on my ideas as has, say, Gary Becker so effectively. One reason is that though I am confident of the soundness of my ideas, I know what rough sledding the ideas face, and I am reluctant to induce any graduate student (or young colleague) to swim in such dangerous waters. Additionally, I do not have the sort of personality that attracts followers, partly because I do not seek them. And last, the subjects I work on have shifted radically over time and have spanned several disciplines, so that even if I created a group within my department, in a few years the subject of that group would not be my own focus any longer. This movement among topics has also prevented me from banding together with a small group of like-minded faculty members. This also reduces the advantage to me of being at a first-class institution.

Every college and university has many excellent undergrads. Even at a mediocre institution, there are some undergrads who are the equal of the best at the top universities. The universities differ in the breadth of their talent distributions; at mediocre institutions ,the bottom 80 percent are much less good students than the top 5 or 10 percent, whereas at the best schools, even the least good are pretty good.

When I came to the University of Maryland, I asked to teach the Introduction to Business course which then enrolled 500 students (the number fell as the course was no longer an easy B), so that I could feel I was making a contribution to the college even if I did not do committee work. This course was very demanding to teach at first because it covered a wide range of subjects, as well as because of the difficulty of keeping students' interest in the worst lecture hall I have ever seen, at a time (starting 1984) when student indiscipline was rife at Maryland. So I had to learn about new topics, which I greatly enjoyed. The first semester or two, I had guest lecturers discussing the law, for example. Later on I mastered enough of the subject to prefer doing it myself.

It was a great shock for me to experience the undisciplined conditions in that huge classroom. I had never had to give a moment's thought to discipline at Illinois, and now I had students reading newspapers in class, putting feet up on the chairs, walking in and out and chatting at will, eating and drinking and throwing the trash on the floor. The first semester, I asked one student to leave after I warned him twice about disruptive behavior, and he refused to leave. So I went outside and phoned a state police officer to come and pull him out, then returned and kept on lecturing.

Eventually I learned how to deal with the matter with fast-paced lectures, strict rules, and sufficiently tough grading so that people stopped taking the class for a soft spot in their schedules.

I'm a pretty good teacher, and in some ways I've gotten better over the years. My strengths are my animated manner, my unwillingness to continue on the same line when the listeners show boredom, and my use of visual aids and other teaching devices. I also work hard to put everything I say into concepts and words that every single person in the class can understand fully; I refuse ever to ask anyone to take anything on faith or ever to say "It can be proven that . . . " or "More advanced texts show that . . . " or any other such buck-passing. This is part of what led me into inventing the resampling method for teaching (and doing) basic statistics. (See Chapter 00).

My shortcomings include my not marching down a tight outline point by point and not worrying enough that the students will feel good about the examinations and their grades; research seems to show that the exams are the biggest factor in explaining how well students rate instructors, and I fail to invest enough effort into exam-making. Many students—especially those recently out of high school—feel uncomfortable with this style, however, and perceive it as a lack of organization. I taught a small "honors" section of the introductory business course in 1996, and it was a resounding failure. It did not require very much to become part of the honors program, and the students were very young, and they did not enjoy the freedom and the spontaneous atmosphere that I maintained in the first half semester. In the second part of the semester, I had to go to formally structured lectures, and in a small class that is very dull for both students and teacher.

Many or most students may also consider it a weakness that I am willing—in fact, often anxious—to show in which ways the subject we are discussing is unclear. I believe that it is important that college teachers make clear to students how different university learning—and learning in general—is from high school, where the material tends to be cut-and-dried, where there are straightforward right and wrong answers, and where the students can often rely completely on the validity of material being taught—as, for example, in classes in language, arithmetic, other school math, geography, the details of local history, and the like.

The best part of my courses—especially those that teach skills, such as managerial economics, statistics, and research methods—is the content itself. My approach to managerial economics is fundamentally different from the standard course, in replacing formulas and the notion of marginal magnitudes (marginal revenue and marginal cost) with tables and total magnitudes; this and related ideas constitute a textbook I wrote on the subject. Predictably, when I first lectured on this material to business students in Jerusalem in 1968, they were not interested because it made the subject seem too simple; it required no mental struggles to obtain sound answers. And teaching the resampling approach to statistics has been one of the handful of most important activities of my life, involving books, computer programs, the business with Peter Bruce, huge expenditures of money and time—all because I want so badly to teach a better way of doing things not just to my students but to the entire world. (See Chapter 00).

Always I have wanted to teach material that would be useful to students. When in 1968 at Hebrew University, my students in advertising and marketing seemed very distant from that subject, I asked myself what would be most relevant to their situation. I decided that discussing entrepreneurship—how to start a new business—would be most helpful to them. So I set the task for each student to develop a real plan for a real prospective business. And that led to several actual businesses being started.

When I first started teaching at the University of Illinois in 1963, perhaps a quarter of my students had grown up on farms. By the end of my time at the University of Illinois in 1983, almost none were farm kids. In those first years, the farm kids made a big difference in the way I taught and talked, even though the subject was advertising and they were only a quarter of the class. They tended to be practical and down-to-earth (a meaningful expression) in a way that the city kids were not. Even though I had never lived on a farm, I related to them better both intellectually and sentimentally than I did to the kids from upper-middle-class city families. Why?

The young woman who served as Miss Pork, 1981 (or some nearby year) was in a class I taught because she was majoring in agricultural economics. Laugh at the moniker, but she was one of my best students—very competent as well as very pleasant; in the Navy we would have said that she was very squared-away.

Rita and I visited her uncle's nearby farm not long before we moved; he taught me a lot about his operation, which I enjoyed. I tried to convince him that farmland prices were too high, by reference to Colin Clark's law that the value of a farm should be about 3.5 times the gross value of a year's output. But the uncle said he could not afford to sell; prices were already below the peak. Prices then proceeded to fall to half what they then were. That's the classic trap of not treating sunk costs as sunk.

19

Research 1963–1967: Advertising Economics, Research Methods, and Other Topics

This chapter begins discussion of the academic research that—along with my family—has absorbed most of my life energy. My senior thesis in college had been serious research in an academic mode, though in psychology. The experiment I conducted on improving pistol shooting among the Marines also was professional in attitude and practice. Later, my Ph.D. thesis was a many-sided piece of work, but I thought of it more as operations research than as "pure" academic research, and I had done it as a job rather than because I chose the problem for its inherent fascination and theoretical importance. But now research was to be my life, not just casual amateur work or a for-pay job.

My first main subject of academic research, beginning in 1963 at the Department of Advertising of the University of Illinois, was the economics of advertising. That is what I knew most about, and it was the subject of the department I was in.

The first study eventuated in an article entitled "Are There Economies of Scale in Advertising?" The work arose out of a comment in December 1962 by another seeker of a job teaching marketing, while we were waiting together in a Pittsburgh hotel for an interview. He described his thesis and mentioned an S-shaped advertising response function (the curve showing the quantitative relationship of advertising to sales) as a key assumption. The S-shape is consistent with the idea that twice as much advertising produces more than twice as much sales. The image that advertising salespeople have used since time immemorial is that of the rock that eventually is shattered all at once by a stream of drops of water.

I replied that the curve does not have that shape, as is well known in the mail-order business (which I was then working at), where the data are clear and sharp. That is, the second ad on average produces less sales than the first ad. He shrugged off my assertions and insisted that the S-shaped function was crucial to his work.

This is just one of the many times that I have heard contrary-to-fact assumptions justified as necessary for mathematical or other convenience. Any competent academic can cite many other examples. I once showed a paper-giver that the implications of a model of the patent process were exactly the opposite of what he thought they were, making the model useless. "Maybe it can be used for something else," he said, without much sign of disappointment. Another example is the model of an airplane to determine optimum overbooking that had flexible seating—add seats one at a time; this preposterous assumption was justified by the need for mathematical tractability.

My interlocutor in Pittsburgh suggested that perhaps mail-order advertising is different from other advertising in respect to the shape of the response function. So I now proceeded to address the matter, and my first research task in academia was to tackle this topic—which should have been settled once and for all by the excellent small book that mail-order businessman William Shryer published in 1912.

The evidence is all consistent with the no-S-curve conclusion. But the belief in an S-curve will never die, both because it is "logical" and because it is a crucial element in the sales pitch of those who sell advertising space and time.

This was the first professional article I submitted to a technical journal since I wrote up my senior thesis (on concept formation) in experimental psychology and sent it to a technical journal. (If you remember, that one was quickly rejected on the grounds that it lacked proper literature citations, etc., and surely also because it did not look professional). This first piece on advertising was quickly rejected by the *American Economic Review* on grounds that it did not "meet the competition."

I have gone back several times to the topic of the advertising response function, in a variety of ways. I hope to do so once more before I check out.

It boggles my sense of perspective that it is more than 80 years now since Shryer published his excellent book showing the absence of economies of scale in mail-order advertising, asserting that the contrary idea was a fraud perpetrated by sellers of advertising. Since then, no one has shown any solid evidence to the contrary. Yet the theory and the belief continue. Over this period of time our transportation has gone from the horse and the railroad to automobiles and airplanes; our energy sources have gone from coal through oil to nuclear power; our medical practice has gone from a situation in which Abraham Flexner commented, I believe, that it was about 1912 before a random patient seeing a random physician for a random ailment had a better than 50 percent chance of benefiting from the encounter, when the notion of tinkering with our genes would have seemed entirely far-fetched given that Mendelian genetics had not long before been resurrected; and so forth. All those changes in knowledge have occurred since 1912, but nothing has changed with respect to general knowledge about the advertising response function since Shryer's book.

Other studies in the economics of advertising occupied most of my time during my first three years as a professor. Next I worked on the problem of how much money business should expend in advertising. This is another study that arose out of my experience in the mail-order business. It came out of the talk that I gave to Joel Dean's class at Columbia in 1961, in which we likened the advertising expenditure decision in mail order to the capital-budgeting decision in investments; Dean himself had pioneered this logic in his text, *Managerial Economics*, the first such text ever written. (See Chapter 00 for the chance event of that lecture that changed the entire course of my life.)

Deciding on the potential profitability of mail-order advertising is straightforward. The decision about how much to spend for mail-order advertising is simple: One simply does not make any aggregate decision at all. So my thoughts turned to the more difficult problem: How much should non-mail-order general advertisers expend on advertising? This problem turns out to be much more difficult. The key difference is that a mail-order advertiser can trace the results of an individual ad very precisely; a general advertiser ordinarily cannot do so, and therefore must connect the firm's total advertising to total sales. But advertising in one year affects sales in subsequent years as well as that year, which makes the relationship complicated, indeed. Nevertheless, I found a way to solve the problem for general advertising with a mode of thinking analogous to mail-order advertising.

I remember the morning hours at our dining room table, the first year in Urbana, trying to work out the formal statement of the solution—my first formal mathematical work—as among the most pleasurable hours of my life. In moments like that, work provided the rare surcease from depression. Nowadays, I could deal with such a problem in a much shorter period of time, with much less effort, because I have learned some simple tools of thought that enable me to see the fundamentals more quickly and more surely.

I entitled the paper "A Simple Model for Determining Advertising Appropriations," and I thought that it surely would be an academic and practical success. It turned out to be hard to publish (as with almost everything I write), and even after publication it made practically no impression; it has mostly been ignored to this day.

I am not surprised that advertisers still use the same crude rules of thumb that have been around for a hundred years, rather than rational methods for budgeting. I was surprised—and disappointed, of course—that my article did not at least catch on with academics who work in the field.

Later, Haim Levy and I generalized that article to a wider variety of situations, including some interactions among the variables, which required some complex algebraic manipulations. The formal elegance of our joint work—which undoubtedly was the cause of its being awarded the prize of "Best Theoretical/Empirical Research Paper," at a conference at which we gave it in 1977 (my only such elevation to even this modest height of honor), is all due to Haim. Notwithstanding this accolade, the paper fell unread to the bottom of the sea.

That collaboration with Haim was one of the joys of my intellectual life. It was like two jazz musicians who pass the theme back and forth from one to the other, so enhancing it in each transition that each is startled at how much good stuff the other has added. I am less sure about the practical usefulness of the article, however, a matter which always concerns me even if it does not concern others.

In 1964 the Surgeon General's famous report on cigarettes and health appeared. I think that I got hold of it and read it primarily because I was then a smoker, though I had sworn it off once in New York for quite a while; I read it and was convinced enough to write a short letter to *American Statistician* arguing with the great statisticians Fisher and Brownlee who were not yet convinced of the causal effect of smoking.

I was also interested in the report because of its connection with cigarette advertising. I naturally wondered about the effect of a ban on that advertising, so I worked out a cost-benefit analysis of cigarette smoking, leading to the conclusion that for every dollar of earnings that would be lost to people in the industry, 100 minutes of human life would be gained. Unfortunately I published this in the *Illinois Business Review*, because I was in a hurry to get it into print. IBR's editor V. Bassie told me that 10,000 copies were mailed out regularly, many to Washington, but I doubt that anyone paid any attention during the public discussion of the issue, judging by the absence of any feedback from it.

Necessary for that cost-benefit analysis was an explicit demographic analysis of the quantitative effect of various amounts of smoking on life expectancy. I was sure that this quantity had to have been calculated. But as I came to find out many more times in my work life, it is often the case that scientific studies that *must* have been done because they seem so logical, have in fact never been done. The estimates of the effect of smoking on life expectancy, in the appendix, were the first such estimates ever made.

I made them simply because I needed those magnitudes when writing about the ban of cigarette advertising. When I got over being amazed to find that no one had previously computed them and having made the estimates, I wrote the paper on "The Health Economics of Cigarette Consumption" as a vehicle for publishing the estimates to a wider audience. But because I published this as an appendix to an article on the economics of smoking, it disappeared from sight. I did not have the wit to try to publish them in a journal of demography and public health; these are the hazards of work by a young, ignorant researcher who does not know how to find wise advisors and ask them for advice—in fact, does not even have the wisdom to realize that he should do so.

Interestingly, I think my friendly and much-respected colleague in later years, physicist Bernie Cohen, later was the first to rediscover the same quantities.

During the first years at the University of Illinois, I explored a wide variety of other topics in connection with advertising. One set of studies asked the same questions about advertising that economics asks about prices and costs; for example, how do forces such as *(a)* cost, and *(b)* the number of competing firms, influence the amount of advertising that firms do? Another set of studies used data from the advertising industry to throw light on more general questions in microeconomics, such as: how is the price of retail newspaper advertising affected by the number of newspapers in a city? I did many of these studies together with master's degree students in advertising doing their theses.

One of these studies looked at mergers among advertising agencies as a source of information on the disputed topic of whether mergers have a positive or negative effect on the merging entities. Advertising agencies have a major research advantage that they are much more like each other than almost any other collection of firms that might be studied; therefore, comparisons among them are relatively clean and easy. The result seemed to be in favor of firms that did not merge, but the sample of mergers was too small to be very conclusive. At the end of the 1980s, however, my son Daniel came back to the topic for a bachelor's honors thesis at the University of Wisconsin, using the much larger sample that had accumulated over the years. Afterwards, he and I and Manouchehr Mokhtari cleaned up the work, found that the merging firms really do worse, and published the results as an article, a nice thing to do with one's son.

I always find it useful to estimate a writer's general excellence by his or her soundness on a subject I know well. As I noted in Chapter 00, John Galbraith frequently wrote about the power of advertising over people as if commercial speech has the power of a Svengali. Clearly Galbraith had never himself attempted to persuade people to buy a commercial product with advertising; if he had, he would have known how difficult it is to do so. As from time to time I have read him on other subjects, too, I concluded that he was the "wrongest" economist of our times, with the exception of (the legacy of) John Maynard Keynes. I'd love to write an article assessing Galbraith's record if I could find a journal or magazine that would print my views. (But I am saved by the difficulty of finding publishing outlets from wasting an even bigger part of my life than I do on such foolish forays.)

Here arises a most interesting question: So what if someone is wrong every time? Does that mean that one does not enjoy life, a professorship at Harvard, become president of the American Economic Association, and be appointed ambassador of the United States to India? Of course not; a lifetime replete with gross error—even containing *only* errors—is no bar to success with the mass media, the public, and even academic professions.

Galbraith's one useful discovery was about how to influence an academic profession such as economists by way of a book widely read by the lay public. I read his comment about that and remembered it later; it was the basis of my strategy with population economics and *The Ultimate Resource*; I'll say more about this later.

In trying to understand the nature of advertising, I found that advertising was sometimes said to be an *example* of something called "product differentiation" and sometimes a *cause* of it. So I tried to make sense of the confusing concept of product differentiation. For a long time I struggled without success. Then the answer hit me in the midst of a boring movie, and I remember being hardly able to wait for the show to end so that I could get home and set pen to paper. Grappling with the notion of product differentiation was one of the most frustrating and enjoyable experiences of my life.

The solution lay with looking for an operational definition of the concept. Or if one chooses, one may think of this as philosophical linguistic analysis, showing that "product differentiation" in Chamberlin's original usage is simply a tautology. Though the linguistic analysis itself is not simple because the concept was originally set forth in exquisitely complex fashion, the philosophical principle is clear-cut.

After one takes into account Stigler's criticism of the concept of the "group" in Chamberlin's supposed classic work and the concept of product differentiation as I discussed it in my paper, I don't think there is anything much left of Chamberlain's monopolistic competition except an idea that everybody thinks he or she understands but does not understand.

But of course the paper was not suitable for an economics journal, being only "philosophic" in its mode of analysis. So I had to publish in the excellent philosophy journal *Ethics*, which took it because of its linguistic analysis. The many negative referee's comments I received in the process of seeking publication exemplified two well-known remarks on innovation: Schopenhauer said that every original idea is first ridiculed, then attacked, then taken for granted; and Charles F. Kettering remarked, "First they tell you you're wrong, and they can prove it. Then they tell you you're right, but it's not important. Then they tell you it's important, but they've known it all along." I got all of these responses, and two exactly contradictory ones arrived with the same rejection letter.

It would be interesting to trace systematically the history of the concept of product differentiation. For years product differentiation was the rage; the only economist who stayed away from it was Milton Friedman. Then, without controversy—and certainly with no reference to Stigler's or my attack upon it—the concept began to fade. After appearing in several editions of Samuelson's *Principles*, for example, it disappeared. It would be illuminating to understand how this came about.

In 1970 the University of Illinois Press published a book of my collected studies of advertising. Before it came out, I stood in the shower and imagined a review in a technical journal that would begin, "This is a masterpiece." Then I laughed at how the imagination can create flights of delicious fancy no matter how unlikely they are. The first (and only) review a year later began, "This is a disappointing book."

The only positive notice of the book came in a newspaper column in a Chicago paper. The columnist noticed that I had ended the book, not with the obligatory, "This subject needs more research", but rather with "[T]he economic study of advertising is not deserving of great attention." I appreciated his fine eye for a remark that few would notice. But he didn't bother to mention the name of the author of the book in the column; an acquaintance guessed the identity by chance. Such is the life of academic book scribblers. I began to think that I have a special genius for obscurity, a conviction that was deepened by my experiences throughout the 1970s. It didn't end quite that way, though.

Before leaving the subject of advertising, here is summary at the end of the book:

NUTSHELL SUMMARY

This is my overall assessment of advertising in the economy and society.

First, there is no question but that much of advertising is useful and important economically and without grave danger to society; industrial advertising and department store advertising are leading examples. In the main, no one objects to either the presence or the nature of these branches of advertising, and hence there is no issue for analysis and argument.

Second, those branches of advertising which are most in dispute—advertising for such products as beer, autos, soap, and aspirin—do not seem to have much

> effect upon the economy in any way, direct or indirect, and hence from an economic point of view it is immaterial whether they are present or absent. (However, it must be noted that it would be operationally difficult to get rid of any branch of advertising without also getting rid of branches of advertising that are valuable.) All this implies that the economic study of advertising is not deserving of great attention except for special problems, e.g., the television rate structure. (As the reader may realize, this is not a congenial point at which to arrive after spending several years working on the subject.)
>
> Third, it follows that if there are important issues in advertising they concern esthetics and morals, and advertising should be studied in those contexts. (Simon, Julian L., *Issues in the Economics of Advertising*, 1970, pp. 284–5).

Given that conclusion about the study of advertising, I began to look for another main subject of inquiry. A wise step would have been to identify some great figure in economics whose work I particularly respected and apprentice myself to him or her. But this thought never occurred to me. It was entirely foreign to my life—one of the ways in which my independence has been too great and therefore costly.

In my first semester I was assigned to teach a course to masters and Ph.D. students on research methods. I also taught a course in advertising media, a topic about which I knew nothing, and I studied the textbook just ahead of the class, probably the only time in my professorial career that I did this. I was delighted to teach research methods because the topic had always interested me. When at the University of Chicago and still a graduate student, Phil Ennis was about to teach such a course, I gratuitously gave him an outline of what I thought such a course should include.

As I proceeded through the semester, I got the idea that the research process embodied a series of efforts to surmount obstacles to knowledge. Once this thought came to me, I found the same idea expressed in various forms in books on research methods in various fields. But I decided to proceed beyond the observation and organize the course around the various obstacles rather than various techniques, the traditional mode of organization. (Later I read George Stigler cleverly defining a business as a collection of devices to overcome obstacles to profit, and I have since quoted that many times though it is really a very partial definition.)

The second year I taught the course, 1964, I decided to write a text using the obstacles approach. As I proceeded with it, I found it necessary to modify that approach and make it only part of the book, but I was, and am, still satisfied with the value of this approach.

Because I considered that I was being paid to do research on advertising, I wrote the textbook in the evening, on my "own" time. I put great pressure on myself to do so. Rita was pregnant, but we still had no children, so outside distractions were at a minimum.
Work was the only way to hold my depression at bay, even a little. So I pressed on and on, harder and harder.

After awhile, I began to feel some stomach pains and experienced some diarrhea. And it got worse. But still I pressed on. Eventually I went to a doctor and he diagnosed a nervous stomach—essentially exhaustion of my insides from the overly hard work I was forcing on them.

In the short run, I had almost no ability to work for a few weeks. Then I could work only for a relatively short time before needing to stop for a rest. And true to the doctor's diagnosis and a description I read in (I thought, but can't find it now) Richard Dana's *Two Years Before the Mast*, it took two years before I was at full strength. Even after that, whenever I pushed myself too hard, my stomach would pain me, making me stop. It therefore served as an excellent warning mechanism, forcing beneficial rest upon me. Later on I adopted the habit of never working when I am tired, but sleeping more frequently. Yet more than 30 years later, my gut still remembers the insult it received then, and I cannot sit comfortably if my belt is tight.

Eventually I completed a short and rough draft of the research methods text that was entitled *Basic Research Methods in Social Science*, and I sent it off searching for publishers. Perhaps in part because the draft I sent out looked so crude (I had not learned how responsive academics are to appearances of copy, unlike magazines and advertising agencies), I got a flock of rejections. Finally I got an acceptance from Random House, which it turned out was a subsidiary (or the reverse) of Alfred Knopf which had already rejected it, and the editor who signed the contract was the same one who had signed the rejection for Knopf.

The book was accepted because it was sent to Hanan Selvin for review. Hanan was a fine sociologist, statistician, and methodologist, as well as a remarkable (and voluminous—actually sometimes his comments were *too* voluminous) academic editor. He also appreciated at least one of the understated throwaway jokes he found in the typescript, drew a happy face next to the joke, and wrote on the typescript,

"This will be fun to edit." Hanan and I later became and remained close friends until his death.

Another line of work also came out of my business experiences before becoming a professor. Alfred Marshall advised every economist to read regularly the trade journals for at least one industry, but this wise dictum is widely honored in its breach.

While I was still in the mail-order business on my own, I did some consulting for a liquor trade association. The elasticity of demand—the extent to which liquor sales are affected by a change in price—is a key issue in industry lobbying against tax increases. In advance of a legislative hearing, the director asked me to prepare a statement. In the past the association had offered some carefully chosen examples, apparently showing that the elasticity with respect to price is high, and therefore states would lose revenue if they raise taxes. When I went to the literature to find scientifically solid estimates, I found lots of fancy econometric studies, but none that seemed reliable. None of the many methods tried, many of them extremely complex, seemed very persuasive to me. So I went back to first principles—as is my wont, and as has proven to be the greatest strength of my work, and a source of the novelty that it possesses.

After much meditation, it occurred to me that with a simple set of adjustments, comparison of the sales before and after state changes in liquor tax laws should yield a reliable answer. But before I had an opportunity to do the research, I was fired, for reasons I never understood; the likeliest explanation is that my poking around in the files for data of various kinds that would support basic research in the economics and marketing of liquor was interpreted as suspicious activity.

The next year, after I began teaching advertising at the University of Illinois, I did the simple calculations for the liquor study. After writing up the results, I sent the study to *Econometrica*, then the most high-powered mathematical-statistical journal. To my great surprise and delight, after a good many months the article was accepted for publication. This was amazing because the article contained not a single equation in algebra (though it did contain an equation in plain English), probably the first time in the history of the journal that such a "mathematically unsophisticated" article had been published.

Sidenote: Even with the total absence of algebraic notation, I erred in one of the key words in the single formula, interchanging one variable for another. Luckily, the obvious error is easy for anyone to spot who might later choose to use the method.

The explanation for the happy accident of the article being accepted is that the referee was the world-class statistician Herman Wold, too capable a man to be put off by the lack of mathematical dazzle. He requested the editor to put me in touch with him because he wanted to tell me about a similar piece of work he had done in Sweden with postal rates, though he had never analyzed the method or written it up.

In the course of correspondence with Wold, he sent me a couple of papers on the formal analysis of causality. These led to my most challenging and deepest work, that on causality, discussed in Chapter 00.

Another sidenote: I hired the wife of another young professor to perform the algebraic calculations on the liquor elasticity study. But when she finished I noticed that her work was shot through with errors. So I hired another person. When the second person was finished, and her work seemed clean, I compared her estimate with the estimate calculated by the first woman. They were almost identical—a nice demonstration of the important "law of errors" (with maybe some luck thrown in).

Twenty years later, Badi Baltaggi brought this work up-to-date and ingeniously allowed for interstate movement of sales. It pleased me greatly that his estimate was much the same as mine; together, the results still constitute the best estimate of this socially important parameter, I believe.

It was happenstance that I chose the same title—"quasi-experimental method"—as did the wonderful methodologist Donald Campbell working in psychology and sociology. He meant something a bit different than I, however; all interrupted time-series are included in his concept, whereas I include only those situations where there are nonchanging "control" situations against which to compare the "experimental" situation.

Given that the quasi-experimental method worked so well for liquor, why not use it for cigarettes, whose tax situation is much the same as that of liquor? So I again illustrated its power with a product similar in its regulatory conditions. The work was "The Price Elasticity of the Demand for Cigarettes in the United States," (with Herbert C. Lyon). This study provided an opportunity to develop additional ways to exploit the method.

In 1963 George Stigler gave a lecture at the University of Illinois in which he said that regulation does not affect the price outcome in an industry. The liquor industry seemed to contradict this statement; where the retail stores were state-owned (16 states) prices tended to be lower than where they were privately owned (26 states), I thought. I guessed that the study would take a day to do; it took months. But the answer did shake out that way—at that time.

In the 1980s, my son David (as part of a senior honors thesis at Johns Hopkins) and I (after he turned in the thesis) returned to the topic. We found that the situation as of 1983 had changed drastically since my original publication in 1966. The states had reduced the extent of regulation on private stores that had kept the prices higher in the 1960s, and the result came to be what free-market economists would expect.

20

Research on Population Economics

Again the serendipity of negative events: If my department head Charles Sandage had not tossed me out of the Department of Advertising at the University of Illinois, I would not have been free to wind down my studies of advertising and move on to other topics. After he had done so and I had moved to the College of Commerce, I could comfortably choose to work on whatever I liked.

Once I had decided that I would stop working on the economics of advertising and turn my attention to another topic, I began a mental survey of possibilities. For two years, I devoted the last hour of almost every evening to mulling the question: What topic should I study? For example, I seriously considered health economics, but I decided that the major questions had already been asked and answered.

Perhaps it would have been better if I had considered this question at an hour of the day when my mind was fresh and not just when I was tired; this aspect of time use became decisive in my conquest of depression, as you may read in Chapter 00. The difficulty to be overcome is that I always am constrained by a powerful drive to do *productive* work in my prime time when I am fresh, and I feel as if I am cheating someone or something if I use that time for such matters as thinking about my research future—or writing this autobiography! Only telling myself that I am "retired" will ever relieve me of that pressure.

When I began the study of demographic economics in 1966, continuing until about 1968, I believed that rapid population growth was the main obstacle to the world's economic development and one of the two main threats to humankind (nuclear war being the other). I had recently come across an article on population growth in the *New York*

Times Magazine that showed the usual scary graph of supposed exponential growth in world population size, and I had assumed that the accepted view, as presented in that article, was scientifically sound. It seemed obvious that the world's population was growing too fast, and I decided to use my skills in economics and marketing to help the world contain its "exploding" population. So I enlisted in the great war to have fewer human beings. My work was intended as a contribution to that cause.

It has been of some importance to my credibility that I began to work in the field of population economics for the same reason that many others do: I thought population growth, along with all-out war, to be one of the two fearsome threats to mankind and civilization; I did not come from another ideological direction. And I could not be accused of going in the direction I did because of Catholic religious views, a stick that was used to beat Colin Clark, a great pioneer in the field.

My first article was in the Population Association of America's journal *Demography* (in 1968). Entitled "Marketing Correct Methods for Promoting Family Planning," it was a rejoinder to an article by Donald Bogue, the editor of *Demography* and a well-known sociologist-demographer, entitled, "Some Tentative Recommendations for a 'Sociologically Correct' Family Planning Communication and Motivation Program in India". Bogue's piece was entirely innocent of advertising and marketing knowledge, and it reached unsound conclusions about how to market birth control, so I decided to correct it.

I requested of Bogue that the piece be published under a pen name, because I was afraid that an advertising-related article as my first entry in the field would typecast me incorrectly as a marketer rather than an economist. My request must have reached him too late, because the piece ran under my name. Lo and behold, a quarter-century later those anti-population-growth and anti-immigration persons (such as Paul Ehrlich) and organizations (such as Federation for American Immigration Reform in a 1996 pamphlet) attacked me on just those grounds, by writing:

> Simon is little more than an information packager, i.e., a 'spin control' expert. This should come as no surprise. Simon is a professor of marketing, not a demographer or labor economist. Nevertheless, his writings appear to have had a disproportionate impact in shaping public and policymaker views on immigration when compared with the work of the academic experts whose works he selectively quotes and whose data he selectively repackages. (p. 30)

(The FAIR pamphlet also suggests that "Julian Simon should be exiled from any serious discussion of the effects of immigration on the United States, past, present, or future" [p. 1]. I'm flattered.)

I then set forth to produce new empirical and theoretical research from the standpoints of both economics and marketing. And miracle of miracles! When for a brief time (and luckily I published almost no work on the subject before I learned better), I joined the population-control movement—it was and is a "movement" in the sociological sense. For the first time in my life I found myself part of a mutual support group. For example, Steven Enke, an economist who had written a famous article showing how to calculate the value of averted lives had made a fundamental technical error, I found. I analyzed the matter and found an ingenious and technically correct procedure (though one I would certainly not advocate today), and I sent the article to him privately. I quickly received a phone call, saying, "That's wonderful, you've discovered an important error." That sort of behavior in the academic profession is exceedingly rare. I basked in the warmth of the sense of community, as never before. I was so glad to be part of such a network of mutual support and encouragement that I made mention of that fact in a footnote in the article.

As of 1967 I even felt that vigorous population-control action was called for. Frank Notestein had founded the Population Council and also the preeminent Office of Population Research at Princeton. I ran into him in an elevator at a meeting about 1968, and I seized the opportunity to recommend the urgency of starting money-incentive programs in India and elsewhere to induce couples to refrain from having more than (say) two children. Notestein responded to me with the calmness of age, not disagreeing with the point but suggesting that it was worth proceeding deliberately with such matters. Of course I silently criticized his caution in the face of what I considered to be a raging inferno of a social problem. Because of my own experiences, I understand the impetuousness of environmental activists now.

As late as 1969, Parker Mauldin of the Population Council arranged a trip for me to India to look over prospects for incentive schemes, though about that time my ideas were changing rapidly. And Bernard Berelson, who then ran the Population Council, offered me a job that would put my marketing skills to work; we had met when he came to Chicago as the member of the oversight committee at the completion of the Library Use Study.

I set forth to master the literature of population economics, the theory and facts of my intended life work. The then-standard formal economic theory of population (which had hardly changed since Malthus and of which there was little except for the book by Ansley Coale and Edgar Hoover, which adds little to Malthusian diminishing returns) asserted that a higher population growth implies a lower standard of living due to capital dilution. Before he invented "Keynesian economics," J. M. Keynes was one of the most fervent of all Malthusians, but later recanted for a while when it seemed to him as if population growth could, within the Keynesian framework, cure economic stagnation, but he later reverted back to Malthusianism.

While in Israel in 1968 I began a long treatise on the economics of population, taking as my point of departure the Coale-Hoover simulation model of the effects of population growth in India. Ansley Coale may remember a discussion between us in his office in June 1967 to that effect. That volume was the origin of my 1977 book, which arrived at quite contrary conclusions.

By 1969, however, my reading on the effects of population growth had led me into confusion. The first challenge to my beliefs came from the empirical correlations (or rather, noncorrelations) between the observed simple relationship of population growth and the rate of economic growth. The then-recently-published cross-sectional and time-series studies of nations presented by Simon Kuznets and Richard Easterlin, together with the historical allusions of Alfred Sauvy and Colin Clark, did not confirm the conventional theory. These data did not then persuade me that population growth is good; I thought that the data were too weak for that. But the data were strong enough to cause me to distrust the Malthusian theorizing which is the basis of almost all academic strictures about population growth's ill effects. Shaken by this contradiction between the bare theory and the bare facts, I sought a reconciliation. So I dropped my original, unthinking assumption about the evils of more people. My work in the field since then has followed that course, and by 1972 or 1973 I was satisfied that I had found a better theory.

The difference between me and most others was that I took the data seriously, whereas they assumed that the Kuznets-Easterlin conclusion must be some sort of an aberration and paid them no attention. It is important that I reached the conclusions and beliefs that I now hold because of the facts and analyses contained in the writings of my predecessors and because of the results of my own work as summarized in my 1977 book (which had largely been completed by 1973), rather than because I started with an ideological predisposition toward them. As I have said, I began this work with the prevailing popular view: that population growth is a menace to the world. It was this concern over that supposed menace that led me to the study of population economics in the first place. Furthermore, my early articles in this field were straightforward efforts to help reduce population growth, though luckily I had no opportunity to do so.

Again, it was only when I could not square the statistical facts with the standard theory that I was led to question the prevailing view and also to inspect my own values. One does not change one's mind easily about a subject like this, especially when one has made a professional investment in a viewpoint. To repeat once more, it was not my preexisting beliefs, either philosophic or religious, that altered my assessment, but rather the statistical facts as I saw them.

Studies based on as many countries as possible, showing the lack of correlation between a country's population growth rate and the rate of its economic development, have continued to be the most important evidence in population economics through the 1990s because of their generality and their analytical dominance over conclusions drawn only from handpicked samples of countries. The absence of a negative statistical relationship shows that within a century, or within even as short a time as a quarter of a century, the positive benefits of additional people at least balance the short-run costs. Much of the work that I did in the 1970s—both theoretical and empirical—was intended to illuminate this fundamental broad fact by studying the forces that offset the simplest Malthusian diminishing returns. These factors include longer hours of work, additional investment in private holdings and public infrastructure such as roads, and the creation and implementation of new technology.

To bring out the main idea, over the years I have sought various other methods than these aggregate correlations for economic growth with population growth and density. One such method was to marshal data on the three available pairs of otherwise-comparable countries—East and West Germany, North and South Korea, China and Taiwan—that differ in their political structures. The rates of economic development since their splits after World War II were much higher for the "free-enterprise" members of the pairs than for the "central planning" members, though their fertility patterns were not different. This demonstrates both that population growth does *not* account for economic development and also that political structure *does* influence it heavily.

Now back to the later 1960s and how my thought developed about the consequences of population growth. (It is difficult to proceed at once on the two paths of logical substantive development and chronological development without creating confusion.)

I found my way to Ester Boserup's *The Conditions of Economic Growth*, which directly contradicts first-edition Malthusianism with respect to subsistence agriculture. A work I did not find then, because it was too far ahead of its time, was Theodore Schultz's article showing that farmland was becoming less scarce and less important over time, despite increasing population—a truly amazing and prescient conclusion when it was published in 1951.

My reading included the great 1963 book *Scarcity and Growth* by Harold Barnett and Chandler Morse, which showed that natural resources were becoming more available rather than more scarce. The data and analyses of Barnett and Morse seemed completely persuasive to me, but most of the profession continued to think as it always had. I remember taking a walk with David Levhari, visiting from Israel about 1972, talking about population and resources, and then finding a secondhand copy of Barnett and Morse in the YMCA's basement bookstore, which I bought for him; I was disappointed that when I asked him about it later, when he had at least looked at it, that the book had not effected any change in his thinking, though his own work touched near the subject.

One spring day about 1969, while my thoughts about population growth were still in flux, I visited the U.S. AID Office on the outskirts of Washington to discuss a project intended to lower fertility in less-developed countries. I arrived early for my appointment, so I strolled outside on the plaza in the warm sunshine. As I leaned over the rail, I noticed below the plaza a road sign that said "Iwo Jima Memorial." There came to me the memory of reading a eulogy delivered by a Jewish chaplain over the dead on the battlefield at Iwo Jima, saying something like, "How many who would have been a Mozart or a Michelangelo or an Einstein have we buried here?" Then I thought, have I gone crazy? What business do I have trying to help arrange it that fewer human beings will be born, each one of whom might be a

Mozart or a Michelangelo or an Einstein—or simply a joy to his or her family and community, and a person who will enjoy life?

Even after I learned that the standard outlook was ass-backwards, I still held the view that the U.S. as a nation, and each of us as individuals, could, with clear conscience, help foreign countries attain the population goals they set for themselves. Indeed, much of my 1977 book *The Economics of Population Growth* is concerned with devices—cost-benefit analysis and marketing plans—that could help other countries make decisions and plans to lower population, though between the time of submission of the typescript and its publication, my beliefs were still evolving. Of course I still believe it is one of the good works of all time to help families have families the size they wish, either by helping limit fertility or cure infertility by making knowledge and aids available. This is very different from much of what emerges as a result of present national policies.

Starting about 1970, I set out on a series of studies, lasting through the 1970s and into the 1980s, to test, one by one, the key elements in the Malthusian analysis of the effect of population growth. At first the studies were mostly empirical but later many were also theoretical. I and collaborators (mostly students) examined various of the underlying relationships concerning population growth, size, and density, and economic growth. These included the effect of population growth on the construction of irrigation systems, the proportion of the labor force in agriculture, the amount of education students receive, and the effect of density on the rate of economic growth.)

An example of these studies: Because prices for copper, wheat, oil and other resources are much the same all over the world (aside from tax and transportation costs), there is no obvious way to examine, in a sample of independent locations, how population growth affects those prices. And the Barnett and Morse book mentioned earlier shows very convincingly that the historical course of all those prices is downward even as world population has been growing. Therefore I turned to the effect of population growth on agricultural productivity.

I experienced great difficulty in publishing my work. An example was a critique of the central study in the field, the book by Coale and Hoover. I made an argument—very strong, I think—that that book was fundamentally flawed in a variety of ways; most obviously, the book added up to not much more than that the same postulated total output would be divided by a larger number of persons, yielding a lower calculated per-person income; this "conclusion" derived from the fact that the analysis is mostly confined to a sufficiently short period of time that additional births have an effect on consumption but no effect on production. The piece was rejected by journal after journal, and only appeared at last in my 1977 book. Of course one should not be surprised at the inability to publish such a criticism of the dominant (indeed the *only*) viewpoint. But the inevitability makes the outcome no more welcome.

For two years or so around 1969, late each evening I would wander around the living room and kitchen and puzzle about how to reconcile (a) Malthus's view of innovation as a cause of increasing population growth, with (b) Boserup's view of innovation as a result of population growth. Boserup's model of population-pushed adoption of techniques from an already existing reservoir of technology is not consistent with observed ups' and downs' in the standard of living throughout history—perhaps most notably in Ireland in the decades around the Famine, and in Europe in the centuries before and after the Black Death. Finally I realized that Malthus and Boserup had in mind different sorts of innovations. The paper I wrote showed how the analyses of both Malthus and Boserup are correct descriptions for particular types of innovations, and how together they convey a more general and sound (though more complex) picture of the overall process of demographic economic growth than either alone.

Boserup's theory that increasing population density causes shifts to more labor-intensive agricultural techniques has been one of the keystones of my overall thought since I learned that the aggregate data did not square with the conventional received theory. The theory I just described fit Boserup's theory into a more general framework that also includes Malthus's theory, and therefore makes it even stronger. Boserup's empirical evidence was comprised of case studies, and one inevitably desires a more "objective" and systematic test. I therefore undertook a systematic, cross-country test of one measurable step in agricultural intensification, the extent of irrigation. I found that population density has a strong positive relationship to the proportion of a country's cultivated land that is irrigated. In light of the fact that agriculture typically at that time accounted for half or more of the value of a poor country's output and given that irrigation systems are a key element of capital used in agriculture, this finding suggests that additional people lead to an increase in agricultural saving. The paper goes on to compare this partial savings effect with estimates of the aggregate savings effect of population growth presented in the literature.

The endpoint of greater population growth is greater population density. So Ph.D. candidate Roy Gobin and I examined the data relating density in various countries to rates of economic growth. We found a positive rather than negative relationship; higher population density conduces to faster growth.

For years I tried to convince people working with cross-national data to include a density variable to recheck this result. It was gratifying, therefore, when in a careful study with additional data done in the early 1990s, Allen Kelley and Robert Schmidt confirmed this finding.

Taking a different tack, Ph.D. candidate Douglas Love and I studied the relationships among "City Size, Prices, and Efficiency for Individual Goods and Services." This is another exercise in checking out the supposed negative effects of population growth. Doug did this work for a thesis in 1976. A paper by him containing the price results appeared in the 1977 annual *Research in Population Economics* that I edited. But it took us thirteen years and about twenty rejections before any journal agreed to publish the main paper.

A contemporary version of the Malthusian nightmare imagines that additional people cause more congestion in public facilities and does not take into account the increase in public facilities induced by the additional people. A study with master's student (in advertising) Donald Glover of the effect of population density on road building came next. The results were astonishingly neat: At any level of income, higher population density is associated with a higher level of road density, which is important because the presence of roads is a crucial element in agricultural and economic development.

Eventually, some economists who believed that population growth was a bad thing (especially those who worked for the World Bank and similar organizations) recognized that natural-resource shortage was not a vital issue, because resource supplies were increasing rather than decreasing. They then turned to the purported ill effect of population growth by way of reducing the quantities of education that people get. Therefore, Adam Pilarski and investigated whether population growth diminishes the amount of education children get, comparing nations with different amounts of population growth. We found no negative effect, counter intuitive though that may be; countries with higher population growth somehow find the resources to provide as much education as other countries.

Then I did another study with Adam Pilarski of the unemployment effect. Writings about population economics by non economists, and even by economists, are full of propositions simply assumed to be true because they are "obvious common sense." Too often "common sense" means looking only at the immediate direct effects and neglecting the indirect and diffuse effects; this is the defect in thinking illuminated by Bastiat.

The effect of population growth upon unemployment is a classic example of this fallacy. People have worried since time immemorial that a greater supply of labor would result in greater difficulty in finding jobs; this proposition makes perfect common sense. It is implicitly assumed—by too many economists along with laypersons—that the number of workplaces is fixed, in the same fashion that the number of niches for particular species of bird are fixed in a given area. An increased number of potential workers must therefore imply more people without jobs. Wholly neglected is job *creation*, which is the central process in an advancing, growing economy. Additional workers not only take jobs, they make jobs. They spend their earnings, thereby increasing the demand for goods and for workers to produce them, which in turn produces more income and more new jobs. This process continues until the economy approaches a new equilibrium, with the same rate of unemployment as before. This is why unemployment is no higher in large countries than in small countries, and no higher (probably much lower) now than in past centuries, on broad average.

The article with Pilarski subjected the "commonsense" proposition to systematic test. It examined the rates of unemployment in countries with differing relative sizes of youth cohorts. Looked at by itself as a partial effect, there is some negative relationship between the number of youths and the unemployment rate. But when a fuller model of the economy is specified and the offsetting positive effect of labor-force growth upon the rate of economic development is taken into account, much of the observed negative effect disappears. We also worked out a nice, simple theory to fit with the observed data.

The most important economic effect of a person in the long run is the new knowledge that the person creates. Of course not everyone supplies new knowledge, but a wide variety of people do improve the techniques with which they work and pass on the improved technique to others; it is not just the exceptional "geniuses" who advance technology; I originally owe this observation to Kuznets, but since then I have seen it made by others as well, for example, by Nathan Rosenberg. Nowhere is this more likely to be true than in farming.

It would not seem to require proof—except that various "authorities" did not accept the validity of the proposition—that if two countries are at similar levels of economic development, the country with the larger population will produce (that is, "supply") more new knowledge. But even respected scholars have argued against the plain meaning of this proposition. One argument (made by Ansley Coale) has been that the classical contributions of Greece arose from a tiny population and that small interwar Hungary produced a remarkable group of scientists; it is inferred that those populations were "sufficiently" large. But this line of thought stands up against neither simple logical analysis nor data showing that in those periods when Greece (also true for Rome) had a larger population, its discoveries were greater in number (Simon, *The Ultimate Resource* 1980; 1981, pp. 201–202).

So Doug Love and I studied "The Effect of Population Size and Concentration Upon Scientific Productivity". We found that the number of scientists is proportional to population, holding income constant. That is, *ceteris paribus*, a larger population implies more scientific activity. Scientific activity is roughly proportional to population size; that is, there is evidence for neither diseconomies nor economies of scale when the income level is allowed for. This piece was written under the pen name "Lincoln Pashute"—the first part being my middle name due to being born on Lincoln's birthday and the second part being Hebrew for "simple"—because it appeared in a volume of *Research in Population Economics*, which I edited and which contained two other of my articles. I did not think it looked good for the series to have so many pieces by one author, especially the editor. Also, I did not want it to appear (as was actually the case) that we were short of good submissions. Curious the devices that critics will use. In 1980 I referred to this selection in an article in *Science*, where I noted in the citation both the pen name and my own name as author. A critic of that same *Science* article subsequently charged me with concealing my authorship of the article for dishonest purposes.

Another thread in the general argument is the *demand* for new knowledge as a function of population size. An additional person spurs the creation and adoption of new knowledge through the demand mechanism as well as through the supply side. The demand effect should be especially operative in agriculture, particularly in earlier centuries when food accounted for the largest part of a person's consumption in value terms. So Richard Sullivan and I examined the relationship between the amount of new agricultural technology—as indicated by the number of patents and books published—and the population size of Great Britain between the middle of the sixteenth century and the middle of the nineteenth century. A model of the invention-innovation process is applied to the technological development of English agriculture between 1541 and 1850 to explain the amount of invention in farming. We use the number of titles of didactic books published on farming techniques and the number of agricultural patents issued as alternate measures of invention. Population, accumulated technology, and fluctuations in food prices are significant explanatory variables. Population growth speeds technological advance, we find. Though the data are crude, we detected an increase in technology production when population is larger and when food prices are higher. A larger stock of prior knowledge also increases the flow of new knowledge.

***

A fascinating episode in the sociology of thought occurred among economists at large and among many population economists in particular at the end of the 1960s. Though economists certainly did not exhibit the intensity of environmental alarm evident in the rest of the academic community—perhaps their views were moderated by the fundamental economic understanding that shortages lead to adjustments—even most economists forecast increasing shortages of natural resources. As Schumpeter put it about the propopulationist attitude in the seventeenth and eighteenth centuries, "Economists fell in with the humors of their age" (*Economic Doctrine and Method*, 1954, p. 251).

The saddest part of all this was how quickly economists departed from the fundamental intellectual glory of the field, the conception—dating back to David Hume and Adam Smith (or perhaps to Bernard Mandeville)—of macro adjustment to disequilibrium brought about by the spontaneous micro responses of individuals seeking to profit from the situation. In the case of natural resources, this social adjustment has in the past tended eventually to outweigh the forces that set in motion the movement toward greater scarcity.

I choose Paul Samuelson as an example of this dismaying phenomenon because his colleagues have regarded him as the most brilliant star in their firmament.

The span of time within which one considers the effects of the number of people upon the standard of living is a central issue. The most important effects are those that occur in the intermediate and long run, rather than in the very short run before there is an opportunity for society to adjust to the additional people. One of my main aims was to enlarge the time span within which the economics of population growth is commonly discussed. The too-short horizon of most conventional previous work such as the Coale-Hoover book that influenced world policies for a quarter century in population and various environmental works—30 years or less and sometimes as short as a single hot summer—has often led to fear-induced, overreactive governmental policies that have been costly in human lives as well as material.

More than a century ago, Frederic Bastiat's famous essay, "What is Seen and What is Not Seen," taught that economic policy analysis frequently is led into error by disregarding effects which are "unseen" because they are remote either in time or in causal nexus. Population economics requires the long view even more than do most other fields in economics, if for no other reason than that two decades must pass following the birth of a child before the important effects of that child begin to manifest themselves, effects that are easy to overlook when focusing attention on the costs incurred during childhood. Yet the field of population economics perversely has mostly stayed in the self-imposed straitjacket of short-run analysis, the "commonsense" period that so appeals to journalists; that short-run analysis boils down to the deduction that more people sharing the same output, or the same land and tools, implies less output per person.

Though the day-to-day work I have done in population economics has been intended to produce new knowledge by using technical analysis of models and data, the conclusions often have emerged as implicit criticisms of faulty thinking, especially the bad thinking that people consider to be "common sense" (for example, there *must be* a limit to agricultural production).

Since World War II, the fallacy of focusing on the short-run effects of population growth has caused (or allowed) such institutions as the World Bank, the U.S. State Department's Agency for International Development (AID), the United Nations Fund for Population Activities (UNFPA), and the environmental organizations to mis-analyze such world development problems as supplies of natural resources, starving children, illiteracy, pollution, and slow growth. Because these institutions have focused their attention on population growth, they have not recognized that the key factor in a country's economic development is its economic and political system. The centrality of the economic-political structure of a country is no longer the subject only of theory and ideology but now has been demonstrated conclusively by empirical analysis. This misplaced attention to population growth has resulted in disastrously unsound economic advice being given to developing nations.

Erroneous belief in the malign effects of population growth on economic development also has been the intellectual foundation for inhumane programs of coercion and the denial of families' freedom to make their own decisions about the number of children that they wish to bear and raise. At various times such policies have operated in the United States to sterilize blacks and the poor, as well as operating with particular severity upon the population-at-large during recent decades in China, Indonesia, and India. Many countries' use of government propaganda to have fewer children, programs which violate traditional values and cause lives never to be lived, also are based on this erroneous belief. Ironically, the long-run effect of these programs of propaganda and coercion is likely to be a lower standard of living than would otherwise be the case. This is another case of governmental infringement on liberty which is motivated by zeal but misdirected by ignorance. (It must be noted, however, that along with ignorance, religious animus, racism, and unscientific racist beliefs also are frequently implicated in these population-control activities).

When in later work I extended the horizon even further, one can see that the long-run effects of additional people are positive on balance and not just neutral, which is quite in contradiction to the conventional wisdom.

The most abstract outline of the central process that links population growth to long-run economic development is as follows: Increased numbers of consumers and/or an increase of income expand the demand for raw materials as well as finished products. The resulting actual and expected shortages force up prices of the natural resources. The increased prices trigger the search by business and scientists for new ways to satisfy the demand, and sooner or later new sources and innovative substitutes are found. Eventually these new discoveries lead to cheaper natural resources than existed before this process began, leaving humanity better-off than if the shortages had not appeared. Increased productivity of land and the development of new sources of energy moving from wood to coal to oil to nuclear power exemplify this process.

The long view in population economics includes long-run structural change that does not fit comfortably within the standard economic framework of optimal allocation of a given set of initial resources. New structural and technological developments often seem to appear unbidden and unbought, rather than as a deliberate tradeoff with other uses of inputs. Indeed, new developments often stem from human resources that would otherwise be devoted to leisure or to thinking about other intellectual subjects such as art and religion, unlike short-run investment which is often at the cost of consumption in industrial society.

The very long-run effects of demographic change—which occur over hundreds or thousands of years—include such phenomena as changes in the disease environment in response to changes in population density, structural alterations in the organization of society, and the development of cultural practices such as habits and rituals. These developments, particularly of cultural changes, may be thought of as evolutionary. I undertook systematic study of these phenomena only much later in the late 1980s and 1990s, in the context of understanding the causes of the long-run progress of humanity.

The field of population economics is striking for the number of propositions that everyone "knows" are true, which upon empirical investigation turned out not to be true at all. Most of the empirical studies mentioned above are exercises of that sort.

By the end of a long series of such investigations, I thought it safe to predict that each such expected negative effect would not appear. I also worried that arriving at this conclusion would lead to ill effects in my research, perhaps to snap judgments that are unwarranted. Luckily, this fear has not been realized—so far.

About 1972 I got to thinking more about the element of population growth in connection with what is called "neo-classical growth theory."

Because knowledge develops autonomously in that body of work that began with Robert Solow, that theory implies that faster population leads to a lower rate of economic growth. So I thought to make the growth of knowledge a function of the number of potential knowledge creators, which it clearly is.

My 1977 book, *The Economics of Population Growth*, included the results of some simulations of a macromodel with technological progress endogenous. The model's aim was to show that the standard result of growth theory—a faster rate of population growth implying a lower rate of growth of consumption—depended upon the absence of more people producing more knowledge.

In 1973, I think, I came to wonder about the possibility of an "optimum" rate of population growth in the context of such an abstract growth model. At first I thought that this was a wholly new idea. After digging deeper into the literature on growth theory, I found that the same idea had occurred to other writers earlier, including Kaldor and Nordhaus and especially Phelps, though the idea was more implicit than explicit in Phelps's model of optimum research and development. In sifting through this literature, I realized that the function I had earlier used is unreasonably responsive, whereas the function Phelps used could be admirably adapted to my purposes. I therefore went to work with the simulation method, broadening Phelps's function to include arguments for income and education. The simulations not only showed that the results converged to meaningful theoretical outcomes which had the properties of the "optimum" I sought, but also allowed intermediate-run (say, 30 to 200 years) assessments of the present value of different rates of population growth.

The reception of the paper by referees was horrendous. Mercifully, I cannot find them for publication.

About then, I asked Gunter Steinmann if he could solve the system analytically. And he did so. This time, the first journal to which the paper was sent accepted it, exceedingly speedily and without any revision required—an outcome almost unprecedented in my prior experience.

That model then became a centerpiece in my 1986 book on population growth and economic growth theory.

The second main line of theoretical analysis in my 1986 book mentioned above is a reexamination of the proposition implicit in Arrow's famous 1962 paper on learning-by-doing that more people do not imply a higher level of consumption. It turns out that Arrow's conclusion results from his use of equilibrium analysis, which is inappropriate for the purpose at hand. If one starts from first principles, one immediately sees that this is wrong, as can be seen in this analogy of haircutting: If Father Alpha has one son and Father Beta has twin sons, and both cut their sons' hair, both starting from the same level of skill, Father Beta will shortly have a higher level of skill than will Father Alpha due to more learning from more doing, leading to a higher level of consumption. (Inclusion of the role of capital in the analysis does not alter this conclusion.) The confusion arises from the fact that after the first haircut, the *rate of change* of skill will be the same for the two fathers, even though the *absolute* increases will be greater from week to week by Father Beta. This is a good example of how equilibrium growth-rate analysis can bewitch and obscure.

In light of this last remark, the reader may wonder why I wrote a book on growth theory. One reason is that nothing could have a prayer of altering belief in the standard growth-theoretic conclusion except another theory; empirical data alone will not suffice. Also, when the same framework is used for *short* periods to compare rates of increase—either of native births or of immigrants—the framework is not without meaning.

Referees insist that equilibrium analysis is the only acceptable way to view the problem, which, of course, leads them to accept Arrow's implicit conclusion and to reject that of Steinmann and me; they have not been troubled by the fact that equilibrium analysis conflicts with the simplest model of what the relevant facts are. They also have been distressed by this "attack" upon Arrow, a Nobel prizewinner. I have no rebuttal to that. The referees also objected with great vigor to my saying that Arrow's formulation misleads thought, and they seemed to take personally my criticism of him.

Prior to Steinmann joining me in this work, referees complained that the paper was "unfinished" and lacked "sophistication." Well, yes. Of course the main point was there, with sufficient argument to prove it. That is not enough, however, which seems to me a major problem with the economics publication system.

My writings in population economics have been evolutionary, and therefore each successive book contained material from articles and preceding books. The articles written in the 1970s provided background theory and empirical results for my 1977 book *The Economics of Population Growth* and my 1981 *The Ultimate Resource*. And the crude growth model in my 1977 book evolved into a spate of articles with Steinmann and then the 1986 *Theory of Population and Economic Growth*, which dealt with more-developed countries.

Population economics certainly is inherently interesting—its mechanisms, its contemporary phenomena, and its history of events and ideas. But it also is an intensely practical discipline. Its doctrines affect human life in the most fundamental sense: for example, millions of Chinese who would otherwise be brought into life are not born each year because of Chinese government policies based on unsound ideas about the effect of numbers upon the rate of economic development.

The work I have mentioned so far has been "positive economics"—that is, studies of how things are, rather than how they ought to be, or of whether an outcome is good or bad. Especially in the case of population growth, people want to know whether the effects of additional people on others are benign or malign.

My attention to the issue addressed here began when I read someone writing that "science shows" population growth to be a bad thing. One key idea arrived as I was dreamily looking out the window of the car as Rita was driving us through the Missouri Ozarks. The outcome of the analysis is stated in the title of the article (in hopes that this would attract attention to the article): "The Welfare Effect of an Additional Child Cannot be Stated Simply and Unequivocally".

The approach of that article typifies many pieces of my work: Resolve arguments by showing that there are many different cases to which different answers apply. It differs from the hundreds of other welfare analyses in that it examines a wide variety of cases and reaches different conclusions about different cases. I remember using this general approach as early as my second course in finance in 1958, when the instructor showed several "competing" methods of thinking about the cost of capital. I argued—using Ovid on love as an analogy—that the different methods are appropriate for different situations. But people involved in controversies like their controversies, and they don't want to have them resolved by someone showing that both sides are partly right.

***

The extent to which the course of economists' thinking about population changed in the 1980s, following *The Ultimate Resource*, which brought my work to the attention of the profession (see Chapter 00 popdiff) still is unclear, and the connection to my work is less clear still. In 1984, Lee wrote: "I think most scholars [population economists] would agree that rapid population growth is a development problem, but certainly not all do" (p. 130). The latter clause in Lee's assessment would not have been true ten or even five years earlier than 1984. Also in 1984, the World Bank—for many years the strongest and shrillest voice calling for reduction in the rate of population growth—did a complete about-face in its 1984 *World Development Report* and said that natural resources are not a reason to be concerned about population growth. On the other hand, in that year, as well-respected an economist as Nobelist Jan Tinbergen wrote: "[*C*]ontinued population growth constitutes a threat to humankind's welfare. . . . It is . . . highly desirable—in fact inescapable—that population growth be stopped as soon as possible . . . Among governments the one extreme is represented by the Chinese government, whose attitude is to be applauded . . . " (pp. 137–138).

In 1986, the National Research Council of the National Academy of Sciences went even further. A report on *Population Growth and Economic Development*, whose primary draft was written by Samuel Preston, almost completely reversed a 1971 report on the same subject from the same institution. On the specific issue of raw materials that has been the subject of so much alarm, NRC-NAS concluded: "The scarcity of exhaustible resources is at most a minor constraint on economic growth."

By the time of writing this in 1994, the intensity of concern clearly has diminished enormously, even among those economists who consider population growth a problem. It is safe to say that whereas most scholars in the field of population economics, along with most other demographers and laypersons writing about population, assumed through the 1970s that views on the subject were settled, all now agree that the subject can be described as "controversial."

U.S. foreign aid policies since the 1950s have been based on the version of the Malthusian theory provided by Coale and Hoover (1958). Therefore I took up the matter of population growth policy in less-developed countries. With the use of simple theoretical comparisons, I arrived at these conclusions: (1) A country's political and economic organizations—particularly market processes and the institution of private property—are the main influences upon the speed of a country's economic development, (2) A more dense population does not hamper population growth, and (3) U.S. foreign aid programs for "family planning" cause damage along with their benefits, and are politically dangerous.

Just for fun, I speculated that faster population growth leading to higher population size and density will, all else equal, lead to a lower propensity to make war for economic reasons. The reasoning is that the larger the population, the faster will operate the various mechanisms described in earlier essays that lead to growth in knowledge and increase in income.

***

When I have reviewed my work in the economics of population, it has seemed to me that I have simply pulled together theoretical links suggested by others into a more general theoretical structure and adduced chunks of empirical evidence developed by others and by myself in order to make the theoretical links credible. On rethinking, however, it seems to me that I may also claim credit for one or two of the links in the theory (though they may be pairs of smaller links). More generally, my contribution may be linking the various elements into a coherent structure.

***

What effect has my population work had? This is a difficult and delicate question for any author; one's hopes and fears cloud one's vision. In the introduction to my 1977 book that I asked him to write (after Kuznets turned me down), Joseph Spengler was kind enough to write: "*The Economics of Population Growth* is a path-breaking work . . . Simon advances what may be treated as a new paradigm in the Kuhnian sense" (Joseph J. Spengler, ex-president, Population Association of America), but there was absolutely no reaction other than a review in the *Journal of Political Economy* that got the key issue quite wrong, written by a student of Ansley Coale's, who was given the task when Coale turned it down. It is clear that, as recently as 1981, the point of view presented here was at the far outskirts of the field of population economics, espoused mainly by Colin Clark and (in muted fashion) Simon Kuznets. The "mainstream" economic demographers in the 1970s ranged somewhere between viewing population growth as *(a)* the *most* important, and *(b)* a *very* important, problem in economic development. Only a handful of economists or demographers then agreed with the general conclusions that emerge from this work.

There undoubtedly has been considerable change since then. The settled wisdom concerning population growth has been increasingly questioned in the 1980s, especially with respect to less-developed countries. It is not at all clear just how great that change has been. As of 1988, I read most writers on population economics as ranging somewhere between considering population growth *something* of a problem to considering it *totally unrelated* to economic development.

The shift in the mainstream viewpoint is evident in the great difference between the 1971 and the 1986 reports on the subject of the National Academy of Sciences. It is also evident in other recent representative reviews of the field, most of which remark on the changes in thinking that have occurred, though they themselves differ in their assessments of the extent of change as they also differ in their substantive conclusions; examples include Preston (1986); Kelley (forthcoming); Birdsall (forthcoming); McNicholl (1984); Horlacher (1986); Ahlburg (1987); McKellar and Vining (1987); Horlacher and McKellar (1987); also instructive is the variation in reviews of the 1986 NAS study, e. g. the symposium in *Population and Development Review* (1987).

I despair sometimes because I see no sign of it in citations in technical economic work. A few economists, however, have been kind enough to suggest that my work has had great influence.

> "Allen Kelley, an economist at Duke University, said [Simon] has 'mounted a challenge to the popular conception about population' that caused 'a rethinking of almost the entire scientific literature' . . . Fifteen years ago, Dr. Kelley said, economists thought that rapid population growth always led to economic decline. Thanks to Dr. Simon, 'maybe the majority' of academics studying population issues don't believe it anymore." Douglas Birch, *Baltimore Sun*, July 29, 1995, p. 2.

Few other economists are as generous in print as is Kelley, though some may say such things in private. Winston Churchill once remarked about the people who praise him privately to his face in the men's room and then abuse him in the press. He said he would prefer if they would abuse him in the men's room and praise him in the press. But no such luck. Some nonconomists have been more generous

"Julian Simon has been the dominant world figure in population economics over the nearly two decades that span the publication of these essays." Bill Gould, U. of Liverpool, in *Third World Planning Review*, Vol. 16, No. 1, p. 90

"Julian Simon . . . almost single-handedly transformed academic discourse on population issues." Doug Bandow, "A New Aid Policy for New World," *Policy Analysis*, May 15, 1995, p. 28.

***

Since Malthus and his frightening analysis, economics has been known as "the dismal science." It was only after working in the field for some time that I realized that the data point away from dismal conclusions by showing that population growth can contribute to a better future. So my work in economics is cheerful rather than dismal. My traverse from simple Malthusianism to the conclusions I have held since then shifted my worldview from pessimism to optimism. Now I believe that we need only forestall war to achieve a bright future for mankind.

I also believe that helping people fulfill their desires for the number of children they want—whether it be to increase or decrease fertility—is a wonderful human service. To persuade or to coerce couples to have fewer children than they would individually like to have—that is something entirely different.

In 1742 (first edition), David Hume wrote: "Multitudes of people, necessity, and liberty, have begotten commerce in Holland." That says a lot.

21

Reaching the Public with Facts about Population and Resources

Take your mind back to the period before the first Earth Day, April 19, 1970. It is difficult to imagine the feverish mood of the country then.

[T]he top-of-page headline story in the *Chicago Tribune* was "The Pollution of Earth: `I'm scared,'" with the subheadline "Air, Sea and Land—All Being Strangled." The story was typical of headlines all across the country: "I'm scared," said Joseph Sauris, 16, a sophomore at Maine East Township High School, Park Ridge. . . . "I don't like the idea of leaving a dead world to my children. That might sound like a cliché, but it may be the truth someday."

In Champaign-Urbana, the main activity for Earth Day itself was to be an address in an auditorium of about 2500 people by Alan Guttmacher of Planned Parenthood. The organizers wanted some discussants for a panel after Alan Guttmacher gave the main speech, and of course as an organizer you always want to find at least one discussant who will not agree with the speaker. It had already gotten about that I didn't share the mainstream view, so they asked me to be the token opposition.

When an organizer called, I asked who else would speak. When I was told that one of the speakers would be a professor named Paul Silverman, I declined the invitation. He asked why. I explained that one of Silverman's students had invited me to speak to a large popular New Age class that Silverman gave on social issues connected with biology. When I did so, I found it a very ugly experience because of Silverman's remarks to the class—at very great length, and with a very personal cast. I didn't want to subject myself to that sort of thing again, and before a very large audience.

So the man on the phone went back to the committee of organizers, and then he called again and said, "Look, we'll fix it so we all win."

I said, "How are you going to do that?"

"You tell us what rules you want for the discussion, and we'll make them so," he said.

Though with trepidation, I specified that each of the panelists would get to speak exactly the same length of time and no more, which they said would be ten minutes. I also specified that each speaker must address himself (all men) to the main speaker and not to me. And I also specified that Silverman would speak before and not after me. It is a sign of my concern that I made these arrangements; I have never done anything like this before or since.

So I did it, and it was much worse than I imagined. After Guttmacher spoke the moderator called on me, and I made the mistake of not saying that it was Silverman's turn; in front of 2000 people, I had no such poise. So I spoke. I provided some facts about population and resources—the same facts that have been the staples of my general talks on the subject since then—plus a few remarks pointing out that any conclusions about population policy must rest on values as well as scientific analysis, because scientific analysis by itself cannot serve as such a basis. The applause was very tepid.

Silverman then spoke and immediately addressed himself to me. He continued to speak for some twenty-odd minutes saying some rather ugly things about me. Upon ending he received a thunderous ovation.

There follows a large chunk of Silverman's talk, transcribed from a tape of the radio transmission. So much space is devoted to it here because it is an excellent example of the sort of discussion this topic provokes; this talk can serve as an exemplar for thousands. It also will show you the comments that incensed me. I do not have Silverman's permission to print it, but I doubt that it was copyrighted, and it was broadcast over the radio.

Paul Silverman:

Ladies and gentlemen, fellow students and Biology 199, we are honored indeed to have you with us tonight and this week, as you know, we are talking about matters existing of concern to you for many years. Your humanity and your expertise are invaluable resources not only internationally but to us as Americans.

We are faced with a crisis involving the future of our country and indeed the world, the seriousness of which cannot be exaggerated. Scholarly studies by a wide variety of organizations which include among them the World Academy of Art and Science, the National Academy of Science, the National Research Council, the Food and Agricultural Organization, the World Health organization as well as numerous other groups and individuals, all one that we are in the process of destroying and polluting our environment at a rate which may soon put its redemption beyond human intervention. All these studies agree that inextricably involved in the pollution of our environment is the growth of our population. These two interrelated problems cannot be dealt with independently. While it is possible to develop the technology and to apply it and detoxify pollutants and transform organic wastes into inoculate by-products, the rate of increase of pollution makes the task increasingly difficult. All these studies conclude that the population growth rate must be reduced. Hopefully this can be accomplished through education, and by the provision of economic incentives, and through the kinds of events under way this week. If voluntary restraints on population growth are not forthcoming, we will be faced with a need to consider coercive measures. If immediate and substantial efforts are not taken to purify our air, water, and land, we will leave very little for our children to inherit. Population increase has resulted very largely from work by life scientists who have reduced deaths from infectious diseases and prolonged life. Vaccine, wonder drugs and insecticides, hormones as well as new technology have been developed by scientists to protect against disease and to increase food supplies. In this regard, life scientists, whose work has contributed to the problem, have a special responsibility for concern about the uncontrolled increase in population and the growing pollution. Life scientists by training and involvement are particularly aware of the problems that arise from overpopulation. It is our duty to identify those problems and to suggest solutions. We have literally made life possible where it might not have existed, and we are therefore partially responsible for its qualities and its future. We have before us the specter of the destruction of our environment in the foreseeable future. Lake Erie is dead, Lake Michigan is dying, our air is polluted with hydrocarbons from cars and jet aircraft, and the Earth is poisoned with lead from gasoline and by excess fertilizer. We may recall the warnings of physicists about fallout from atomic bombs and the subsequent accumulation of radioactive strontium in milk and finally in the bones of children. Scientists have foreseen many events which we now see before us today. Many of the warnings in the past have been ignored, but today we can no longer be indifferent to the danger signals of overpopulation. In opposition to these warnings and in contrast to the declaration for the concern about the future of our children and this earth there have been voices largely representing the religious groups declaring that science is overly concerned and we need not worry.

Very recently another voice claiming scholarship has declared and I quote: "It is wrong, outrageously wrong, to say that science shows there to be overpopulation." Professor Julian Simon, in a talk on "Science does not show that there is overpopulation," has taken issue with the overwhelming facts and figures provided by the wide variety of studies which I have listed earlier. Indeed Professor Simon has declared and I quote: "Overpopulation cannot be decided on scientific ground alone. This decision," he says, "depends upon one's values in matters about which science must be silent." He goes on to declare that biologists and those who are concerned with overpopulation are coercionists. This label he has applied to people such as Paul Ehrlich, and Allen Guttmacher and presumably myself, who out of our great concern for the future of the world and the threat to the quality of life, and in order to avoid introduction of coercive measures have urged that voluntary means be adopted for bringing about restraints on the overburdening of our environment by overpopulation. This misrepresentation by Professor Simon has no claim on scholarship. Among the numerous unsupported assertions in his speech, Professor Simon claims the following factual basis for his optimism about the food supply in the world. He has stated, and I quote: "We now know that protein can be made from fishmeal, oil, soybeans, cottonseed, and many other sources for almost insignificant costs, say two cents per day per person, and in quantities from sources that seem almost inexhaustible, for example, oil and seaweed." The whole question of resources, both renewable and unrenewable, is being discussed in detail this week. I shall be extremely surprised to learn whether fishmeal, oil, soybeans, and cottonseeds are available in an inexhaustible supply. The National Research Council for example, has indicated in their recent study that 80 percent of our total potential oil reserves will be gone, 80 percent will be gone, in 20 to 30 years time. Soybeans and cotton seeds depend upon agricultural limits which are clearly defined by a variety of obvious factors, and fishmeal is anything but inexhaustible. Fish from the ocean currently represent no more than four percent of the world's total diet, and this supply is rapidly decreasing. What is remarkable about Professor Simon's claim is that he not only has somehow learned of an inexhaustible supply of protein but has ascertained that it will cost no more than two cents per day per person to provide. His scholarship on this point has extended, I learned, to a conversation with a local businessman, who is a producer of fishmeal and who suggested that he could produce the fishmeal protein at two and a half cents per day per person. Professor Simon has applied this estimated cost for the preparation of fishmeal protein to oil, soybeans, cottonseeds, and treeleaves-substances which, unlike fishmeal, must be converted to protein by a yet-to-be-developed technology. There are numerous other assertions and statements made in Professor Simon's speech which I do not have time to discuss in detail, but I must turn my attention to his most remarkable of all statements, and I quote: "For the very long run I think it is safe to predict," he says, "that if the population stabilizes at say 30 billion, the standard of living will be higher than if it were to stabilize at 7 billion." Now, this is a monumental piece of scholarship. In order to arrive at the figure of 30 billion as being sustainable on this earth numerous calculations concerning a wide variety of requirements to sustain life will have to be made. These include among others, energy and power requirements, for just one example. Calculations such as these are currently baffling numerous engineers and scientists whose preliminary work is suggesting that serious problems will be faced by an increase of just a few billion people, let alone the 27 billion people which Professor Simon safely predicts can be added to our earth. As an example, the need for water as a coolant for power stations, whether they are of the conventional or nuclear type, is already placing severe burdens upon the major river systems of North America. In the USA these power stations will have to be increased by eight times to meet the needs which are projected over the next 30 years. And river systems, such as the Columbia River, are already becoming unsuited for any form of biologic life because of thermal pollution alone. The safe prediction made by Professor Simon obviously must have included some kind of calculation of a helocalorie required per person per year, and the means by which this can be supplied, not only by an ocean which is dying, but by the increasing crop land and animals grazing on earth that is increasingly polluted by heavy metal poisoning and residual pesticides. It is presumed that Professor Simon has also been able to calculate how other renewable resources will be provided in the form of wood and building products as well as demands for the production of steel, aluminum and other non-renewable resources. Presumably he has calculated the effects of an increase in such manufacturing processes and the ability of our environment to sustain them. These problems which are exercising concerned scientists and engineers for which there are only fragmentary data and computer models currently available, these problems have made the prediction of population optima extremely hazardous. Some of the evidence indeed suggests that the USA may already be overpopulated if we intend to maintain the current standard of living. Nevertheless, Professor Simon has obviously developed some method by which he can predict safely not only what the carrying capacity of the world will be but that it will be maintained at a higher standard of living than if it were to stabilize at 7 billion people, which is twice that which now obtains. I urge Professor Simon to review the method by which he has been able to make this safe optimistic prediction. I predict that this remarkable prediction technique is worthy of at least a Nobel prize. I sadly suspect, however, that like so many other of his assertions and statements this prediction lacks scholarship or substance to support it.

At this point I think it necessary to ask why Professor Simon has made this kind of prediction, why he has denied the facts on overpopulation in spite of the confessional he made at the beginning of his talk, why he has dismissed pollution as a red herring. He himself proclaims to answer that question. He has stated that the really tish-tee issue concerning judgments about population growth is one's values about people. This, he says, is the ultimate issue. Indeed, this is a matter on which those of us who he describes as coercionists agree with him. It is because we are concerned about people that we are now trying to alert them to the dangers which face us. Apparently, however, there is a basic difference in our value systems. The value system which Professor Simon wishes to use as a criterion for decisions about population growth is, and I quote: "The value about people and life that is found in the Bible." Professor Simon points out that the Bible teaches us to abort killing and asks a question: "Why should one feel so strongly that murder is bad and then not want to bring more people into the world?" He carries on his reasoning to conclude, and I quote: "It seems to me that there is no difference between murder, abortion, contraception, and abstinence from sex." This in spite of what Professor Simon has said tonight. "If I were an Asian," he said, "then I would be for abortion and contraception. But apparently in this country, it seems to me there is no difference to me between murder, abortion, contraception and abstinence from sex." Now, although this doctrine may have been inspired by Professor Simon's contact with the Bible, it is a doctrine that goes far beyond the Old or the New Testaments. In fact it goes beyond any of the doctrines contained in Eastern or Western religions as I have come to know them. Indeed, a new religious doctrine has been enunciated in which murder and abstinence from sex are not distinguishable. Personally I find this religious doctrine abhorrent and retrogressive in terms of the kinds of value systems about the quality of life which civilization has built up over the Millennia. He makes it clear, for example, that all life, no matter how brief or miserable it is destined to be, is worth living, and in his speech he has given examples in India of a toothless crone of an undetermined age living on wet cow dung, or the fourteen-year-old girl catching bricks at a construction job for 30 cents per day as her baby, covered with flies, lies on a burlap sack. If this religious doctrine is sincerely believed by Professor Simon, then I respect his right to express these views. But I find it difficult to discover any consistency

> in his writings to build confidence that this is so. For example, in 1968, writing in *Demography*, he chastised family-planning campaigns in the following way, and I quote: "The social psychologists and sociologists who have done yeoman work in the family planning movement would benefit from an examination of the principles of advertising and marketing as derived from many years of hard-nosed experience." Professor Simon continues, "It might also be well if family planning campaigns took advantage of the experience of professional creators of advertising and of qualified managers of marketing campaigns rather than depending on their own amateur talents." This paper has as a reference handbook for family planners, a book called: *How to Start and Operate a Mail-Order Business,* written by Julian L. Simon. It is also curious that a man who proclaims the ultimate sacredness of potential human life, last year in *Population Studies,* Volume 23, published a paper in which he down-values the worth of an avoided birth in India, in spite of inflation since Steven Enke published his higher estimate in 1963. Just last year Professor Simon argued persuasively that it was well worth the payment of such bonuses to prevent a birth permanently. Possibly Professor Simon has got religion since he wrote those articles in 1968 and 1969. I find it hard to relate this new religious doctrine to the hard-nosed manager of advertising campaigns, as Professor Simon describes himself, unless, of course, he's convinced that the economics of a stable society threatened the mail-order business. Whatever the explanation, let us not be deflected by false prophets from the serious task which we must sustain for the rest of our lives. We have to educate, to research, and to promote concern about our environment and the size of our population. We must, we can, and we will achieve a fine and beautiful world for ourselves and our children to inherit. I am optimistic that it can be done based on an intelligent and a humanistic approach. We can realize a new quality of life, free from avarice which characterizes our current society. Thank you.

Please note Silverman's remarks about my view's apparent connection to the Bible, about the new religious doctrine I enunciated in which murder and abstinence from sex are not distinguishable, and the refrain, "this has no claim in science."

After Silverman sat down, I was in shock. It was impossible to rebut him; I had four full pages of notes. So I simply stood up and stated that before this talk, arrangements had been made to avoid what happened, and Silverman had violated the agreement. I then sat down. To my amazement, I received an overwhelming ovation—the only time in my entire life that this has happened. Clearly, Silverman had so overstepped the bounds of decency that I had gained the sympathy of the audience. It was heartening that there was this much sense of fair play.

In 1970 I sent an article to *Science* magazine pointing out that those whom I referred to as "population controllers" were wrong on the facts, and misleading in making apparently objective statements that were really based on value judgments about the worth of human life.

Despite generally favorable referee reports, the article was turned down apparently because the term "population controllers" was unwarranted.

In 1972 I, together with Rita, gave a talk at the PAA on the rhetoric surrounding population and why we hear the kind of language about population growth that is heard, and even that was a hot session. My talk evoked a comment denouncing me as a "defrocked priest" by sociologist Lincoln Day.

Then I didn't speak about population for years. I gave a talk to some young women at the Lincoln Avenue Residence Hall at the University, a block from home, but that was about all for the ten years between 1970 and 1980. I later told Walt Harrington of the *Washington Post* that one of my strengths is that I could live for a long period without love from communities, but that does not mean it is enjoyable or easy. I was living without much encouragement professionally even before I got involved with population studies.

After being three years in press, *The Economics of Population Growth* came out in 1977. It had the advantage of coming out under Princeton University Press's auspices, rather than an unknown publisher, which could easily have happened. It was sponsored by Sandy Thatcher, a wonderful editor who became a long-time trusted friend. Nevertheless in David Hume's immortal phrase, the book "fell deadborn from the press," as he referred to the fate of his own first book, it seemed. Nothing happened with respect to the book; absolutely nothing.

About the time my book was published there appeared a book on population growth by John Pitchford. It was a neat enough review of the standard Malthusian thought, but nothing new. It received a fair amount of attention, but my 1977 book went apparently unnoticed.

So I decided to write a popular book to bring the message to a wider audience, both for its own sake and as an implementation of the Galbraith strategy. I'm not a great fan of Galbraith in most respects, but he was a very clever marketer of books. As I remember, he somewhere described what he did with his 1950-something book called *The Affluent Society*. He thought that he wouldn't be able to reach the academics directly; they wouldn't be interested because the book would be insufficiently technical. So he would try to reach a sufficiently wide audience that readers would publicly go to the professionals and say, what about this book of Galbraith's? So I wrote the 1981 book, *The Ultimate Resource*.

In the course of that writing, I excerpted four pages of highlights, and at the 1977 Population Association meeting I put 500 copies of this broadside onto a chair. The 500 disappeared, all right, but I didn't hear a single word from anybody.

I also sent copies to four general publications, including the editor of *Science*, Philip Abelson. Abelson replied that he would be willing to consider an article based on the four pages and the book. So I worked on the article and sent it off to him.

Eventually Abelson sent me referees' reports that said terrific, you ought to publish this, and Abelson said he was going to publish it, but then it never seemed to get published. Month after month after month passed. (It was two and one-half years in press, an unprecedented length of time, a *Science* editor told me.) Finally I heard through a third source that he said to somebody else about the article, "I've got to crap or get off the pot." Finally he did publish it, and I suppose I should be grateful. I'm not because it was so painful a process.

Immediately upon publication there was an explosive reaction, the sort of thing every author dreams about. My new telephone answering machine served yeoman duty. (That's a Navy pun; "yeoman" is the label for administrative enlisted men.) By the time I'd go to the office in the afternoon for weeks, each day the machine had accumulated ten, twelve, fifteen messages. People were calling and writing, "I knew this was true all along! I had nobody else to talk to about it." It turned out that there were (and are) a lot of people spread around the country who shared my conclusions on these subjects on the grounds of personal experience or general intuition, and they felt lonely and sometimes a bit nuts. They didn't know anybody else in town who shared these ideas. They were very glad when they finally found a kindred spirit in my article.

There were lots of invitations to lecture, some at fancy prices. It was a nice opportunity to take one of the kids to those opportunities that were reasonably close so that we could make a day of it.

The reaction to John Tierney's 1990 article in *The New York Times Magazine*, famous as it still is, did not produce a fraction of the action that followed the *Science* article.

The article also had the wonderful effect of bringing me in touch with a lot of interesting and amusing people—Herman Kahn for one, with whom I later collaborated. Some of these people became close friends—including Petr Beckmann and Aaron Wildavsky, both now dead. Along with some of the amusing people, I also heard from every crank in the world who had an idea that was rejected by the rest of the world; they wrote and sent me manuscripts and books, and so on. I kept reading what they sent, hoping that I'd find somebody who really did have some terrific unknown ideas, as Hardy found Ramanujan, because I greatly sympathize with people who cannot get their ideas published. But none turned out to be the real thing, so far as I could tell.

The article was then quickly reprinted in many magazines and newspapers with a total circulation of many millions, vastly multiplying its impact.

When I saw the actual printed copy of *Science* containing the article, I had a rare sense of triumph, and I said to myself, "I beat the bastards." I thought that the data would matter—that the exposure of the facts would be devastating, and the false assertions that I attacked would be laid to rest. Was I wrong! That was the worst forecast I ever made. The article had shock value, produced lots of letters and phone calls. It raised the blood pressure of people like Garret Hardin. But it made little difference, at least in the short run. Aside from immediate republication in newspapers and magazines, it was not reprinted—never in a single collection, I think.

Lest I seem elsewhere in my book to be parading my failures, here are some of the quotes from reviews of *The Ultimate Resource* that the Princeton University Press publicist found and put on the jacket of a subsequent book:

> "... There is little in this book that can be ignored. What is most startling is its deep-rooted optimism about the human condition—a position that has not been seriously entertained in American thought for almost 20 years. Whether its principles are widely accepted or not, *The Ultimate Resource* is a landmark book."
> —*The Washington Post Book World*

> "... The main weight of [Simon's] argument rests on the evidence of the past and on general economic reasoning, both of which are often neglected or undervalued by the pessimists, and which the author presents extremely well. Unfortunately, the views that he attacks are widely held and influential. By challenging them so effectively Simon has performed a real service."
> —*Nature*

> "Compelling and often brilliantly original. . . . His economic analysis will leave a lot of readers revising their thinking about the world around them."
> —*Fortune*

> "On the whole, I can think of no very recent book in demographic economics . . . that is so well documented and has so logical a core, and yet will begin to stir such passionate disagreement. If one does not mind controversy, even vehement differences, and wishes to learn about the current state of the debate, then this is an optimal book to buy, read, and recommend to others."
> —*Population Studies*

Then out of the blue came a letter from Friedrich Hayek, with whom I had had no contact but whom I had recently begun reading seriously. This most valuable letter of my life read as follows:

URACHSTRASSE 27
D–7800 Freiburg (Breisgau)
77216

March 22, 1981

Professor Julian L. Simon
1105 S. Busey
Urbana, Ill., 61801
Dear Professor Simon,

I have never before written a fan letter to a professional colleague, but to discover that you have in your Economics of Population Growth provided the empirical evidence for what with me is the result of a life-time of theoretical speculation, is too exciting an experience not to share it with you. The upshot of my theoretical work has been the conclusion that those traditional rules of conduct (esp. of several property) which led to the greatest increases of the numbers of the groups practicing them leads to their displacing the others—not on "Darwinian" principles but because based on the transmission of learned rules—a concept of evolution which is much older than Darwin. I doubt whether welfare economics has really much helped you to the right conclusions. I claim as little as you do that population growth as such is good—only that it is the cause of the selection of the morals which guide our individual action. It follows, of course, that our fear of a population explosion is unjustified so long as the local increases are the result of groups being able to feed larger numbers, but may become a severe embarrassment if we start subsidizing the growth of groups unable to feed themselves.

Sincerely,
F.A.Hayek

22

Philosophical Analyses of Basic Conceptual Issues: Causality

This and the following chapters required tougher editorial decisions than any other chapters. They deal with some of the fundamental issues in my life. Yet the subjects are inherently difficult for the reader to understand, no matter how clearly I set forth the content—because the very essence of the issues is their deep and complex philosophical natures.

These and most other philosophical problems I have dealt with are not "ivory tower" issues, however. All arise out of dealing with the practical questions of the day in economic research.

Leaving out these topics, or simply mentioning them in vague terms, would be like an early astronaut briefly mentioning that s/he had gone into space but supplying no details, a surgeon simply noting that s/he had performed operations and moving on to his/her golf game and PTA activities, and Casanova confining himself to a one-line statement that he had chased and seduced women. For me to tell the story of my life, philosophical content must be included here, though of course many readers may choose to skip over it. The question is: how much to say?

The Analysis of The Concept of Causality

Linguistic analysis in the best philosophical sense—more specifically, close examination of the term "simultaneous"—was the tool Einstein used to build the theory of special relativity, and the heart of his analysis. The importance of such "philosophical" analysis is an important lesson about scientific method that physics can teach other sciences, including economics. Bohr also emphasized the fundamental importance of semantics in physics generally and in quantum theory in particular.

Economics often suffers from confusion of some key concepts because economists do not worry about the definitions and meaning of the concepts. This can and does lead to irrelevant empirical work, unsound forecasts of economic phenomena, and misunderstanding in the structure of economic theory. There is no sure-fire cure for such confusion except careful analysis of the language used in discussion of the concepts. It can help economists, however, to be alert to two frequent sources of confusion discussed in the philosophy literature—tautology, and lack of measurement orientation (operational definition) for concepts that are intended to bridge theory and empirical work.

The philosophical technique that Einstein pioneered with his analysis of the concept of simultaneity—the measurement-oriented operational definition—is at the base of my analysis of causality and utility and the non-finiteness of natural resources. First I'll talk about causality.

Starting with Bridgman's explication of Einstein's analysis of simultaneity, many philosophers and scientists concluded that "operationalizing" all scientific terms would reduce confusion in scientific discourse. This led to a philosophical program called "operationalism," which has often played the red herring. Calling for the discipline of measurement-oriented definitions *where theorizing abuts with economic phenomena and their empirical investigation* is very different than asking that *all* concepts used in the process of theorizing be defined operationally. By now, as Machlup (1978, Part 3) has eloquently discussed in the context of economics, there apparently is reasonable consensus among philosophers of science that it is both unnecessary and counter-productive to call for operational definitions of purely theoretical terms. But this should not be construed as philosophical license to assume that *no* terms in economic theorizing need to be specified with respect to practical measurement; such an assumption would point the way to irrelevant abstraction. This idea is successively applied to the examples of utility, causality, and finiteness with respect to future natural resource supply.

In the course of correspondence in 1964 when he refereed my paper

("The Price Elasticity of Liquor in the U.S. and a Simple Method of Determination," Vol. 34, No. 1, January, 1966) for *Econometrica,* the famous econometrician Herman Wold revealed his identity and enclosed a mimeo draft of a paper about causality in statistical investigations. Flattered by the thought that he sought comments from this young punk, I read the paper carefully. It was a huge struggle, however, to figure out what the term "causality " meant in the context of that paper.

I finally understood that Wold's work, as with considerable other useful work starting with Paul Lazarsfeld and continuing through Nobel prize winner Herbert Simon, addresses the problem of *which* among a set of variables should be considered to be causal. These writers developed a body of statistical techniques for unraveling the skein of causality in available statistical data series. They studied how to disentangle the relationships within a complex set of variables, and how to understand the *relative* causal status of a *closed set* of relationships. Their works *assume* causal relationships within the system and consider *which variable causes which*, i.e., the *direction* of causality.

Wold's paper led me to wonder about a more general—and more commonsensical—concept of causality that would be appropriate for economics. After the hardest intellectual work I have ever done (and the work has gotten much easier as I have gotten older), I realized that what I sought to do, as also Hume sought to do, is to classify *whether or not* one variable causes another. That is, my purpose is to better understand the nature of the relationship between two given variables, though with reference to other relevant variables, of course. The Lazarsfeld-H. Simon-Wold sort of analysis resembles the advances made by experimenters in biology and agriculture who have developed methods for effectively arranging experiments so as to determine which among a set of fellow-traveling variables are the operative ones, e.g. is it the paper or the tobacco that causes cancer? Implicit in such experiments, without explicit justification, is the notion that if you manipulate an independent variable and the dependent variable changes in response, the independent variable may be called "causal." (As we shall later see, however, this implicit definition of causality as experiment does not cover some crucial situations, which require a more explicit and more extended treatment of the concept of causality.)

After wrestling with Wold's paper for a while, I went back to David Hume's seminal discussion. (This is the first time I have used the word "seminal," but if ever it was appropriate, now is the occasion; Hume's treatment of the concept is indeed the seed from which all subsequent work has grown.)

Hume did not replace the material-property definition with a concept that fits the needs of the working scientist. And it is that nut that I sought to crack when I first began to think about the matter in the early 1960s.

It was heady excitement for me to find myself, a second-year professor of advertising who until two years before had thought of himself as a businessman by occupation, challenging a fundamental idea of the man whom I regard as the greatest philosophical mind of all time, and as great a mind as the best in any field. The result, I then believed and still believe, is the first major improvement in the concept of causality since David Hume's breakthrough.

I now understand the matter a bit better than when writing the paper. Though Hume's discussion of causality is not perfectly clear in all respects, and may even be a bit self-contradictory in some secondary issues, this much is crystal clear: All that can ever be known about events is what can be observed. And the most that can be observed is that there is a "constant conjunction" between events, a statistical correlation. Hume specifically denied that a causal relationship can be established by *a priori* logical analysis of the features of events or objects.

In retrospect, I see that Hume went no further because he did not recognize the role of theory as an element to be combined with the observed data. This element of theory in scientific thinking and in the explication of the concept of causality is perhaps the biggest difference between Hume's thinking and contemporary thinking. He approaches the concept of theory when he talks of "reason" in contrast with experience (*Treatise*, p. 214 Open Court Ed), but the full-blown concept is not there; rather, it is likened to analysis: "All kinds of reasoning consist in nothing but a comparison"; *Treatise*, p. 199, Open Court edition).

Markowitz noticed this, too:

> The reason that Hume's view needs modification—really amplification—is that science does not merely catalog cause and effect. Rather it develops theories, what I would now refer to as models, sometimes mistakenly thought to be inevitable universal laws. (Markowitz, 1993, p. 3.)

Hume focused on each relationship all by itself, and all by itself it is indeed so that there is no more that one can say except that there is "constant conjunction". But the presence or absence of other statements of relationship that are either connected to the relationship in question by commonsensical logic, or even more strongly by an integrated body of theory, is very important in deciding whether it is sensible to think that the statement in question should be considered as only a predictive relationship, or whether one should go further and call it "causal". One likely reason for the absence of this consideration in Hume's thinking is that in his time there was no branch of science, except perhaps physics, that possessed such an integrated body of theory. Economics lacked an integrated body of theory until Adam Smith came along to weld together the various fragmentary observations that already existed. William Letwin (1975) has persuasively argued that this was Smith's greatest achievement. Certainly there was at that time no philosophy of science that analyzed the importance of an integrated theoretical framework, as has been done for us by recent writers. Indeed, none of the social sciences other than economics yet has a well-developed body of deductive theory, and hence this criterion of causality is not weighed as heavily in those social sciences. Rather, the other social sciences seem to substitute a weaker and more general criterion—whether the statement of the relationship is accompanied by other statements that seem to "explain" the "mechanism" by which the relationship operates.

Consider, for example, the relationship between the phases of the moon and the suicide rate. The reason sociologists do not call it "causal" is because there are no auxiliary propositions that sensibly "explain" the relationship and describe an operative mechanism. On the other hand, the relationship between broken homes and juvenile delinquency is often referred to as causal, because a large body of psychological theory serves to explain why a child raised without one or another parent, or in the presence of parental strife, is not likely to "adjust" readily.

Depending on who is reading him, it might be argued that Kant sensibly brought theory back into the discussion of causality. But if he did so, it was in such a confusing fashion that progress was not made, but rather the opposite. Hence Hume remained the pertinent endpoint in the development of the causality concept when I first began to think about it.

The only other difference between what Hume wrote and what is possible for us to understand now is that he lacked the idea of an operational definition, as discovered by Einstein with respect to time and distance. Hume had no model for defining causality by the way that one would "measure" or classify it in actual operations. Instead, he was stuck in the consideration of properties, and hence he could get no further than the negative work of denying that there was any property corresponding to the idea of causality—that is, that there was nothing discernible other than the properties of contiguity and priority in time (*Treatise*, pp. 202–203 Open Court Ed).

The result of my application of the concept of the operational definition, together with the study of a variety of examples of causal analysis in economics, led me to this definition:

> To explicate the term 'causality' and the concept for which it stands in economics, we must start with the most basic notion in economics and other sciences—the observed association or correlation or relationship. Many—but not all—observed associations can be interpreted as predictions. A prediction is an association that the predictor believes will also hold in the future; he makes the prediction if he believes that the general background conditions will not change drastically from the observation period to the prediction period. For example, if one observes that sales of Drug D have been associated with the number of cases of angina pectoris in previous years, one might predict that if angina pectoris cases rise this year, sales of Drug D will also rise—if one has no reason to doubt ceteris paribus. But if one learns that some important condition no longer holds—for example, that a new drug for angina pectoris has been introduced—one will no longer interpret the past observed association as a prediction. To put this another way: one is willing to make a prediction if one believes that the future is an unbiased sample from the same universe as the past period on which the prediction is based.

Some persons would say, with respect to dealing with the concept of causality by means of an operational definition: but you're not getting to the bottom of the matter of causality. My response (following after Zen Buddhism on esoteric mysteries—the answer is, that this is all there is) is that this is as much of a bottom as one can get to.

After working out this analysis, I read the study by Hirschi and Selvin of the use of the concept of causality in juvenile delinquency research, where the issue is particularly troubling. And a few years ago I came across a similarly-spirited discussion of the concept in the context of cigarette smoking. In connection with the famous Surgeon General's Report of 1964, the following criteria for a causal relationship were stated: consistency, strength, specificity, temporal relationship, and coherence. Then I found a very similar definition in an epidemiology text, stated without fanfare in a practical fashion (Mausner and Bahn, 1974). Epidemiology shares with many social-science situations the characteristic that experiments cannot be undertaken with human subjects. But these discussions apparently have never entered the literature of philosophy. One reason may be that the writers did not seem to realize that their analyses had something fundamental to contribute to philosophy, but rather assumed that they were working out a tool for the benefit of working scientists in their own field. Another reason may be that they did not frame their analyses in terms of a general concept such as the operational definition, as I did.

For several years I attempted without success to publish the analysis in a philosophy journal. Eventually *Kyklos* published the piece. (That journal has my gratitude for being hospitable to many kinds of work which are not in fashion elsewhere in economics). There was one comment on the article, and my reply. Other than that, to my knowledge there has been no further notice taken of the article. And discussion of the concept of causality, among philosophers and others, continues to be much the same as it was.

My concept of causality has been almost completely ignored from then until now. Nevertheless, my belief in it is as strong now as then—stronger. But is it not the mark of a quack to continue to hold a belief even though all the "experts" in a field pay no attention to the idea, even after a long time? Well, maybe so; that is for you to judge.

There are several possible explanations for the article's lack of acceptance, of course: 1) Perhaps the analysis is without merit, despite my claim. 2) It is the only article I wrote on the subject. Such an "orphan" has a poor chance of attracting attention. 3) The author is not a philosopher, and did not cry the idea's wares at philosophy meetings and seminars. 4) The article was not written within any one of the then-contending schools of philosophy. 5) It employed a then-commonly-despised concept, the operational definition, as a key tool. 6) A strong claim for its originality and importance—as in the first sentence above—was not then made, but instead the merits were left for the reader to discover. 7) The piece did not use any formal technical apparatus (except for cybernetics notation in an appendix), but rather used only the "vulgar instrument" (George Stigler's term) of prose rather than algebra and calculus. This is more than a matter of taste and knowledge of tools. The essence of the paper is that *in principle* a formal definition is not possible.

Another matter: The operational-definition approach to causality has the mortal flaw that at its heart it is judgment and not technique. That implies that other writers cannot pick up on it and add their own twists of technique, the sort of thing on which one builds a career. Hence the work is not of interest to them.

23

The Joy of Studying Immigration

Son David suggested using the following opposite the title page of my 1989 *The Economic Consequences of Immigration*:

> When in the Course of human events, it becomes necessary for one people to dissolve the political bands which have connected them with another . . . a decent respect to the opinions of mankind requires that they should declare the causes which impel them to the separation . . .
>
> The present King of Great Britain . . . has endeavoured to prevent the population of these States; for that purpose obstructing the Laws of Naturalization of foreigners; refusing to pass others to encourage their migration hither.
>
> The Declaration of Independence
> July 4, 1776

The preface then continued: I am grateful that it is my lot in life to write a book about immigration into the United States. People's lives and personalities, their creations and tragedies, can be seen and felt more clearly amidst immigration data and analyses than when writing about most topics in economics.

Immigrants' voyages to this land, following upon preparations that required extraordinary effort and often pain, have been among the most exciting and noble of human endeavors. Women and men and children have been strong and brave. They have undertaken their inevitably-frightening transits to a new place for the best of motives: the desire to improve their own lot and that of their families; the urge to leave countries whose governments they could not abide; and the willingness to help build another country where persons can live in freedom and dignity. Our country has often acted with generosity beyond what it conceived to be its national self-interest, even though its self-interest was thereby served better than most citizens imagined. Perhaps most noble of all have been those immigrant families who, while themselves still struggling to keep together body and soul—a particularly apt description of so many—drew upon their meager resources to help relatives and friends pay for passage and then become established so that they, too, could share the blessings of liberty and opportunity.

I am blessed to have known two cohorts of these people—my grandparents and their kin who came early in this century, and recent immigrants from Viet Nam and from the Soviet Union. This acquaintance surely has influenced the questions that I ask about immigration, and it may also have influenced the answers at which I arrive.

The study of immigration arose out of a conversation at about 5 a.m. walking on a Jerusalem street with an antiquated rifle on my shoulder along with my companion civil guard, Yehoshua Arieli, a well-known professor of American history (though a native Israeli) at Hebrew University. We were acting as the sort of adjunct police force that Israeli cities had at least up until 1975.

Arieli casually expressed concern to me about the economic effect of the large number of Russian immigrants that had been arriving. I replied that those immigrants had a good deal of education, and would be likely to have a very positive effect. He then responded, "Yes, but they are all professors of Russian language or music ethnology."

I said, "But education implies the power to learn new things. So even if there are too many students of Russian language among them, they will be able to learn new valuable skills." Privately I was dismayed that a university teacher held the power of education in such low esteem that he thought it to be of negative rather than positive value.

I then argued to him that in general, additional people are beneficial rather than detrimental in the long run, and most especially in Israel, and that immigrants are, above all, people in their economic impacts. But he countered with worries about housing, social services, and the like.

Next day I realized that I had to think about the topic in a more systematic way, gathering appropriate data. I proceeded to do so for the case of Israel, focusing especially on the flow of public funds to and from the Russian immigrants, taking into account their age distribution and the like. And having published that material in the Hebrew-language *Economic Quarterly*, and then returning to the United States,

I picked up the topic in a more general way for the U.S. and for other countries. That led me to other topics, and eventually to a full-scale treatment in my book *The Economic Consequences of Immigration* in 1989.

One of my first studies was an overall aggregate simulation model along the lines of my general population model, especially taking into account effects on the public coffers as well as knowledge effects.

There are two main economic objections raised about immigration: use of government funds, and displacement of natives from jobs. With respect to the former, in 1981 I did a study called "What Immigrants Take From, And Give To, The Public Coffers" for the Select Commission on Immigration and Refugee Policy Papers on Legal Immigration to the United States (April 1981, pp. 145–174). This paper would not have been done without the last grant that I received from the federal government, in about 1979. There had only been two or three other grants before it during my entire work career, despite numerous applications. And this one happened because it did not pass through peer review, but was dispensed by Guillermina Jasso and Mark Rosenzweig when they were co-research directors of the Select Commission on Immigration and Refugee Policy. I am grateful to them for their courage in making the grant.

The paper first appeared in print as my report to the Commission. Then an article was published in a professional journal from which the editor dropped some data in the tables because I said in the text that those data are not relevant. I had to agree with the editor that those data are not important to the analysis, but I warned the editor that critics would jump on the omission if those data were omitted. The editor prevailed, as editors too often do (and when they don't prevail about such a matter, the paper may simply not be published, a painful event that has occurred to me several times.) And the critics did indeed jump on the omission. It then took me endless months and trouble to get a correction published 12 years later.

The mode of analysis is shaped to fit a very specific policy question: Would present residents be made better off if additional immigrants are excluded? This dictated that a present-value analysis is needed, and that the relevant universe is the entire collection of immigrants rather than particular ethnic groups (the latter a subject which attracts researchers like moths to a flame). Making those kinds of choices correctly was a surprisingly difficult part of the paper, but subsequent work mostly ignored those crucial distinctions because of the unavailability of data.

When Steve Moore, as good a student as I had at the University of Illinois, wanted to work on a senior thesis, the other major hot immigration topic—the effect on native unemployment—seemed a natural. But the available data were a poor lot. The only data on year-by-year inflows of immigrants pertained to totals for various cities, and we therefore examined their possible connection to unemployment rates in those cities. Our inquiry was extremely inelegant, but we tried every one of the many reasonable approaches we could think of. After the long gestation period of more than ten years, we published a short answer: No effect, or not much. The result squared with many other studies using other methods, most of which were much more elegant in their use of micro-data from the censuses, but none of which seemed as germane to the topic because the data are collected only at ten-year intervals.

Economists tend to think of international trade and international migration as similar phenomena, to be analyzed with the same theory that considers movement of workers and movement of capital to be alternative routes to the same production end; the modern theory for trade is mostly a gloss on what Ricardo gave us early in the 19th century.

In a paper entitled "Trade Theory Throws No Light On Migration" so as to put its basic idea right out front, however, I showed (I think) that the analogy is not sound. International trade and international migration are theoretically different phenomena rather than similar. The gains from trade are quite unlike the gains from migration. Consumers do not obtain the same sort of gains from the international movement of people as they do from international exchange of goods, though there are important gains from immigration to the countries of destination through mechanisms other than trade-like effects. And the "explanation" of movement of people is different from the explanation of movement of goods.

Trade theory refers to goods which can be sold separately from the services of the persons who own the means of production of these goods. In contrast, the benefit which the migrant confers upon the person or organization that pays the migrant for her/his services cannot be delivered at a distance. That is, trade theory deals by definition with internationally traded goods, while international (economic) migration is a response to the fact that that person's output cannot be directly sold at a distance. It should not be surprising, then, for trade theory to be silent about the immigration that takes place.

The gains to consumers from *trade* result from differences in the structures of production before and after trade—a supply-side phenomenon. The gains to immigrants result from differences in demand for labor in the two countries, and the supply structures are unchanged (except in size) in the before-migration and after-migration equilibrium situations.

People either immigrate, or they do not. Trade theory explains why one group of people does *not* immigrate—those who make internationally traded goods and whose wages therefore become (theoretically) equal in both countries. (Not only is this not very likely in practice, but in principle we can never know whether the wages really are equal). Another set of people who do not immigrate are those whose earnings would be less in the rich country than in the poor country because their productivity is so low—well below the average in the sending country.

The people who do immigrate are those whose productivity is average or above in the old country, and who could earn more in the new country for that reason and/or because of the difference in price structures in the old and new countries. These are necessarily people whose earnings are not equalized in the two countries. (For example, sculptors who sell their sculpture on an international market and who can live and work anywhere will not migrate.) Trade theory says nothing about this latter group who do immigrate.

This analysis strikes most economists at first hearing as wildly strange. Nobel prize-winners have said publicly that it is wrong and promised to send counter-examples. But I have yet to receive such counter-examples, and with every successive interchange, the theory seems more sound to me, and at least a few of my favorite economists either agreed immediately or came around after discussion. It is fun to challenge existing thought in this sort of way, but frustrating when no journal will publish the result because they think it is either wrong or necessarily unimportant because it contains no fancy mathematics or data. I did publish it in my 1989 book to get it on the record, but topics more relevant to economic policy have dominated reviews and comments on the book.

When "Auctioning Immigration Visas: Doing Well While Doing

Good" appeared in *The New York Times*, this scheme seemed so preposterous to Russell Baker that he wrote a *Times* column ridiculing it. Peculiarly, though Baker is a humorist, the column hardly made fun of the scheme, but instead criticized it seriously, denouncing the idea of trafficking in human flesh—the perfectly predictable reaction on the part of those who are full of compassion.

It is worth recalling that some schemes which seem politically impossible when proposed sometimes become feasible decades letter. Friedman's school voucher scheme is an example.

Even before I got interested in the effects of immigration on the persons in the country of destination (and secondarily, the country of origin) I was interested in the effect of migration on the migrants themselves.

The nexus of knowledge, culture, economic and social structure, and economic development is puzzling. The one sure fact is that people originating in a poor country often have extraordinarily different economic outcomes if they live out their work lives in developed countries rather than in their poor home countries. They not only do well by the poor-country standards, but also by the rich-country standards. This is true of China, India, the Caribbean, Eastern Europe, and elsewhere, and hence must be largely independent of the sending country's "culture." The question is: How can the human community employ this phenomenon in a more general fashion? In "A Scheme to Promote the World's Economic Development With Migration," I suggested one policy that might answer the question—improbable in present political terms, but perhaps illuminating nevertheless.

The idea first came about as a result of living in Israel in 1968, and seeing how different were the economic lives of Jews of North African origin than were the lives of Jews of the same stock whom I had seen and met while passing through Morocco in 1956, in transit from my ship before being discharged from the Navy. The poor, sick, aged Jews, with every manner of eye disease and gait defect that I saw walking in the street and sitting desolately on the curb on the street in front of a synagogue in the mellah in Rabat, left an indelible impression upon me, as did such poverty as seeing water sold from carts, and knowing that there was no schooling available beyond the elementary level unless the student went to the middle-class area of the city to study.

The scheme, therefore, is simply to move people from poor countries to rich countries—and an international fiscal mechanism that would induce rich countries to accept the immigrants. At the time I wrote the paper in 1971, I thought that an international taxing authority might arise in the foreseeable future, even though it then seemed improbable—as the disappearance of kings and queens as rulers seemed improbable before World War I, and as the disappearance of empires seemed improbable before World War II. By 1996, however, I think that the appearance of such an international taxing authority is not probable, despite the call for just such a thing by Secretary-General Boutros Boutros-Ghali of the UN at the beginning of 1996. Furthermore, I now believe that such an international taxing power would not be good for the world community in the long run, because independence of nations is valuable and a monopoly of power is dangerous. But this matter disappears into the mists of the future, and is outside the domain within which I feel reasonably comfortable that I know what I am talking about.

A similar scheme to move people from poor central-city areas to more affluent areas, by paying the affluent to pay the poor to live next door, has many of the same properties. I once wrote this up and sent it to a few journals, but was somewhat relieved when none wished to publish it. My libertarian anti-government friends would have been against it on the grounds that government has no business with such interventions, and others would be publicly against it on grounds that it is demeaning to the poor people, while some of them and many others would be against it on simple grounds of racism.

George Stigler somewhere wrote, in a comment on Malthus and perhaps somewhat jokingly, that travel has never improved any economist's thinking. For my part, I consider it as important to travel—and to live and work in another country—as to know first-hand about a particular industry and to follow its happenings, as Albert Marshall urged that an economist should.

Studying a topic as a scientist and having a passionate feeling about governmental policies related to the topic introduces complexities into one's scientific life. Many or most people assume that if one allows a preference to be seen, one's work inevitably will be shaped to promote one "side" of the issue. Because my work tends to show that immigrants are good for U. S. natives, and I (separately) hope that more immigrants will be admitted, journalists assume that my work is advocacy rather than as dispassionate presentation as one can present—the extent to which it is dispassionate depending upon my skill, just as with every other researcher. The journalists assume that those who hide their preferences (or really have none) are "neutral" and therefore more reliable.

Deciding one's policy preferences is unusually complicated with respect to immigration, because some of the policies one believes both make sense and are desirable lead to long-run results in other policies which have the opposite results. And the persons whom one feels sympathetic to in such matters themselves advocate policies that would injure people almost exactly like them.

The key to sorting out the tangle of policies and interests is, I think, making sure that all the parties who have a stake in the matter are represented in one's thinking, and that all their interests are considered. Specifically, the group that most complicates one's analysis consists of persons who are outside of the U.S. and who might immigrate here in the future. And if they do immigrate, they might or might not be eligible for certain benefits, depending on U. S. immigration policies. The joker in the deck is that if one tries to ensure that they—and immigrants already here—will be eligible for certain benefits, one may reduce the likelihood that those potential immigrants will be able to immigrate even without any social benefits at all. And the persons whom one might expect to understand this and to act in a fashion helpful to the potential immigrants instead advocate policies that may well lead to less immigration. And their leaders seem blind to this possible outcome, and talk as if they are acting in the interests of compassion toward the needy.

Another complication is the lumping together of various social policies toward immigration that have different meanings and effects. Specifically, policies toward children are a tough issue here, as they are in all welfare policies and have been since long before the welfare debates in England around the time of Malthus.

Debate on this subject is hampered because it brings into conflict individuals and groups who would otherwise be friends and allies. Hence they prefer not to air their disparate views in public.

The nub of the problem is that—being human, and ordinary members of a democratic society in which government dispenses various kinds of benefits—immigrants who are already in the country scuffle to get just as much of the public purse as they can. And they use every form of political rhetoric to do so—just as everyone else does. And they assume that such scuffling for a place at the public trough is righteous behavior and the basic stuff of democratic politics. Indeed, such attempts to get as much as one can for one's group is such an accepted definition of politics that if you question it, you will be looked at with incredulity.

The Hassles of Studying Immigration

One of the joys of studying immigration is that a clearcut scientific finding that shows some aspect of immigration to be beneficial to natives, if it reaches the newspapers, produces a strong reaction. Some of these reactions are from ordinary readers, like this one scrawled on an op-ed of mine on immigration:

> "Left Wing, Liberal, Illegal Alien Lover."
> "Keep (Retire) the tired image of (immigrants) Illegal Aliens
> By Julian L. Simon — Commie."
> "Communist Scum—Deport Simple Simon."
> "*Leftist, Liberal, Commie.*"
> "Democrats love illegal aliens (like you do). Democrats kiss Hispanics, hate U.S. citizens (like you do). Hispanics don't want a illegal alien bill because 99% of illegals are Hispanic. Deport all left wing, liberal, anti-America Commies (like you)."
> "Why isn't Proof of U.S. citizenship required when registering to vote?"
> "Make English the official language of the U.S.A." Write to:
> U.S. English
> 1424 16th St., N.W.,
> Washington, D.C. 20036
> ANC—TUTU—MANDELA ARE ALL COMMUNIST PUPPETS. DEPORT ALL LEFTIST LIBERAL ILLEGAL ALIEN LOVERS (YOU FIRST). DO YOU SLEEP WITH REP. ED ROYBAL?

More important are the responses of the anti-immigration organizations. These organizations have considerable payrolls employing staffs of full-time people whose business it is attempt to discredit such findings, and the individuals who produce such findings.

For example, at the end of 1995, with an eye to the upcoming immigration legislation, I prepared a booklet of nothing but the bare demographic and economic facts, and it was presented by the libertarian Cato think tank and the liberal National Immigration Forum, together with about 20 other organizations across the various spectra. Despite my radical eschewing of any analysis or advocacy, this produced the response by the anti-immigration organization Federation for American Immigration Reform (FAIR) shown on the next page. I'm sure the director, a man named Dan Stein, thinks that he manages to call me a liar while being able to claim that he does not do so; when I asked him on the phone about a report from Steve Moore that he had explicitly called me a liar on the radio in several places, Stein reacted in mock horror, saying that he had never called me a liar. The reader may judge for him/herself. And apparently in frustration at being unable to find any real points of argument, the attack begins with the usual ad hominems. The remark that Simon "is a marketing professor" is lifted from Paul Ehrlich's frequent use (and, of course, it is patently false; the last time I taught marketing was at the end of the 1960s). And then refers to my not having degrees in economics or demography. (It's even worse than he thinks; I never even had a course in demography and only two in economics at any level, but let that go.)

FAIR head Dan Stein headlines [a press release] "Julian Simon is not a liar." These are quite some sweet gentlemen I have fallen in with.

"Behind the Curtain—Julian Simon's Manipulation of Immigration Studies," published by the Federation for American Immigration Reform, February 1996:

> Preface
>
> Last December, Julian Simon, A University of Maryland business professor and noted apologist for large-scale immigration, unveiled a pamphlet, published by the Cato Institute, entitled "Immigration: The Demographic and Economic Facts." Simon says that: "It aims to be entirely factual. It does not contain any advocacy or ideology . . . " However, Simon is far from a reliable source of information and analysis on immigration, as we shall show.
>
> The new Simon tract is designed to strengthen the position of opponents of immigration reform. Unfortunately, many busy decisionmakers will not be familiar enough with the facts to be able to see through the distortions in Simon's manipulation of economic and statistical data. The following analysis is designed to raise the curtain on Simon's misleading assertions and set the record straight.
>
> We will first highlight the most egregious distortions in Simon's pamphlet. Then, for quick reference we provide a topical discussion that follows Simon's claims to what he has found in his "new" research effort. Each of his broad-brush assertions is noted and discussed.
>
> Finally, for those who have the time to look in greater depth at how Simon has succeeded in the past in pulling the wool over the eyes of immigration policymakers and commentators, we examine in detail Simon's questionable selective use of statistics to bolster his arguments. We think that the record will be clear from this analysis that Julian Simon should be exiled from any serious discussion of the effects of immigration on the United States, past, present, or future. (FAIR, 1996, p. 1.)

Conclusion

What stands out after a detailed examination of Julian Simon's most recent whitewash of immigration-related problems that require national attention and remedial action is that he is not a serious researcher. His work is replete with errors. More seriously, he misrepresents the research of others by glossing over findings that conflict with his own mindset.

Our analysis of Simon's "new study" supports the conclusion that, in his writing on immigration, Simon is little more than an information packager, i.e., a `spin control' expert. This should come as no surprise. Simon is a professor of marketing, not a demographer or labor economist. Nevertheless, his writings appear to have had a disproportionate impact in shaping public and policymaker views on immigration when compared with the work of the academic experts whose works he selectively quotes and whose data he selectively repackages. (FAIR, 1996, p. 30.)

Peter Brimelow cutely writes (in the *National Review*), "Simon is not, surely, being dishonest here. No crook would be so blatant. We're talking *serious*—What?—wishful thinking? Intellectual paralysis? creeping distaste for debate?"

"[L]unatic pro-immigration economist . . . " Peter Brimelow.

The following is my letter to the *Atlantic Monthly* about whether it would run one of my immigration articles:

Mr. William Whitworth, Editor
The Atlantic Monthly

Re my interactions about the subjects of population and immigration. When I queried you about them, you said that you prefer a journalist who could provide a more "balanced" account, if memory serves.

It is my aim as an economist and social scientist to present the most balanced account of the subject that I can. I believe that my book, *The Economic Consequences of Immigration* is as balanced as anyone could make it, and I include two new theoretical ideas which imply that immigration is less favorable to natives than the body of theoretical work before that. I certainly fail to provide a perfectly balanced account, but to the extent that such failure occurs it is a failure in my skills as an economist and social scientist, and has nothing to do with "where I am coming from."

It seems to me that when you say "balance" you mean *politically balanced*. To the extent that a politically-balanced article differs in emphasis from an economically balanced treatment, the politically-balanced article deviates from the economic truth. Therefore, if you explicitly seek a politically-balanced treatment of the economics of this subject, you will cause there to be distortion.

24

The Airline Oversales Auction System

In 1978, the (later abolished) U.S. Civil Aeronautics Board (CAB) mandated an auction plan to reduce the number of involuntary bumpings. Since then, whenever there is an oversale, airlines have been required to ask for volunteers to wait for a later flight, using whichever incentive system the airlines choose. This chapter is about the history of how that regulatory reform came about, and its results.

Until 1978, travelers being involuntarily bumped from flights for which they possessed a reservation and a paid-for ticket was a long-time difficult problem in the airline industry. Each airline had arbitrarily removed excess passengers with any selection policy it preferred. For example, United Air Lines instructed its staff to bump old people and Armed Services personnel, on the assumption that they would be least likely to complain. But this policy produced trouble and outrage for many involuntarily bumped passengers.

The airlines publicly proclaimed that they never intentionally oversold a flight. But at the same, they circulated among their employees elaborate instructions about how to handle oversales and bumping incidents. Here are some excerpts from the American Airlines Operations Manual (various 1974 and 1975 dates):

> American Airlines never deliberately causes a passenger to be oversold. We tolerate a limited number of oversold and inconvenienced passengers only because we must allow some margin for error in our operation . . .

> Reservations will select for removal, the most recently sold locally boarding passenger, whenever good judgment dictates that this passenger will be less inconvenienced than some other passenger, except when undue hardship will be incurred . . .

> If none of the alternatives provide a satisfactory solution and there are to many passengers on board, advise all passengers that their flight cannot be operated with more than the authorized number of passengers and request the proper number to deplane . . .
>
> In extreme cases it may be necessary to actually cancel the flight until all passengers have deplaned, after which, the flight can be reoriginated as an extra section and conformed to capacity. This action should be used as a last resort.

The manual included this precaution: "Never give an oversold passenger anything in writing which admits an error on the part of American Airlines". Marvin Rothstein, a member of American's Operations Research group, later wrote about their overbooking system that "The scheme was never spoken of openly as overbooking; instead, we employed the euphemism 'revenue coordination'".

The Eastern Airlines procedures included seeking a volunteer to deplane (though without recompense). If that ploy did not work, passengers who were not yet in their seats were the first to be bumped. And the employees were instructed to "never use the words `oversale' or `overbooked' in conversation with the passengers denied boarding or within hearing distance of anyone except the company employees involved."

The oversales problem fed on itself. The larger the probability of being bumped, the greater the passenger's incentive to make multiple reservations on different flights under a variety of names to insure getting onto at least one flight. And the greater the extent of this practice, the greater the need for the airlines to overbook to ensure a decent load factor. In this fashion, the vicious cycle got worse and worse.

I learned in the late 1950s about the United Air Lines bumping policy from a friend who had been a stewardess, Betty Glad. The conversation lay dormant in my memory until sometime around 1965 or 1966 when I heard at a party a sad saga of how someone had been summarily kicked off a plane and forced to endure a costly and unpleasant delay. The next day when shaving it occurred to me that there must be a better way; indeed, an auction market could solve the problem by finding those people who least mind waiting for the next flight. The practical details fell into place before the shave was complete.

The scheme is simply a reverse auction, asking each ticket holder to write down the lowest amount she or he would be happy to accept in return for waiting for the next flight. In case of an oversale, the airline agent would simply proceed from lowest bidder upwards until the requisite number of bumpees is achieved. Low bidders would be given the amounts they bid (or the amount that the highest-bidding bumpee bid, if that version is deemed more equitable and attractive) and they take the next flight, happy about it. All other passengers fly as scheduled, also happy. The airlines can overbook more, which aids them, too. Literally everyone is better off except the railroads and bus companies who compete in the transportation market—a true "Pareto improvement" in economists' lingo, a scheme that benefits all parties concerned—a rare situation indeed. A cruder version is for the airline to cry a price and to ask for takers.

Trying to Get the Scheme Adopted

In 1966 and 1967 I wrote to all the airlines suggesting the scheme. The responses ranged from polite brushoffs, to denials that they overbooked, to assertions that the scheme could not work, to derision. The letter from Pan American was more colorful than most, but otherwise not untypical:

> Dear Mr. Simon:
> Mr. Shannon, our Senior Vice President-operations, asked me to thank you for your most practical solution to the reservations booking problem. Of course, we instituted the procedure immediately, after having the instructions for bidding translated into eighteen languages.
>
> We are unable to tell you of the expected excellent results as yet because the first flight on which the system was tried was on St. Patrick's Day, the 17th. The plane hasn't left as of this writing [March 22, 1967], since the passengers keep changing their bids. We feel it's highly unfortunate also that the first occasion for using the procedure should happen on a flight destined for Ireland that day, and some of the passengers were in rather unusual condition!
>
> We will keep you advised.
>
> (Seriously, it was refreshing to have an objective view of airline reservations, and I would like to discuss it further with you over lunch next time you visit New York!)
>
> Sincerely,
> A.W. Leonard
> Director—Reservations & Ticket Offices
> Pan American World Airways

It seemed to me that the first airline to implement a volunteer scheme could reap an enormous marketing bonanza by advertising that on its flights a person would be safe from the hated bumping—unlike all other airlines. But my suggesting this opportunity to them did not convince any airline, perhaps because such a marketing device was regarded as unsportsmanlike in the old clubby days of CAB regulation.

The Civil Aeronautics Board showed no interest. And the airlines' responses made clear their belief that an outsider could not understand their industry well enough to develop a workable idea. Most of us believe that we know our own situations so much better than another person can know it that we quickly reject advice and ideas about our situations. Sometimes this is well-warranted because the advice-giver really does know too little about the situation at hand to offer good advice; this disregard of dispensed knowledge is one of the main reasons that socialist centralized economic planning fails. But sometimes the advice-giver *does* know enough about the situation to offer useful advice on the basis of general knowledge, yet is rejected without sufficient hearing. "You don't understand my industry" or "my family" is too often an automatic response, and often a costly one. That was the universal reaction when I proposed the volunteer auction plan to the airline industry. And it is the reaction of my close friend T when I suggest to him that he do a bit of market research about what consumers like in the garments he sells; he is sure that his accumulated knowledge is sufficiently great that it is not worth spending even a bit of money and time in systematic investigation, though this seems never to have been done in his industry.

In a professional journal article just two pages long entitled "An Almost-Practical Scheme to Solve the Airline Overbooking Problem" I described the idea. The article noted that in extreme circumstances airlines had occasionally sought volunteers with satisfactory results.

The scheme was labeled "almost practical" partly as an (unsuccessful) eyecatcher, but more importantly because—as the article explained—its chances of adoption were almost nil despite its practicality and ease of implementation and operation. I speculated that the lash of competition in the airline industry (as regulated by the CAB) simply was not severe enough to move anyone to bother with the scheme, even though it could be adopted unilaterally and with the possibility of a promotional coup.

Former airline executive Blaine Cooke later offered another explanation: the NIH factor ("not invented here").

> I greatly fear that your Overbooking Auction Plan suffers from a flawed premise and a fatal defect. The flawed premise is that you assume that airline management and regulation is a rational exercise. It is not; it is more accurately described as an exercise in applied insanity. The defect is your plan offers a market sensitive and sensible solution to a real problem but a solution not conceived by an airline. Accordingly, the idea must be disallowed since it is well established in airline marketing that only ideas which originate within the airlines are permissible.
>
> Cooke also added:
>
> Somewhat more seriously, your plan can't possibly be tried since the CAB would have to provide an exception from its denied boarding policy—a process which theoretically could happen but practically would probably take five years.

The scheme did not find publication easily in a professional journal. One never knows why an article does not catch referees' interest. Possible drawbacks in this case were brevity (only two pages), simplicity (equated with unimportance by many), absence of mathematics (absence of "sophistication", "rigor" and "elegance" is considered unprofessional and lacking in skill), and lack of connection to any ongoing work tradition among economists. The only apparent advantages were some novelty in the form of the auction, the scheme's rarity as a policy that constitutes a "Pareto improvement," and (an advantage to my mind, at least) brevity and simplicity. Eventually in 1968 it found its way into print in the *Journal of Transport Economics and Policy*. Later, Visvabharathy and I offered empirical evidence of the scheme's likely ability to attract people with low incentive payments, using the technique of the hypothetical question.

The scheme was received mostly with derision, both by the academy and by industry. Even the table of contents in the *Journal of Transport Economics and Policy* referred to the scheme as "light-hearted"—that is, not exactly serious. With engaging frankness, Rothstein of American Airlines wrote about his reactions at the time:

> In 1970 . . . I discovered a short article in an obscure journal . . . that contained a remarkable proposal for solving the overbooking problem: if too many reserved passengers show up at flight time, the airline agents should conduct an auction among them . . . Simon claimed that his solution would satisfy everybody: those left behind, those boarded and the air carriers too. Nevertheless, he stated that "of course this scheme will not be taken up by the airlines" because it will "not seem decorous" or they will allege "administrative difficulties." . . . Amused, I imagined that the world would hear nothing more of the "almost practical solution," as he termed it.

Over the years, whenever there were CAB hearings on the oversales and bumpings, I wrote to anyone whom I thought might have some influence. Before the hearings scheduled in 1977 or 1978, I systematically wrote to a great many more persons—legislators, trade associations, financial analysts, Ralph Nader's Aviation Consumers Action Program (ACAP), and so on. All this activity availed naught, however.

In all my discussions, I insisted that the appropriate way to deal with an idea like this one is not to decide about it in the abstract, or even on the basis of hypothetical experimental data, but rather to conduct an actual experiment. And such an experiment could be conducted very cheaply. But I was unable to persuade any airline (or the CAB) to conduct an experiment for even one day on a single airline at a single airport at a single boarding gate—an experiment that I believed would be sufficient, even with the inevitable breakdowns in any new activity. Rather, the industry and the bureaucrats preferred to proceed on the basis of their "logic" alone that the scheme could not work. The airline officials said that I did not understand their problems. That was frustrating.

One of the groups I wrote to was composed of eminent economists—all the ex-presidents of the American Economic Association, and the current members of the Council of Economic Advisors; I asked them to write an endorsement to the CAB. Several did indeed write, including some very forceful statements.

But the reactions of the man I consider the greatest economist now alive (and the greatest spirit), and another of those economists whose work I honor most, were unusual and therefore particularly interesting. The latter, George Stigler, wrote that the scheme would not work because the passengers would form cartels and hold up the airlines for very high prices. (I quote publicly because he is no longer alive to be embarrassed.)

> [Since your scheme strikes me as intellectually admirable and administratively impossible, I shall not write to the CAB. You should explore the possibilities of collusion by a group of 40 unemployed people. (January 7, 1977).
> Milton Friedman wrote as follows:
> [If the plan is as good as you and I think it is, I am utterly baffled by the unwillingness of one or more of the airlines to experiment with it. I conclude that we must be overlooking something. I realize that you have tested this quite exhaustively, and I have no reason to question your results; yet I find it even harder to believe that opportunities for large increments of profit are being rejected for wholly irrational reasons. (January 18, 1977)

Surely nothing would have come of the scheme except for an extraordinary happening: For the first time in history, an economist was appointed to head the CAB.

On the news that he was a candidate I wrote to Alfred Kahn, and before his appointment (with notable lack of bureaucratic reticence) he wrote me that the idea made obvious economic sense. Kahn announced something like the scheme in his first press conference. He also had the great persuasive skill to repackage it as a "voluntary" bumping plan, and at the same time to increase the penalties that airlines must pay to involuntary bumpees, a nice carrot-and-stick combination.

The Results

The voluntary bumping plan has now been in operation for over twenty years, with excellent results. Everyone is delighted with the various versions of the plan that the airlines use. The people who care least about waiting for the next plane select themselves to get a payoff that they prefer to flying as scheduled. Neither arbitrary airline agents nor bureaucratic policy decide who gets thrown off, willy-nilly. And the airlines have increased their efficiency by being able to overbook to a much higher extent than before, and therefore they now fly with fewer empty seats.

Half a year after inauguration of the scheme the Senior Vice President-Marketing of American Airlines, who was in charge of passenger operations, wrote:

> We've been very pleased with the results of our voluntary approach to denied boardings. . . . [M]ore than 85 percent of our denied boardings are now voluntary—a dramatic improvement which has yielded important dividends in the form of fewer dissatisfied customers.

Year by year since 1978, the airlines have been increasing the extent of overbooking, from 6.4 oversales per 100,000 passengers in 1978 to 15.1 in 1991. This practice—which the law and the Nader-type reformers formerly condemned—has enabled the airlines to raise the capacity level at which planes fly, hence increasing their efficiency and ultimately lowering costs. Yet with the volunteer system the rate of *involuntary* bumpings per 100,000 passengers has fallen sharply—from 6.4 per 100,000 in 1978 to 1.1 per 100,000; this is the most important measure of the improvement in airline service from the point of view of passengers. To put it in absolute terms, as total passenger volume has almost doubled, the number of people booted from planes against their will has dropped from 155,507 to 46,879, and the number who happily accepted a windfall they never expected rose from zero in 1977 and 15,733 in 1978 (the first year of operation) to 599,205 in 1991.

Not a single flaw in the system has turned up, to my knowledge. No one has claimed to be damaged by it. Even Ralph Nader praises it now, after opposing it before adoption.

After the scheme had been working successfully, I wrote to Milton Friedman roughly as follows: "About the airline oversales scheme: I'm not given to I-told-you-so's, but . . . I told you so." And he replied (in a fashion that will surprise no one who knows Friedman in person or by correspondence): "Many thanks for your `I told you so'; you are entitled to it." (September 26, 1979). I would not tell this story publicly except that Friedman himself—again, typically for him—told the story on himself at a large banquet, and then wrote me as follows: "There is no reason why [the story] should be kept private. It is something that actually happened." (June 27, 1989).

So: The volunteer system for handling airline oversales exemplifies how markets can improve life for all concerned parties. As theory and empirical study predicted, the rate of oversales has increased since the system was mandated in 1978, while involuntary bumpings have greatly diminished, and capacity utilization has increased which results in cheaper fares to passengers.

25

My Depression and the Theory of Negative Self-Comparisons: The Story

"Life is hard," someone said to Voltaire.
"Compared to what?" Voltaire answered.

The book *Good Mood: The New Psychology of Overcoming Depression*, my new theory of negative self-comparisons, emerged from the body of scientific discoveries starting in the 1950s and 1960s by Aaron Beck and Albert Ellis called "cognitive therapy," together with my own experience of deep and prolonged melancholy.

"Physician, heal thyself!" At the least, the doctor should be sure that the cure works on himself or herself before prescribing it to others. I have healed myself. That's why I tell you my story here.

I was depressed—badly depressed—for thirteen long years from early 1962 to early 1975. When I say that I was depressed I mean that, except for some of the hours when I was working or playing sports or making love, I was almost continuously conscious of being miserable, and I almost continuously reflected on my worthlessness. I wished for death, and I refrained from killing myself only because I believed that my children needed me, just as all children need their father. Endless hours every day I reviewed my faults and failures, which made me writhe in pain. I refused to let myself do the pleasurable things that my wife wisely suggested I do, because I thought that I ought to suffer.

As I look back now, in comparison to re-living the *better* of the days when I felt as I did then, I'd rather have a tooth pulled and have the operation bungled, or have the worst possible case of flu. And in comparison to re-living the *worse* of those days in the first year or two, I'd rather have a major operation or be in a hellish prison.

Over the years I consulted psychiatrists and psychologists from several traditional schools of thought. A couple of them left me with the impression that they didn't have a clue about what I was saying and had simply somehow passed the necessary exams to get into a well-paying business. A couple of them were human, understanding, and interesting to talk to, but could not help me. And toward the end of that time, the psychiatrists and psychologists did not even offer me hope, and certainly no hope of a quick cure. My own training in psychology was no help, either.

Then I read about what was, at that time, a new and different approach to psychological problems—Aaron Beck's Cognitive Therapy, which in Albert Ellis's somewhat different form is called Rational-Emotive Therapy. (I shall consider them together under the label "cognitive-behavioral therapy" or just "cognitive therapy," along with Frankl's Logotherapy, recent variants such as Interpersonal Therapy, and also behavioral therapy.)

The core of cognitive-behavioral therapy is a thoughtful problem-solving procedure that quickly can get to the root of the depression, and directly yank out that root. Within that vision of the individual as *able to change his or her depressed thinking*, I then developed an analysis of the cause of depression centering on the depressed person's negative self-comparisons. And I worked out the logic of what I call "Values Treatment," which can provide a powerful force for people to use the resources of cognitive therapy and thereby cure themselves of depression; that is what Values Treatment did for me.

Within two miraculous weeks I banished my depression, and I have since then been able to keep depression at bay. (Such a quick cure is not usual, but it is not wildly exceptional, either.) Starting April, 1975, I have almost always been glad to be alive, and I have taken pleasure in my days. I have occasionally even been ecstatic, skipping and leaping from joy. And I am joyful more often than most people, I would judge. Though I must still fight against depression from time to time, I have not lost more than a minor skirmish since then, and I believe that—if my family and community stay safe from catastrophe—I have beaten depression for life.

After I had cured myself, I wondered: Could I use my new advances in cognitive therapy—Self-Comparison Analysis and Values

Treatment—to help others, too? I proceeded to counsel with other persons who were depressed, and I found that these ideas could indeed help many of them get over their depression and find new joy in life. Then I wrote a short version of this book, and leading psychiatrists and psychologists who read it agreed with me that the book—including Self-Comparison Analysis, and the therapeutic approach derived from it—makes a new contribution not only to sufferers from depression but also to the theory of the subject. And people to whom I have given early copies, some of whose cases I'll mention later, have reported dramatic salvation from their own depressions—not in every case, but often.

I ended the Introduction as follows: I hope that there will soon be a smile on your face, too, and laughter bubbling inside you. I don't promise you an instant cure. And you will have to work at overcoming the depression. You must exercise your intellect and will in outwitting the traps that your mind lays for you. But I *can* promise you that cure and joy are possible . . . A tip for the road: Try treating your fight to overcome depression as an adventure, and think of yourself as a valiant warrior. More power to you, and luck.

My Misery, My Cure, and My Joy

This is how my life seemed to me in March, 1975, when I was living for a year in Jerusalem. The first-draft notes for this description were written while I was still depressed, based on what I said to a family physician in December, 1974. The purpose of the writing was to serve as the basis for consulting one or more famous psychotherapists by mail—that's how desperate for help I had become—before finally concluding that my depression was incurable. Shortly after I made these first notes I went through the process of thought that removed my depression immediately, the first time I had been free of depression in thirteen years.

As of December, 1974, my external situation was the best it had been in thirteen years. I had just finished what I hoped would be an important book, and I had no troubles with health, family, money, etc. Nevertheless, there was no day that I wanted to see. Each morning when I awoke, my only pleasant expectations were taking a nap early in the evening, and then (after more work) finishing the day gasping with relief like an exhausted swimmer reaching shore, then having a drink and going to sleep. Looking ahead to each day I had no sense of accomplishment in advance, only the expectation that I might finish a little bit more of what I considered to be my duty.

Death was not unattractive. I felt that I had to stay alive for my children's sake, at least for the next ten years until the children would be grown, simply because children need a father in the house to constitute a complete family. At many many moments, especially in the morning when waking, or when walking back home after taking the children to school, I wondered whether I would be able to get through that ten years, whether I would have strength enough to fight back the pain and fears rather than to simply end it all. Those next ten years seemed very long, especially in the light of the past thirteen years that I had spent depressed. I thought that after that next ten years I would be free to choose to do what I wanted with my life, to end it if I then wished, because once my children would be sixteen or seventeen years old they would be sufficiently formed so that whether I would be alive or not would not make much difference in their development.

To repeat, as I thought about the day ahead I saw nothing pleasurable. When I had talked to a psychologist a few times about a year and a half earlier he had asked me which things I truly enjoyed in this world. I told him that the list was short: sex, tennis and other sports, poker, and at some happy times in my past when I had been working on new ideas which I thought might result in some impact on the society, the work was really fun, too.

I remember as early as 1955, when I was in the Navy, noticing that I get pleasure from very few things. At sea one Saturday or Sunday, sitting on the ship's fantail, I asked myself what I really enjoyed. I knew that I did not get much pleasure out of what gives most people the most pleasure—just sitting around talking about the events of the day, and about the doings of themselves and other people around them. The only conversations I really looked forward to with pleasure were those concerning some common project in which I was engaged with the other person. But now (as of 1975) I had even lost the pleasure of such joint-work conversations.

My depression had its proximate cause in an event in 1962. I was then a businessman running my own new small business, and I did something that was morally wrong—not a big thing, but enough to throw me into the blackest depths of despair for more than a year, and then into an ongoing gray depression thereafter.

Of course, the long-run causes of the depression—and in every way I fit the textbook description of a depressive personality—were more basic. I lacked a basic sense of self-worth. I did not esteem myself highly, as do so many people whose "objective" accomplishments might be considered small compared to mine. My work did not, and still does not, fill me with a sense of what a fine fellow I am. For most people in the university occupation I'm in, a tenth of the books and articles that I've written would enable them to feel that they had done a lifetime's worth of scholarly work, enough to enable them to claim with a straight face the highest rewards a university can offer. But for me it all seemed hollow. I asked myself (and continue to ask myself) what real impact upon society my work has had. When I can't point to some substantial change, I feel that the work is all a waste. And in truth, up to 1975 a fair amount of my work had not been received well or much esteemed, and this had given me a sense of futility toward those of my writings that were about to appear, or those which I considered writing in the future. (To get ahead of the story, starting in 1980 some of my work brought me wide recognition. From time to time I believe that I affect some people's thinking and perhaps public policy. This was delightful at its height for a few years, and gave me much pleasure. It still gives me much pleasure even though the effect has paled, and brought considerable negative reaction with it. But the change this has brought about in my daily feeling about my life is small compared to the change brought about by my recovery from depression in 1975.)

To give you an idea of how my depression swallowed me up: The day in 1962 when the U.S. confronted the USSR over the Cuban missiles is indelibly imprinted on the mind of almost everyone who was then an adult. But I was so deep in the pit of depression that even though I was then living in New York City—where people seemed particularly frantic about the situation—I was almost unaware of the world crisis, and I was little affected by it.

People who have never been severely depressed sometimes pooh-pooh the pain the depressed person suffers. But experienced psychiatrists know better:

> The emotional pain experienced by a depressed person can easily rival the physical pain suffered by a cancer victim. The suffering of a depressed person is difficult for his healthy colleague to appreciate. Sometimes the complaints of the depressed seem absurd and childish. You may wonder whether the patient is behaving much

> like the "Princess and the Pea"—overreacting to subjective feelings which could not possibly be so terrible as the patient describes them.
>
> I doubt that depressed patients are playing games with their friends and physicians.

The following comparisons may make depression more vivid and understandable to the non-depressive. In 1972 I had a major surgical operation, a spinal fusion, serious enough to keep me on my back almost constantly for two months. The day of the *operation* was worse for me than most of my depressed days, made so by the fear that the operation might be disastrously botched and leave me permanently disabled. But though I was full of pain and discomfort, the first day *after* the operation (when I already knew that there had been no disaster) was easier to get through than were the run-of-the-mill days of my first couple of years of black depression, and was about the same as the average days in my later depression years.

Another example: A day in which a wisdom tooth was pulled had about the same pain content for me as a day in my later "gray depression" years. The nice side of an operation or of a tooth-pulling is that when you are already safe, though in pain and confined to bed or crutches for months, you know the pain will end. But my depression went on for month after month and year after year, and I became convinced that it would *not* ever end. That was the worst of all.

I refused to let myself do the pleasurable things that my wife wisely suggested I do—go to the theater, take a walk on a sunny day, and so on—because I thought that I ought to suffer. I was superstitiously operating on the nutty presumption that if I punished myself enough, no one else would punish me for my misdeeds. And later on I refused to do these casual pleasurable things because I thought that I would be kidding myself by doing them, covering up the symptoms of my depression and therefore preventing a real cure—more bad depressive-type thinking.

During my first year of depression there was one good day. My wife and I went to visit overnight at a country shack with friends. In the morning when we woke in sleeping bags I heard a bird and saw the trees against the sky, and I felt exquisite joy of relief—the relief that one feels at the finish of a long exhausting ordeal of physical or mental work when you can at last rest, lightened of your burden. I thought, maybe it is over. But after a matter of hours I was again full of fear and dread and hopelessness and self-loathing. And even an hour of such relief did not return for perhaps another full year. (The next good moment was the night our first child was born, about two years after the depression began. Incidentally, I will seldom mention my good wife because it is not possible to do justice to one's spouse in an account such as this one.)

Though the pain grew less acute with time, and my outlook came to seem only a constant gray rather than totally black, after six to eight years of it I became more and more convinced that I would never escape. Such prolonged depression is medically unusual, and physicians can honestly reassure patients that they may expect relief within weeks or months, or a year or so at most, though the depression may return. But that was not the case with me.

For a while I dreamed about entering a monastery, perhaps a silent monastery, where there would be no burdens or expectations. But I knew that I could not run away until the children would be grown. The prospect of hanging on for that long period of future depression depressed me more.

Upon awakening every single morning for all those years my first thought was, "All those hours! How am I going to get through them?" That was the worst moment of the day, before I could get my fear and sadness under conscious control. The best moments of the day were crawling into bed finally to go to sleep, at night or for a nap in the late afternoon.

You may doubt that I was really depressed for so long or that my depression was deep. How could anyone be continually depressed for thirteen years? In fact, there *were* hours when I was not depressed. Those were the hours when I was deep enough in my work and in creative thinking that I forgot about my depression. These hours happened almost every morning, once I had gotten myself started on the day, provided that the work I was doing was reasonably creative rather than just such routine work as editing or proofreading—and providing, also, that I was not overly pessimistic about the probable reception of that particular piece of work. This meant that for probably half the days during the year I had a couple of hours in the morning, and perhaps an hour late in the evening after I had a drink, when I was not consciously sad.

Only work helped. For a long time my wife thought that she could distract me with movies and other entertainment, but it never worked. In the midst of the movie I'd be thinking how worthless a person I am, and about the failures of all my efforts. But in the midst of work—and especially when I would have a beautiful hard problem to think through, or a new idea would come to me—my depression would ease. Thank goodness for the work.

You may wonder, as I did: If the sadness and self-loathing hurt so much, why I didn't resort to liquor and tranquilizers (the new drugs were not then available) to cut the pain? I didn't do so, even during the worst half-year or year at the beginning, for two reasons: First, I felt that I had no "right" to use artificial gimmicks to escape from the pain because I felt it was my own fault. Second, I was afraid that tranquilizers or other drugs would interfere with the one part of me that I continued to respect, my ability to have ideas and think clearly. Without explicitly recognizing it, I acted as if the only possible avenue of escape for me, in the short run and the long run, was to be able to think well enough to involve myself in some work for a while every day, and maybe eventually to do enough useful work to bring about self-respect. Booze or pills could ruin that avenue of hope, I thought.

All those years I concealed my depression so that no one except my wife knew about it. I was afraid to seem vulnerable. And I saw no benefits in revealing my depression. When occasionally I hinted about it to my friends, they did not seem to respond, perhaps because I did not make clear how badly off I really was.

In December, 1974, I told the family physician that I had reduced my possibilities of happiness to "two hopes and a flower." One of the hopes was a book which I hoped would make an important contribution to people's thinking and perhaps to some government policies. I worried that the book was not written in a sufficiently attractive manner to make any impact, but it was one of my hopes anyway. The second of my hopes was that sometime in the future I'd write a book about how to think, how to use one's head, how to use one's mental resources, in such a way as to make the best use of them. I hoped that that book would put together a lot of what I've done and what I know into a new and useful form. That book became *Developing Decision-Making Skills for Business*.)

The flower was a flower that I often looked at while I was meditating. In that meditation I could let everything go and feel that there is absolutely no "ought" of obligation upon me—no "ought" to continue meditating, no "ought" to stop meditating, no "ought" to think about this or to think about that, no "ought" to telephone or not to telephone, to work or not to work. The flower was for that moment an enormous relief from "ought," the flower that demanded nothing yet offered great beauty in quiet and peace.

About 1971, give or take a year, I decided that I wanted to be happy. I had figured out that one cause of my depression was my self-punishment for what I felt were my bad deeds, in the superstitious belief that if I punished *myself* this might ward off *other people's* punishment. And I then concluded that I no longer felt the need to be unhappy as a way of punishing myself. So, the first thing that happened in this sequence of events was that *I decided explicitly that I wanted to be happy*.

Starting perhaps 1972, I tried a variety of devices to break through my depression and give me happiness. I tried Zen-type concentration on the moment to prevent my thoughts from slipping to anxious memories of the past or anxious fears about the future. I tried think-happy exercises. I tried breathing exercises, separately and also together with concentration exercises. I started a list of "good things that I can say about myself" in those moments when I felt low and worthless and devoid of self-esteem, to pep myself up. (Unfortunately, I only managed to get two things down on the list: a) My children love me. b) All students who have done theses with me respect me, and many continue our relationship. Not a very long list, and I never managed to use it successfully. None of these schemes helped for more than half a day or a day.)

Starting in the summer or fall of 1973, a revolution lasting one day each week came into my life. An Orthodox Jewish friend of mine told me that it is one of the basic precepts of the Jewish Sabbath that one is not allowed to think about anything that will make him or her sad or anxious during that day. This struck me as an extraordinarily good idea, and I tried to obey that rule. I tried to obey it not because of a sense of religious dictate, but rather because it seemed to me a wonderful psychological insight. So on the Sabbath I have tried to act in ways that would keep me thinking in a friendly and happy manner, ways such as not allowing myself to work in any way, not think about work-connected things, and not letting myself be angry with the children or other people no matter what the provocation.

On this one day a week—and *only* on this one day of the week—I found I could usually fend off depression and be content and even joyful, though on the other six days of the week my mood ranged from gray to black. More specifically, on the Sabbath if my thoughts tended to drift toward things which were unhappy, I tried to act like a mental street-sweeper, using my broom to gently deflect my mind or sweep away the unpleasant thoughts, and to nudge myself back to a pleasanter frame of mind. The fact of knowing that there was one day in which I would do no work probably was itself very important in alleviating my depression, because an important factor in my depression has been my belief that my hours and days should be devoted entirely to work and to the duty of work. (It's worth noting that I've often had to *struggle* to keep myself from being depressed on the Sabbath, and sometimes the effort of the struggle seemed so great that it just wasn't worth it to keep struggling, but rather seemed easier just to give myself over to the depression.)

After that I'm not sure exactly in which order things happened. Starting September, 1974, the work-load felt lighter than for many years. (Of course my work-load is largely self-imposed, but deadlines felt less pressing.) Starting in 1972, I began no new works, and instead tried to finish up all the things which were in my pipeline so as to get my desk clear. And starting in September, 1974, the various books and articles and research that I had in process were, one by one, getting done. From time to time, of course, I was jerked up short by a new set of proofs or a new deadline for something that I had set in motion a long time before. But for the first time in a very long time there were at least some interludes during which I felt unrushed and free. I also had the feeling that I really was approaching that nirvana when I really would be very free, and able to feel a sense of relaxation. But still I was depressed—sad, and full of self-loathing.

Starting about the middle of December, 1974, I had a special feeling of nearing completion, and I felt that in many ways it was the best period that I had had for the past thirteen years. Because I had no troubles with health, family, or money, nothing pressed on me from outside my own psychology. That certainly did not mean that I was happy or undepressed. Rather, it meant that I was sufficiently undepressed that I was willing to spend some time on myself and my depression.

I therefore determined that if I was *ever* going to rid myself of depression, then was the time to do it. I had the time and energy. And I was in a cosmopolitan city (Jerusalem) which I thought (wrongly) was likely to have more possibilities of help than my small home city in the U.S. I decided to look for someone who might have the wisdom to help me. I thought to consult some eminent psychologists in person, and others by mail. And at the same time I went to a family physician to ask him to refer me to someone—physician, psychologist, religious wise man, or whatever—who might help. All this should illustrate how desperate I was to get rid of my depression. I figured that it was my last chance—now or never: If it didn't work then, I'd give up hope of ever succeeding. I felt like a man in a movie hanging by his fingertips to the edge of the cliff, figuring he has strength enough for just one more try to pull himself up and over to safety—but the fingers are slipping . . . his strength is waning . . . you get the picture.

The family physician suggested a psychologist, but one visit convinced us both that—good as he probably is—that he was not the right man for my problem. He in turn suggested a psychoanalyst. But the psychoanalyst suggested a long course of therapy which exhausted me just thinking about it; I didn't believe it would succeed, and it didn't seem worth spending the energy or money to try.

Then in March, 1975, about four weeks before writing the first draft of this account, I felt that my current work was really complete. I had no work laying on my desk, all my manuscripts had been sent to publishers—simply nothing pressing. And I decided that now I owed it to myself to try to spend some of my "good time"—that is, the time when my mind is fresh and creative in the morning—thinking about myself and my problem of depression in an attempt to see if I could think my way out of it.

I went to the library and took out a bag of books on the subject. I began to read, think, make notes. The book which made the greatest impression upon me was Aaron Beck's *Depression.* The main message I got was that a person can alter one's thinking by consciously working at it, in contrast to the passive Freudian view with its focus on the "unconscious." I still didn't have much hope that I could work my way out of depression, because many times I had tried without success to understand it and deal with it. But this time I decided to devote my full energies to the subject when I was fresh, rather than thinking about it only at those times when I was exhausted. And armed with that key message of Beck's cognitive therapy, I at least had *some* hope.

Perhaps the first big step was my concentrating on the idea—which I had understood for a long time but had simply taken for granted—

that I'm never satisfied with myself or what I do; I never allow myself to be satisfied. I have also known the cause for a long time: With all good intentions, and though we were (until her death in 1986) quite fond of one another even if not very close, my mother (with the best of intentions) never seemed satisfied with me as a child (though perhaps she really was). No matter how well I did something, she always urged that I could do better.

Then this startling insight came to me: Why should I still pay attention to my mother's stricture? Why should I continue to be dissatisfied with myself just because my mother had built that habit of dissatisfaction into me? I suddenly realized that I was under no obligation to share my mother's views, and I could simply tell myself "Don't criticize" whenever I begin to compare my performance to the level of greater achievement and perfection urged by my mother. And with this insight I suddenly felt free of my mother's dissatisfaction for the first time in my life. I felt free to do what I wanted with my day and my life. That was a very exhilarating moment, a feeling of relief and freedom which continues until this moment, and which I hope will continue for the rest of my life.

This discovery that I am not *obligated* to follow my mother's orders is exactly the idea that I later discovered is the central substantive idea in Albert Ellis's version of cognitive therapy.

But though this discovery helped a great deal, by itself it was not enough. It removed some of the knives I felt sticking into me, but it did not yet make the world look bright. Perhaps the depression persisted because I felt I was not succeeding in making a real contribution with my research and writings, or perhaps it was because of other underlying connections between my childhood and my present self-comparisons and mood which I do not understand. Whatever the reason, the structure of my thinking was not giving me a happy life-loving life, despite my discovery that I need not keep criticizing myself for lapses from perfection.

Then came another revelation: I remembered how my depression lifted on one day each week, on the Sabbath. And I also remembered that just as Judaism imposes an obligation not to be anxious or sad on the Sabbath, Judaism also imposes an obligation upon the individual to enjoy his or her life. Judaism enjoins you not to waste your life in unhappiness or to make your life a burden, but rather to make of it the greatest possible value. I am here using the concept of obligation in a rather vague and unspecified fashion. I am not using the concept in the way that a traditional religious person would use it—that is, as a duty imposed upon a person by the traditional concept of God. Nevertheless, I did feel some kind of a vow in which there is a compact, an obligation which goes a little bit beyond me and me.

After it occurred to me that I have a Jewish obligation not to be unhappy, it occurred to me that I also have an obligation to my children not to be unhappy, but rather to be happy, in order to serve as a proper model to them. Children may imitate happiness or unhappiness just as they imitate other aspects of their parents. I think that by pretending not to be depressed I had avoided giving them a model of unhappiness. (This is the one part of our relationship in which I have falsified and play-acted, rather than being openly and truthfully myself.) As they would have gotten older they would, however, have seen through this play-acting.

And like the happy ending of a fairy tale I promptly became undepressed and have (mostly) stayed undepressed. It was a matter of pitting one value against another. On the one side was the value of trying with all my strength, and damn the personal consequences, to create something of social value. On the other side was the value that I derived from Judaism: life is the highest value, and all have an obligation to cherish life in others and in oneself; to allow oneself to be depressed is a violation of this religious injunction. (I also got some help from the sage Hillel's injunction. "One may not neglect the work, but one is not required to finish it, either.")

Those, then, were the main events in my passage from black despair, then to constant gray depression, then to my present state of non-depression and happiness.

Now a few words about how my anti-depression tactics work out in practice. I have instructed myself, and have pretty much got into the habit, that whenever I say to myself "You're an idiot" because I forgot something or don't do something right or do something sloppily, I then say to myself, "Don't criticize." After I start to browbeat myself because I didn't prepare a class well enough, or I was late for an appointment with a student, or I was impatient with one of my children, I say to myself, "Lay off. Don't criticize". And after I say this it's like feeling the yank of a reminder rope. I then feel my mood change. I smile, my stomach relaxes, and I feel a sense of relief run all through me. I also try the same kind of plan with my wife, whom I also criticize too much, and mostly for no good reason. When I start to criticize her about something—the way she cuts the bread, puts too much water on to boil, or pushes the children to get to school on time—I again say to myself "Don't criticize."

Since the start of my new life, there have been several family problems or work failures which previously would have deepened my depression from gray to black for a week or more. Now, instead of these events throwing me into deep and continuing depression, as would have happened before, each of them has caused me some pain for perhaps a day. Then after doing something active to deal with the event—such as trying to improve the situation, or writing a letter blowing my top at the responsible person (usually not mailed)—I have been able to forget the matter, and to leave behind the pain caused by it.

That is, I'm now able to get over these unpleasantnesses fairly easily. And taken together, this means that I enjoy most of my days. When I wake up—which has always been the hardest time for me, as for many depressives—I'm able to draw a mental picture of the oncoming day which seems reasonably free of events that I'd have to criticize myself for, such as not working hard enough. I look forward to days mostly of freedom and tolerable pressures and burdens. I can tell myself that if I really don't want to do all the things that are more-or-less scheduled for that day, I have the right not to do a fair number of them. In that way I can prevent much of the dread I used to have when looking forward to duty-filled days with no sense of coming pleasure.

* * *

That ends the description of my life written just before and soon after my release from depression. Here are a few reports on my progress later on, as they were written at various times:

March 26, 1976

It is almost a year from the time my new life began. Inscribing the date makes me think with pleasure that tomorrow is my youngest son's birthday, and that gives me a joyful apprehension of life such as I never had before April of 1975. I am able to smile, close my eyes, feel melting tears and inner pleasure when I think—as I did just now—of one of the children's birthdays.

I am, by now, less often ecstatic with my new joy of living than I was at the beginning of this new life. Partly that may be due to getting used to my new life without depression, and accepting it as permanent. It may also be partly because

I'm no longer in Jerusalem. But still I have these ecstatically-joyful skipping-and-leaping feelings probably more often than most people who have never been severely depressed for a long time. One has to have experienced pain for a long time to be able to be wildly joyful just from noticing the absence of pain.

January 16, 1977

Soon it will be two years since I decided to get rid of depression, and did so. There still is a constant running skirmish between me and the wolf that I know still waits for me outside the door. But aside from a two-week period that followed an accumulation of professional problems, when my spirits were sufficiently low that I worried I was relapsing into permanent depression, I have been undepressed. Life is worth living, for my own sake as well as for my family's sake. That's a lot.

June 18, 1978

No news is often good news. I've hit some bumps in the past three years, but I've recovered each time. Now I think of myself like a buoyant swimmer. A wave can force me below the surface, but my specific gravity is less than that of water, and eventually I'll float back up after each ducking.

I remember the years when, except for stretches during hours when I was writing, not fifteen minutes of a day would pass without my reminding myself how worthless I am—how useless, unsuccessful, ridiculous, presumptuous, incompetent, immoral, I am in my work, family life and community life. I used to make an excellent argument for my worthlessness, drawing on a wide variety of evidence, and constructing a watertight case.

One important reason that I castigated myself so often and so well was that I believed that I *ought* to keep telling myself how worthless I am. That is, I made sure that I escaped no punishment for my many sins. I functioned as an ever-diligent avenging angel. Then I would finish off the job by being depressed because I felt so depressed in response to all these reminders of my worthlessness. (Being depressed because of being depressed is a common routine with depressives.)

The only force inside me that opposed the gloom was my sense of the ridiculousness of it all—the vision of myself as avenging angel, perhaps, or the jest of carrying the process to absurdity with jokes like titles for an autobiography, "Ten Thousand Leagues Up the Creek Without an Ego." That humor did help a bit, though, by giving me some perspective on how silly it was for me to take myself and my worthlessness so seriously.

Now that I am undepressed I still acknowledge myself to be less than a success with respect to the goals I struggle to attain. But now I only infrequently tell myself how worthless and failing I am. I can sometimes go through an entire day with only occasional remembrances of my worthlessness. I avoid these thoughts by banishing them at first appearance with repression, humor, and misdirection (depression-fighting devices I tell you about in the book) and by reminding myself that my family is well, I am suffering no pain, and the world is mostly at peace. I also try to keep in mind that I'm not a bad father, in my family's eyes as well as in my own.

One important reason that I now act as I do is that I now believe that I *ought not let myself* dwell on my being of little worth, and that I ought not to be depressed by it. And that "ought" comes from the Values Treatment that was an essential part of my salvation.

October 18, 1981

I have hit the jackpot. The world has now made it easy for me to remain undepressed. I no longer must deflect my mind from my professional difficulties in order to stay happy, but instead I can now dwell on my worldly "success" and take pleasure from it.

It is important for both you and me to remember that before my ship came in I had many days in the past few years when I said to myself that I could be no happier. I remember a Thursday in the Spring of 1980 when I was walking to my office and I thought: The trees are lovely. The sun feels good on my back. Wife and children are physically and mentally well. I feel no pain. I have a good job and no money worries. I see peaceful activities on the campus around me. I'd be a fool not to be happy. And I *am* happy, as happy as one could be. In fact, this is the best day of my life. (On other days since 1975 I had also said to myself, this is the best day of my life, or the best Sabbath of my life. But there is no contradiction among such superlatives.)

Then starting June, 1980, many good things happened to me professionally. It started with a controversial article that immediately became very well-known, and led to many invitations to speak and write; that represented a chance for me to reach a wide audience with a set of ideas that had previously fallen mostly on deaf ears, or more exactly, on no ears. Each new writing expanded my possibilities and invitations even more. Then a book on these ideas came out in August, 1981, and immediately was taken up by magazines, newspapers, radio and television. Journalists call me frequently for my views on happenings in this field. My work has come to be seen as legitimate though controversial. My friends joke that I'm a celebrity. Who wouldn't find this easy to take?

But my happiness is not based on this "success." I was undepressed before it happened, and I'm rather confident I'll be undepressed after all this blows over. Being happy because of what is happening outside you is too shaky a basis for happiness. I want the joy and serenity that comes from within me, even despite adversity. And it is that joy and serenity that the methods of this book brought to me—and perhaps will bring you, too. With all my heart I hope that you, too, will soon reflect on some days as being the best days of your life, and that the other days will be without pain. Please struggle to reach that peaceful shore, for your own sake and for me.

October 12, 1988

In 1981 I *thought* I had hit the jackpot. And in perhaps the most important respect this was so: My main professional work had a large effect in changing the thinking of both academic researchers and the lay public. But for a variety of reasons, some of which I think I understand and some of which I surely do not understand, my profession did not take me to its bosom on this account, or make the way easier for my subsequent professional work; access to the non-technical public did become easier, however.

The organizations that oppose my viewpoint continue to dominate public thinking, though the scientific basis for their arguments has been eroded. I have had to conclude that though I may have made a dent in the armor of the opposing viewpoint, and perhaps provided some ammunition for others engaged on the same side of the struggle as I am, the opposing viewpoint will continue to roll on inexorably, though perhaps with a bit less exuberance and carelessness than in the past.

These outcomes have pained and frustrated me. And I have had to keep my pain and frustration to myself lest my unbuttoned words and acts seem "unprofessional" and therefore work against me. (Indeed, I am being careful in these very words on the subject.)

The pain and frustration have taken me to the brink of depression many times

> during the years since about 1983 or so. But the methods for fighting depression described in this book—and especially my basic values about human life, even though it is no longer necessary for my grown-up children's sake that I remain undepressed—have pulled me back from the brink again and again. That is a lot to be thankful for, and perhaps as much as a human being can expect. As to the future—I must wait and see. Will continued unsuccessful struggle make me feel so helpless that I will feel driven from the field, and therefore escape from the negative self-comparisons into either cheerful or apathetic resignation? Will I re-interpret what has happened as success rather than failure, as acceptance rather than rejection, and therefore have positive self-comparisons with respect to this work?

I end with an open question: If I had continued to experience complete lack of success with my main work, rather than the breakthrough that occurred around 1980, could I have continued to maintain my underlying cheerfulness, or would the quagmire of rejection have sucked me inexorably into depression? Perhaps I could have escaped by giving up that line of work entirely, but that would have meant giving up some of my most cherished ideals, and it is not at all sure that I could have produced more positive results in any related field of work that I enjoyed and respected.

I began this epilogue by saying that I healed myself. But healing is seldom perfect, and health never is forever. I hope that you can do even better than I have done. It will make me happy if you do.

26

Why do so Few Nonreligious (and Religious) People Enjoy a Sabbath?

The Sabbath is the most important day in the week for Rita and for me. Our way of enjoying it seems strange to most other persons, Christians and also nonreligious Jews—and even to religious Jews. By telling you about the Sabbath and our ways I can proselytize a bit for the institution of the Sabbath as well as describe a crucial part of my life.

As you read this chapter, however, please understand that I do not believe the observance of the Sabbath implies anything about the religious beliefs of the observer. I believe that there is no necessary connection between enjoying a Sabbath and religious belief. Rita has a fairly traditional Jewish religious belief, whereas I am a radical atheist along the lines of Buddha. But we both enjoy the Sabbath in a fairly similar fashion.

Also, please be aware that many orthodox persons would be horrified by my (our) free interpretation of the Sabbath. For them it is very different in practice, and regrettably (in my view), for many of them it also is different in spirit. I think that many of them miss the spirit of the day, as Hillel and Jesus told them (about which more below).

This is what the Sabbath is *not*: It is not a grim day. It is not a day of mourning (in fact, Jews are not allowed to mourn a death during the hours of the Sabbath). It is not a day of austerity; just the opposite; whatever opulence even the poorest family can afford should be enjoyed on the Sabbath. Though strict Jewish law includes many prohibitions for the Sabbath, the (true, I say) aim is not to make it an unhappy day, but rather to make it the most enjoyable of the days.

The Sabbath is not similar to meditation, though meditation may be a part of the Sabbath. In the early 1970s, I would meditate with a candle or with a flower for 15 or 20 minutes late Friday evening.

The Sabbath is not a vacation, in the fashion that we take secular days off from work. It is not a day for heavy chores. It may be a day for light, casual ball games but not for the strain of competition.

When I was growing up, Saturday was not a good day for me because it consisted mainly of don'ts. Don't ride your bike. Don't use a pencil. Don't, don't, don't. It need not and should not be that way. Prohibitions that make the Sabbath onerous are in the opposite spirit of the Sabbath.

As I understand the original Jewish conception of it, the Sabbath should not be a grim day fenced about with these "don'ts." Rather, it is a day of delight, where the choices not to do this or that are made in order to enhance that delight.

As I understand the spirit of the day, there are no particular "rules" that—if one does not follow any or all of them—one should not consider that one abuses the Sabbath. The Sabbath is not a pane of glass that can be shattered by one or another minor act.

More generally, as Jesus (and Hillel before him) put it, the Jew was not made for the Sabbath, but rather the Sabbath was made for the Jew, meaning that the Sabbath is not a religious duty or sacrifice to God. Rather, it is a great gift of religious thought (or of God, if one prefers) that can enhance one's life.

That's what the Sabbath is *not*. Now about what the Sabbath *is*: It is a day when you do not work and do not even think about work. By "work" is meant any act that *creates*, that builds or fixes or takes care of things, whether part of your job or your home life. On the Sabbath you don't fix a squeaky screen door or plant flowers in the garden or buy a new muffler. If a practical idea comes into your head you try to push it out again, as if to say, come back later. You try not to let yourself think about plans for a meeting or an idea for an article; if thoughts about these activities came into your mind, you politely tell the thoughts to come back after the Sabbath is over. If one of these thoughts comes into your mind nevertheless, you have not "sinned" and you should not criticize yourself. And you'll write it down rather than have it floating in and out.

You also do not worry about debts or the children's schoolwork or not getting promoted or a sickness, because such thoughts are inconsistent with the peaceful feeling and sense of pleasure with life that you try to cultivate on the Sabbath. It is a day when you try to be conscious of the goodness of life in general and of your life in particular, when you try to find elements in your world that make you feel the sweetness of being alive, a day when you try to savor every moment and wish that the hours did not pass so rapidly.

The Sabbath should be the day of the week that you most look forward to.

What might you do on the Sabbath more specifically? You might read poetry or prayers or history or science (if they are not part of your job). You might go to religious services. You make love to a beloved spouse if it is humanly possible to do so, and twice is better than once. You might joke with the children, or play ball with them—but probably not so vigorously that you forget that it is the Sabbath. You should eat the best food in the house. You may have one, two, or three Sabbath meals of particularly choice foods with your family, perhaps with some ritual and if at all possible with happy songs. You might take a long serene walk looking at trees or water. You might talk with friends or relatives about non-argumentative matters, perhaps in a reflective fashion. Sometimes you will do some things that you ordinarily prefer not to do on the Sabbath because you feel a pressing need or desire to do so: play ball hard, or drive a friend to the airport, or write a note to yourself about some work to be done tomorrow. But these unusual acts don't "desecrate" the Sabbath, they just reduce it a little.

These are some of the things Rita and I do: All business-related papers are cleared from sight, and we close the doors to workrooms. I wear a white V-neck shirt instead of the colored one I wear in the summer (when I wear any shirt at all), and a white shirt under a sweater in the winter whereas I usually wear just a sweater the rest of the week; I also wear different shoes, different pants, and bathe and change my underwear before the Sabbath begins. Of course we make love Friday night. I have wine at lunch on Shabbat, but not the rest of the week. And I eat a variety of very fat delicacies that would drive a nutritionist to despair, whereas the rest of the week I eat simple staples and lots of vegetables. I do no writing except if some thought comes to me that otherwise the fear of forgetting would bother me. I try not to look at the clock, and I don't rush for anything. During the warm half of the year I try to sit in the garden rather than on the deck, where

I work on the other six days. I read different books than the rest of the week—classics, mathematics, and other departures from everyday fare. I call relatives and friends on the phone and chat calmly. I usually don't exercise until the day is over.

A high point of our Erev Shabbat dinner is the blessing over the children. Because Rita did not like the characters and actions of the "Mothers" mentioned in the blessing—Sara, Rebecca, Rachel, and Leah—we developed a list of other persons we would like our children to take after, and we always invited guests to contribute names with the sole criterion that the person no longer be alive (and subject to Rita's vetoes). Some of the public personages on the list (I omit the relatives and friends) tell something about us, I believe. Here is some of the list:

Women: Miriam; Naomi; Ruth; Anne Hutchinson; Hannah; Deborah; Harriet Tubman; Emma Lazarus; Henrietta Szold; Jane Adams; Hulda, the Prophetess; Rachel, wife of Rabbi Akiva; Judith Resnick; Dorothy Thomas; Jane Austen; Vashti; Lillian Wald; Marian Anderson; Eleanor Roosevelt.

Men: William James; Benjamin Franklin; Albert Einstein; Abraham Lincoln; King David; Hillel; Adam Smith; David Hume; Martin Luther King; Winston Churchill; Mark Chagall; Spinoza; Maimonides; Daniel; Jonathan; Louis Brandeis; Jesus; Martin Buber; John Locke; Jackie Robinson; Hank Greenberg; Malcolm X; Ahad Ha'am; George Washington; Thomas Jefferson; Arthur Ashe; Frederick Bastiat; Warren Brookes; Friedrich Hayek; William Shakespeare; Thurgood Marshall; Raul Wallenburg; Harry Truman; The Buddha; John Marshall; Morris Cohen; Bayard Rustin.

I admire many (though not all) of these persons.

Some people say: There is no reason for me not to work on the Sabbath because I *like* my work. Rita and I are lucky enough to like our work as much as anyone can, and we probably do too much of it six days a week. But the Sabbath is a *different* part of life. It is not just a day to enjoy yourself, it is a day to enjoy yourself in a special way. It is another dimension of life.

It is not a day of "fun"; that usually means a good television show or noisy partying or reading a mystery novel. Those are good things to do, but they are not Sabbath activities because they are too absorbing and keep you from conscious awareness of the Sabbath mood. The minutes go too fast when engaged in those activities, whereas your aim is to make the Sabbath stretch out as long as you can, the better to taste its bliss.

A couple of anecdotes may show you what the Sabbath has meant to us: As described in Chapter 00, I first came to enjoy the Sabbath during a very long period of deep depression. Seven days a week, I spent most of 16 or 18 hours a day castigating myself for my shortcomings of skill, conscience, and behavior. When I learned from Nat Leff in the summer of 1970 that on the Sabbath one is "supposed" not to think anxious thoughts, it was like coming to an oasis in the desert. I remember getting up at five one Saturday morning to go to the toilet, and automatically I began to dwell on all the horrible aspects of myself. Then I suddenly remembered: This is the Sabbath; I don't have any obligation to remember what a miserable person I am. I instantly felt joyous relief, a sense of peace that I almost never had in those years. By enabling me to be safe from my need to punish myself one day in seven, to alleviate my gloom, the Sabbath may have saved my life.

The one problem that the Sabbath created for us that we would not have had otherwise was an occasional special difficulty with the children when they were growing up. We did our best to make it the best day of the week—taking the trips that were the most fun, and so on. But the kids knew that on the Sabbath they could expect us to be more pleasant than on other days, and we wanted to avoid saying harsh or punishing words to them at all costs, and being human and children, this sometimes led them to do things that they otherwise knew we'd jump on them for—deeds, sometimes, but more often words and demeanor.

The meaning of the term "Sabbath" may be illuminating. The root word in Hebrew simply means "to rest," in the sense of stopping work. When workers strike, the term used in Hebrew comes from the same root. It is a putting down of one's tools, a ceasing from the activities of creating and making things happen.

People sometimes say they don't take a Sabbath because they feel they need seven days to get the weeks' work done. This is a matter of priorities, of course, deciding whether the work that is done on the Sabbath is more or less important than the human experience of the Sabbath that one would otherwise have. But there is also the practical consideration that one does not always get more or better work done by working seven days rather than taking a Sabbath one day and working the other six. The human mind and body are not so purely mechanical that the total output is a simple function of the number of hours of time spent working.

It may be that some people need, and can benefit from, a Sabbath more than other people. It may be that—to use William James's term—the "healthy souls" have less use for a Sabbath than do the twice-born people. Interestingly, it is the "sick souls" (again James's phrase) that Jesus addressed his mission to. Those who are not naturally healthy souls—though they may be in perfect health, just as an alcoholic who has completely stopped drinking is still an alcoholic—may have special need to enjoy a Sabbath.

A related point: When one feels heavy-laden, the Sabbath is especially welcome. I can remember feeling about the Sabbath as an exhausted, frightened swimmer feels when finally reaching and crawling up on the beach, after feeling that you would never make it. Perhaps it is so that when one is living off the fat of the land—when the work goes well, when success crowns your endeavors, and when you and your loved ones are healthy and flourishing—the Sabbath may not seem so precious because it does not then represent sheer salvation. But if you try feeling about it as you feel about a friend who has helped you greatly when in need, and is therefore too valuable to abandon when times are good, you will find that your delight in the Sabbath can still make your life much the richer, even if it does not now feel like a lifesaver. At those times it can help, too, if you can remember in gratitude how the Sabbath did save your life earlier, or can save your life later when again you are in trouble and need.

Friends ask: But how do you manage to observe a Sabbath? The answer is: It's easy; you just do it. When late Friday afternoon comes, we turn off the computers, tell anyone who calls about business that we'll call back on Sunday or Monday, don't take the mail in, and ignore the fax. It sounds impossible, but in fact the problems it presents are minuscule. Once in a while a real problem arises. For example, I was asked to be on Louis Rukyser's very widely watched *Wall Street Week* television show to discuss immigration, and I felt that it was important to do so in the midst of a hot public debate about impending legislation. When I told the producer of my quandary and my decision not to do the show, it turned out that one Thursday a year they tape the show instead of doing it live on Friday evening, and that Thursday was coming up soon. Bingo.

Events don't always turn out that neatly. But I have found that it is only once in several years—and at longer and longer intervals—that I choose to work on the Sabbath.

The only time I choose voluntarily to work at home on the Sabbath has been on two or three occasions when I was suffering so much pain from a family altercation that the only way I could reduce the pain was by immersing myself in work. It didn't seem to make sense to spend the Sabbath suffering, and given that I was unable to control my mind to shut out that suffering, I chose—and wisely, I believe—to turn on the computer and dive into some creative work.

Many Christians go to church every Sunday whether they "want" to or not. ("Want" is in quotes to indicate that the term is ambiguous in this context as in so many others.) Orthodox Jews take upon themselves a commitment not to ride or write or flip a light switch on their Sabbath, even though they recognize that any of these acts might be enjoyable or useful at a given moment. And even Rita and I make a habit of doing or not doing certain things on the Sabbath. You may wonder about the sense of making these "rules" for invariable behavior on the Sabbath.

Consider the Jew's choice between forswearing ever riding on the Sabbath, and allowing herself or himself to choose whether or not to ride on any given Sabbath. The cost of not riding on particular occasions is obvious, though it is hoped that on balance, the person is better off for not doing so. But choosing on each individual occasion reduces the positive balance by imposing a decision-making cost when the choice would eventually be made against riding anyway. A binding commitment never to ride, which avoids these costs of deciding, may be preferable.

Should you read this prayer or not, observe this Sabbath rule or not? The Sabbath-observing person suspends such decision-making, perhaps as an implicit contract between the person and her/his God, or simply as a decision that *taken as a whole* the body of rules is good. Making a cost-benefit analysis of one part or another would be inconsistent with the already-made decision to accept the entire package. The wholeness of the overall package commitment is a key element in the package.

Furthermore, the choice must be nearly irrevocable, because when there should be an occasion when the individual might want to ride, she or he might not choose to do so by *breaking* the rule but rather by *changing* the rule.

If you do decide to try a Sabbath, don't go overboard for it all at once; if you do that, you risk disappointment. An entire day all at once can be a shock, and the results may not seem sufficiently dramatic. Rita and I eased into a full Sabbath over about three years. First we started by just putting aside work for Friday evening. Then Friday evening and Saturday afternoon; at that time, I still chose not to "lose" prime thinking hours on Saturday morning. Then eventually we set aside the full 24 (or 25 or 26) hours. And we have never regretted it, or felt any sense of loss. I can say honestly that there has never been a time when after a Sabbath was over that I have wished that I had worked that day. What happens (or does not happen) on the Sabbath always seems more valuable than any extra work I might have done on that day.

Of course it is true that our occupation—scholars, writers, teachers—and our time in history in the late 20th century, when the gentile world does not keep office hours on either Saturday or Sunday—makes it much easier for us to celebrate the Sabbath than if we were factory workers 75 or 100 years ago who would lose our jobs if we did not work on Saturday. I don't know how I would have acted then. The fact that our times are congenial to enjoying the Sabbath does not make it any less reasonable to take as full advantage of the Sabbath as we can, given our privileged circumstances.

27

How did My Economics Get to be What It Is?

If one is out of step with the rest of the world, one wonders why. So let's try to figure out why many of my economic studies disagree with those of my colleagues. It should be noted before beginning, however, that I am a very mainstream economist in the most fundamental respects—in my concept of the field and of the methods we should use to study economics. But my "mainstream" is that of the great economists of the ages and of those recent economists such as Theodore Schultz, Milton Friedman, Simon Kuznets, Friedrich Hayek, and James Buchanan perhaps, who also are in the mainstream of the greats; I clearly am not in the mainstream of the fanciest trendy movements of the day.

Let's review some of the relevant facts: First, an important cause of my writing what and how I do is that I was not trained as an economist. Rather, I studied experimental psychology as an undergraduate. Then, after three years in the Navy and a year in business, I took a four-quarter masters degree in business administration, plus one more quarter's worth of courses to study for "preliminary" examinations in marketing. Then I wrote a thesis on systems of optimal storage of books in university libraries, based on surveys of book use that I did in conjunction with Herman Fussler. That research finished, I went into the mail-order business on my own.

I never intended to be an academic, let alone an economist.

One of the reasons I intended not to be an academic was that I knew myself unsuited for the kinds of politics found in universities; as it is said, the politics in universities are so vicious because the issues are so trivial. If governmental politics in the U.S. are getting more vicious in the 1990s, as many assert, perhaps it is because the issues are becoming less important. I only began to teach after I realized that researching and scribbling is the work I enjoy best.

I began in 1963 in the Department of Advertising in the College of Communications at the University of Illinois, but was kicked out (told I'd never get tenure) in 1966 by the department head, ostensibly for lack of research (see the list of my publications at the back of the book concerning the plausibility of this assertion). I then moved in 1966 to the Department of Marketing in the College of Business Administration, still at the University of Illinois. In 1969 I became a half-time member of the Department of Economics at the University of Illinois. I've also taught business for two-and-a-half years in three stretches at Hebrew University.

In 1983, I moved to the University of Maryland by way of an open-ended appointment in the Division of Social Sciences. As part of a complex administrative reorganization, my services (that is, an additional "budget line," in academic lingo) were twice offered (without my knowledge) to the economics department for free, a deal which any department would ordinarily grab if the professor in question is capable of doing long division and reading at the eleventh grade level. But the Maryland economics department turned down the offer, mobilized by a professor who regarded my work on population as akin to the seductions of the devil. The College of Business and Management at the University of Maryland (really, Dean Rudy Lamone) was happy to get my services, and I'm happy to be in it.

When I was young, I wrote some nonfiction articles for mass magazines and fiction for "little" magazines; I did legal and engineering work as well as (mainly) line officer's work aboard a Navy ship and while attached to the Marines; and I have always read some in philosophical methods.

All this means is that my head is a ragbag. In academic terminology, my thinking is "eclectic," about which nothing is thought to be worse. Many economists have opined that such diversity makes for good economics. Marshall quoted Mill with approval: "A person is not likely to be a good economist who is nothing else" (*Principles of Economics*, 1920, p. 771). And Hayek made it stronger:

> The physicist who is only a physicist can still be a first-class physicist and a most valuable member of society. But nobody can be a great economist who is only an

> economist—and I am even tempted to add that the economist who is only an economist is likely to become a nuisance if not a positive danger. (quoted by Machlup, *Essays on Hayek*, 1976, p. 49).

Or, as Hutchinson quoted Viner:

> Men who have been trained to think only within the limits of one subject, or only from the point of view of one subject, will never make good teachers at the college level even in that subject. They may know exceedingly well the possibilities of that subject, but they will never be conscious of its limitations, or if conscious of them will never have an adequate motive or a good basis for judging as to their consequences or extent.

Such diversity may be good for one's understanding. But it may also be disastrous for one's ability to relate (in both senses of the word).

My thinking may not be as scattered as it seems on the surface, however. Hayek writes of some scholars that "many of their particular ideas in different fields may spring from some single more general conception of which they are themselves not aware but which, like the similarity of their approach to the separate issues, they may much later discover with surprise." And indeed, a few years ago I noticed that underlying all of my work on population, resources, and environment (though not most of the work in this volume) is the idea of progress—that (as individuals and as groups) people gradually and erratically, but surely, move toward greater efficiency, a higher standard of living, and a better living environment.

Lack of training as an economist has meant that I am without some technical skills that help one pass for an economist. Once in a while this lacuna has even slowed up my work. I have also remained unacquainted with various standard concepts and chunks of economic literature, though I have tried to learn piecemeal what seemed valuable; therefore I have sometimes reinvented old ideas, but this happens even to people who have been conventionally trained.

On the positive side, this lack of graduate training has saved me from getting stuck with some conventional ideas that are wrong, especially the conviction that allocation of fixed resources should be the central interest of economists, and that all theoretical speculation should be done within closed systems (of which more below). It has also led me to use a variety of empirical methods rather than just the single method of regressions based on published economic data.

A shortcoming of the socialization that comes with graduate training in economics is that people begin their inquiry into puzzling real-world situations with standard concepts, rather than with more primitive unstructured curiosity. For example, if one asks why competition produces more effort than monopoly, the trained economist is likely to begin with demand functions, cost functions, and utility functions, rather than wondering: If I were a businessperson, what would the situation look like, and how would I view it, with one competitor compared to no competitor? The former mental habit constrains the imagination from dreaming up radically new analytic approaches which—though *usually* not warranted—may *sometimes* be crucial. As Buchanan says about the conventional thinking:

> Economics seems unlikely to escape from this chaos for many years, if indeed it survives at all as an independent discipline. . . . For myself, I advance no claim that my own thinking has yet fully rid itself of the paradigms of neoclassical orthodoxy. (*What Should Economists Do?*, 1979, p. 63)

The other side of the matter is that many of my colleagues in economics—and even more astonishing, many of my colleagues who teach business administration—have never worked in business. Many have never in their whole lives even worked at any noneducation job, such as a retail food establishment or the armed services or school-teaching or the Peace Corps or anything else; they've never been away from school for more than a summer. Yet they teach others about business—even how to practice "business policy." Firsthand experience in business certainly would produce unwelcome confusion to most economists and would undoubtedly interfere with the practice of conventional career-oriented allocation-of-resources research. But it would lead to better economics.

Speaking of allocation of resources, which is the concept that now defines the study of economics: For at least a century, economists have illustrated the process of allocation of resources among competing uses with the story of Robinson Crusoe. And increasingly, economists have turned away from Alfred Marshall's definition of economics as the study of how people fulfill their material needs. They have turned instead to Lionel Robbins's definition of economics as allocation. But the key element in Crusoe's improvement of his situation was not better allocation. Rather, impelled by need and sparked by imagination, Crusoe developed his "economy" by adapting existing knowledge that he brought with him and by creating new techniques.

The difference between these competing concepts of economics is particularly important in the study of natural-resource development. A focus on allocation points away from understanding the process by which growth in population and income leads to higher prices of resources, which then leads to a search for new ways to satisfy demand. After this search is successful—as it inevitably is after some time—humankind is left better off than if the initial resource problem had never arisen; this is the core of the appropriate theory. The development of new energy sources in response to increased demand and decreasing supplies of the currently—used fuel illustrates that model.

To illustrate that an allocation framework founded on the assumption of maximization of personal gain is inadequate for the purposes at hand: Would anyone assert that the great economists to whom this book and two of my other books are dedicated—all of them in their seventies or eighties—continue to labor at developing ideas that will improve human welfare in order to obtain personal monetary gains from the effort? Of course not.

In my view, not to understand that the motivations of these persons are much broader, and probably include elements of the desire to contribute to (rather than to take from) the human enterprise and also include the element of "honor" that Adam Smith judged to be fundamental, is simply to be blinded by a false narrow view of economic theory. Much of the great work of discovery during the history of civilization certainly has been motivated in whole or in part by considerations other than personal income. This does not call into question the enormous motive power of the demand for improvements and the opportunity for gain, but the gain may be measured in many other sorts of coin than the kind that one puts into one's pocket.

My personality surely is a second important element in determining how I got to be the way I am professionally. I'm comfortable neither as follower nor leader. I'm best suited by nature to be the equivalent in the knowledge enterprise of a freelance prospector for semirare metals, the kind of person who won't stop with small veins but rather keeps trying to trace back the veins to the mother lode. Sometimes when I have what seems to me a really good fundamental idea, I feel like a prospector who has found the mother lode but can't find a way to transport it out of the jungle or desert and into the market. Nowadays, though, I'm rather glad when a small vein peters out before it leads me to chase after a more fundamental idea where I will again feel stuck away from civilization without transport back to the market. I get myself into the same sort of difficulty as do those who have the tastes of the rich but the pocketbook of the poor; I have the aspirations and the intellectual habits but not some other powers of the great social scientists.

I grew up thinking that no one, and certainly not the world as a whole, has a burning need of my work or of me personally, other than as a member of a family and as a friend. A fair amount of evidence in adulthood—in my relations with institutions, groups, and professions—has tended to confirm that childhood view. I expect to lose out in whatever the competition or tussle is, and I go quietly—up to a point. But at some point I'll go to the mat with the fight, and I won't give up until the time is up (or sometimes even after the time is up, as this volume shows). Then the guerrilla side of me emerges.

A key element in my thinking is that I believe (along with diverse writers, the most famous of whom are Einstein and Bohr) that scientific propositions are inventions that arise from the interaction of human imagination with natural and social reality, rather than being "laws" that inhere in the natural and social reality and which the scientist "discovers." In the latter view, the world is a system having inherent order, and the task of the scientist is to uncover the "true" propositions and relationships in that system. For example, one may think that the speed with which a body falls due to gravity is one of the underlying propositions that characterize our world, and if we diligently seek after such propositions and relationships we can eventually discover them all, and then we will have a complete understanding of the universe. To put this view another way, at the beginning the universe was created or evolved according to a set of equations, and it is our job to discern the equations. Lynn White notes that

> The consistency with which scientists during the long formative centuries of Western science said that the task and the reward of the scientist was "to think God's thoughts after him" leads one to believe that this was their real motivation (*The Historical Roots of Out Ecological Crisis,* 1967, p. 1206).

The other view—the one which I find more helpful—is to assume only that *(a)* the universe is not perfectly formless or chaotic, though it may once have been and *(b)* the regularities and generalizations that we discover follow from our interests and perceptions as well as from the "out there" features of the world. That is, we invent and develop the relationships we find, rather than merely discovering them. For example, what shape is the earth? To a firm that manufactures cheap globes it is round and smooth, but it is bumpy to a manufacturer of more expensive globes. To a surveyor or farmer, it is flat. For geologists, its circumference is greater at the equator than elsewhere. To an aviator, it is an unsmooth, unround set of upcropping mountains. And so on. The earth does not have one shape but rather many, and the relevant "model"—flat, round, bumpy, or whatever—depends upon your needs and interests. No "model" of the earth captures all its features, because then it would not be an abstracted model, but the earth itself. As Georgescu-Roegen put it:

> [A]ctuality is a seamless whole we can slice . . . wherever we may please. And, Plato to the contrary, actuality has no joints to guide a carver. . . . Only our particular purpose in each case can guide us in drawing the boundary of a process. So, every scientist slices actuality in the way that suits best his own objective—an operation that cannot be performed without some intimate knowledge of the corresponding phenomenal domain. . . . " (*Entropy Law and Economic Progress*, 1970, p. 3).

It follows from this latter view that when systems are logically closed, they are so because we close them for our convenience, rather than because they are "naturally" so. The mathematics and the other logical techniques that we apply to these systems result in approximations—good approximations if we close the systems sensibly, and silly approximations otherwise. This is quite the opposite of the view that God (or an original force) made the lawful universe, and left it to us to discover the laws, the view that Keynes attributes to Newton:

> He regarded the universe as a cryptogram set by the Almighty—just as he himself wrapt the discovery of the calculus in a cryptogram when he communicated with Leibnitz. By pure thought, by concentration of mind, the riddle, he believed, would be revealed to the initiate (*Essays in Persuasion*, 1963/1951, p. 314).

The view I hold is consistent with Einsteinian operationalism. Percy Williams Bridgman, the explicator of this idea, put it this way: "The proper definition of a concept is not in terms of its properties but in terms of actual operations." He pointed out that definitions in terms of properties constituted the barrier that held physics back and took Einstein to crack through.

Related to the closed-system way of thinking is the notion that available resources are finite and countable. This is simply a prejudice, and a prejudice which leads to unsound long-run forecasts. In Einstein's words, "Even scholars of audacious spirit and fine instinct can be obstructed in the interpretation of facts by philosophical prejudices" (quoted by Clark, *Einstein: The Life and Times*, p. 90).

And elsewhere Einstein wrote:

> Concepts which have proved useful for ordering things easily assume so great an authority over us, that we forget their terrestrial origin and accept them as unalterable facts. They then become labelled as 'conceptual necessities,' 'a priori situations,' etc. The road of scientific progress is frequently blocked for long periods by such errors. It is therefore not just an idle game to exercise our ability to analyze familiar concepts, and to demonstrate the conditions on which their justification and usefulness depend, and the way in which these developed, little by little . . . (as quoted by Holton, *Thematic Origins of Scientific Thought*, 1973).

Of course I, too, am constrained by predispositions and prejudices, but at least mine have the virtue that they differ considerably from the consensus of the economics profession.

***

Ever since I was a child and probably before, there have been rumors about a conspiracy in the auto industry to suppress gasoline additives that would make cars run three times as far at the same cost. In spring, 1996, I had a call from Paul Pantone, who has a design, he says, that will run engines on a third as much fuel of any kind, even old paint thinner, as standard engines, but the big companies have frozen him out; it was quite unclear to me why he could not organize the clear-cut test that would prove his claims, but he insisted it would be too expensive. People of this type occasionally seek me out after reading something about me in the newspaper or seeing me on television because they think that my counter-establishment ideas will make me sympathetic to their projects.

Even as a kid I realized that such a conspiracy was likely to be nonsense; if there really were such an additive, someone could find a good way to make a buck out of it, and hence such a substance probably has never existed. And I'm sure there was not a conspiracy in the auto industry to keep seat belts from being mounted on cars for many decades after everyone knew that they would save lives; it simply was in no one's self-interest to do anything about it.

Re seat belts, consider this bit of history. In 1963, when Rita and I bought our first new car to travel across country in the summertime when she was pregnant, I had to go to a mechanic to get a hole drilled in the door frame so there could be a shoulder harness rather than the standard belt harness across her pregnant belly. How many years was it by then that race drivers had worn shoulder harnesses for protection?

Though I was born an economist in the sense of early recognizing the need for tradeoffs and constantly thinking of more efficient ways of allocating (as well as other efficiency methods), I never believed in simple single-valued measures of efficiency, especially the measure of speed. I remember being charmed when in college by the joke about the young woman who reported to her friend on her visit to the Louvre during her summer abroad. She told her friend how many pictures the Louvre holds, and she bragged that she had been in every room and stood before every picture. Then she added: "And I could have done it even faster if I had had roller skates."

Speed reading struck me as an unlikely improvement in a person's mental equipment. I once read of a man in prison who had only one book and therefore practiced what he called "super slow reading." He found great benefits in his invention, as one can imagine, and he said that he continued the practice in later life. Also, being quick to reach an answer to a question has always struck me as usually being not only useless but also dangerous; one of the best devices I know of as a teacher is to hold back the blank answer books on essay examinations until five or ten minutes after distributing the questions; that device forces people to think before they start writing. "Put brain into gear before putting mouth into motion" is a great slogan.

***

I think of myself as being in the great economic tradition of Hume, Smith, Menger, and Hayek, following the clue given by Mandeville. Here is a short statement of my economic vision:

Until the advent of Communism in the USSR in 1917, all economies had developed almost entirely as a result of individual investment decisions in a regime of private ownership, free markets, and uncontrolled prices. Yes, there have always been government-owned enterprises, especially in transportation, and there have been government regulations of some business practices—including wage and price controls—for at least the past 4,000 years (Schuettinger and Butler, *Forty Centuries of Wage and Price Controls*, 1979). And under systems of feudal ownership of farmland, peasants were hardly free. Yet before 1917, no country had had central planning and control of production, or unified ownership of land and capital. It was taken for granted that the initiative for opening and closing enterprises would come from private individuals.

Socialist thinking of the nineteenth century concluded that government ownership would increase efficiency and equity by substituting "rational" planning and large-scale enterprises for an enterprise system. This system is termed a "command" economy because instructions about who is to produce what come from a central authority.

Persons who consider themselves the "social engineers" of such command systems usually take physics as their model. In that science, the number of crucial variables is far smaller than in economics, and their interactions are simpler. To understand the movement of a billiard ball you need take into account only the table, the force of the stick, the weight of the balls, and the initial position of the balls. But to fully understand and predict the behavior of a single economic actor in a market, you would need to know all the contents of all the participants' minds and all the interactions among them. The individual, however, does not need most of this knowledge in order to do her or his business successfully.

Integral to the thinking of those who favor a command economy is concern about what they perceive to be the "chaos" of an "uncontrolled" economy and society. Perhaps this fear of "chaos" arises out of the engineering bent of mind that transfers the idea of planning from the individual enterprise (where it is necessary and inevitable) to the context of an economy, without even questioning whether this is a sensible intellectual transfer. Another impetus to centralized control is lack of belief in the rational capacity of individuals and of people's willingness to exert their rationality—especially individuals with less education and wealth than the person who is doing the worrying. People who espouse central planning also tend to believe, as Hayek paraphrases W. C. Mitchell, that "since man has himself created the institutions of society and civilization, he must also be able to alter them at will so as to satisfy his desires or wishes."

But this lack of confidence in private initiative does not accord with experience. Certainly there are individuals who cannot fend well for themselves. But anyone who has close acquaintance with squatter settlements in, say, Latin America, or with immigrants who have come to the United States with no skills or even knowledge of the language, has learned that these people organize themselves as individuals and as groups, and in the main they pursue their and their families' lives with intelligence and energy.

It is also clear that the absence of central direction does not mean "chaos." Indeed, chaos almost never is met with in an economy, though it is constantly worried about by politicians. Chaotic conditions are only found in suddenly arising and rapidly changing situations such as a gold rush or a government homestead land sale in the nineteenth century in the U.S. West. And the chaos only lasts briefly. Because individuals and businesses can reap windfall benefit from a disequilibrium, they rush to exploit it, and by so doing they remove the disequilibrium and transform chaos into order and stability. That is, true chaos represents a grand economic opportunity, and as soon as entrepreneurs respond to the opportunity, the chaotic elements disappear into an orderly market pattern. Markets are the most effective devices for the elimination of chaos.

Nor is confidence in the power of "rational" central planning warranted by their results. For some years now, there has been ample statistical proof that planned economies are far less efficient than are market-oriented economies, which, in addition, provide the most important benefit of freedom. But with the collapse of the Eastern European economies in the 1980s, the abysmal failure of Communism became unmistakable. So goes one more idea cooked up and perpetuated (and still taught in American universities) by those with too much faith in their own reason and too little faith in the accumulated patterns of human experience.

Most interesting about a command economy are the two reasons why it cannot succeed in achieving economic efficiency—the lack of *incentive by individuals* to invest their energies and their talents in producing goods that other people are willing to pay for, and the inability of a centrally planned system to take advantage of the *information that individuals possess* about the special productive characteristics of the people and equipment with which they work, as well as information about the demand for goods and services in their locality. This theoretical explanation for this failure of central planning has been known since David Hume and Adam Smith, and it was refined into modern form by Karl Menger, Ludwig von Mises, and Friedrich Hayek.

Even in principle, the amount of knowledge necessary to run a modern economy efficiently on the command principle exceeds the possibility of collection of information by any central planning organization. Efficient central planning would require complete understanding of the operation of the entire mechanism as it now exists, as well as the process by which each aspect got to be what it is. If it makes sense to rank impossibilities, this would be far more impossible than gathering the information necessary for efficient control of every car in highway traffic.

Interestingly, the more advanced the society, the more difficult it is to efficiently control the society with central planning, and the more crucial is decentralization. This contradicts the intuition that greater complexity requires a higher degree of planning and organization; that intuition may be sound for most subgroups and enterprises within a society, but not for the society itself. Nor does the great computational power of the supercomputer alter this conclusion. No conceivable amount of computing power could possibly ascertain and sort out all the changes in preferences and circumstances as they happen instantaneously.

To recognize and accept this limit on our human capacities requires a certain amount of humility. Many find intolerable Hume's dictum that though the evolution of society takes place by human *action*, its basic structure has not—and cannot—advance solely by overall human *design*. Our society was not constructed from scratch by a mastermind, nor could any mastermind have conceived its fullness and richness. People do not enjoy recognizing and accepting our inevitable ignorance and fallibility which follows inexorably from the wide dispersion of information and knowledge among the participants in our society and economy. And our traditions and values cannot be fully understood because they evolve by a survival process of trial-error-success.

This does not imply that careful, thoughtful persons and groups cannot make changes in the society that will improve it. Rather, it implies that changes should be made with due recognition of the complexity of the system, and of the possibility that some patterns that seem to be useless or counterproductive may have hidden uses. It implies proceeding with extreme care in dumping existing patterns of organization. Again in Robert Frost's words, one should try to find out why a fence was put up before tearing it down.

It is important to understand that the problem of effectively organizing a country is *not* the problem of learning how to carry out centralized control more effectively, as Soviet reformer Mikhail Gorbachev still seemed to think that it was, as of 1988.

> With a grin and a wink, the Kremlin boss flattered one capitalist tycoon at his table, General Motors chairman Roger Smith, declaring that the Soviet economy should be run more efficiently—"just like GM!" *Newsweek*, December 21, 1987, p. 15.

Gorbachev's vision was central control with efficient coordination. But effective centrally controlled organization is *impossible in principle* because of the lack of coordination that only a market provides. Only a market can equate supply and demand effectively.

The vast quantity of widely dispersed knowledge about individuals' preferences and abilities is communicated automatically in a decentralized society through the price signals that are transmitted by markets. The entire intricate system is built up spontaneously by people responding only to the signals in their own spheres. Any barrier to signals passing unimpeded introduces distortion into an economy and interferes with its efficient working. Such distortion is a malign effect of regulations that forbid individuals from freely setting prices and supplying goods according to the demands of the public. Business people who conspire to fix prices in an industry similarly interfere with price signals and the working of the price systems.

Even a command economy such as the Soviet Union continued to be, as of 1990, needed price signals to indicate to potential purchasers which goods are available in larger and smaller supply. It is a major defect of command economies that they do not have markets to generate such price signals automatically. Socialist economies often are forced to refer to prices set in market economies. For example, the prices Eastern European countries charged each other for such commodities as oil and natural gas were set on the basis of world market prices. The prices themselves may be the most important product that command economies cannot produce.

A second fatal flaw of socialism is its abnegation of human property and work incentives. For example, for the North Korean communist party, "Market incentives . . . are bourgeois ideas, to be stamped out. People should work hard because they are building communism, not because of some special reward for hard work." (*Wall Street Journal*, Aug 15, 1989, p. 1).

Different views of the role of private property follow from different views of how malleable is human nature. For Mandeville, Hume, and Smith (as for Locke) the origin of their interest in economics and society was their interest in human nature. They sought to *understand* human nature. (In contrast, for Godwin, Marx, Engels, Lenin and their followers, the focus of interest is how to *change* human nature.)

The importance of the malleability of human nature in socialist theory is revealed in the USSR's bizarre and tragic course of action with respect to the study of genetics, and especially the Lysenko incident. The USSR was willing to pervert that entire scientific field to fight against the idea that some human propensities might be affected by a person's genetic makeup. (I note this even though I think there is little or no reason to believe that children's mental capacities are genetically connected to their parents' capacities, which does not include the effect of parental influence after birth. Of course this proposition is exceedingly difficult to test and in no way suggests that genes do not influence mental capacity.)

Even in the U.S., private property became less respected in the 1960s. Often after a riot, it was written that "only" property was damaged, as if property does not matter much. But property rights are fundamental to any society. And property includes not just physical goods, but also intellectual property. Property, and the rules surrounding property and business activity, are the substrate for market activity. As Hume and Smith pointed out, if there is no protection for property, there is no liberty. Property is not just wood and concrete and paper and steel; it is the right to arrange one's life, privacy, and work in such ways as one chooses, free of the interference of others.

A market system can aim to achieve equality of *opportunity*, which certainly is a wonderful goal if you care about human liberty. A market system cannot achieve equality of *results*. Equality of results requires that the society *treat* people unequally, and that is not compatible with equality of opportunity, by definition.

Milton Friedman emphasizes that the main benefit of a market economy is the freedom and liberty that accompany it. The argument is strong and persuasive that there cannot be personal freedom without economic freedom, and economic freedom implies free market relationships. The *economic productivity* benefits of a market system are a bonus for those of us who care most about individual liberty. Friedman (and I, following him) would be for a market system even if it were less efficient. In addition, a market system offers the best protection of the economic situation of minorities, as well as of their liberties.

Another disadvantage of a market system is the absence of treatment fitted to individuals' needs in the way that a family or small society can provide for its members. The related advantage is the greater sense of justice in the Anglo-Saxon fashion of treatment by rules rather than authorities; this is a major gain conferred by a market system. Those who hanker for the sort of justice promised (though not actually brought about) by socialist societies—treatment based upon need—may not agree that in this respect the market enhances fairness and personal freedom. A market society offers personal liberty in the sense that an individual can know what the rules are and behave according to them, without having to worry about having his or her fate depending upon a personal relationship with arbitrary authorities.

The main direct *economic* advantage of a larger impersonal society is that it makes possible the multitudinous activities which support large-scale production of a variety of technologically advanced commodities. As noted earlier, only such a society offers individuals a wide range of opportunities to sell their skills freely.

28

This I Believe: Values and Attitudes

Some critics of my work in population economics have said that my views on population growth, immigration, and related issues are the result of my values, "ideology," and/or political views. It is more the other way around. Especially my political views over the years have been affected by what I have learned about the economics and demography of population. This statement should also serve the more general purpose of telling you something about why I do what I do—or at least why I *try* to do what I try to do. I'll also try to dig down to find the roots of these beliefs.

These now are my values and the main elements in my social outlook:

1. *Freedom* is my most fundamental value—with as few ifs and buts as humanly possible. Here I mean *personal liberty* in the Anglo-Saxon sense, the freedom from the coercion of others and of the government. The phrase "My liberty ends where your nose begins" goes a long way to describing what I mean by liberty.
2. *A dislike of privilege and elitism.*
3. *Equal opportunity* for everyone in my country—including, where possible, people now in other countries. I want our society to give people opportunity as much as possible and to treat people equally to the extent that that is possible. Equality of opportunity rather than equality of outcomes is what I seek. A border is seldom a more valid excuse for denying someone an opportunity in another country than is the color of a skin or a sex.

   I think that my history shows that in my public roles I mostly treat everyone the same, irrespective of their backgrounds, educations, sex, age, and so on. In my private role, I believe that I have an obligation to be particularly helpful to those who are close to me.

4. I am greatly in favor of *progress and creating*, as distinct from simply saving and preserving.
5. My sympathies usually are *on the side of the underdog and against the powerful*, but I don't want to rig the game to help the underdog. I don't want us to patronize the underdog—just give him or her an even chance.

   Every time I take out the garbage, I think about our garbage men—what they'll be thinking as they pick up my and others' waste today; whether it will be very hot or very cold and I should therefore leave them some hot coffee or cold drinks; that they are remarkably reliable and that society is much more dependent on them doing their job every day than on academics or State Department administrators or auto salesmen. Why are sanitation workers paid so much less than professional basketball players? The answer is not that the demand for their services is less, but that the supply of their services is more substitutable for in the intermediate run.
6. *Discomfort with big institutions* of any kind.
7. *Dislike of finagling* of any kind. I recognize that this is an inevitable and necessary aspect of any functional society, but I despise achieving one's ends this way. This goes hand-in-hand with my preference for market allocation over political allocation.
8. *Live and let live.* To the maximum extent possible, letting the other person live his or her life without trying to push him or her to live according to your moral standards and way of life. A key theme in my "political" thinking is that I do not want some people using the government to force other people to live the way the first group thinks is moral. Examples: Coercive recycling programs (which have no economic justification); banned travel and shopping on the Sabbath (a day on which I happen to rest from work but do not force others to); subsidizing car pooling or bicycling or mass transit at the expense of driving; encouraging drinking alcohol and forbidding smoking marijuana; legislating against various forms of ugly speech; requiring one to vote; and a long list more. If I am not to be classed as a "liberal," this is the main respect in which I differ with the people who choose that label in the U.S.

   This goes hand-in-hand with my confidence that most people—no matter what their education or income levels—will live their lives in reasonably sensible and creative fashion without instruction from their "betters." Or perhaps more generally and certainly more operationally, I believe that people's lives will not on average be improved by government attempting to influence or coerce them into ways of life they would not otherwise freely choose.
9. Day after day I comfortably trust my life to people who get low scores on IQ tests (whatever that implies)—and you do, too, if you ever drive on a highway. On the other hand, I note how much destruction, confusion, and bad policy has been wrought by people with high IQs—Marx and Keynes being prominent twentieth-century examples of such havoc, Plato being an interesting question mark in this respect. Cleverness in school may correlate very low (and perhaps zero) with wisdom.
10. Concerning the label "conservative": Along with Friedrich Hayek and Milton Friedman, I disavow the label "conservative." I note that for decades Stalin and orthodox communists and other socialists were labeled "progressive" and "left-wing"; now purveyors of the same doctrines are labeled "conservative" and "right-wing"—at least, in other countries.

    I certainly am not for the conservation of resources for themselves, over and beyond what the relevant costs and benefits dictate to the individual decision-maker (putting aside external matters such as pollution). I am not in favor of any public attempts to conserve existing values or culture or ways of life. Generally, I am against "controlling" individuals and boundaries (such as borders). I do not worry about the loss of control by governments.

11. I believe that David Hume, William James, and Friedrich Hayek were the greatest social scientists of their centuries. I am most in tune with the intellectual frameworks and attitudes in the philosophy of science of Hume, James, Albert Einstein (as interpreted by Bridgman), and Simon Kuznets. The economic philosophy and analysis of Adam Smith, Hayek, and Milton Friedman fit me most comfortably.
12. Games always need good rules, and sometimes they need referees (but it is noteworthy how seldom opponents-partners who frequently play together in racket sports and other games need referees). Games seldom need, and are often made worse off, by owners and managers. Games may seem zero-sum in their point scores, but games usually produce benefits for both players, as do markets.
13. Learning from Hayek, I put great stress on the *distinction between the public and private spheres*. In one's role as a public servant—and this public sphere includes being a Little League coach—one ought to act as disinterestedly as possible with respect to persons. In the private sphere, loyalties properly begin at home, as Adam Smith told us that sentiments do.
14. I am in favor of *safety nets* provided by the government, to the extent that the public wishes to be charitable. But I believe that such safety nets can best be credited by giving people the most generalized kind of purchasing power, rather than making decisions paternalistically for them. I have great faith in the capacity of most people, irrespective of education and income levels, to run their lives wisely, and more wisely than others could do it for them.
15. Government is all-important in maintaining order and providing such "night watchman" services as fire protection (though under some conditions private fire protection might even be better). But I have little faith in the efficiency of government doing those things that might be done alternatively by private firms and individuals. Or rather, I have great faith that government will do such things *worse*—less efficiently, and with more corruption, and at the cost of individual liberty.
16. Tolerance for others' way of life is high in my scheme of values. The notion of live and let live is allied with the value of liberty. And it fits with my belief that a major reason that people condemn others' ways of lives is that by doing so they make themselves feel more virtuous and more valuable. I confess to being intolerant of intolerance.
17. A country should provide *enough* opportunity, but it is hopeless to attempt to provide equal opportunity at birth. I am frequently impressed and moved by the extent to which the United States provides educational opportunity widely. There is hardly a place in the United States where a person cannot reach a junior college by commuter car. And the facilities and faculties of junior colleges and public senior colleges are extraordinarily impressive—even or especially in states like Arkansas and Georgia, where I have given talks in recent years. In many ways the faculty there are better for students than they are at universities where second-rate intellects focus themselves on "research" to get tenure. And the physical facilities at these places are much better than at my home institution of the University of Maryland.

This goes back to the policy early in the century and before, that every child should be within walking distance of a school. It was this that led to the one-room country school that was only superseded when school buses could make it through muddy roads to consolidated schools.

18. I believe that it is each person's duty to serve others, at least to some extent. I think it is each person's duty, also, to enjoy his or her life rather than to be unhappy. And I don't think that it is anyone's duty to live a life of austerity. If one is able to do so without inordinate sacrifice, I believe that one should be useful, and employ one's gifts for the benefit of others as well as for oneself. I believe that this urge is felt by a great many people, and here I hark back to Hayek's observation about the great sadness of a person who is not able to put his or her talents to work.

More and more as I have gotten older, and consistent with my belief that progress is not only possible but inevitable, and probably irreversible by now, the crucial philosophical element in my work life has been the desire to be useful. The sage Rabbi Tarphon enjoined, "One may not neglect the work." I am comforted, however, that he added, "but one is not required to finish it, either." Here I consider "work" to be that which aims to produce something useful to others or to oneself.

The value of doing something useful led me to stop working on the economics of advertising, my first major topic.

I may have succeeded in being of some use to the larger society. My reverse-auction "volunteer" scheme to resolve the problem of involuntary bumping of passengers from oversold airline flights and the lengthy and strenuous promotion of the scheme have been a complete and unmitigated success starting the very first day it was inaugurated—after 12 years during which everyone (except economists, I'm proud to say) asserted that it was ridiculous in principle and could not possibly work in practice. My studies of immigration may have had some effect on federal legislation regulating the volume of immigration into the United States—at least Senator Rudy Boschwitz (the only immigrant then in the Senate) told me so, and the anti-immigration organizations have paid me the tribute of calling me a liar and a profiteer. Any maybe my work on population and resources has had some salutary effects. But it is very easy to fool yourself that you have been more important than you really have been in such matters where causal influence is so indirect.

I judge, however, that I have failed abysmally in what I have spent 90 percent of my work effort trying to do—being useful to my fellow economists and statisticians and social scientists by providing to them theoretical ideas, frameworks, data, and methods that would help them in doing more advanced work.

When I say I have aimed to do work that is "useful" to *economists*, I do not mean work that other economists would simply *consider* valuable, but rather work that would advance other economic work that would be useful to *society*. In a memorable interchange in their 1960s presidential addresses to the American Economic Association, Paul Samuelson and Kenneth Boulding proposed very different tests of the value of economic work. Samuelson stated his criterion to be the approbation of one's peers: "In the long run the economic scholar works for the only coin worth having—our own applause." Boulding then replied that "I did not become an economist for anybody's applause; I became an economist because I thought there was an intellectual task ahead, of desperate importance for the welfare and even the survival of mankind."

Boulding's criterion appeals to me, and I suspect that it appeals to Samuelson, too. But Samuelson's criterion is much more easily measurable—with citations, for example, or speaking invitations or salary offers—than is Boulding's criterion, which helps Samuelson's criterion to dominate the profession. Any many of those who espouse Samuelson's criterion say that the acceptance of the profession is in fact the best available proxy for Boulding's criterion of usefulness.

***

People on the "other side" of some ideological fence find it impossible to believe that people on "this side" can have values that they approve of, including many of the above. They also disbelieve that I am in favor of all people having the family size which they want, and they attribute to me an opposition to contraception methods, which I have disavowed as explicitly as it is possible to do in print.

Therefore they disbelieve that my most fundamental value is liberty. They also disbelieve that in addition to liberty, my main values are protecting the weak from being stomped on by the strong, providing opportunity to those in most need of it, being concerned more about the poor than about the rich, and so on. Indeed, so-called "liberals" are much more likely to be elitist than I, and they do not believe that I believe that talent is distributed equally among all human groups, and that the achievements and the status of the parents predict absolutely nothing about the talents of the offspring.

***

I am exceedingly grateful for many small things in life. I take enormous delight in the snooze button on my alarm clock that gives me one or two or three delicious opportunities to go back to sleep after it wakes me. Because I sleep in three separated periods a day, this gives me a good many opportunities to use the snooze bar. This little device wasn't available to human beings twenty years ago. And it seems so minor. Yet it is capable of giving so much pleasure.

I can even enjoy (at least a bit) the head cold that I have as I write this. I am very pleased with this cold because it is the cleanest, neatest, least offensive cold I have ever had—or so it seems. It came on with a big rush of sneezes, immediately proceeded to a torrent, and left me strong enough to play racquet ball (I have shifted from squash; another story). The first day of the cold passed without any loss of energy. The next three days were mild, and it looks ready to end—the best cold of my life. Furthermore, this is probably the first cold I've had in a year, and it will inoculate me against other colds for a while. How can you beat it?

Of course the other side of the coin is that I can be incredibly annoyed at some little thing for some short period of time—a bunch of books that got disturbed, or an idiot telephone receptionist who doesn't give a damn about the public, or being put on hold for too long. But these are like summer squalls in the tropics—they blow up rapidly, they have spectacular heights, and they revert to calm shortly. And I tend not to vent my annoyance at those who are close to me (though there may be some dissent from my family about that).

Values and Character

Because I write that I have a value for doing or being something, you should not conclude that I manage to live up to that value. As I look back on my life, I realize that there were too many times and places when I did not know right from wrong, or more specifically, I did not recognize that what I was doing was wrong. An example was my amoral attitude toward the provision of evidence for the value of prescription drugs when I wrote advertising copy in 1956. I know that I have had larceny in my heart at various times. And sometimes I have imagined myself committing some crimes in the name of "good causes"—for example, robbing British banks in Palestine in 1947. When I read newspaper accounts of people being tried, convicted, and sent to jail for various offenses, I find myself saying, "There go I but for the grace of God." I do know, however, that I am not capable of such acts as child abuse and torture.

As I imagine many other people do, I perform some generous acts simply because it is cheap and easy for me to perform them; even psychopaths are likely to give you street instructions or the time of the day because they can get the benefit of feeling generous and experiencing the pleasure of human gratitude without making any sacrifice. I can be open-handed about money because I've got enough of it and don't care much about it. I also take some pleasure in overcoming the baser side of my nature, as when I give a deserved compliment to someone toward whom I am not well disposed at the moment.

A Note on Abortion

The issue of abortion has arisen frequently in public discussion in recent years, and everyone asks where everyone else stands. It's really no one's business, but maybe I should answer, anyway. The following is from a letter to my friend Bill McGurn, with whom I see eye-to-eye on many issues:

July 13, 88
Dear Bill:

I think that some part of the cause of difference between us may be a different way of thinking generally. It seems to me that you first decide whether a fetus "is" or "is not" a child, and then deduce from that definition. I am persuaded by various writers that the word "is" is (sic) the worst word in the English language. I recognize that the law requires one to make such categorizations. But apart from the law, I seldom find it necessary, and usually it is (sic) confusing when one is talking of morals.

Rather, I think that it is better to make judgments about the individual case, taking all its characteristics into consideration. This is likely to lead you to say, "But this means everyone should take the law into his or her own hands with respect to such matters." I agree that this is embarking on a perilous course. But it is a course that I am often prepared to undertake for myself, for example in religion. Judaism makes it very clear that the individual should *not* pick and choose which religious laws one should obey. And I understand the wisdom of that in many cases. Nevertheless, I have chosen to pick and choose—and I write that sentence with full awareness of the words it contains. Indeed, I have made a metachoice about choosing. And other choices that I can imagine making—heaven preserve me from having to make them, but I can imagine making them anyway—would horrify you.

> An interesting trivial case is whether one would go through a red light in the middle of the night when you can see in all directions that there are no cars coming. (Sometime I will tell you about Hayek's fascinating response to my question about this, and I hope to retrieve the letter that he wrote about it.) To me it is an easy question. The red light would be no different than a stop sign if the physical conditions would be the same; the labeling would matter little to me.
>
> More generally, I don't see many black-white distinctions in these connections. As I wrote in *The Ultimate Resource*, I see a continuum from abstinence to contraception to infanticide.

In connection with the discussion with Hayek of going through red lights and the discussion of the specified rules for the Sabbath: I always believed that most rules we encounter make sense, and therefore I never had any inclination to challenge them, even if they seemed annoying to me. On the other hand, I never had any sense of the sanctity of rules, and if, upon as thorough an inquiry as I could make, there seemed no good reason for my following it, I have had no compunction about breaking the rule or evading it. Thus for me the answer about going through the red light at midnight on a deserted road was easier than for Hayek. If I could see neither traffic nor police, I would immediately go through it without a second thought.

Index